THE REPTILES
AND AMPHIBIANS
OF ALABAMA

THE REPTILES AND AMPHIBIANS OF ALABAMA

Robert H. Mount

The University of Alabama Press
Tuscaloosa and London

in cooperation with
Alabama Agricultural Experiment Station
Auburn University

The 1996 reprint edition is published by The University of Alabama Press,
Tuscaloosa, Alabama 35486-0380.

∞

Library of Congress Cataloging-in-Publication Data

Mount, Robert H. (Robert Hughes), 1931–
The reptiles and amphibians of Alabama / Robert H. Mount.
p. cm.
Originally published: Auburn : Auburn University,
Agricultural Experiment Station, 1975.
Includes bibliographical references and index.
ISBN 0-8173-0054-6
1. Reptiles—Alabama. 2. Amphibians—Alabama. I. Title.
QL653.A2M68 1996
597.6'09761—dc20 95-46581
British Library Cataloguing-in-Publication Data available

CONTENTS

PREFACE TO THE 1996 REPRINT EDITION

During the twenty years following the first printing of this book, a great deal of new information on the life histories, ecology, and geographic distributions of our state's reptiles and amphibians has been acquired. Three previously named species, unrecorded from Alabama in 1975, are now know to occur here. They are the one-toed amphiuma (*Amphiuma pholeter*), razorback musk turtle (*Sternotherus carinatus*), and pine barrens treefrog (*Hyla andersonii*), all in southern Alabama. These species were mentioned in the first printing in the section "Problematical Forms."

The recently described Appalachicola dusky salamander (*Desmognathus appalachicolae*) is recorded from southeastern Alabama and can be added to the state list, as can a map turtle, *Graptemys ernsti,* from the Conecuh and Yellow rivers in southern Alabama. This turtle is a first cousin of the Alabama map turtle, to which species *G. ernsti* was formerly assigned.

Other additions to the state list include a frog and a lizard, both introduced exotics. All the new information is being incorporated into a revision of this book being prepared by Dr. Craig Guyer of Auburn University. Publication of the revision is anticipated a few years down the road.

In the original preface I noted that increasing numbers of people were appreciative of the creepy and crawly critters that make up our herpetofauna. I am happy to report that this trend has continued, particularly among members of the younger, more enlightened generation.

It saddens me, however, that the changing attitude has not resulted in a reversal of the declines occurring in so many of our species. Especially troubling is the deteriorating status of most of our reptiles. Only a few of us old-timers realize how precipitous some of the declines have been and fret about them.

Dr. Archie Carr, my Ph.D. adviser, in his book *A Naturalist in Florida, a Celebration Eden* (published posthumously by Yale University Press), lamented the decrease in numbers of wild ducks using his pond. He wrote: "Ducks have suffered grievous depletion in Florida, and to watch this decline has been one of the penalties of living a long time in the same locality." I guess that's my problem as I observe what is happening to so many of Alabama's reptiles.

The problems confronting our reptiles and amphibians are much the same as I reported twenty years ago—with one important addition, the red imported fire ant. Evidence is mounting that this alien predator is the major contributor to declines in a host of ground-nesting animals, including reptiles that lay their eggs where fire ants can find them. I fail to understand for the life of me why we are smart enough to send a man to the moon but cannot figure out an environmentally sound way to get rid of fire ants.

Nevertheless, healthy populations of frogs of the expected varieties can still be found in many of the same places I could find them in 1975. Also, in forested lowlands and in creeks that have not yet been polluted with chemicals or clogged with sediment, salamanders are doing reasonably well.

For snake lovers, I should point out that at least one of our species, the gray rat snake, is about as easy to find as it has ever been.

PREFACE

The reptiles and amphibians, as a group, continue to be the least appreciated of Alabama's native vertebrate animals. Although a few are perhaps as numerous now as ever, most have apparently declined in numbers, some to the point of rarity or possible extinction. Several reptiles and amphibians are rare in Alabama because of factors unrelated to man or his activities. But in too many cases the plight of threatened or declining forms is due to mindless destruction or degradation of their habitats — or more regrettably, to deliberate persecution.

Much of the detrimental habitat manipulation is the result of the increasing human population and its demands on the natural environment. Extensive land clearing, whether for housing, industry, mineral exploitation, or agriculture, takes a heavy toll of many forms of reptile and amphibian life. Increasingly, our forest lands are being clear-cut and prepared for row-crop production of pine pulpwood, a practice that is devastating to many forms of low mobility and to those that require a humic, forest-floor habitat. The Red Hills salamander, whose entire range is confined to a small area of southern central Alabama, has both of these limitations, and the acreage of habitat suitable for this animal has greatly diminished due to clear-cutting.

The destruction of natural streams and stream-associated habitats by stream channelization often eliminates some aquatic and semi-aquatic species, such as hellbenders, seepage salamanders, and waterdogs, as well as a number of species that rely on natural floodwater pools for breeding sites. Damming creeks and rivers, while favoring some species, is detrimental to others. Unfortunately, the former are usually those already present in reasonable abundance, while the latter are more frequently in the threatened category. The hellbender, for example, apparently was common at one time in the Tennessee River in Alabama, but with the construction of the TVA dams, this species is now restricted largely, if not entirely, to a few of the river's free-flowing tributaries. Impoundment may also be detrimental to the flattened musk turtle, a form whose entire range is limited to streams in the upper portion of the Black Warrior River system in Alabama.

The extent to which environmental contaminants, such as pesticides and other potentially dangerous chemicals, constitute a menace to the reptiles and amphibians of Alabama has not been ascertained. It is reasonable to assume that the effects vary widely with the pollutant as well as with the species. Some forms not killed outright by a harmful chemical may be affected adversely in subtle ways. Reproductive functions may be impaired, or the chemical may reach toxic levels through bioaccumulation. Some pollutants may not affect a reptile or amphibian directly, but may reduce or eliminate its food supply. It is not unlikely that environmental contaminants are responsible for many of the cases in which certain species are declining when other adverse factors are not apparent.

In the Lower Coastal Plain of Alabama and in portions of Georgia and Florida, the decline of some reptiles and amphibians is probably being accelerated by events called "Rattlesnake Roundups." These galas, one of which is held annually in Opp, Alabama, encourage the capture of eastern diamondback rattlesnakes and other snake species by awarding prizes and publicity to the captors. The usual method of capture involves the introduction of gasoline or gasoline fumes into burrows of gopher tortoises, which rattlesnakes and several other animals use as overwintering retreats. Dan Speake and I (1973) reported on the effects of this kind of "gassing" on some of the animals that overwinter in gopher tortoise burrows. Our findings indicated that indigo snakes and pine snakes, both of which are declining in the affected regions, are likely to be killed outright by the "gassing." We concluded that the rattlesnake roundups, as they are now conducted, pose an ecological threat that warrants concern.

In some places in Alabama, especially along rivers in the less densely populated areas, the practice of shooting aquatic turtles with a rifle is popular. The relative scarcity of turtles along some stream stretches, and the high incidence of large turtles having scars from bullet wounds suggest that this practice may be responsible for significant reductions in the populations of certain species. These species include the Alabama red-bellied turtle, a form whose range is limited to a small area of southwestern Alabama.

Over-collecting by amateur and professional herpetologists may be a factor in the decline of some species. Forms that exist in relatively small numbers, such as the Red Hills salamander, are particularly vulnerable to over-collecting. Gopher tortoise populations have been reduced or eliminated in certain areas of the state by people who collect them for food.

While the overall outlook for the future of the herpetofauna of Alabama is not reassuring, there are a few bright spots. The public is becoming increasingly better educated, and with education, people tend to lose unfounded fears and prejudices. Numerous farmers in Alabama now refrain from killing certain harmless snakes on their premises, either through realization of their economic value or appreciation of the contribution they make toward healthy, diverse ecosystems. In some other states, indications of the new, enlightened attitude are much more apparent. Arizona, for example, has extended legal protection not only to the venomous Gila monster but to three of its eleven species of rattlesnakes as well. Florida protects the indigo snake, alligator snapping turtle, and gopher tortoise. It is illegal in Texas to collect Texas gopher tortoises and horned lizards. In Illinois the U.S. Forest Service recently closed a road to protect migrating snakes. Closer to home, an Auburn student was recently reprimanded by a Mississippi game warden for catching turtles in that state!

Legislation was recently enacted at the Federal level to enhance the welfare of threatened and endangered forms of wildlife. Under the act, entitled the Endangered Species Conservation Act of 1973, species designated "threatened" or "endangered" by the Secretary of the Interior will receive Federal protection. Financial assistance is provided to states on a cost-sharing basis to develop programs to study and protect their own endangered forms.

Alabama has made some progress in this area. In 1972 a symposium was held under the sponsorship of the State Department of Conservation and Natural Resources and Birmingham Southern University which resulted in a publication entitled *Rare and Endangered Vertebrates of Alabama.* Included among the forms considered rare or endangered were 23 reptiles and amphibians. In 1975 another symposium was held, under the sponsorship of the Department of Conservation and Natural Resources and the Alabama Museum of Natural History, for the purpose of up-dating the 1972 list and considering, in addition to vertebrates, plants and some invertebrate groups. The results of that symposium are to be published by the Museum of Natural History. Included on the list will be 16 Alabama reptiles and amphibians considered threatened or endangered, and another 17 that will be placed under a category of "special concern." (The species and subspecies to be included on the new list can be found in the appendix of this report.)

Another forthcoming publication will consider threatened and endangered vertebrates of the Southeast. This will be published by Tall Timbers Research Station of Tallahassee, Florida, and will present the results of a 1974 workshop co-sponsored by Tall Timbers and the Southeastern Section of the Wildlife Society (see Appendix).

Despite all the clamor over endangered species and other such favorable signs, many highly placed people continue the ruthless war against nature, scorning anything which cannot be assigned a direct dollars-and-cents value or exploited for monetary gain. If we wish to retain anything more than vestiges of our rich natural heritage, we must temper that callous attitude with ecological reasoning and strive to find better ways to live at peace with the wild things around us.

ACKNOWLEDGMENTS

During the 13 years this undertaking was underway, I have been assisted by literally hundreds of contributors. Heading the list of those whose efforts I can acknowledge in the space permitted are James Dobie and George Folkerts. These colleagues have contributed hundreds of specimens, freely given me their thoughts and opinions virtually on a day-to-day basis, and read and criticized the manuscript. Lacy Hyche, another Auburn faculty member, spent weeks on a painstaking, sentence-by-sentence critique of the manuscript, which vastly improved its accuracy and readability. My long-time friend and associate, Dan Speake, contributed in numerous ways to the project. The influence of that outstanding naturalist was largely responsible for my having developed an interest in Alabama biogeography.

I deeply appreciate the efforts of my present and former graduate students who spent many long hours both in the field and in the laboratory working on problems related to this study. They are Ralph Jordan, Jr., William Redmond, Robert Shealy, Terry Schwaner, Ronald Estridge, John Davidson, Richard Little, Kelly Thomas, Hugh Hanlin, and William Phillips.

Thomas Yarbrough of Anniston and James Keeler of the State Department of Conservation and Natural Resources, both of whom have long been interested in the herpetology of Alabama, not only advised me throughout the study period, but donated their personal collections to the Auburn Museum. I am especially grateful for their generosity.

I am thankful to the following for permitting me to examine specimens in their care: Jack Brown, Florence State University (now University of North Alabama); Donald Tinkle, University of Michigan; Clarence McCoy, Carnegie Museum; Walter Auffenberg, University of Florida; L. G. Sanford, Jacksonville State University; Herbert Boschung, University of Alabama; Michael Howell, Samford University; Harold Dundee, Tulane University; Hymen Marx, Field Museum of Natural History; and Donald Linzey, University of South Alabama.

Numerous people made special efforts to supply specimens or records from critical areas. They include John Ramsey, Harold Walquist, Floyd Scott, Winston Baker, Billy Hillestead, James Adams, J. L. Dusi, Ronnie Horton, Roy Hyde, James English, Lee Barclay, Jr., Ron McKitrick, Fred Cox, Gary Breece, Thomas French, James Byford, Charles Turner, David Thrasher, David Bayne, David Smith, Darrell Bateman, Nalria Wisdom, Lois Donavan, Rhett Barnes, John Gwaltney, Robert Shoop, James Peavy, Mike Hopiak, Robin Russell, Reo Kirkland, David Nelson, Hector Harima, Faye Williams, Patrick McIntosh, and Joseph T. Collins. I am grateful for the thoughtfulness and generosity of these people.

Several times I sought and received advice or information from herpetologists outside of Alabama in attempting to solve problems I encountered. Those who were helpful in this respect include John Mecham, Jack Fouquette, Richard Highton, Roger Conant, Ronald Brandon, Denzel Ferguson, Phillip Smith, George Pisani, Ray Ashton, Joseph Collins, Bruce Means, Douglas Rossman, William Brode, William Palmer, and Francis Rose. Samuel Telford, Bernard Martof, Jack Fouquette, and Phillip Smith kindly supplied information on the reptiles and amphibians of the states in which they reside.

Kelly Thomas and Robert Shealy contributed several photographs. John Hopkins, Gerald Edmondson, Gene Widders, James Jenkins, and Robin Russell did much of the routine museum work. The line drawings and some of the maps were prepared by Terri Glasscock, of the Agricultural Experiment Station's Department of Research Information.

Finally, I wish to thank my wife, Rena, for the many services she performed during every phase of the study, and my son, Robert, who helped on many of my collecting trips.

INTRODUCTION

People enlightened in the area of natural history seldom fail to develop responsible attitudes with respect to man's role as the dominant member of the earth ecosystem. Moreover, a knowledge of natural history provides an opening into a vast new world full of endless opportunities for soul-enriching experiences that are virtually unknown to the uninitiated. This publication is designed to provide a basis for an understanding of the extant reptilian and amphibian components of Alabama's natural history. It is a compromise of sorts, in that it was prepared for use by the layman and the serious student of southeastern herpetology as well.

My research on the reptiles and amphibians of Alabama began at Alabama College (now Montevallo University) in 1961 and continued there through 1966. In 1967 I moved to Auburn University, where the research continued thereafter as Agricultural Experiment Station Project No. 13-025. During the study period, over 24,000 preserved specimens were examined. About 20,000 of these are now in the Auburn University Museum (hereinafter designated AM); the remainder are in collections at other institutions.

I am disappointed in having been unable to reach firm conclusions that might solve several vexing problems pertinent to Alabama herpetology. The relationship between the toads *Bufo terrestris* and *B. americanus* in Alabama remains poorly understood, as does that between the cricket frogs, *Acris gryllus* and *A. crepitans*. I have been able to add but little to an understanding of the relationships among the salamanders of the genus *Necturus* in Alabama. Solutions to these and numerous other problems will require an attack of a much broader scope than I was able to mount.

As will be ascertained from examining the distribution maps, several areas of the state remain inadequately surveyed with respect to their reptiles and amphibians. The most poorly known of these are in extreme western Alabama. It will also be noted that details of the life histories of many forms are lacking. I hope this work will provide a stimulus for future researchers to fill some of the obvious gaps in our knowledge of Alabama herpetology.

HISTORY OF HERPETOLOGY IN ALABAMA

Despite its richness and diversity, the herpetofauna of Alabama received relatively little attention until recently. One of the earliest significant contributions to Alabama herpetology was the description of *Emys* (now *Pseudemys*) *mobilensis* from the Mobile area by Holbrook (1838). In 1857 Agassiz described *Cistudo* (now *Terrapene*) *major* from the Mobile area and *Goniochelys* (now *Sternotherus*) *minor* from specimens collected in Georgia, Alabama, and Louisiana. Cope (1880) described *Eumeces pluvialis* from Mobile County, and his works of 1889 and 1900 contained a number of herpetofaunal locality records from Alabama, as did that of Yarrow (1882). Baur (1893) described *Graptemys pulchra* from Montgomery and *Pseud-*emys alabamensis from the Mobile area.

Brimley (1904, 1907, 1910, 1920, 1928) made important contributions to the herpetology of the Southeast, most of which were pertinent to the Alabama fauna. In two of these (1910, 1920), Alabama locality records were specified. Holt (1919, 1924a, 1924b) contributed locality records for several forms, as did Dunn (1920 and 1940) and Howell (1921).

The first comprehensive report on the herpetology of Alabama was an annotated list by Löding, which appeared in 1922. Acknowledged by Löding as having made important contributions to his work were Julius Hurter, E. R. Dunn, Thomas van Aller, Eugene A. Smith, Herbert H. Smith, Thomas M. Owen,

FIG. 1. Counties of Alabama.

and Frank N. Blanchard. Several of Blanchard's outstanding monographs were valuable to an appreciation of Alabama herpetology, including those on *Lampropeltis* (1921), *Virginia* (1923), *Carphophis* (1925), *Tantilla* (1938), and *Diadophis* (1942). In addition, Blanchard published the first paper on the "black *Pituophis*" from Alabama (1920), which he later (1924) described as *Pituophis lodingi*. *P. lodingi* was relegated to subspecific status under *P. melanoleucus* by Stull (1929).

In 1931 Haltom published his illustrated bulletin on the reptiles of Alabama. Although valuable to the layman as a basic reference, it contributed little new information. In 1937 Viosca described *Necturus alabamensis* from the Warrior River in Tuscaloosa County and *N. lodingi* from Eslava Creek in Mobile County. Viosca's 1938 report on the winter frogs of Alabama included the first state record for *Pseudacris brachyphona*.

Taylor's (1935) monograph of the genus *Eumeces* clarified relationships within the *fasciatus* group, three species of which occur in Alabama, and placed *pluvailis* in the synonymy of *E. anthracinus*. Goff (1936) described *Natrix cyclopion floridana*, but failed to clarify relationships among Alabama populations of *N. cyclopion*.

Numerous other works in the 1930's dealt with species that occur in Alabama, and several provided distributional data for the state or elucidated other aspects of natural history that contributed to our knowledge of the herpetology of Alabama. These include the following: Carr (1937, 1938), on *Pseudemys*; Gloyd (1935a, 1935b, 1940), on rattlesnakes; Gloyd and Conant (1938, 1943), on *Agkistrodon*; Smith (1938), on *Farancia abacura*; Burt (1939), on lizards; and Cahn (1939), on *Hyla gratiosa* (first record of species from northern Alabama).

In 1940, Penn published his observations on the herpetofauna of DeKalb County. This work, in addition to providing a wealth of other locality data,

included the first state record for *Lampropeltis t. triangulum* and the first record for *Agkistrodon piscivorus* from the northeastern portion of the state. Goin and Netting in 1940 described *Rana sevosa*. Additional notes on *sevosa* were published by Goin in 1942. Kauffeld (1941) first recorded the presence of *Eumeces egregius* in Alabama. Carr and Marchand (1942) described *Graptemys barbouri* from the Chipola River in Florida. Middlekauff (1943) confirmed the presence of *Eurycea lucifuga* in Alabama, and Shreve (1945) provided the first record of *Pituophis melanoleucus mugitus*.

Snyder (1944, 1945a, 1945b) made observations on the herpetofauna of southeastern Alabama and provided a number of locality records. Trapido (1944) described *Storeria dekayi wrightorum*, allocating all Alabama specimens he examined to that subspecies. In the same publication, he listed several Alabama localities for *Storeria occipitomaculata*, assigning the specimens to the nominate form after having first described the new subspecies *S. o. obscura*. Conant (1949) elucidated geographic variation among populations of *Natrix erythrogaster* in the mid-Gulf area in describing *N. e. flavigaster*.

In 1950 *Desmognathus chermocki* was described by Bishop and Valentine from specimens collected in Tuscaloosa County. Grobman in 1950 published on *Desmognathus* of the southeastern United States, and recognized not only *D. fuscus fuscus* and *D. f. auriculatus* as occurring in Alabama, but *D. f brimleyorum* as well. In the same year, Goin described *Ambystoma cingulatum bishopi* and allocated Alabama specimens to that form. Dowling in 1950 published the first record of *Eumeces anthracinus* from Alabama since 1880.

Ralph Chermock's key to Alabama reptiles and amphibians appeared in 1952. This work, which included rather general statements on the distribution of each form, replaced Löding's catalogue as the definitive work on Alabama herpetology, and it remains so at the time of this writing. Chermock, who was affiliated with the University of Alabama during the period 1947 to 1956, published several other papers on Alabama herpetology, including the first state record of *Pituophis m. melanoleucus* (1955). Chermock's enthusiastic interest in natural history influenced the careers of many students with whom he came into contact. Herpetologists who studied under Chermock include Jack S. Brown, University of North Alabama; Barry D. Valentine, Ohio State University; J. W. Cliburn, University of Southern Mississippi; James Boyles, University of South Alabama; and Whitfield Gibbons, University of Georgia.

Cagle (1952) published on the relationship between *Graptemys pulchra* and *G. barbouri*, and in 1954 described *G. nigrinoda* from the Mobile Bay drainage in Alabama. Neill (1954) published on the ranges and taxonomic allocations of several southeastern forms, and included Alabama locality data for *Ambystoma maculatum* and *Drymarchon corais*. Also included was a recommendation that *Sistrutus catenatus* be dropped from the Alabama herpetofaunal list.

Additional locality records for *Gyrinophilus porphyriticus* were provided by Thurow in 1954 and 1955. Tinkle and Webb (1955) described *Sternotherus depressus* (*S. minor depressus*) from a locality in Walker County in the Warrior River system. Keeler (1955) gave a new state record for *Pituophis m. lodingi*, and Conant's paper on pine snakes in 1956 contained a summary of the information available on Alabama *Pituophis*. Carr and Crenshaw (1957) recommended removing *Pseudemys alabamensis* from the synonymy of *P. floridana mobilensis* and restoring its status as a species. Tinkle (1959) established the zoogeographic importance of the Fall Line as it relates to the distribution of turtles, basing his conclusions chiefly on observations made in Alabama.

Several monographic studies published in the 1950's contributed significantly to an appreciation of Alabama herpetology. They were as follows: McConkey (1954),

on the North American *Ophisaurus;* Mecham (1954), on *Rana clamitans;* Auffenberg (1955), on *Coluber constrictor;* Tinkle (1958), on *Sternotherus carinatus* complex; Hecht (1958), on *Necturus;* and Huheey (1959), on *Regina rigida.*

Probably the most significant herpetological event of the 1960's in Alabama was the discovery and subsequent description of *Phaeognathus hubrichti* (Highton, 1961). Other works related to that species have been those by Valentine (1963c, 1963d), Brandon (1965, 1966b, 1966c), Mount and Schwaner (1970), Schwaner and Mount (1970), and Jordan and Mount (1975).

Also of importance during the decade was Mecham's study of introgression involving *Hyla gratiosa* and *H. cinerea* in Lee County, Alabama (1960a). Mecham, now at Texas Technological University, taught herpetology at Auburn University from 1956 to 1965, during which he published several other works dealing with hybridization among hylid frogs (1957, 1960b, 1965), a study of the ecological and genetic relationships between *Acris gryllus* and *A. crepitans* in Alabama (1964), and the first report of *Eumeces egregius* from above the Fall Line (1960). In addition, Mecham began the Auburn University Museum herpetology collection.

Valentine, in addition to his contributions on *Phaeognathus hubrichti* (cited above), published several other reports dealing with Alabama amphibians, including the first state record of *Desmognathus ocoee* (*D. ochrophaeus*) (1961), a study of intergradation between *Eurycea l. longicauda* and *E. l. guttolineata* (1962a), one on the range of *Eurycea lucifuga* in Alabama (1962b), and a study of early life history of *Desmognathus aeneus chermocki* (1963b).

Brandon, whose contributions on *Phaeognathus* were mentioned previously, worked at the University of Alabama during 1962 and 1963. His publications also include a note on the occurrence of *Ambystoma texanum* in Greene County, Alabama (1966a), and a monograph of the genus *Gyrinophilus* (1966d), which contained Alabama records for both *G. porphyriticus* and *G. palleucus*.

The descriptions of *Natrix septemvittata mabila* by Neill and *Eurycea aquatica* by Rose and Bush both appeared in 1963. *N. s. mabila* was placed in the synonymy of *Regina septemvittata* by Spangler and Mount in 1969. Folkerts and Mount described *Graptemys nigrinoda delticola* from the lower portion of the Mobile Bay drainage in 1969.

Two papers appeared expressing conflicting views on the taxonomic status of *Necturus alabamensis*. Neill (1963b) favored restoring it to species rank; Gunter and Brode (1964) recommended relegating *N. punctatus lodingi* to the synonymy of *N. b. alabamensis*, retaining the latter as a subspecies of *N. beyeri*.

Holman (1961) reported on the herpetofauna of the Howard College natural area; Ernst (1967) noted that *Chrysemys p. picta* intergrades with *C. p. dorsalis* in Alabama. Cooper and Cooper (1968) and Cooper (1968) contributed to our knowledge of *Gyrinophilus palleucus* and its relationship to *G. porphyriticus*. Gloyd (1969) described *Agkistrodon piscivorus conanti* and made general statements concerning its influence in cottonmouth populations in southern Alabama.

Several notes were published during the decade on new locality records and range extensions within the state. These were: Jackson (1962), second state record for *Pituophis m. melanoleucus;* Mount (1964), range extensions for several frogs; Rossman (1965), report of *Eurycea bislineata wilderae* from the Red Hills; Caldwell and Howell (1966), new locality records for *Siren intermedia;* Blaney and Relyea (1967), *Plethodon dorsalis* from the Red Hills; Mount and Folkerts (1968), first state records for *Trionyx ferox, T. muticus calvatus, Rana heckscheri,* and *Plethodon cinereus,* with clarification of the ranges of several other forms; Horton (1968), first state record of *Seminatrix pygaea;* and Mount (1969), range extension for *Trionyx*

muticus calvatus and *Chrysemys picta dorsalis.*

Monographs that appeared in the 1960's, other than the aforementioned one on *Gyrinophilus,* that contributed substantially to the knowledge of the Alabama herpetofauna were: Webb (1962), on *Trionyx;* Highton (1962a), on *Plethodon;* Rossman (1963b), on *Thamnophis sauritis;* Mount (1965), on *Eumeces egregius;* Neill (1964), on *Farancia erytrogramma;* Telford (1966), on southeastern *Tantilla;* Myers (1967), on *Rhadinaea flavilata;* Williams and Wilson (1967), on *Cemophora;* and Milstead (1969), on *Terrapene.*

Mount and Schwaner in 1970 published on the distributional relationships between *Natrix rhombifera* and *N. taxispilota,* and Mount (1972) reported on subspecific variation among Alabama populations of *Carphophis amoenus.* Walquist's paper on sawback turtles (1970) contained pertinent information on *Graptemys nigrinoda* in Alabama. Jackson and Jackson (1970) surveyed the reptiles and amphibians of Dauphin Island, Mobile County. A publication on poisonous snakes of Alabama by Wimberly (1970) contained a good account of snakebite treatment, but contributed nothing else of scientific value. Dobie (1972) clarified a misconception of the range of *Graptemys barbouri* in Alabama. New locality data for *Ambystoma texanum* and *Trionyx ferox* were supplied by Scott and Johnson (1972) and Scott (1973), respectively.

In addition to the works cited above, a number of theses and dissertations, unpublished at the time of this writing, deal mostly or entirely with Alabama reptiles or amphibians. The most important of these include those by Boyles (1952), on *Natrix;* Brown (1956), on frogs and toads; Folkerts (1968a), on *Desmognathus;* Schwaner (1969), on *Natrix sipedon* and *N. fasciata;* Estridge (1970), on *Sternotherus minor depressus;* Davidson (1971), on *Pseudemys scripta;* Thomas (1972), on *Pseudemys floridana;* and Shealy (1973), on *Graptemys pulchra.*

ABOUT SUBSPECIES

Generally speaking, all individuals of a given species within an area of reasonably good habitat constitute a population. The individuals of a population differ from one another. Usually the differences are subtle, but in some cases they may be striking, as with the different color phases of the eastern hognose snake, *Heterodon platyrhinos* (p. 192). Populations also differ from one another, but the differences may be so slight that they are detectable only when large samples are compared. When variation within a species produces recognizably distinct geographic races, the races may be described as subspecies and receive formal taxonomic recognition. Thus, *Farancia abacura abacura* and *Farancia abacura reinwardti* are, respectively, the nominate, eastern race, and the western race of the mud snake, *Farancia abacura*. The third name or epithet in each case designates the subspecies.

Situated between the ranges of subspecies of the same species are, in most instances, zones of intergradation. Within these zones the resident populations, though not necessarily every one of the constituent individuals, show influence of each of the intergrading subspecies.

Each individual belonging to one of these populations, regardless of its appearance, is properly termed an intergrade. Ordinarily, more than one subspecies of the same species cannot occur in the same area in the same habitat. One of the rare exceptions to this general rule is the overlap of subspecies of *Lampropeltis triangulum*, which is dealt with in the account of that species (p. 201).

There are numerous cases in which the subspecies concept has been misapplied, resulting in confusion and misunderstanding. Many such errors of interpretation were made by taxonomists who had only a fragmentary knowledge of variation within the groups with which they were working. When a subspecies is determined to be invalid, it should be promptly discarded. Taxonomists have in some instances depicted zones of intergradation between subspecies as being much narrower or less extensive than they actually are. This practice has also resulted in confusion. The growing skepticism of the value of the subspecies taxon will be curtailed only if its advocates apply it more judiciously in the future than they often have in the past.

CLIMATE OF ALABAMA

The climate of Alabama is mild and humid. The mean annual temperature is approximately 64°F. Below-zero temperatures are rare in the southern half of the state and infrequent in the northern half. Average January temperatures range from 53°F near the coast in Mobile to 42°F in Valley Head, DeKalb County, in northeastern Alabama. Length of the frost-free period ranges from 298 days in Mobile to 191 days in Mentone, DeKalb County.

Alabama summers are relatively hot, but temperatures above 100°F are infrequent. Afternoon thundershowers, providing relief from the heat, are common, especially near the coast. July tempera-

ture averages for most localities are between 78°F and 82°F, with somewhat lower readings at high elevations.

Average annual precipitation for most inland reporting stations in Alabama is between 48 and 54 inches. The average increases from about Montgomery southwestward, with some stations in Mobile and Baldwin counties reporting averages in excess of 66 inches. Almost all precipitation in Alabama occurs as rain. Measurable snowfalls are exceedingly rare in the southern half of the state, and annual totals of more than 6 inches are seldom recorded even for the northernmost stations.

March and July are typically the wettest months in every part of the state.

The relative proportion of rain falling during the summer is generally greater in southwestern Alabama than elsewhere. Occasionally a late-summer hurricane will strike the northern Gulf Coast and bring excessively heavy rains to southern Alabama; deluges of more than 15 inches have been reported in several such instances. Moderately severe droughts with up to 4 to 6 rainless weeks occur in some years. Such droughts are most frequent during the period August through October, but May and June may also be droughty.

THE HERPETOFAUNA—REGIONAL COMPOSITION

In the overall diversity of its plant and animal life, Alabama is rivaled by few other areas of comparable size in the United States. Several interrelated factors combine to produce this diversity: the state's strategic location with respect to species and subspecies range limits, its remarkable geologic and physiographic variability, and its surface drainage pattern, which involves eight isolated river systems (Fig. 2).

Among the notably diverse biotic groups in Alabama are the reptiles and amphibians. Exclusive of the sea turtles and introduced forms, at least 134 species are represented. A taxonomic breakdown of the state's herpetofauna is compared with those of four other states in Table 1. Within Alabama, at least 34 species, or 25 percent of the total, are either represented or are influenced substantially by 2 or more subspecies, and 12 species by 3 or more. One or 2 species and 2 subspecies are endemic to Alabama. Sixty species occur statewide or nearly so.

The southernmost point in the ranges of at least 9 species are in Alabama, reflecting to a considerable extent the deep intrusion of the Appalachian Plateaus and other upland provinces into the central portion of the state. At least 10 species reach the westernmost limits of their ranges in Alabama.

The range limits of many species and subspecies of reptiles and amphibians in Alabama coincide closely with physiographic boundaries. Harper (1943) divided the state into forest regions primarily on the basis of physiography, and it is likewise possible to divide it into herpetofaunal regions which correspond

TABLE 1. NUMBERS OF SPECIES AND SUBSPECIES OF REPTILES AND AMPHIBIANS NATIVE TO ALABAMA, FLORIDA, ARIZONA, ILLINOIS, AND NORTH CAROLINA

	Native species and subspecies									
	Alabama		Florida[1]		North Carolina[2]		Illinois[3]		Arizona[4]	
Order	Spp.	Spp. & ssp.	Spp.	Spp. & ssp.	Spp.	Spp. & ssp.	Spp.	Spp. & ssp.	Spp.	Spp. & ssp.
	No.	No.	No.	No.	No.	No.	No.	No.	No.	No.
Sirens	2	3	3	6	2	2	1	1	0	0
Salamanders	30	37	21	24	36	51	17	18	1	1
Frogs	28	30	30	34	29	31	18	21	18	19
Turtles[5]	22	33	23	35	15	15	16	17	4	4
Lizards	11	13	18	22	10	10	7	7	43	61
Snakes	40	65	43	63	39	47	38	46	49	76
Crocodilians	1	1	2	2	1	1	0	0	0	0
TOTALS	134	182	140	186	132	157	97	110	115	161

[1] Compiled with the aid of a checklist supplied by Samuel R. Telford, Jr., University of Florida.
[2] Figures supplied by Bernard Martof, North Carolina State University.
[3] Figures supplied by Phillip W. Smith, Illinois State Natural History Survey.
[4] Figures supplied by M. J. Fouquette, Arizona State University at Tempe.
[5] Excludes sea turtles (families Cheloniidae and Dermochelidae).

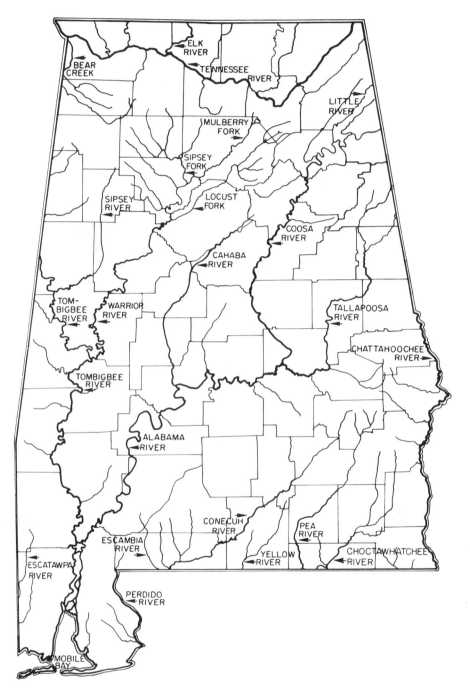

FIG. 2. Major streams of Alabama.

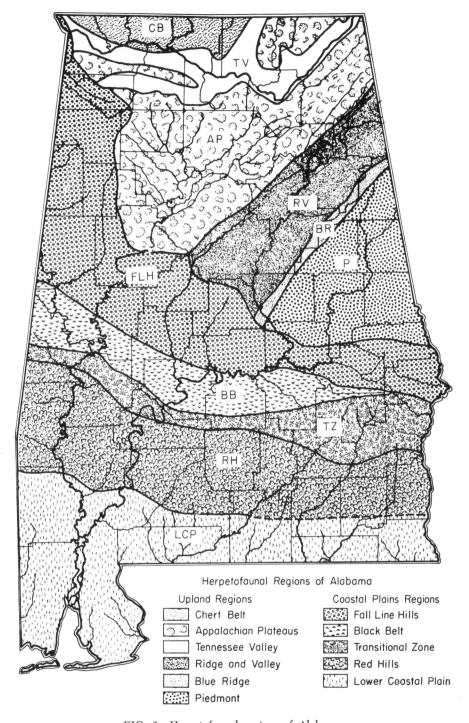

FIG. 3. Herpetofaunal regions of Alabama.

roughly, and in some cases almost precisely, with physiographic subdivisions. I have attempted to do this (Fig. 3) and have relied heavily, though not wholly, on Fenneman (1938) for physiographic interpretations.

The nomenclatural system used is that which I consider most biogeographically appropriate and does not, to my knowledge, conform precisely to that of any other author.

The Fall Line as a Barrier to Dispersal

Extending in an arc from the northwestern corner of Alabama generally southeastward across the state, the Fall Line marks the separation between the Coastal Plain to the south and southwest and the older, upland provinces to the north and northeast. Rather sharply defined in some areas but vaguely so in others, the Fall Line in Alabama, or some segment thereof, is a barrier to the dispersal of about 24 species of reptiles and amphibians. As such, it is the single most important physiographic feature determining herpetofaunal distribution patterns in the state.

The Coastal Plain

The Coastal Plain in Alabama is distinctly belted and is physiographically more variable than it is in either Georgia or Mississippi. Topographically it varies from flat to almost montane. The soils vary from acid sands and sandy loams to heavy, calcareous, alkaline types. Most of the latter appear best suited agriculturally to pastures, and indications are that some of them supported prairie communities at the time the first white settlers came to Alabama.

FIG. 4. Sandhill or "high pine-turkey oak" association near Citronelle, Mobile County. This habitat type occurs on well-drained, sandy soils in the Coastal Plain and is usually dominated by turkey oak (*Quercus laevis*) and longleaf pine (*Pinus palustris*). It is the preferred natural habitat of the gopher tortoise in Alabama. Periodic burning is essential for the maintenance of sandhill associations.

Rocks and rock outcrops occur in some portions of the Coastal Plain, but seldom to the extent that they do in provinces above the Fall Line. Most streams of the Coastal Plain are fairly sluggish and have sand, silt, or gravel bottoms, but a few flow over bedrock. Several of the streams have broad, low floodplains with sloughs and oxbows. Swampy habitats are fairly common, many of them having been created by beaver dams.

Forty-three species of reptiles and amphibians, constituting about 32 percent of the state's herpetofauna, occur exclusively or almost exclusively within the Coastal Plain. These include 5 of the 8 frogs of the genus *Hyla*, the 2 amphiumid salamanders, the 2 sirenids, 8 turtles (excluding sea turtles), and 10 snakes. The Coastal Plain is separable

into 4 distinct major regions: Lower Coastal Plain, Red Hills, Black Belt, and Fall Line Hills (Fig. 3). A wide transitional zone occurs between the Black Belt and Red Hills, and is so designated on the map.

Lower Coastal Plain

The Lower Coastal Plain (Fig. 3) corresponds to the Saballian Zone of some authors and, roughly, to the Gulf Strip of others. It extends completely across the state and includes, essentially, the southernmost tier of counties and the lower portions of some of those in the second tier. The relief varies from flat to gently rolling. Soils are sands, sandy loams, and sandy clays, with occasional gravelly phases.

Much of the Lower Coastal Plain is cleared for pasturage and cultivation,

FIG. 5. Pine flatwoods area near Citronelle, Mobile County. A "pitcher plant bog" is situated in the foreground and a flatwoods pond in the background. The microhabitats in pine flatwoods associations provide optimal living conditions for a number of reptiles and amphibians, including the scarlet kingsnake, flatwoods salamander, and dwarf salamander. Pine flatwoods associations, found mostly in the Lower Coastal Plain, need periodic fires for their existence as distinctive community types.

the greatest proportions so altered being in the eastern segment and in southern Baldwin County. The dominant forest communities on the upland sites are fire subclimax types, such as longleaf pine-turkey oak ("sandhills") (Fig. 4) and pine flatwoods (Fig. 5), although a variety of other types are also represented. Intensive forestry is practiced in much of the Lower Coastal Plain, with a growing tendency to replace existing forest types with planted pine stands. The intensive mechanical site preparation which often precedes replanting tends to eliminate a number of native plant species, including wiregrasses (*Aristida stricta* and *Sporobolus junceus*), the dominant herbs in many natural communities within the Lower Coastal Plain.

Characteristics of streams of the Lower Coastal Plain are highly variable. The major rivers flow generally southward and along some stretches have broad, low floodplains. The smaller streams are typically sand-bottomed and tea-colored (Fig.

6). Some stretches of the latter have typical floodplain forest development along them, while others have high banks forested with pine or live oak. Swampy places along the smaller streams may be dominated by thickets of titi (*Cliftonia monophylla* and *Cyrilla racemiflora*). Most natural ponds and lakes are of sinkhole origin, with clear, shallow water and abundant aquatic vegetation. The largest of these is Lake Jackson, which is situated on the Alabama-Florida boundary at Florala, Covington County.

The dominant feature of the coast of Alabama is Mobile Bay. To the southeast, the bay is delimited by Fort Morgan peninsula, a narrow strip of land extending westward from the body of the mainland for about 18 miles. Fort Morgan peninsula, as well as the remainder of the coast of Baldwin County with which it is contiguous, is dominated by dune communities and xeric pine flatwoods, with some salt marsh habitat on the leeward side. West of Mobile Bay,

FIG. 6. Escatawpa River near Citronelle, Mobile County. This stream, with its dark-stained water and sandy shores and bottom, is typical of many that arise within the Lower Coastal Plain. Aquatic reptiles and amphibians are often somewhat scarce in such streams.

in Mobile County, the coast of the mainland is low with extensive salt marsh communities. Several islands lie offshore of Mobile County, the largest of which is Dauphin Island. Dauphin Island is about 5 miles long and about 1½ miles wide at the widest point. The island has beach and dune habitat, as well as pine flatwoods and salt marsh. There is one small freshwater lake.

Jackson and Jackson (1970) prepared an annotated list of the reptiles and amphibians of Dauphin Island, but the herpetofauna remains inadequately studied. At least 2 of the components suggest a closer affinity with the mainland region to the east (Baldwin County) than with that to the north (Mobile County), even though the island is usually considered most closely associated with Mobile County. The eastern kingsnake (*Lampropeltis getulus getulus*) and the eastern mud snake (*Farancia abacura abacura*), both of which occur in southern Baldwin County, are also found on Dauphin Island. The subspecific counterparts of these forms on the mainland of Mobile County are the speckled kingsnake (*L. g. holbrooki*) and western mud snake (*F. a. reinwardti*). It appears on the basis of

this evidence that Dauphin Island was, in the relatively recent past, the western extremity of what is now Fort Morgan peninsula.

Fourteen species of reptiles and amphibians (excluding sea turtles) are restricted to the Lower Coastal Plain, some of which are encountered only rarely. The latter include the flatwoods salamander and pine woods (yellow-lipped) snake, forms which inhabit low pine flatwoods; the river frog, which prefers titi swamps; and the indigo snake. The indigo snake, along with the eastern diamondback rattlesnake, dusky gopher frog, and Florida pine snake, frequently takes shelter in the burrows of the gopher tortoise. Also restricted to the Lower Coastal Plain are the North Florida black swamp snake and the little grass frog, two forms whose ranges barely enter Alabama from the southeast.

Several species are not restricted to the Lower Coastal Plain but are much more frequently encountered there than elsewhere. These include the pine woods treefrog, oak toad, chicken turtle, southern hognose snake, coral snake, and eastern diamondback rattlesnake.

The northern range limits of several

TABLE 2. HERPETOFAUNAL COMPOSITION OF REGIONS OF ALABAMA IN TERMS OF NUMBERS OF NATIVE SPECIES IN MAJOR GROUPS

Region	Native species by group[1]							
	Sirens (2)	Salamanders (30)	Frogs (28)	Turtles[2] (22)	Lizards (11)	Snakes (40)	Crocodilians (1)	Total (134)
	No.	No.	No.	No.	No.	No.	No.	No.
Lower Coastal Plain	2	17	24	20	11	40	1	115
Red Hills	1	20	22	16	11	35	1	106
Black Belt	1	17	19	14	9	29	1	90
Fall Line Hills	1	20	20	15	11	34	0	101
Piedmont	0	15	16	10	10	27	0	78
Blue Ridge	0	17	14	12	10	28	0	81
Ridge and Valley	0	16	20	13	10	28	0	87
Appalachian Plateaus	0	18	17	11	9	26	0	81
Tennessee Valley	0	17	13	11	8	24	0	73
Chert Belt	0	15	13	12	8	23	0	71

[1] Numbers in parentheses are totals for state.
[2] Sea turtles excluded.

subspecies coincide roughly with the northern boundary of the Lower Coastal Plain. These subspecies are the southern red salamander, southern dusky salamander, yellow-bellied pond slider, southern copperhead, and dusky pigmy rattlesnake.

The Lower Coastal Plain is delimited above by its boundary with the Red Hills region. The transition is rather abrupt west of the Conecuh River. Eastward the distinction is not well defined, and in eastern Alabama the Red Hills region tends to lose its biogeographic and physiographic integrity. This is reflected in the distributional relationships between the southern chorus frog, a species predominantly of the Lower Coastal Plain, and the closely related but more northerly distributed upland chorus frog. West of the Conecuh River the ranges of the two forms meet along the regional boundary with very little overlap, whereas they overlap by approximately 80 miles

east of the river. The number of species within the different groups of reptiles and amphibians found in the Lower Coastal Plain, along with corresponding numbers for other regions, are shown in Table 2.

Red Hills

The Red Hills region (Fig. 3) is a belt of Eocene age, 30 to 40 miles in width. Much of the region has deeply dissected topography, relatively fertile soils, and frequent outcrops of siltstone, claystone, or limestone. In places in Choctaw, Clarke, and Monroe counties, it is almost montane in character (Fig. 7), with rocky bluffs, deep ravines, and clear, rock-bottomed brooks. Some of the ridge tops rise as high as 300 feet above the floors of the intervening valleys. The ridge tops and upper ravine slopes tend to support communities with mixtures of pine and hardwood, while the coves and lower slopes often have luxuriant hard-

FIG. 7. Vegetation on a ravine slope in the Coastal Plain Red Hills near Dozier, Crenshaw County. The habitat type shown here supports a forest dominated by hardwood trees and is the type to which the Red Hills salamander is confined. Other reptiles and amphibians found in this habitat type in the Red Hills include the worm snake, pickerel frog, zigzag salamander, and seal salamander, forms that are more often associated with areas above the Fall Line. (Photo by Ralph Jordan, Jr.)

wood forest stands, with oaks, hickories, beeches, and magnolias predominating.

Many elements of the biota of the Red Hills are some of those usually associated with regions above the Fall Line, and some are found in no other Coastal Plain province. Among the latter are the pickerel frog and zigzag salamander. The seal salamander is locally common in the western portion of the Red Hills, and except for one other locality, the Coastal Plain part of its range in Alabama is confined to the Red Hills. The entire range of the Red Hills salamander lies within the region. A large measure of the region's biological interest is being lost as vast tracts of forest are converted to pine plantations (see Preface).

Black Belt

The Black Belt is roughly crescent-shaped and extends almost continuously from western Tennessee southward through Mississippi and generally east-southeastward across central Alabama (Fig. 3). Its eastern terminus is poorly defined, but lies well west of the Chattahoochee River. The region is about 35 or 40 miles wide at its widest point, in extreme western Alabama.

The Black Belt is characterized by a predominance of heavy calcareous soils of Cretaceous origin, gently rolling topography, and intensive agriculture (Fig. 8). Rankin (1974) summarized the literature on the physiography and agriculture of the Black Belt and included several of his own interpretations. Formerly the Black Belt was devoted largely to cotton production, but today most of it is pasture.

Scattered through the Black Belt are inclusions of acid soil, some of which is sandy in texture. Several reptiles and amphibians commonly associated with light, friable soils in the Coastal Plain, however, appear to be scarce or absent from much if not all of the Black Belt. These include the mole skink, pine snake, pine woods treefrog, and southern hognose snake. The lack of extensive upland forests also contributes to the scarcity of some forms. The numerous farm ponds and lakes, however, often support an abundance, though not a great variety, of water snakes, frogs, and turtles. Among the larger terrestrial snakes, the copperhead and speckled king-

FIG. 8. Prairie habitat in the Black Belt, Montgomery County. Large areas within the Black Belt are devoted predominantly to row crops and improved pasture and are relatively poor habitat for most reptiles and amphibians.

snake are relatively common in the Black Belt. Amphiumas reportedly are common in many of the aquatic habitats, and the small-mouthed salamander seems fairly well adapted to the Black Belt.

Between the Black Belt and Red Hills is a belt which some authorities have termed "the Blue Marl Region." Zoogeographically, it appears to be irregularly transitional between the Black Belt and Red Hills and is so designated in Fig. 3. Also included within the "transitional zone" is the Post Oak Flatwoods (not indicated on map), a small area in western Alabama occupying portions of Sumter, Choctaw, Marengo, and Wilcox counties (see Harper, 1943).

Fall Line Hills

The Fall Line Hills, called Upper Coastal Plain by some authorities and Central Pine Belt by others, lies between the Black Belt and the Fall Line (Fig. 3). Topographically it varies from moderately hilly in the west to gently rolling in the east (Fig. 9).

The soils are Cretaceous in origin, mostly well drained, and vary from clay to sand. Gravelly phases are common. The sandy, well drained sites often support communities dominated by longleaf pine and turkey oak, the best developed and most extensive of these being in Autauga and Russell counties. These communities are generally similar to those that occur on dry, sandy sites in the Lower Coastal Plain, and some support populations of pine snakes, mole skinks, and oak toads. The gopher tortoise apparently ranged over much of the Fall Line Hills region until fairly recent times, but it exists today in this region only in a small area of Russell County.

Other forms of notable occurrence in the Fall Line Hills are the coal skink, mountain chorus frog, and seal salamander. The coal skink is locally common in the central and western portions, and an apparently disjunct population of this species inhabits an area in Russell County in the eastern portion. The mountain chorus frog, a species distributed rather generally above the Fall Line, oc-

FIG. 9. Open pine forest in the Fall Line Hills, Macon County. The Fall Line Hills region probably contains a greater diversity of habitat types than any other region of the state.

curs locally in the Fall Line Hills southward nearly to the edge of the Black Belt. The seal salamander, whose range includes several of the upland regions and a portion of the Red Hills, is known from one locality in the Fall Line Hills.

In the Fall Line Hills in northwestern Alabama, there are a number of areas where streams have cut through the Coastal Plain sediments into the underlying sandstone, producing habitats similar to many of the gorges in the Appalachian Plateaus region to the east. Such habitats are exemplified by "The Dismals" in Franklin County. Physiographically similar sites can be found at several other places in the Fall Line Hills in Franklin County, as well as in Colbert, Marion, Fayette, and Tuscaloosa counties. Green salamanders and spring salamanders, forms usually associated with habitats above the Fall Line, occur at some of these sites.

The Upland Regions

The upland regions, considered collectively to include the herpetofaunal provinces above the Fall Line, include the Piedmont, Blue Ridge, Ridge and Valley region, Appalachian Plateaus, Tennessee Valley, and Chert Belt (Fig. 3). The ranges of 11 species, or approximately 8 percent of the Alabama herpetofauna, are limited essentially to one or more of these regions. These species include 7 salamanders, 2 turtles, and 2 frogs. Seven of these species occur southward to the Fall Line, at least in some part of the state, while the ranges of the other 4 fail to reach it.

Piedmont

The Piedmont extends into Alabama from the east and occupies a triangular area of about 5,000 square miles in the eastern central portion (Fig. 3). Along its lower margin where it makes contact with the Coastal Plain, the transition is relatively abrupt, biotically and physiographically. To the north, the Piedmont borders the Blue Ridge. The transition there is not abrupt, and the northern portion of the Piedmont and the Blue Ridge have several features in common.

The Piedmont is hilly for the most part, with clay soils that tend to be rocky. The farms are relatively small, and much of the land is forested (Fig. 10). The ecology favors pines on the ridge tops and hardwoods along lower slopes and in the bottomlands. Several of the more extensive tracts of forest land are being clear-cut and replanted to loblolly pine.

The herpetofauna of the Piedmont is somewhat less rich than those of adjacent regions. In eastern Alabama at least 15

FIG. 10. Typical scene in the Piedmont near Gold Hill, Lee County. Relatively heavy, rocky soils predominate in the Piedmont. Several species of reptiles and amphibians, including the pine snake and spring salamander, are notably scarce or absent from the Piedmont.

species that occur in the Coastal Plain are not found in the Piedmont (or are limited to its lower edges), whereas only 2 species that occur in the Piedmont do not extend into the Coastal Plain. At least 4 species, the wood frog, the spring salamander, red-backed salamander, and pine snake, are present in the Blue Ridge, but apparently absent from the Piedmont. The seepage salamander, pickerel frog, and worm snake have been found in the upper Piedmont but not in the lower portion.

Blue Ridge

Above the Piedmont is a ridge, or series of ridges, extending approximately 100 miles southwestward which is herein designated Blue Ridge (Fig. 3). Whether this designation is physiographically correct is debatable. The region is included by some physiographers within the Piedmont and by others within the Ridge and Valley region. From the standpoint of the herpetofauna, however, the Blue Ridge designation seems appropriate.

The Blue Ridge gives way abruptly to the Coosa Valley, the main body of which lies to the northeast. As previously noted, the transition to Piedmont is

rather gradual. The highest point in Alabama, Mt. Cheaha (elevation 2,407 feet), is a component of the Blue Ridge, as are a number of other peaks in the region that exceed 2,000 feet in elevation (Fig. 11).

The soil tends to be rocky and fairly friable, with some sandy phases. A great majority of the region is devoted to forestry, and a variety of forest habitat types are represented. Longleaf pine seems to be one of the most abundant trees on the drier sites. The small streams arising within the region are cool and clear, and those which are unaltered by channelization, impoundment, or pollution support an abundance of salamander life.

As noted earlier, the region has several species of reptiles and amphibians that either do not occur in the Piedmont or occur only in its uppermost portion. Several species are notably absent from both the Blue Ridge and Piedmont, although they occur in some of the other upland regions. These include the green salamander, mountain dusky salamander, Tennessee cave salamander, and milk snakes (*Lampropeltis t. triangulum* and *L. t. syspila*). The northernmost record of the mole skink is located in the Blue

FIG. 11. View from Mt. Cheaha, the highest point in Alabama. (Photo by William Redmond.)

Ridge, as is the southernmost record for the spring salamander. The spring salamanders of the Blue Ridge are recognizably different from populations elsewhere in the state in showing strong influence of the subspecies *Gyrinophilus porphyriticus dunni*. (See account of the species p. 126.) The wood frog, a form of northern affinity, has been collected in Alabama only from the Blue Ridge around Mt. Cheaha.

Ridge and Valley Region

The Ridge and Valley region lies between the Blue Ridge and the Appalachian Plateaus (Fig. 3). It extends southwestward to the Fall Line. The region is considered here to consist of the Coosa Valley, the Cahaba Valley, and the uplands arising within these valleys. The soils range from gravelly loams to clay. The rocks at the lower elevations are mostly limestone and shale, with sandstone and chert at the higher elevations. Over one-half of the region is open.

The Coosa Valley occupies the largest area (Fig. 12). The most prominent ridge is Double Oak Mountain, most of which lies in Shelby County, near the region's southwestern terminus. Springs are common and include some of the largest in the state.

The herpetofauna of the Ridge and Valley region is unique among those of the upland subdivisions in having populations of at least 5 species which are usually associated with the Coastal Plain and not known to occur elsewhere above the Fall Line. These are the chicken turtle, eastern glass lizard, southern hognose snake, oak toad, and pine woods treefrog. Another form usually associated with the Coastal Plains, the dusky gopher frog, has been collected on one occasion in the region, but the presence of a breeding population has not been substantiated.

A related peculiarity of the region was noted earlier by botanists. In the upper reaches of the Coosa Valley, in Cherokee and Etowah counties, there were at one

FIG. 12. The Coosa Valley, the largest component of the Ridge and Valley region in Alabama. The Coosa Valley and some of its associated upland areas are inhabited by a number of reptiles and amphibians that do not occur elsewhere above the Fall Line. The Talladega Mountains, components of the Blue Ridge, are in the background. (Photo by William Redmond.)

time sizable areas of longleaf pine flatwoods with sandy or gravelly soil, similar
in many respects to some of the Lower
Coastal Plain flatwoods communities.
Harper (1943) mentions these and cites
earlier references to them.

Several reptiles and amphibians are
notably absent from the Ridge and Valley region. They are the green salamander, the mountain dusky salamander,
and the milk snakes. All of these occur
in the Appalachian Plateaus region,
which lies to the northwest.

Appalachian Plateaus

Lying immediately above the Ridge
and Valley region are the Appalachian
Plateaus (Fig. 3). Physiographically
these plateaus are often considered subdivisions of the Cumberland Plateau.
They include Lookout Mountain and
Sand Mountain below the Tennessee Val-

ley, and several broad fingers of the
main body of the Cumberland Plateau
above the Tennessee Valley.

Lookout Mountain originates in Tennessee, extends southwestward across the
northwestern corner of Georgia and into
Alabama, where it narrows and gradually
loses its identity around Gadsden in
Etowah County. Sand Mountain lies
to the west and northwest, across the
valley of Big Wills Creek. At the Ala-
bama-Georgia boundary, Sand Mountain
is about 15 miles wide. Southwestward it expands to occupy much of the
northern central portion of Alabama
above Birmingham. A small outlier of
Sand Mountain, Chandler Mountain, lies
along the southern edge.

The integrity of Sand Mountain as a
plateau is maintained westward to within about 20 miles of the Fall Line before it breaks up into an area of deeply

FIG. 13. Forest in a cove in the Bankhead National Forest, Lawrence County. The Bankhead is situated along the western edge of Sand Mountain, a component of the Appalachian
Plateaus region. Habitat such as that depicted here is common in the less accessible portions of the Plateaus region and supports a rich and diverse assemblage of forest- and
stream-dwelling reptiles and amphibians. Green salamanders, coal skinks, worm snakes,
and copperheads are among the forms that are notably abundant.

dissected terrain in Lawrence and Winston counties. Much of this rugged terrain is now included within the Bankhead National Forest. Several authorities
exclude a large area of Jefferson, Walker,
Winston, Cullman, and Blount counties
from the Appalachian Plateaus region,
designating it "coal basin" or "coal meas-
ures." From the standpoint of the herpetofauna, this distinction is unwarranted.

Lying north of Sand Mountain, from
Morgan County westward, is Little
Mountain. This narrow, somewhat irregular ridge has biogeographical characteristics similar to those of Sand Mountain;
it is separated from the latter by Moul-
ton Valley, a narrow, low-lying intrusion
of the Tennessee Valley. In Fig. 3, Little Mountain is shown as a portion of
the Appalachian Plateaus region.

The soils of the Appalachian Plateaus
are mostly sandy loams, although clay

soils are not uncommon in the southern
portion and at some of the lower elevations in the north. Rocky phases are
found at many sites. Throughout most
of the region, sandstone is the dominant exposed rock. Shale and limestone
as well as chert, however, are common
in the southern portion.

The gently rolling tops of the plateaus,
especially portions of Sand Mountain,
are often intensively farmed, but the
edges and sides have much of the natural habitat remaining (Fig. 13). The
streams draining protected watersheds
are clear with rock and sand bottoms
(Fig. 14). Caves and overhangs are
common. Most of the coal deposits in
Alabama are situated within this region,
and strip mining has drastically altered
the ecology at many localities.

Several forms of reptiles and amphibians are either confined to the Appalachian Plateaus or are much more likely

FIG. 14. Thompson Creek in the Bankhead National Forest, Lawrence County. This
stream is typical of many in protected watersheds within the Appalachian Plateaus region.

to be found there than elsewhere in Alabama. The mountain dusky salamander occurs only in the northeastern portions of Sand Mountain and Lookout Mountain. The entire range of the flattened musk turtle, a subspecies of *Sternotherus minor*, is included within the Appalachian Plateaus region. The cave salamander, Tennessee cave salamander, green salamander, and the large-headed, orange or brown morphotype of the two-lined salamander may occur in other regions, but are most frequently associated with habitats in the Appalachian Plateaus.

Subspecific influence from the northern brown snake (*Storeria dekayi dekayi*) and northern ringneck snake (*Diadophis punctatus edwardsi*) is evident in populations of their respective species in the northeastern portion of the region in Alabama. Notably scarce in most parts of the Appalachian Plateaus is the seal salamander, and it may be absent altogether from the western portion.

Tennessee Valley

The main body of the Tennessee Valley is a broad expanse of relatively level, fertile land which lies along much of the Tennessee River (Fig. 3). On the east and south where it meets the Appalachian Plateaus, there are bluffs and steep slopes, the lower reaches of which have extensive limestone outcrops. The soil of the valley is mostly red clay of limestone origin. The province is devoted largely to farming and industry (Fig. 15). The few remaining forests are composed mostly of hardwoods and scattered patches of red cedar.

Because so little of the natural habitat remains, the herpetofauna of the Tennessee Valley, on the whole, is relatively depauperate. Several species of turtles and snakes are abundant in the river and its associated backwaters, and the expected species of lizards, frogs, and salamanders are present in suitable habitats. The mole salamander, which is unknown from the other upland regions, occurs locally within the Tennessee Valley, and the small-mouthed salamander and Tennessee cave salamander have been collected at several sites. The seal salamander is absent, and the spring salamander does not occur in the valley proper.

The Tennessee River is impounded throughout its course in Alabama and bears little resemblance to its former state. The shoals which once contributed to a diverse aquatic fauna are now all under deep water. The most common turtles in the river are pond sliders, river cooters, painted turtles, common musk turtles, Ouachita map turtles, and midland smooth softshells. The most com-

FIG. 15. Typical scene in the Tennessee Valley, Jackson County. Most of the rural land in the Tennessee Valley has been cleared for pasture or row crops.

mon snakes are queen snakes and midland water snakes.

In Alabama, hellbenders are confined to the Tennessee River drainage system, where they occur mostly in well-oxygenated, cool-water streams that have not been channelized, impounded, or excessively polluted. Little suitable habitat remains, however, in the streams after they flow onto the floor of the Tennessee Valley. It is doubtful that breeding hellbender populations still persist in the Tennessee River itself.

Chert Belt

Above the Tennessee Valley in northwestern Alabama is the Chert Belt (Fig. 3). Physiographically the Chert Belt is the southernmost subdivision of a vast province whose components are termed collectively the Interior Low Plateaus. In our state, the Chert Belt occupies most of Lauderdale and Limestone counties, extends into northwestern Madison County, and includes small portions of Colbert and Lawrence counties south of the Tennessee River.

The Chert Belt is a moderately elevated region, with topography varying from hilly to nearly flat. The greatest relief is typically found near the streams.

The soils are mostly heavy and fairly fertile, but row-crop agriculture is difficult on many sites because of an abundance of chert fragments. The areas that remain forested are mostly in Lauderdale County and have a preponderance of hardwood trees, except where pines have been planted (Fig. 16).

The Chert Belt in Alabama lies entirely within the Tennessee River drainage area. There are several important streams, including Cypress Creek, Little Cypress Creek, Shoal Creek, Elk River, and a short segment of the Tennessee River.

The herpetofauna of the Chert Belt is poorly known. Hellbenders are present in several of the streams, and several species of aquatic turtles are fairly common, including pond sliders and the map turtle (*Graptemys geographica*). The "cave-mouth phenotype" of the northern dusky salamander (Folkerts, 1968a), which resembles the seal salamander in some respects, is locally common. The northern pine snake is known to occur in the region, and it is likely that milk snakes are there also. The green anole is scarce in the Chert Belt and the coachwhip is either scarce or absent.

FIG. 16. Hardwood forest in the Chert Belt, Limestone County.

PROBLEMATICAL FORMS

A number of species of reptiles and amphibians have ranges whose limits are known to lie very near Alabama but not known with certainty to include any portion of the state. Some of these may not now be present in the state but may extend their ranges into Alabama in the future. Others may now be present, but undetected. All these forms are listed below. In a separate subsection are forms of doubtful taxonomic validity that have been considered to occur in Alabama in relatively recent times.

Valid Forms Whose Ranges Closely Approach Alabama

Pseudobranchus striatus spheniscus Goin and Crenshaw — Dwarf Slender Siren. Occurs in Florida northwestward at least to the vicinity of Chipley, Jackson County. Inhabits weed-choked lakes, ponds, and swamps.

Amphiuma pholeter Neill — One-toed Amphiuma. Known to occur in Florida near the southeastern corner of Alabama (Bruce Means, personal communication). Inhabits mucky areas near small streams.

Haideotriton wallacei Carr — Georgia Blind Salamander. Has been collected from aquifers and cave pools in lime-sink areas of southwestern Georgia and adjacent portion of Florida. The north-westernmost record is from near Marianna, Jackson County, Florida.

Pseudotriton montanus diastictus Bishop — Midland Mud Salamander. Reported to occur in northern Alabama (Conant, 1958), but documentation is lacking. This form is rather strikingly different from the other subspecies of *P. montanus* and may in fact deserve species status. Except for some large individuals which become brownish, the ground color is a clear pinkish or salmon red. The dorsum and sides have a few well-separated black spots, usually ranging from 20 to 40 in number.

Hyla andersoni Baird — Pine Barrens Treefrog. An apparently isolated population of this frog was reported by Christman (1970) from near Dorcas, Okaloosa County, Florida. Attempts to locate it in nearby areas of southern Alabama have so far been unsuccessful.

Rana areolata circulosa Rice — Northern Crawfish Frog. Occurs in bottomland areas in Mississippi at least as far eastward as Columbus, Lowndes County. Probably occurs in Alabama in some suitable habitats in the Lamar-Pickens County area, but documentation is lacking.

Rana pipiens pipiens Schreber — Northern Leopard Frog. Range approaches Alabama from the north. Some unsampled populations of leopard frogs from near the Tennessee boundary may be of this subspecies or may be influenced by it.

Lampropeltis calligaster calligaster (Harlan) — Prairie Kingsnake. This subspecies may occur in extreme northwestern Alabama or may influence populations of *L. calligaster* in the area. Additional specimens are needed to assign these populations a subspecific designation.

Graptemys flavimaculata Cagle — Yellow-blotched Sawback. Known to occur in some streams of the Pascagoula River system in Mississippi, but has not yet been found in streams of that system in Alabama. This is also true of the turtle, *Sternotherus carinatus*.

Pseudemys floridana hoyi (Agassiz) — Missouri Slider. Possibly occurs in southwestern Alabama, although I have seen no specimens that so indicate. (See account of *P. f. floridana*, p. 291.)

Pseudemys nelsoni Carr — Florida Red-bellied Turtle. Apparently a close relative of *P. alabamensis* (the Alabama red-bellied turtle), this form occurs in Florida northwestward at least to the Chipola River in Jackson County, near the southeastern corner of Alabama. Possibly occurs in southeastern Alabama.

Forms of Doubtful Taxonomic Validity Reported in Alabama

Pseudemys concinna hieroglyphica (Holbrook). See pages 287-290.

Pseudemys concinna mobilensis (Holbrook). See pages 287-290.

Eurycea aquatica Rose and Bush. This form, described in 1963 from specimens obtained from springs and small streams 2 miles west of Bessemer, Jefferson County, was said to resemble *E. bislineata* but to differ from it "in coloration, in being much stockier, having a shorter tail, fewer prevomarine teeth, high percentage of adults with continuous prevomarine and parasphenoid teeth, fused nasal processes of the maxilla, and prominent prootic-squamosal crests." *Aquatica* was said to produce more eggs per individual than *E. bislineata* and to be permanently aquatic as opposed to predominantly terrestrial as is *E. bislineata*.

The type locality of *aquatica* is in the Ridge and Valley region. Its central feature is a spring choked with watercress (*Nasturtium officinale*). Since the discovery of *aquatica*, I have examined numerous salamanders referable to it from other localities within the Ridge and Valley region. Most were from springs and spring runs similar to those at the type locality. In nearly every instance, however, individuals intermediate between *aquatica* and *E. bislineata* were collected either at the sites or nearby, along with "typical" *E. bislineata*. Individuals intermediate in color pattern are most often intermediate in other respects also, including tail length and, in the case of gravid females, in number of yolked eggs.

Specimens referable to *aquatica* have been found on land under rocks and logs, as well as in the water among the underwater portions of aquatic plants. Not all springs within the Ridge and Valley region have populations referable to *aquatica*. Many are inhabited by "typical" *E. bislineata*.

The evidence thus far accumulated suggests that *aquatica* represents either an ecotype of *E. bislineata* or possibly a relict phenotype of that species which has maintained its integrity in certain situations where the geography tends to insulate it from an influx of obliterative genes. (See remarks under *E. bislineata*, p. 119.)

Eurycea bislineata cirrigera (Green). See page 119.

Eurycea bislineata wilderae Dunn. See page 119.

INTRODUCED SPECIES

Each year in the United States, many individuals of exotic species escape from their keepers or are released by well-meaning individuals. Others are brought in inadvertently in imported cargo. The vast majority of these aliens die sooner or later and leave no trace of their former presence. In several instances, however, breeding populations of exotic species have become established. Most such cases have occurred in Florida and California, but at least 1 species, and possibly 2, have 1 or more colonies in Alabama.

There is evidence that the Mediterranean gecko, *Hemidactylus turcicus*, has established a breeding population in Eufaula, Barbour County. On 2 occasions more than 1 individual of this small, nocturnal lizard have been seen around a restaurant in the northern outskirts of that city. The lizard, which has become rather common in many areas of Florida, is insectivorous and perfectly harmless. It can be distinguished from our native lizards in having a warty skin and elliptical eye pupils.

Sphaerodactylus lineolatus, another gecko, appeared on one occasion in Mobile, Alabama, but there is no indication of a breeding population there.

The Texas horned lizard, *Phrynosoma cornutum*, is known to have become established in several localities in Florida. This species, the "horned toad" that is most common throughout much of Texas and the Southwest, is often collected along the coast in the Florida Panhandle and might be expected to occur in the Alabama coastal area as well. A hatchling of this species, suggesting successful reproduction, was collected in a field near Siluria, Shelby County, in central Alabama. The Texas horned lizard, despite its formidable appearance, is harmless and feeds almost entirely on ants.

SPECIES ERRONEOUSLY REPORTED FROM ALABAMA

A number of apparently valid species have been reported erroneously from Alabama. Neill (1954) properly deleted *Sistrurus catenatus* and *Natrix kirtlandi* from the state list. *Plethodon jordani* (as "*P. metcalfi*") was reported from Jackson County by Holt (1924). This record was discredited by Bailey (1937). Although Conant (1958) reported *Graptemys kohni* in Alabama, the species apparently does not occur in the state.

Haltom (1931) leaves the implication that *Opheodrys vernalis* ("*Liopeltis vernalis*") may occur in Alabama, but no supporting evidence has appeared. Löding (1922) mentions a specimen of *Crocodylus acutus* collected near Mobile. This record, from well outside the natural range of that species (Neill, 1971), apparently was based on a released captive or a straggler.

ACCOUNTS OF TAXA

Within each of the orders or suborders, the constituent families are arranged in alphabetical order, as are genera within families. The species and subspecies, respectively, are placed in alphabetical order except for the nominate subspecies, which, if included, is the first one treated. The intrafamilial organization results in "cutting across" some subfamilial lines, but makes for easier reference.

Scientific Names

The generic, specific, and subspecific names applied are, in most cases, those in current usage by the majority of herpetologists. A few generic designations, such as *Pseudemys* instead of *Chrysemys* for several emydid turtles, *Manculus* instead of *Eurycea* for the dwarf salamander, and *Regina* instead of *Natrix* for the queen snake and Gulf glossy water snake, are used as a matter of personal choice between alternatives in cases where a clear consensus has not yet emerged. The reader should keep in mind that scientific names and taxonomic allocations of the various groups are subject to change as knowledge of their genetic interrelationships increases.

Common Names

Common names used are those recommended by the Committee on Common Names, American Society of Ichthyologists and Herpetologists, unless there are overriding reasons for not doing so.

Descriptions

The descriptions are intended to provide sufficient information to enable the reader to distinguish the form from all others occurring within the state. Each description is based on a composite of specimens representing a population or a group of populations, and it should be kept in mind that occasional individuals belonging to the described taxon will not conform to the description.

Included under the description of certain forms are occasional references to tables, and in some instances comments on taxonomic problems. The meanings of technical terms used in the descriptions and not clarified by illustrations are defined in the glossary.

Distribution

In addition to a general statement describing the distribution of each form occurring within Alabama, a spot map is included for each species, except marine turtles, depicting the range in the state and, if applicable, subspecies distribution. Specific localities from which specimens have been examined by the author are indicated. Also indicated are literature records in cases where they help to clarify distributional patterns. A smaller map depicts the approximate range of the species within the coterminous United States.

Habits

Information provided on habits is in most cases fairly general. When details are given, they often constitute significant new discoveries.

Photographs

Unless otherwise indicated, the photographs were taken by the author using 35 mm Kodak Plus-X film. The county from which each specimen photographed was collected is indicated, with the exception of the indigo snake in Fig. 203, for which there is no locality datum.

CHECK LIST OF THE REPTILES AND AMPHIBIANS OF ALABAMA

This list includes only the forms known to be native to Alabama or, in the case of some subspecies, to have substantial influence on Alabama populations. It incorporates, where appropriate, superfamilial and subfamilial groupings. Thus, the sequence in which the forms appear on the list differs from that in which they are treated in the accounts sections (see p. 26).

CLASS AMPHIBIA — AMPHIBIANS
Order Anura — Frogs and Toads

Family Bufonidae — Toads

Bufo americanus americanus	American Toad
Bufo quercicus	Oak Toad
Bufo terrestris	Southern Toad
Bufo woodhousei fowleri	Fowler's Toad

Family Hylidae — Hylid Frogs

Acris crepitans crepitans	Northern Cricket Frog
Acris gryllus gryllus	Southern Cricket Frog
Acris gryllus dorsalis	Florida Cricket Frog
Hyla avivoca	Bird-voiced Treefrog
Hyla cinerea	Green Treefrog
Hyla crucifer crucifer	Northern Spring Peeper
Hyla femoralis	Pine Woods Treefrog
Hyla gratiosa	Barking Treefrog
Hyla squirella	Squirrel Treefrog
Hyla versicolor (and *H. chrysoscelis?*)	Gray Treefrog
Limnaoedus ocularis	Little Grass Frog (Least Treefrog)
Pseudacris brachyphona	Mountain Chorus Frog
Pseudacris nigrita nigrita	Southern Chorus Frog
Pseudacris ornata	Ornate Chorus Frog
Pseudacris triseriata feriarum	Upland Chorus Frog

Family Microhylidae — Narrow-mouthed Toads
SUBFAMILY MICROHYLINAE

Gastrophryne carolinensis	Eastern Narrow-mouthed Toad

Family Pelobatidae — Spadefoot Toads
SUBFAMILY PELOBATINAE

Scaphiopus holbrooki holbrooki	Eastern Spadefoot Toad

Family Ranidae — True Frogs

SUBFAMILY RANINAE

Rana areolata sevosa	Dusky Gopher Frog
Rana catesbeiana	Bullfrog
Rana clamitans clamitans	Bronze Frog
Rana clamitans melanota	Green Frog
Rana grylio	Pig Frog
Rana heckscheri	River Frog
Rana palustris	Pickerel Frog
Rana pipiens sphenocephala	Southern Leopard Frog
Rana sylvatica	Wood Frog

Order Caudata — Salamanders

Family Ambystomatidae — Mole Salamanders

Ambystoma cingulatum	Flatwoods Salamander
Ambystoma maculatum	Spotted Salamander
Ambystoma opacum	Marbled Salamander
Ambystoma talpoideum	Mole Salamander
Ambystoma texanum	Small-mouthed Salamander
Ambystoma tigrinum tigrinum	Eastern Tiger Salamander

Family Amphiumidae — Amphiumas

Amphiuma means	Two-toed Amphiuma
Amphiuma tridactylum	Three-toed Amphiuma

Family Cryptobranchidae — Giant Salamanders

Cryptobranchus alleganiensis alleganiensis	Hellbender

Family Plethodontidae — Woodland Salamanders

SUBFAMILY DESMOGNATHINAE

Desmognathus aeneus	Seepage Salamander
Desmognathus fuscus fuscus	Northern Dusky Salamander
Desmognathus fuscus auriculatus	Southern Dusky Salamander
Desmognathus monticola ssp.	Seal Salamander
Desmognathus ochrophaeus	Mountain Dusky Salamander
Phaeognathus hubrichti	Red Hills Salamander

SUBFAMILY PLETHODONTINAE

Aneides aeneus	Green Salamander
Eurycea bislineata	Two-lined Salamander
Eurycea longicauda longicauda	Long-tailed Salamander
Eurycea longicauda guttolineata	Three-lined Salamander
Eurycea lucifuga	Cave Salamander
Gyrinophilus palleucus palleucus	Tennessee Cave Salamander
Gyrinophilus palleucus necturoides	No common name
Gyrinophilus porphyriticus porphyriticus	Northern Spring Salamander
Gyrinophilus porphyriticus dunni	Carolina Spring Salamander
Gyrinophilus porphyriticus duryi	Kentucky Spring Salamander
Hemidactylium scutatum	Four-toed Salamander
Manculus quadridigitatus	Dwarf Salamander
Plethodon cinereus polycentratus	Georgia Red-backed Salamander
Plethodon dorsalis dorsalis	Zigzag Salamander
Plethodon glutinosus glutinosus	Slimy Salamander
Pseudotriton ruber ruber	Northern Red Salamander
Pseudotriton ruber vioscai	Southern Red Salamander
Pseudotriton montanus flavissimus	Gulf Coast Mud Salamander

Family Proteidae — Mudpuppies, Waterdogs, and the Olm

Necturus beyeri	Beyer's Waterdog
Necturus malculosus	Mudpuppy

Family Salamandridae — Newts

Notopthalmus viridescens viridescens	Red-spotted Newt
Notopthalmus viridescens louisianensis	Central Newt

Order Trachystomata — Sirens

Family Sirenidae — Sirens

Siren intermedia intermedia	Eastern Lesser Siren
Siren intermedia nettingi	Western Lesser Siren
Siren lacertina	Greater Siren

CLASS REPTILIA

Order Crocodilia — Crocodilians

Family Alligatoridae — Alligators

SUBFAMILY ALLIGATORINAE

Alligator mississippiensis	American Alligator

Order Squamata — Lizards and Snakes
Suborder Lacertilia — Lizards

Family Anguidae — Lateral-fold Lizards

SUBFAMILY ANGUINAE

Ophisaurus attenuatus longicaudus	Eastern Slender Glass Lizard
Ophisaurus ventralis	Eastern Glass Lizard

Family Iguanidae — Iguanid Lizards

Anolis carolinensis carolinensis	Green Anole
Sceloporus undulatus undulatus	Southern Fence Lizard
Sceloporus undulatus hyacinthinus	Northern Fence Lizard

Family Scincidae — Skinks

Eumeces anthracinus anthracinus	Northern Coal Skink
Eumeces anthracinus pluvialis	Southern Coal Skink
Eumeces egregius similis	Northern Mole Skink
Eumeces fasciatus	Five-lined Skink
Eumeces inexpectatus	Southeastern Five-lined Skink
Eumeces laticeps	Broad-headed Skink
Scincella laterale	Ground Skink

Family Teidae — Teid Lizards

Cnemidophorus sexlineatus sexlineatus	Eastern Six-lined Racerunner

Suborder Serpentes (Ophidia) — Snakes

Family Colubridae — Colubrid Snakes

SUBFAMILY COLUBRINAE

Carphophis amoenus amoenus	Eastern Worm Snake
Carphophis amoenus helenae	Midwest Worm Snake
Cemophora coccinea copei	Northern Scarlet Snake
Coluber constrictor constrictor	Northern Black Racer
Coluber constrictor priapus	Southern Black Racer
Diadophis punctatus punctatus	Southern Ringneck Snake

SUBFAMILY COLUBRINAE (Continued)

Diadophis punctatus edwardsi	Northern Ringneck Snake
Diadophis punctatus stictogenys	Mississippi Ringneck Snake
Drymarchon corais couperi	Eastern Indigo Snake
Elaphe guttata guttata	Corn Snake
Elaphe obsoleta obsoleta	Black Rat Snake
Elaphe obsoleta spiloides	Gray Rat Snake
Farancia abacura abacura	Eastern Mud Snake
Farancia abacura reinwardti	Western Mud Snake
Farancia erytrogramma erytrogramma	Rainbow Snake
Lampropeltis calligaster rhombomaculata	Mole Snake
Lampropeltis getulus getulus	Eastern Kingsnake
Lampropeltis getulus holbrooki	Speckled Kingsnake
Lampropeltis getulus niger	Black Kingsnake
Lampropeltis triangulum triangulum	Eastern Milk Snake
Lampropeltis triangulum elapsoides	Scarlet Kingsnake
Lampropeltis triangulum syspila	Red Milk Snake
Masticophis flagellum flagellum	Eastern Coachwhip
Opheodrys aestivus	Rough Green Snake
Pituophis melanoleucus melanoleucus	Northern Pine Snake
Pituophis melanoleucus lodingi	Black Pine Snake
Pituophis melanoleucus mugitus	Florida Pine Snake
Rhadinaea flavilata	Pine Woods Snake (Yellow-lipped Snake)
Tantilla coronata coronata	Southeastern Crowned Snake

SUBFAMILY NATRICINAE

Natrix cyclopion cyclopion	Green Water Snake
Natrix cyclopion floridana	Florida Green Water Snake
Natrix erythrogaster erythrogaster	Red-bellied Water Snake
Natrix erythrogaster flavigaster	Yellow-bellied Water Snake
Natrix fasciata fasciata	Banded Water Snake
Natrix fasciata clarki	Gulf Salt Marsh Water Snake
Natrix fasciata confluens	Broad-banded Water Snake
Natrix fasciata pictiventris	Florida Water Snake
Natrix rhombifera rhombifera	Diamond-backed Water Snake
Natrix sipedon pleuralis	Midland Water Snake
Natrix taxispilota	Brown Water Snake
Regina rigida sinicola	Gulf Glossy Water Snake
Regina septemvittata	Queen Snake
Seminatrix pygaea pygaea	North Florida Black Swamp Snake
Storeria dekayi dekayi	Northern Brown Snake
Storeria dekayi limnetes	Marsh Brown Snake
Storeria dekayi wrightorum	Midland Brown Snake
Storeria occipitomaculata occipitomaculata	Northern Red-bellied Snake
Thamnophis sauritus sauritus	Eastern Ribbon Snake
Thamnophis sirtalis sirtalis	Eastern Garter Snake
Virginia striatula	Rough Earth Snake
Virginia valeriae valeriae	Eastern Smooth Earth Snake
Virginia valeriae elegans	Western Smooth Earth Snake

SUBFAMILY XENODONTINAE

Heterodon platyrhinos	Eastern Hognose Snake
Heterodon simus	Southern Hognose Snake

Family Elapidae – Coral Snakes, Cobras, and Relatives
Micrurus fulvius fulvius   Eastern Coral Snake

Family Viperidae – Vipers
SUBFAMILY CROTALINAE – PIT VIPERS

Agkistrodon contortrix contortrix	Southern Copperhead
Agkistrodon contortrix mokeson	Northern Copperhead
Agkistrodon piscivorus piscivorus	Eastern Cottonmouth
Agkistrodon piscivorus conanti	Florida Cottonmouth
Agkistrodon piscivorus leucostoma	Western Cottonmouth
Crotalus adamanteus	Eastern Diamondback Rattlesnake
Crotalus horridus	Timber Rattlesnake
Sistrurus miliarius miliarius	Carolina Pigmy Rattlesnake
Sistrurus miliarius barbouri	Dusky Pigmy Rattlesnake
Sistrurus miliarius streckeri	Western Pigmy Rattlesnake

Order Testudinidata – Turtles
Suborder Cryptodira
Superfamily Chelonoidea

Family Cheloniidae – Sea Turtles

Caretta caretta caretta	Atlantic Loggerhead
Chelonia mydas	Green Turtle
Eretmochelys imbricata imbricata	Atlantic Hawksbill
Lepidochelys kempi	Atlantic Ridley

Family Dermochelidae – Leatherback Sea Turtle

Dermochelys coriacea coriacea   Atlantic Leatherback

Superfamily Testudinoidea

Family Chelydridae – Snapping Turtles

Chelydra serpentina serpentina	Common Snapping Turtle
Macroclemys temmincki	Alligator Snapping Turtle

Family Emydidae – Emydid Turtles

Chrysemys picta picta	Eastern Painted Turtle
Chrysemys picta dorsalis	Southern Painted Turtle
Chrysemys picta marginata	Midland Painted Turtle
Deirochelys reticularia reticularia	Eastern Chicken Turtle
Graptemys barbouri	Barbour's Map Turtle
Graptemys geographica	Map Turtle
Graptemys nigrinoda nigrinoda	Northern Black-knobbed Sawback
Graptemys nigrinoda delticola	Southern Black-knobbed Sawback
Graptemys pseudogeographica ouachitensis	Ouachita Map Turtle (False Map Turtle)
Graptemys pulchra	Alabama Map Turtle
Malaclemys terrapin pileata	Mississippi Diamondback Terrapin
Pseudemys alabamensis	Alabama Red-bellied Turtle
Pseudemys concinna concinna	River Cooter
Pseudemys floridana floridana	Florida Cooter
Pseudemys scripta scripta	Yellow-bellied Pond Slider
Pseudemys scripta elegans	Red-eared Pond Slider
Terrapene carolina carolina	Eastern Box Turtle
Terrapene carolina major	Gulf Coast Box Turtle
Terrapene carolina triunguis	Three-toed Box Turtle

Family Kinosternidae — Mud and Musk Turtles

Kinosternon subrubrum subrubrum	Eastern Mud Turtle
Kinosternon subrubrum hippocrepis	Mississippi Mud Turtle
Sternotherus minor minor	Loggerhead Musk Turtle
Sternotherus minor depressus	Flattened Musk Turtle
Sternotherus minor peltifer	Stripe-necked Musk Turtle
Sternotherus odoratus	Common Musk Turtle (Stinkpot)

Family Testudinidae — Tortoises

Gopherus polyphemus	Gopher Tortoise

Superfamily Trionychoidea

Family Trionychidae — Soft-shelled Turtles

Trionyx ferox	Florida Softshell
Trionyx muticus muticus	Midland Smooth Softshell
Trionyx muticus calvatus	Gulf Coast Smooth Softshell
Trionyx spiniferus spiniferus	Eastern Spiny Softshell
Trionyx spiniferus asper	Gulf Coast Spiny Softshell

TAXONOMIC KEYS TO THE REPTILES AND AMPHIBIANS OF ALABAMA

Following are taxonomic keys to the reptiles and amphibians of Alabama (except sirens), including a species key to the tadpoles. Illustrations are provided where appropriate to facilitate use of the keys.

Key to the Orders of Amphibia

1a. Tailless or if tailed, aquatic with a more or less globular body (tadpole). Order Anura — Frogs and Toads _____(p. 32).

1b. Tailed; body not globular; aquatic or terrestrial_____2

2a. Permanently aquatic; external gills present throughout life; front limbs well developed, hind limbs absent; body eel-like. Order Trachystomata — Sirens_____(p. 145).

2b. Aquatic or terrestrial; external gills present or absent; front and hind limbs present, or, if either pair absent, body not eel-like (except in very small amphiumas). Order Caudata — Salamanders_____(p. 39).

Key to the Orders and Suborders of Reptiles

1a. Limbs present; tail laterally compressed; snout elongate, flattened.

Order Crocodilia — Crocodilians _____ _____(p. 150).

1b. Limbs present or absent; tail not laterally compressed (in Alabama forms); snout not noticeably elongate, or, if so, not flattened (except for somewhat flattened, upturned rostral in *Heterodon simus*, Southern Hognose Snake)_____2

2a. Toothless; body enclosed in a shell. Order Testudinata (Suborder Cryptodira) — Turtles_____(p. 51).

2b. Toothed; body not enclosed in a shell. (Order Squamata)_____3

3a. External ear openings present; with or without limbs. Suborder Lacertila — Lizards_____(p. 42).

3b. External ear openings absent; limbless. Suborder Serpentes — Snakes _____(p. 44).

Key to the Frogs and Toads (transformed individuals)

1a. Undersurface of hind foot with 1 or 2 hard spadelike tubercles on the heel_____2

1b. Undersurface of hind foot lacking hard spadelike tubercles on the heel_____6

2a. Undersurface of hind foot with 1

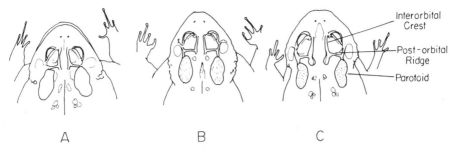

FIG. 17. Cranial crests of 3 toads (*Bufo*) and their relationship to the parotoids: (A) Fowler's toad, *Bufo woodhousei fowleri;* (B) American toad, *B. a. americanus;* (C) southern toad, *B. terrestris.*

hard spadelike tubercle; pupil of eye vertically elliptical in light; hind foot with conspicuous webbing between toes. (Family Pelobatidae) *Scaphiopus holbrooki holbrooki* — Eastern Spadefoot............(p. 83).

2b. Undersurface of hind foot with two hard spadelike tubercles; pupil or eye horizontally elliptical in light; hind foot with scant webbing between toes. (Family Bufonidae)..3

3a. Adult size less than 35 mm snout-vent length; dorsum with paired dark spots separated by a light median stripe. *Bufo quercicus* — Oak Toad............................(p. 58).

3b. Adult size greater than 40 mm snout-vent length; dorsum variously marked with spots, occasionally with a median light stripe............4

4a. Postorbital crest or ridge touching parotoid (Fig. 17A); largest dorsal spots usually with 3 or more warts. *Bufo woodhousei fowleri* — Fowler's Toad...........................(p. 60).

4b. Postorbital crest or ridge not touching parotoid, but having a backward-projecting spur that does (Fig. 17B, 17C); dorsal spots usually with from 1 to 3 warts........5

5a. Interorbital crests or ridges ending posteriorly in pronounced knoblike protuberances (Fig. 17C); large dorsal spots usually with 1 to 3 warts. *Bufo terrestris* — Southern Toad.......................(p. 59).

5b. Interorbital crests or ridges not ending in knoblike protuberances (Fig.

17B); large dorsal spots usually with only 1 wart each. *Bufo americanus americanus* — American Toad ....(p. 56).

6a. Head with a transverse fold behind the eyes (in life) (Fig. 18); head and snout abruptly tapering to a point, tympanum absent; hind foot lacking webbing between toes. (Family Microhylidae) *Gastrophryne carolinensis* — Eastern Narrow-mouthed Toad.............(p. 81).

6b. Head without a transverse fold; head and snout not abruptly tapering to a point; tympanum present; hind foot with at least some webbing between toes...................7

FIG. 18. Dorsal aspect of the eastern narrow-mouthed toad, *Gastrophryne carolinensis.*

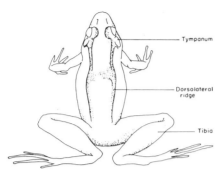

FIG. 19. Dorsal aspect of a frog with dorsolateral ridges.

7a. Belly skin smooth; hind foot with extensive webbing between toes; toes pointed, their tips not expanded. (Family Ranidae)_____8

7b. Belly skin granular; hind foot not extensively webbed; tips of toes (in most forms) expanded into adhesive discs (Family Hylidae)_____17

8a. Back with dorsolateral ridges (Fig. 19_____9

8b. Back without dorsolateral ridges__15

9a. Face with a dark mask extending from snout to behind tympanum — *Rana sylvatica* — Wood Frog_____
_____(p. 96).

9b. Face without a dark mask extending from snout to behind tympanum_____10

10a. Dorsum usually with a row of large squarish spots down each side, some of these occasionally fused. *Rana palustris* — Pickerel Frog_____
_____(p. 92).

10b. Dorsum with or without spots, but if spotted, not marked with a row of large squarish spots down each side_____11

11a. Dorsum with numerous large, rounded, dark spots and scattered smaller dark markings; frog noticeably stubby in appearance. *Rana areolata sevosa* — Dusky Gopher Frog_____(p. 84).

11b. Dorsum without numerous large, rounded dark spots; frog not noticeably stubby in appearance____12

12a. Edge of jaw with alternating light and dark spots (*Rana clamitans* ssp.)_____13

12b. Edge of jaw with an unbroken light line (*Rana pipiens* ssp.)_____14

13a. Dorsum of adults usually green, often spotted, rugose; dark markings on undersurfaces scant or lacking; throat of male bright yellow. *Rana clamitans melanota* — Green Frog_____(p. 88).

13b. Dorsum of adults usually bronze, unspotted, and not rugose; undersurfaces often profusely marked with dark spots and vermiculations; throat of adult male not bright yellow. *Rana clamitans clamitans* — Bronze Frog_____(p. 88).

14a. Snout usually with a dark medial spot; tympanum not conspicuously light-centered. *Rana pipiens pipiens* — Northern Leopard Frog (occurrence in Alabama problematical)
_____(p. 24).

14b. Snout usually lacking a dark medial spot; tympanum conspicuously light-centered. *Rana pipiens sphenocephala* — Southern Leopard Frog
_____(p. 95).

15a. Venter gray to gray-brown with light markings. *Rana heckscheri* — River Frog_____(p. 90).

15b. Venter white or whitish with dark markings_____16

16a. Hind foot with webbing extending to near the tip of longest toe; rear of thigh usually with a light longitudinal stripe or with a longitudinal series of light spots; snout pointed. *Rana grylio* — Pig Frog____(p. 90).

16b. Hind foot with longest toe projecting well beyond limit of webbing; rear of thigh without light longitudinal stripe or suggestion thereof; snout rounded. *Rana catesbeiana* — Bullfrog_____(p. 86)

17a. Rear of thigh with one or more dark, longitudinal stripes or suggestion thereof (Fig. 20); front of snout with light vertical lines. (Genus *Acris*)_____18

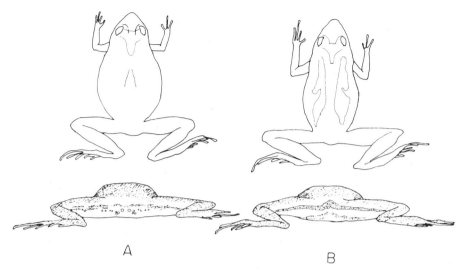

FIG. 20. Dorsal aspect and post-femoral markings of 2 cricket frogs (dorsal markings are extremely variable on both forms): (A) northern cricket frog, *Acris c. crepitans;* (B) southern cricket frog, *Acris g. gryllus.*

17b. Rear of thigh without longitudinal stripes; front of snout without light vertical lines _____20

18a. Body stout; snout rounded; thigh stripe usually ragged-edged or obscure (Fig. 20A); webbing on hind foot usually extending at least to second phalanx of longest toe. *Acris crepitans crepitans* — Northern Cricket Frog_____(p. 62).

18b. Body slender; snout pointed; thigh stripe(s) usually smooth-edged, prominent (Fig. 20B); last 3 phalanges of longest toe on hind foot

usually free of webbing. (*Acris gryllus* ssp.) _____19

19a. Back of thighs with 1 longitudinal dark stripe. *Acris gryllus gryllus* — Southern Cricket Frog_____(p. 64).

19b. Back of thigh with 2 longitudinal dark stripes. *Acris gryllus dorsalis* — Florida Cricket Frog_____(p. 65).

20a. Adult size less than 18 mm from snout to vent; a dark lateral stripe passing through the eye and ending on the side usually visible. *Limnaoedus ocularis* — Little Grass Frog_____(p. 74).

FIG. 21. Dorsal aspect of 3 Alabama chorus frogs: (A) southern chorus frog, *Pseudacris n. nigrita;* (B) upland chorus frog, *P. triseriata feriarum;* (C) mountain chorus frog, *P. brachyphona.*

20b. Adult size over 20 mm; markings various or absent, but if present, not as above_____21

21a. Tips of digits moderately expanded (to less than one-half the diameter of the tympanum), or not at all. (Genus *Pseudacris*)_____22

21b. Tips of digits greatly expanded (to more than one-half the diameter of the tympanum). (Genus *Hyla*)_25

22a. Head lacking a dark triangular blotch or expanded figure between the eyes; body slender; snout pointed (Fig. 21A). *Pseudacris nigrita nigrita* — Southern Chorus Frog_____(p. 77).

22b. Head with a dark, triangular blotch or expanded figure between eyes; body slender to stout; snout rounded (Fig. 21B, 21C)_____23

23a. Tips of digits rounded, but not obviously expanded; body with conspicuous dark blotches on sides and near the groin. *Pseudacris ornata* — Ornate Chorus Frog_____(p. 78).

23b. Tips of digits expanded; body usually with longitudinal stripes, bars, or with longitudinally oriented series of spots_____24

24a. Dorsum usually with 2 longitudinal broad, dark stripes, these typically in the form of "reversed parentheses" (Fig. 21C). *Pseudacris brachyphona* — Mountain Chorus Frog _____(p. 76).

24b. Dorsum usually with 3 longitudinal dark stripes or series of dark spots (Fig. 21B). *Pseudacris triseriata feriarum* — Upland Chorus Frog ____ _____(p. 79).

25a. Face with a light spot below each eye_____26

25b. Face without a light spot below each eye _____27

26a. Light interspaces between dark markings on rear of thigh yellow or orange (in life); skin of dorsum warty. *Hyla versicolor* complex — Gray Treefrog(s) _____(p. 73).

26b. Light interspaces between dark markings on rear of thigh light green or yellowish green; skin of dorsum smooth to slightly papillate or pustulate. *Hyla avivoca* — Bird-voiced Treefrog_____(p. 65).

27a. Rear of thigh with distinct light spots (yellow or orange in life). *Hyla femoralis* — Pine Woods Treefrog_____(p. 69).

27b. Rear of thigh without light spots 28

28a. Dorsum with a conspicuous dark, X-shaped mark. *Hyla crucifer crucifer* — Northern Spring Peeper_____ _____(p. 68).

28b. Dorsum without a conspicuous dark, X-shaped mark_____29

29a. Adult size less than 40 mm from snout to vent; pigmentation variable but never with conspicuous markings on sides. *Hyla squirella* — Squirrel Treefrog_____(p. 63).

29b. Adult size greater than 45 mm from snout to vent; sides with conspicuous markings_____30

30a. Side with a sharply defined, straight, white or yellowish stripe; dorsum bright green, lacking dark spots. *Hyla cinerea* — Green Treefrog_____(p. 67).

30b. Side variously marked, but never as above; dorsum green to brown, usually with dark spots. *Hyla gratiosa* — Barking Treefrog___(p. 71).

Species Key to the Larval Frogs and Toads (Tadpoles)

This key is based chiefly on the one published by Altig (1970). The user should refer to Fig. 22, 23, and 24 for meanings of terms used in key.

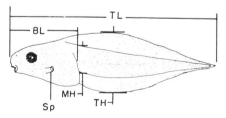

FIG. 22. Lateral aspect of a tadpole (from Altig, 1970). BL—body length; TL—total length; Sp—spiracle; MH—tail musculature height; TH—tail height.

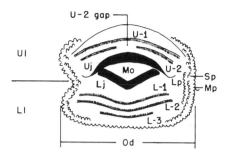

FIG. 23. Tadpole mouth and its associated structures (from Altig, 1970). The left side is emarginate, the right not emarginate. Ul, upper labium; U-1, first upper tooth row; U-2, second upper tooth row; Uj, upper jaw; Lp, lateral process of upper jaw; Mo, mouth; Mp, marginal papilla; Od, oral disc; Ll, lower labium; L-1, first lower tooth row; L-2, second lower tooth row; L-3, third lower tooth row; Sp, submarginal papillae; Lj, lower jaw.

1a. Oral disc lacking; jaws lacking keratinized teeth; labial teeth lacking. *Gastrophryne carolinensis* — Eastern Narrow-mouthed Toad_____ _____(p. 81).

1b. Oral disc present; jaws with keratinized teeth; labial teeth present__2

2a. Anus opening medially_____3

2b. Anus opening to left of ventral tail crest (viewed from venter)_____7

3a. Papillary border of oral disc uninterrupted ventrally. *Scaphiopus holbrooki holbrooki* — Eastern Spadefoot Toad_____(p. 83).

3b. Papillary border of oral disc with a medial gap ventrally_____4

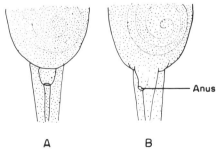

A   B

FIG. 24. Venter of tadpoles, showing anus opening medially (A) and to the left of midline (B) (from Altig, 1970).

4a. First upper labial tooth row with a median gap. *Bufo quercicus* — Oak Toad_____(p. 58).

4b. First upper labial tooth row uninterrupted_____5

5a. Upper and lower tail fins equal in vertical dimension to that of the tail musculature; a light oblique mark present behind each eye in life. *Bufo terrestris* — Southern Toad_____(p. 59).

5b. Upper and lower tail fins subequal in vertical dimension to that of the tail musculature; no light oblique mark behind each eye_____6

6a. Dorsum commonly with light mottling in life; snout rounded in lateral profile; tail length/tail height ratio 2.8 or more; tail height/tail musculature height ratio 2.0 or more. *Bufo woodhousei fowleri* — Fowler's Toad_____(p. 60).

6b. Dorsum unicolorous; snout sloping in lateral profile; tail height/tail musculature height ratio 2.0 or less. *Bufo americanus americanus* — American Toad_____(p. 56).

7a. Papillary border of oral disc emarginate; eyes dorsal. (Family Ranidae)_____8

7b. Papillary border of oral disc entire; eyes lateral. (Family Hylidae)____15

8a. Dorsal tail crest extending anteriorly on body to a point opposite spiracle. *Rana sylvatica* — Wood Frog_____(p. 96).

8b. Dorsal tail crest not extending anteriorly as far as point opposite spiracle_____9

9a. Venter pigmented with black; tail fins dark-bordered (in young, dark borders confined to proximal regions). *Rana heckscheri* — River Frog_____(p. 90).

9b. Venter light or transparent; tail fins lacking dark borders_____10

10a. Tail fins clear or with distinct black dots; blood vessels in fins evident near musculature. *Rana catesbeiana* — Bullfrog_____(p. 86).

10b. Tail fins pigmented but without distinct black dots; blood vessels in tail fins near musculature obscured by dark pigment_____11

11a. Ventral body wall usually transparent in preserved specimens, allowing viscera to show through (except in some *Rana areolata sevosa*)____12

11b. Ventral body usually opaque, viscera not showing through in preserved specimens _____13

12a. Space separating the 2 segments of the second upper labial tooth row no more than one-half the length of either segment; less than 11 marginal papillae below third lower labial tooth row. *Rana palustris* — Pickerel Frog_____ (p. 92).

12b. Space separating 2 segments of second upper labial tooth row more than one-half the length of either segment; 11 or more marginal papillae below the third lower labial tooth row. *Rana pipiens* ssp. — Leopard Frog_____ (p. 93).

13a. Lower beak broadly pigmented; tail roughly triangular. *Rana areolata sevosa* — Dusky Gopher Frog_____ _____(p. 84).

13b. Lower beak narrowly pigmented; tail not triangular_____14

14a. Third lower tooth row only slightly less than half the length of the first lower row. *Rana clamitans* ssp. — Bronze and Green Frogs____(p. 88).

14b. Third lower tooth row about one-third the length of the first lower row. *Rana grylio* — Pig Frog_____ _____(p. 90).

15a. Two rows of teeth on lower labium _____16

15b. Three rows of teeth on lower labium_____18

16a. Right and left segments of second upper labial tooth row narrowly separated; tail tip never black; body globular. *Hyla crucifer crucifer* — Northern Spring Peeper____ _____(p. 68).

16b. Right and left segments of second upper labial tooth rows widely separated; tail tip often black; body somewhat flattened. (Genus *Acris*) _____17

17a. Spiracular tube free virtually throughout its length; throat dark; tail musculature finely flecked. *Acris gryllus* ssp. — Florida and Southern Cricket Frogs____(p. 64).

17b. Spiracular tube attached to body to approximately the mid-point of its length; throat light; tail musculature mottled or reticulated. *Acris crepitans crepitans* — Northern Cricket Frog_____(p. 62).

18a. Third lower tooth row shorter than horny beak and not more than one-half the length of the first lower tooth row_____19

18b. Third lower tooth row longer than horny beak and at least three-fourths the length of the first lower tooth row_____25

19a. Papillae absent below third lower tooth row; tail with a longitudinal brown stripe bordered on each side by a light stripe. *Limnaoedus ocularis* — Little Grass Frog____(p. 74).

19b. Papillae present below third lower tooth row; tail not marked as above _____20

20a. Eye closer to spiracle than to snout; ventral one-half of tail musculature not lighter than dorsal one-half 21

20b. Eye equidistant between spiracle and snout; ventral one-half of tail musculature lighter than dorsal one-half_____22

21a. Body wall and tail transparent; depth of tadpole at eyes about one-half the greatest tail depth. *Hyla gratiosa* — Barking Treefrog____ _____(p. 61).

21b. Body wall and tail not transparent; depth of tadpole at eyes much greater than one-half the greatest tail depth. *Hyla cinerea* — Green Treefrog_____(p. 67).

22a. Dorsal fin high, extending anterior of spiracle; length of tail about twice its greatest depth. *Pseudacris ornata* — Ornate Chorus Frog____ _____(p. 78).

22b. Dorsal fin moderately developed, usually not extending anterior of spiracle; length of tail more than twice the greatest tail depth_____23

23a. Body dark brassy in life; space separating right and left segments of second upper labial tooth row less than one-half the length of either segment. *Pseudacris brachyphona* Mountain Chorus Frog_____(p. 76).

23b. Body not dark brassy in life; space separating right and left segments of second upper tooth row more than one-half the length of either segment_____24

24a. Chest pigmented; dorsum without small black dots. *Pseudacris nigrita nigrita* — Southern Chorus Frog_____ _____(p. 77).

24b. Chest not pigmented; dorsum usually with small black dots. *Pseudacris triseriata feriarum* — Upland Chorus Frog_____(p. 79).

25a. Tail musculature with light (red in life) dorsal saddles; fins without bold dark markings. *Hyla avivoca* — Bird-voiced Treefrog_____(p. 65).

25b. Tail musculature without light dorsal saddles; fins with bold dark markings_____26

26a. Tail musculature distinctly striped. *Hyla femoralis* — Pine Woods Treefrog_____(p. 69).

26b. Tail musculature not distinctly striped_____27

27a. Tail musculature distinctly bicolored; tails of large individuals not reddish in life. *Hyla squirella* — Squirrel Treefrog_____(p. 72).

27b. Tail musculature not distinctly bicolored; tails of large individuals

reddish in life. *Hyla versicolor* complex — Gray Treefrogs_____(p. 73).

Key to the Salamanders (excluding larvae)

1a. Body eel-like; external gills absent; limbs tiny; each foot with no more than 3 toes (Fig. 25). (Family Amphiumidae)_____2

1b. Body not eel-like; external gills present or absent; limbs not tiny; each foot with more than 3 toes____4

2a. Three toes on each foot. *Amphiuma tridactylum* — Three-toed Amphiuma_____(p. 107).

2b. One or 2 toes on each foot_____3

3a. Two toes on each foot. *Amphiuma means* — Two-toed Amphiuma_____ _____(p. 106).

3b. One toe on each hind foot. *Amphiuma pholeter* — One-toed Amphiuma (occurrence in Alabama problematical)_____(p. 106).

4a. Permanently aquatic; external gills lacking in adults; neck with an opening on each side; skin on sides wrinkled and folded; head strongly flattened; eyes greatly reduced. Family Cryptobranchidae: *Cryptobranchus alleganiensis alleganiensis* — Hellbender_____(p. 24).

4b. Adults aquatic or terrestrial; if aquatic, with external gills_____5

5a. Adults aquatic; external gills present; all feet with 4 toes each. Family Proteidae: *Necturus* spp._____ _____(See accounts, pp. 139-144).

5b. Adults aquatic or terrestrial; with

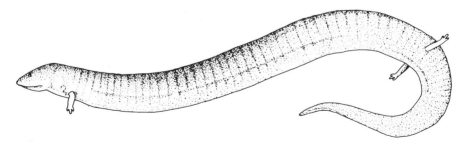

FIG. 25. General aspect of *Amphiuma* spp.

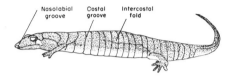

FIG. 26. Lateral aspect of the seal salamander, *Desmognathus monticola* ssp.

or without external gills; if aquatic, hind feet with 5 toes each_____6

6a. Nasolabial grooves (Fig. 26) absent_____7

6b. Nasolabial grooves present (Fig. 26) (Family Plethodontidae)____15

7a. Costal grooves lacking. (Family Salamandridae: *Notopthalmus viridescens* ssp.)_____8

7b. Costal grooves present (Fig. 26). (Family Ambystomatidae)_____9

8a. Dorsum with a row of conspicuous orange-red to red, black-bordered spots down each side. *Notopthalmmus viridescens viridescens* — Red-spotted Newt_____(p. 144).

8b. Dorsum without a row of orange-red to red spots down each side, or, if spots are present, they are reduced in size and incompletely encircled by black. *Notopthalmus viridescens louisianensis* — Central Newt_____(p. 145).

9a. Dorsum with light spots, blotches, or bars_____10

9b. Dorsum with lichen-like markings, reticulate, or unmarked_____12

10a. Dorsum with transverse silvery bars, some or all of which are occasionally broken. *Ambystoma opacum* — Marbled Salamander_____(p. 101).

10b. Dorsum with orange or yellow spots or blotches_____11

11a. Dorsum with distinct round, yellow (occasionally orange) spots, in 2 fairly regular rows. *Ambystoma maculatum* — Spotted Salamander _____(p. 99). (See also couplet 12.)

11b. Dorsum with irregular yellowish blotches, not arranged to form a regular pattern. *Ambystoma tigri-*

num tigrinum — Eastern Tiger Salamander_____(p. 104).

12a. Dorsum without any discernible light markings; costal grooves usually 12, occasionally 11 or 13. *Ambystoma maculatum* — Spotted Salamander (occasional variant)_____
_____(p. 99).

12b. Dorsum with discernible light markings or, if plain, costal grooves 14 or 15_____13

13a. Costal grooves 10 or 11. *Ambystoma talpoideum* — Mole Salamander_____(p. 103).

13b. Costal grooves 13 to 16_____14

14a. Dorsum black with light gray reticulations. *Ambystoma cingulatum* — Flatwoods Salamander_____(p. 98).

14b. Dorsum brown to black, plain or with light, lichen-like patches. *Ambystoma texanum* — Small-mouthed Salamander_____(p. 103).

15a. Face with a light stripe, or suggestion thereof, from the eye to the angle of the jaw (Fig. 26). (Genus *Desmognathus*)_____16

15b. Face without a light stripe from the eye to the angle of the jaw_____ 20

16a. Adults from 18 mm to 30 mm in snout-vent length; tail rounded in cross-section; dorsal surface of each thigh with a conspicuous oval spot; dorsum with a longitudinal stripe. *Desmognathus aeneus* — Seepage Salamander_____(p. 112).

16b. Adults 29 mm to 80 mm in snout-vent length; tail with a dorsal keel; dorsal surface of thigh plain or variously marked, but never with a conspicuous oval spot; dorsum variously patterned_____17

17a. Tail with a weak keel; tip of tail attenuate; width of tail behind vent equal to or greater than its height; commissure of jaw markedly sinuate. *Desmognathus ochrophaeus* — Mountain Dusky Salamander_____
_____(p. 117).

17b. Tail conspicuously keeled; tip of tail not attenuate; width of tail behind vent less than its height; commissure of jaws not markedly sinuate_____18

18a. Venter dark brown or black, speckled with white; dorsum suffused with black, markings usually obscure; sides of body with 2 rows of conspicuous white spots which continue onto tail. *Desmognathus fuscus auriculatus* — Southern Dusky Salamander_____(p. 115).

18b. Venter cream-colored with brown blotches or spots; dorsum with evident markings or, if unmarked, suffused with brown instead of black; sides of body and tail lacking rows of white spots, or with 1 inconspicuous row on body only_____19

19a. Dorsal pigmentation merging gradually or irregularly with ventral pigmentation; a conspicuous dorsal stripe often present; top of head usually lighter in front of eyes than behind them. *Desmognathus fuscus fuscus* — Northern Dusky Salamander_____

19b. Dorsal and ventral pigmentation merging abruptly to form an obvious mid-lateral transition line (Fig. 26); top of head usually darker in front of eyes than behind them. *Desmognathus monticola* — Seal Salamander_____(p. 115).

20a. Hind foot with 4 toes_____21

20b. Hind foot with 5 toes_____22

21a. Venter light with conspicuous dark flecks; tail with a basal constriction. *Hemidactylium scutatum* — Four-toed Salamander_____(p. 128).

21b. Venter lacking conspicuous dark markings; tail without a basal constriction — *Manculus quadridigitatus* — Dwarf Salamander_(p. 129).

22a. Tail neither keeled nor strongly compressed laterally_____23

22b. Tail keeled or strongly compressed laterally_____27

23a. Tips of digits expanded into adhesive discs; dorsal color with yellowish green lichen-like markings. *Aneides aeneus* — Green Salamander_____(p. 110).

23b. Tips of digits not expanded into adhesive discs; dorsal color without green markings_____24

24a. Body noticeably elongate; intercostal folds (Fig. 24) between adpressed limbs more than 12; color dark brown to nearly black, unmarked. *Phaeognathus hubrichti* — Red Hills Salamander_____(p. 130).

24b. Body not noticeably elongate; intercostal folds between adpressed limbs fewer than 7; body usually marked. (Genus *Plethodon*)____25

25a. Color dark brown to black with white or yellow spots and flecks or, occasionally, with diffuse brassy mottling; sides sometimes white frosted; rarely unmarked, but if so, total length of specimen greater than 125 mm. *Plethodon glutinosus glutinosus* — Slimy Salamander_____ _____(p. 134).

25b. Color gray, brown, or black, usually with a cream to red mid-dorsal stripe; if unmarked, total length less than 125 mm_____26

26a. Costal grooves 20 to 22; dorsum with a straight-edged reddish stripe which fails to broaden on the base of tail (dorsum occasionally plain); mental gland of sexually active male shelflike, contacting jaw rami laterally (Fig. 27A). *Plethodon cinereus polycentratus* — Georgia Red-backed Salamander____(p. 132).

26b. Costal grooves usually 18; dorsum usually with a broad, yellow to red, lobed longitudinal stripe (dorsum

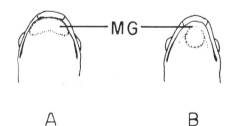

A   B

FIG. 27. Location of mental glands of 2 species of *Plethodon*: (A) Georgia red-backed salamander, *Plethodon cinereus polycentratus*; (B) zigzag salamander, *P. dorsalis dorsalis*.

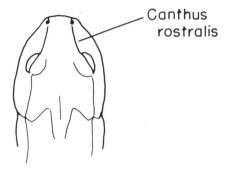

FIG. 28. Head of the spring salamander, *Gyrinophilus porphyriticus* ssp., showing canthus rostralis.

occasionally lacking stripe or having a straight-edged stripe; in the latter, stripe broadens slightly on base of tail); mental gland of sexually active male rounded or oblong, failing to reach jaw rami laterally (Fig. 27B). *Plethodon dorsalis dorsalis* — Zigzag Salamander (p. 133).

27a. Snout with an angular ridge (canthus rostralis) on each side from eye to nostril (Fig. 28). (Genus *Gyrinophilus*)_____28

27b. Snout rounded on side, lacking canthus rostralis_____29

28a. Adults permanently aquatic, with external gills; snout spatulate; eye small, its diameter entering distance from anterior corner of eye to snout tip from 4 to 5 times. *Gyrinophilus palleucus* ssp. — Tennessee Cave Salamander_____(p. 125).

28b. Adults not permanently aquatic, lacking external gills; snout not spatulate; eye larger, its diameter entering distance from anterior corner of eye to snout tip from 1.5 to 3.5 times. *Gyrinophilus porphyriticus* ssp.— Spring Salamander_____
_____(p. 126).

29a. Body relatively stout; costal grooves 16 to 18. (Genus *Pseudotriton*)___30

29b. Body relatively slender; costal grooves no more than 15. (Genus *Eurycea*)_____33

30a. Spots on dorsum and sides usually less than 35 in number. *Pseudotriton montanus diastictus* — Midland

Mud Salamander_____(occurrence in Alabama problematical, p. 24).

30b. Spots or markings on dorsum and sides usually more than 35 in number_____31

31a. Ground color pink to salmon; numerous small dark spots on dorsum and sides. *Pseudotriton montanus flavissimus* — Gulf Coast Mud Salamander_____(p. 136).

31b. Ground color orange to red (brownish red in large individuals); spots fewer, larger, often showing a tendency to coalesce. (*Pseudotriton ruber* ssp.)_____32

32a. Ventral surfaces of legs spotted; dorsal markings often forming a herringbone pattern. *Pseudotriton ruber vioscai* — Southern Red Salamander_____(p. 138).

32b. Ventral surfaces of legs unspotted; dorsal markings seldom forming a herringbone pattern. *Pseudotriton ruber ruber* — Northern Red Salamander_____(p. 137).

33a. Body and tail irregularly spotted and flecked. *Eurycea lucifuga* — Cave Salamander_____(p. 123).

33b. Body with dark stripes or bands, or, if body stripes are lacking, tail with vertical bars_____34

34a. Dorsum with a conspicuous median dark stripe; venter mottled. *Eurycea longicauda guttolineata* — Three-lined Salamander_____(p. 123).

34b. Dorsum lacking a median dark stripe or, if stripe is present, venter clear_____35

35a. Tail with vertical bars, forming a herringbone pattern. *Eurycea longicauda longicauda* — Long-tailed Salamander_____(p. 121).

35b. Tail lacking vertical bars. *Eurycea bislineata* (including "*Eurycea aquatica*") — Two-lined Salamander
_____(p. 119).

Key to the Lizards

1a. Limbless; superficially resembling snakes. (Family Anguidae: Genus *Ophisaurus*)_____2

1b. Limbs present; no resemblance to snakes_____3

2a. Venter with 1 or 2 (most often the latter) longitudinal rows of dark spots, forming stripes, underneath the lateral groove (Fig. 29B); dorsum crossbarred in most adults and in some subadults; light markings on dorsal scales, when present, centrally located. *Ophisaurus attenuatus longicaudus* — Eastern Slender Glass Lizard_____(p. 153).

2b. Venter lacking dark markings below the lateral groove, or with only faint indications of dark pigment (Fig. 29A); dorsum never crossbarred; light markings on dorsal scales, when present, peripherally located. *Ophisaurus ventralis* — Eastern Glass Lizard_____(p. 155).

3a. Dorsal scales shiny. (Family Scincidae)_____4

3b. Dorsal scales not shiny_____10

4a. Lower eyelid with a transparent "window;" maximum size small (50 mm snout-vent length); dorsum lacking conspicuous light stripes. *Scincella laterale* — Ground Skink _____(p. 169).

4b. Lower eyelid lacking transparent "window," maximum size larger than above; dorsum plain or with

A   B

FIG. 30. Chins of 2 species of skinks: (A) coal skink, *Eumeces anthracinus* ssp. (single postmental); (B) five-lined skink, *Eumeces fasciatus* (2 postmentals).

light stripes of varying intensity or otherwise patterned. (Genus *Eumeces*)_____5

5a. Postmental single (Fig. 30A). (*Eumeces anthracinus* ssp.)_____6

5b. Postmentals 2 in number (Fig. 30B)_____7

6a. Light pigment on posterior upper labials continuous; scales at midbody usually 25 or fewer; dorsum usually lacking dark markings between dorsolateral light stripes. *Eumeces anthracinus anthracinus* — Northern Coal Skink _____(p. 160).

6b. Light pigment on posterior upper labials broken by dark pigment along the sutures, producing a spotted aspect; scales at mid-body usually more than 25; dorsum often with dark stripes or rows of dark spots between dorsolateral light stripes. *Eumeces anthracinus pluvialis* — Southern Coal Skink _____ _____(p. 161).

7a. Body slender; limbs reduced in size; tail red or noticeably reddish (occasionally orange); maximum size around 55 mm in snout-vent length. *Eumeces egregius similis* — Northern Mole Skink _____(p. 163).

7b. Body not slender; limbs normally developed; tail not red, noticeably reddish or orange; maximum size greater than 55 mm snout-vent length. (Five-lined Skink group) 8

8a. Median subcaudal scales about the same width as those in adjacent rows (Fig. 31A). *Eumeces inexpectatus* — Southeastern Five-lined Skink_____ (p. 166).

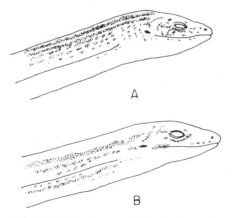

A

B

FIG. 29. Lateral aspect of anterior region of 2 species of glass lizards: (A) eastern glass lizard, *Ophisaurus ventralis;* (B) eastern slender glass lizard, *Ophisaurus attenuatus longicaudus.*

A   **B**

FIG. 31. Undersurfaces of tails of 2 species of skinks: (A) southeastern five-lined skink, *Eumeces inexpectatus* (median subcaudals not widened); (B) five-lined skink, *Eumeces fasciatus* (median subcaudals widened).

8b. Median subcaudal scales noticeably wider than those in adjacent rows (Fig. 31B) _____9

9a. Mid-dorsal stripe on juveniles very narrow; adult males and females large, up to around 130 mm in snout-vent length; adult males patternless, or nearly so, with conspicuously swollen heads; upper labials (Fig. 33) usually 8 in number; enlarged postlabials usually lacking. *Eumeces laticeps* — Broad-headed Skink_____(p. 168).

9b. Mid-dorsal stripe on juvenile relatively wide; adult males and females seldom if ever exceeding 85 mm in snout-vent length; adult males usually showing at least traces of striped pattern; head of adult male usually somewhat swollen, but not conspicuously so; upper labials usually 7; postlabials usually evident and 2 in number. *Eumeces fasciatus* — Five-lined Skink _____(p. 164).

10a. Belly scutes quadrangular, in 8 longitudinal rows; body with 6 longitudinal light stripes. *Cnemidophorus sexlineatus sexlineatus* — Eastern Six-lined Racerunner_____ _____(p. 171).

10b. Belly scutes not quadrangular or in 8 longitudinal rows; body without 6 longitudinal light stripes_____11

11a. Dorsum with spines or spine-tipped scales _____ 12

11b. Dorsum lacking spines or spine-tipped scales_____14

12a. Body greatly flattened; head with

conspicuously enlarged spines. *Phrynosoma cornutum* — Texas Horned Lizard (introduced species) _____(p. 25).

12b. Body not greatly flattened; head lacking conspicuously enlarged spines. (*Sceloporus undulatus* ssp.) _____13

13a. Dorsal scale count, from back of head to a point even with posterior edge of thighs, usually less than 38. *Sceloporus undulatus undulatus* — Southern Fence Lizard____(p. 158).

13b. Dorsal scale count usually 38 or greater. *Sceloporus undulatus hyacinthinus* — Northern Fence Lizard _____(p. 159).

14a. Eyes lidless; pupil of eye elliptical; dorsum warty. *Hemidactylus turcicus* — Mediterranean Gecko (introduced species)_____(p. 25).

14b. Eyes with eyelids; pupil of eye round; dorsum not warty. *Anolis carolinensis carolinensis* — Green Anole_____(p. 157).

Key to the Snakes

1a. Face with a depression or pit between eye and nostril; pupil of eye elliptical (Fig. 32); subcaudal scutes undivided except those near the end of the tail (Fig. 34D). (Viperidae: Crotalinae)_____2

1b. Face lacking a depression or pit between eye and nostril; pupil of eye round (Fig. 33B); all subcaudals divided (Fig. 34C)_____11

2a. Tail with a rattle or button at the end_____3

2b. Tail without a rattle or button at the end. (Genus *Agkistrodon*)_____7

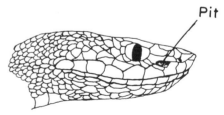

FIG. 32. Lateral aspect of head of pit viper showing location of pit.

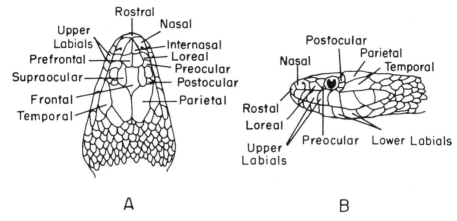

FIG. 33. Head of colubrid snake (*Natrix* sp.) and terminology of scalation.

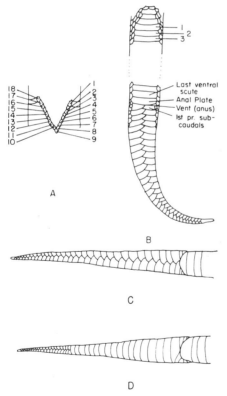

FIG. 34. Scales on body and tail of snakes: (A) method of counting dorsal scale rows; (B) method of counting ventral scutes (after Dowling, 1951); (C) subcaudal scutes divided (Elapidae, Colubridae); (D) basal subcaudal scutes undivided (Viperidae).

3a. Crown of head with 9 large plates (Fig. 35A); rattles very small; size of adults less than 640 mm. (*Sistrurus miliarius* ssp.) 4

3b. Crown of head with many small scales, along with a few plates (Fig. 35B); rattles large; size of adults greater than 700 mm. (Genus *Crotalus*) 6

4a. Dorsal ground color dark gray, heavily stippled with black; dark lateral blotches in 3 series; scale rows at mid-body usually 23 or 25, more often the latter (Fig. 34A); venter white with sharply contrasting dark blotches. *Sistrurius miliarius barbouri* — Dusky Pigmy Rattlesnake.................. (p. 259).

4b. Dorsal ground color light gray to brown, often with pinkish cast; lateral spots in 1 or 2 series; dorsal scale rows usually 21 or 23; venter light with dark markings, but not contrasting sharply as in above 5

5a. Mid-dorsal body blotches usually regularly oval-shaped, about equal longitudinally to light interspaces; mid-lateral blotches relatively round. *Sistrurus miliarius miliarius* — Carolina Pigmy Rattlesnake........ .... (p. 257).

5b. Mid-dorsal body blotches wider than long, irregularly shaped, narrower longitudinally than light in-

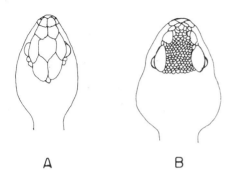

A   B

FIG. 35. Dorsal aspect of rattlesnake heads:
(A) *Sistrurus* spp., (B) *Crotalus* spp.

terspaces; mid-lateral blotches usually higher than wide. *Sistrurus
miliarius streckeri* — Western Pigmy
Rattlesnake_____(p. 259).

6a. Dorsum with yellow-bordered, dia-
mond-shaped markings on an olive
to dark brown background. *Crotalus
adamanteus* — Eastern Diamondback Rattlesnake_____(p. 253).

6b. Dorsum with dark chevron-like
markings on a pinkish to brown
background. *Crotalus horridus* —
Timber Rattlesnake_____(p. 255).

7a. At least one upper labial scale entering the orbit; dorsal scale rows
25_____8

7b. Upper labials separated from orbit
by a row of small scales; dorsal
scale rows 23_____9

8a. Hourglass-shaped crossbars on dorsum strongly constricted in width,
to 2 or 3 scale lengths mid-dorsally,
or the two halves failing to meet
altogether; ventrolateral spots un-
equal in intensity. *Agkistrodon contortrix contortrix* — Southern Cop-
perhead_____(p. 248).

8b. Hourglass-shaped crossbars on dorsum moderately constricted in
width, to 3 to 5 scale lengths mid-
dorsally; ventrolateral spots about
equal in intensity. *Agkistrodon contortrix mokeson* — Northern Cop-
perhead_____(p. 250).

9a. Rostral scute with a conspicuous
dark vertical stripe on each side.

Agkistrodon piscivorus conanti —
Florida Cottonmouth_____(p. 252).

9b. Rostral scute without a conspicuous
dark vertical stripe on each side__10

10a. Top of head uniformly dark brown
to black; body bands often not apparent in adults. *Agkistrodon piscivorus leucostoma* — Western Cot-
tonmouth_____(p. 253).

10b. Top of head often developing light
patches in adults; body bands usually evident throughout life. *Agkistrodon piscivorus piscivorus* — Eastern Cottonmouth_____(p. 251).

11a. All or most of the body scales
keeled (Fig. 36B) (*Elaphe guttata
guttata* has weak keels)_____12

11b. All or most of the body scales
smooth (Fig. 36A) (*Virginia valeriae elegans* has very weakly
keeled scales, but they appear
smooth to the unaided eye)_____41

12a. Rostral scale protruding and upturned or pointed (Genus *Heterodon*)_____13

12b. Rostral scale not protruding (but
see couplet 15)_____14

13a. Rostral scale shovel-shaped, sharply
upturned; undersurface of tail usually not conspicuously lighter than
belly. *Heterodon simus* — Southern
Hognose Snake_____(p. 194).

13b. Rostral scale pointed, not sharply
upturned; undersurface of tail usually conspicuously lighter than bel-

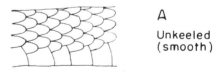

A
Unkeeled
(smooth)

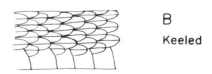

B
Keeled

FIG. 36. Dorsal scales of snakes: (A)
smooth; (B) keeled.

ly. *Heterodon platyrhinos* — Eastern Hognose Snake_____(p. 192).

14a. Dorsal color uniform bright green (bluish in preservative); belly yellowish or whitish, unmarked. *Opheodrys aestivus* — Rough Green Snake_____(p. 222).

14b. Dorsal color not uniform bright green; belly marked or plain____15

15a. Rostral scale enlarged, curving upward around tip of snout, intruding between internasals, and ending in a point. (*Pituophis melanoleucus* ssp.)_____16

15b. Rostral scale not enlarged and intruding between internasals____18

16a. Dorsal color dark brown to black; dorsal blotches, if present, obscure. *Pituophis melanoleucus lodingi* — Black Pine Snake_____(p. 225).

16b. Dorsal color not dark brown or black; dorsal blotches evident, at least posteriorly_____17

17a. Dorsal blotches contrasting sharply with light ground color, at least posteriorly; venter glistening white. *Pituophis melanoleucus melanoleucus* — Northern Pine Snake_____(p. 224).

17b. Dorsal blotches not contrasting sharply with ground color; venter light, but not glistening white. *Pituophis melanoleucus mugitus* — Florida Pine Snake_____(p. 226).

18a. Anal scute divided_____19

18b. Anal scute undivided (Genus *Thamnophis*)_____40

19a. Ventral scutes turning upward abruptly near their ends to form an angle; dorsal scales weakly keeled. (Genus *Elaphe*)_____20

19b. Ventral scutes turning upward gradually near their ends, not forming an angle; dorsal scales strongly keeled_____22

20a. Dorsal blotches bright red to dull red; neck bands uniting on head in a "spear-point." *Elaphe guttata guttata* — Corn Snake_____(p. 183).

20b. Dorsal blotches, if present, dark gray to brownish or nearly black; no neck bands uniting on head to form a "spear-point." (*Elaphe obsoleta* ssp.)_____21

21a. Dorsal ground color very dark gray to black; blotches, if evident, obscure. *Elaphe obsoleta obsoleta* — Black Rat Snake_____(p. 186)

21b. Dorsal ground color gray to light yellowish brown; blotches conspicuous. *Elaphe obsoleta spiloides* — Gray Rat Snake_____(p. 186).

22a. Fifth upper labial scale with a light spot; labials otherwise wholly dark. *Storeria occipitomaculata occipitomaculata* — Northern Red-bellied Snake_____(p. 236).

22b. Upper labials plain or variously marked, but not as above____23

23a. Belly light with 1 or 2 minute black dots near the ends of the ventrals (*Storeria dekayi* ssp.)_____24

23b. Belly uniform or variously marked, but not as above_____26

24a. Paired dorsal spots not connected by crossbars. *Storeria dekayi dekayi* — Northern Brown Snake (p. 234).

24b. Paired dorsal spots usually connected by crossbars_____25

25a. Anterior temporal with diagonal or vertical bar; sixth and seventh upper labials with dark pigment (Fig. 37A). *Storeria dekayi wrightorum* — Midland Brown Snake_____(p. 235).

25b. Anterior temporal with a horizontal bar; sixth and seventh upper labials usually unpigmented (Fig. 37B). *Storeria dekayi limnetes* — Marsh Brown Snake_____(p. 234).

FIG. 37. Lateral aspect of heads of brown snakes: (A) midland brown snake, *Storeria dekayi wrightorum;* (B) marsh brown snake, *S. d. limnetes.*

26a. Adult size small, less than 325 mm; dorsum and venter unmarked except for a light neck ring in young and in some old individuals; head small, snout pointed. *Virginia striatula* — Rough Earth Snake (p. 243).

26b. Adult size larger than 325 mm; either dorsum or venter (or both) with pattern; head large or small; snout not pointed_____27

27a. Dorsal pattern obscure or absent_28

27b. Dorsal pattern easily discernible 31

28a. Venter with 2 rows of conspicuous dark spots, forming stripes, these converging anteriorly and uniting on throat; light ventrolateral stripes absent. *Regina rigida sinicola* — Gulf Glossy Water Snake (p. 228).

28b. Venter not pigmented as above or, if so, body with ventrolateral light stripes_____29

29a. A light ventrolateral stripe on each side. *Regina septemvittata* — Queen Snake_____(p. 229).

29b. Ventrolateral stripes absent. (*Natrix erythrogaster* ssp.)_____30

30a. Venter usually orange or reddish orange. *Natrix erythrogaster erythrogaster* — Red-bellied Water Snake_____(p. 210)

30b. Venter usually cream or yellow. *Natrix erythrogaster flavigaster* — Yellow-bellied Water Snake_____(p. 211).

31a. A series of subocular scales separating upper labials from orbit. (*Natrix cyclopion* ssp.)_____32

31b. Some upper labials entering orbit_____33

32a. Anterior one-third of venter yellowish to white, posterior two-thirds smoky gray to brown with light half moons. *Natrix cyclopion cyclopion* — Green Water Snake_____(p. 208).

32b. Venter predominantly light, including posterior two-thirds. *Natrix cyclopion floridana* — Florida Green Water Snake_____(p. 209).

33a. Dorsum with mid-dorsal and dorsolateral yellow stripes. *Natrix fasciata clarki* — Gulf Salt Marsh Water Snake_____(p. 215).

33b. Dorsum without longitudinal yellow stripes_____34

34a. Parietal scutes fragmented behind; body pattern of mid-dorsal dark blotches alternating with lateral ones. *Natrix taxispilota* — Brown Water Snake_____(p. 221).

34b. Parietal scutes not fragmented behind; body pattern with blotches, bands, or both_____35

35a. Body with mid-dorsal dark blotches connected to alternating lateral blotches, forming a chainlike pattern. *Natrix rhombifera rhombifera* — Diamond-backed Water Snake_____(p. 217).

35b. Body without mid-dorsal dark blotches connecting to lateral blotches to form a chainlike pattern_____36

36a. Body with alternating mid-dorsal and lateral dark blotches anteriorly, banded posteriorly (*N. sipedon pleuralis* may rarely be banded throughout its length)_____37

36b. Body banded throughout its length_____38

37a. Venter with 2 rows of crescent-shaped or half-moon-shaped dark markings. *Natrix sipedon pleuralis* — Midland Water Snake_____(p. 219).

37b. Venter with dark transverse lines or narrow bands, one on anterior edge of each ventral scute. *Natrix erythrogaster* ssp. juvenile (p. 210).

38a. Venter with irregular wormlike markings. *Natrix fasciata pictiventris* — Florida Water Snake_____(p. 217).

38b. Venter with rectangular or squarish blotches_____39

39a. Ventral blotches seldom involving more than 1 scute each, and not showing a tendency to merge extensively. *Natrix fasciata fasciata* — Banded Water Snake_____(p. 213).

39b. Ventral blotches frequently involving 3 or more scutes each, and showing a tendency to merge extensively. *Natrix fasciata confluens*

— Broad-banded Water Snake_____
_____(p. 216).

40a. Venter with 1 or 2 rows of dark spots down each side. *Thamnophis sirtalis sirtalis* — Eastern Garter Snake_____(p. 241).

40b. Venter unmarked. *Thamnophis sauritus sauritus* — Eastern Ribbon Snake_____(p. 240).

41a. Anal scute undivided_____42

41b. Anal scute divided (except occasionally in *Farancia* spp., 65b)_____
_____52

42a. Dorsal pattern of red saddles bordered by black on a yellowish or white ground color; snout red; venter immaculate. *Cemophora coccinea copei* — Northern Scarlet Snake_____(p. 176).

42b. Dorsum plain or variously patterned, but if similar to above, not in combination with immaculate venter_____43

43a. Color pattern of red, yellow, and black bands encircling body; snout black followed by a wide yellow head band. *Micrurus fulvius fulvius* — Eastern Coral Snake_____(p. 246).

43b. Body variously patterned or plain, but if similar to above, not in combination with black snout_____44

44a. Dorsum black or blue-black without yellow markings_____45

44b. Dorsum not black or blue-black or, if so, with yellow markings. (Genus *Lampropeltis*)_____46

45a. Venter predominantly red or reddish; a small aquatic snake. *Seminatrix pygaea pygaea* — North Florida Black Swamp Snake____(p. 233).

45b. Venter mostly dark gray to black, never predominantly reddish; a large terrestrial snake. *Drymarchon corais couperi* — Eastern Indigo Snake_____(p. 182).

46a. Dorsal color black with yellow markings. (*Lampropeltis getulus* ssp.)_____47

46b. Dorsal color not black with yellow markings_____49

47a. Dorsum with conspicuous yellow bands, some of which may be broken; interspaces usually lacking yellow markings. *Lampropeltis get-*

ulus getulus — Eastern Kingsnake
_____(p. 197).

47b. Dorsum lacking conspicuous yellow bands or, if bands are present, interspaces with yellow markings__48

48a. Dorsum with a conspicuous yellow spot on each scale. *Lampropeltis getulus holbrooki* — Speckled Kingsnake_____(p. 199).

48b. Dorsum with small, irregular yellow markings and occasionally with inconspicuous, narrow yellow bands or, more rarely, uniformly black. *Lampropeltis getulus niger* — Black Kingsnake_____(p. 200).

49a. Dorsum plain brown or brown to tan with reddish, transverse dorsal blotches that seldom extend downward past the fifth scale row on each side. *Lampropeltis calligaster* ssp. — Mole Snake (or Prairie Kingsnake)_____(p. 195).

49b. Body ringed or with dorsal blotches or saddles that extend downward past the fifth scale row on each side (*Lampropeltis triangulum* ssp.)__50

50a. Body ringed, with ringed pattern occasionally irregular on venter. *Lampropeltis triangulum elapsoides* Scarlet Kingsnake_____(p. 203).

50b. Body with blotches or saddles on the dorsum, not ringed_____51

51a. Dorsum gray or tan with dark gray, brownish, or red, dark-edged dorsal blotches that extend downward to fourth or third scale row; a medial light spot or a Y- or V-shaped light area on nape or back of head. *Lampropeltis triangulum triangulum* — Eastern Milk Snake (p. 201).

51b. Dorsum tan, yellow, white, or gray, with dark-edged dorsal saddles or blotches (usually red) that extend downward to about the first scale row; nape or back of head usually with a light band or collar. *Lampropeltis triangulum syspila* — Red Milk Snake_____(p. 204).

52a. Dorsum of body (excluding neck) unicolorous or virtually so_____53

52b. Dorsum of body not unicolorous__64

53a. Dorsum dark, with a light, occa-

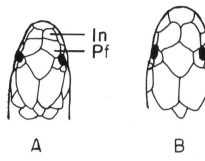

FIG. 38. Dorsal aspect of heads of worm snakes: (A) eastern worm snake, *C. a. amoenus* (internasals and prefrontals separate); (B) midwest worm snake, *Carphophis a. helenae* (internasals and prefrontals fused).

sionally interrupted neck ring. (*Diadophis punctatus* ssp.) _____54

53b. Dorsum not dark with a light neck ring _____ 56

54a. Venter unmarked or with a single median row of dots or small dark spots; chin usually lacking dark spots. *Diadophis punctatus edwardsi* — Northern Ringneck Snake _____ (p. 181).

54b. Venter with relatively large dark spots or otherwise conspicuously marked; chin with dark spots ____ 55

55a. Venter with a single median row of conspicuous dark "half-moons." *Diadophis punctatus punctatus* — Southern Ringneck Snake (p. 179).

55b. Venter with paired dark spots on each scute or with irregular dark markings. *Diadophis punctatus stictogenys* — Mississippi Ringneck Snake _____ (p. 181).

56a. Dorsum dark, venter light, with a distinct separation between dorsal and ventral colors. (*Carphophis amoenus* ssp.) _____ 57

56b. Dorsal and ventral colors similar or, if different, not distinctly separated but with a zone of intermediacy between _____ 58

57a. Prefrontal and internasal scutes fused (Fig. 38B). *Carphophis amoenus helenae* — Midwest Worm Snake _____ (p. 174).

57b. Prefrontals and internasals separate (Fig. 38A). *Carphophis amoenus amoenus* — Eastern Worm Snake ____ _____ (p. 174).

58a. Tail long and whiplike; dorsum tan or brown. *Masticophis flagellum flagellum* — Eastern Coachwhip (an occasional variant) _____ (p. 205).

58b. Tail not long and whiplike; dorsum variously colored _____59

59a. Dorsum of body tan or brown; neck with a conspicuous black collar. *Tantilla coronata coronata* — Southeastern Crowned Snake _____ _____ (p. 239).

59b. Dorsum not tan or brown; neck without a conspicuous black collar _____61

60a. Dorsum plain black (*Coluber constrictor* ssp.) _____61

60b. Dorsum not plain black _____ 62

61a. Enlarged spine at base of male's hemipenis less than 3 times the length of the adjacent spine in the same row (Fig. 39B). *Coluber constrictor constrictor* — Northern Black Racer _____ (p. 177).

61b. Enlarged spine at base of male's hemipenis at least 3 times the length of the adjacent spine in the same row (Fig. 39A). *Coluber con-*

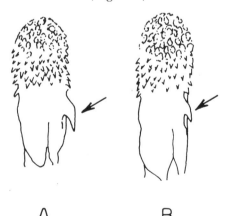

FIG. 39. Hemipenis of black racers. Arrows indicate basal hemipenial spine: (A) southern black racer, *C. c. priapus* (spine relatively long); (B) northern black racer, *Coluber c. constrictor* (spine relatively short).

strictor priapus — Southern Black Racer_____(p. 179).

62a. Dorsum brown or yellowish brown, occasionally with obscure, diffuse longitudinal stripes; upper labials predominantly yellow. *Rhadinaea flavilata* — Pine Woods Snake_____ _____(p. 231).

62b. Dorsum gray, brown, yellowish brown, or pink, frequently with tiny dark flecks; upper labials not yellow (*Virginia valeriae* ssp.)____63

63a. Dorsal scales in 15 rows at midbody, lacking keels. *Virginia valeriae valeriae* — Eastern Smooth Earth Snake_____(p. 244).

63b. Dorsal scales in 17 rows at midbody, with faint keels (visible on close observation). *Virginia valeriae elegans* — Western Smooth Earth Snake_____(p. 245).

64a. Dorsal pattern of dark median blotches or saddles alternating with single or paired lateral blotches; venter with small dark spots. *Coluber constrictor* ssp. juvenile_____ _____(p. 177).

64b. Dorsum not with dark blotches or saddles (but see key couplet 67) _____65

65a. Tail long, whiplike, not terminated by a stout spine. *Masticophis flagellum flagellum* — Eastern Coachwhip (p. 205). (See also key couplet 58.)

65b. Tail short, terminated by a stout spine. (Genus *Farancia*)_____66

66a. Dorsum with longitudinal stripes. *Farancia erytrogramma erytrogramma* — Rainbow Snake _____(p. 190).

66b. Dorsum without longitudinal stripes. (*Farancia abacura* ssp.)__67

67a. Upward extensions of red (rarely white) ventral color forming 53 or more figures with acutely angular apices. *Farancia abacura abacura* — Eastern Mud Snake_____(p. 188).

67b. Upward extensions of red ventral color forming 52 or fewer figures with rounded apices. *Farancia abacura reinwardti* — Western Mud Snake_____(p. 189).

Key to the Turtles
(See Fig. 40)

1a. Shell covered with leathery skin; snout ending in a tubular proboscis. (Family Trionychidae: Genus *Trionyx*)_____2

1b. Shell covered by horny scutes (Fig. 40) (except in the marine turtle, *Dermochelys coriacea*); snout not ending in a tubular proboscis_____6

2a. Leading edge of carapace lacking tubercles or other prominences (*Trionyx muticus* ssp.)_____3

2b. Leading edge of carapace with tubercles_____4

3a. Top of snout lacking stripes; carapace of juveniles and adult males with large, circular spots. (Mature females of this and the following subspecies are often virtually indistinguishable.) *Trionyx muticus calvatus* — Gulf Coast Smooth Softshell_____(p. 310).

3b. Top of snout usually with stripes; carapace of juveniles and adult males with scattered dark dashes and pale spots. *Trionyx muticus muticus* — Midland Smooth Softshell_____(p. 309).

4a. Leading edge of carapace with a marginal ridge; anterior carapacial tubercles low, rounded. *Trionyx ferox* — Florida Softshell_(p. 308).

4b. Leading edge of carapace lacking a marginal ridge; anterior carapacial tubercles often pointed or spine-tipped. (*Trionyx spiniferus* ssp.)_____5

5a. Rear of carapace with one encircling dark line. *Trionyx spiniferus spiniferus* — Eastern Spiny Softshell _____(p. 311).

5b. Rear of carapace with 2 or more encircling dark lines. *Trionyx spiniferus asper* — Gulf Coast Spiny Softshell_____(p. 313).

6a. Limbs modified into flippers; marine turtles. (Families: Cheloniidae and Dermochelidae)_____7

6b. Limbs not modified into flippers 11

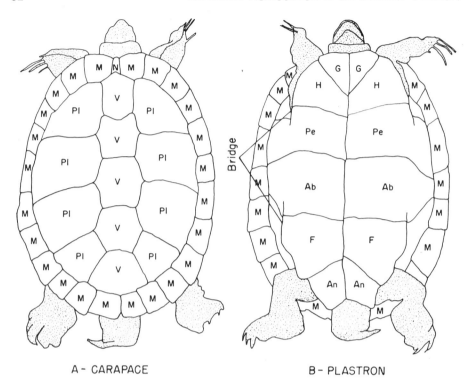

A - CARAPACE   B - PLASTRON

FIG. 40. Turtle shell and terminology of scutes: N—nuchal (cervical); M—marginal; Pl—pleural; V—vertebral; G—gular; H—humeral; Pe—pectoral; Ab—abdominal; F—femoral; An—anal.

7a. Shell without scutes; carapace with 7 longitudinal ridges. *Dermochelys coriacea coriacea* — Atlantic Leatherback_____(p. 267).

7b. Shell with scutes; carapace, if keeled, having no more than 4 keels _____8

8a. Pleurals in 5 or more pairs_____9

8b. Pleurals in 4 pairs_____10

9a. Bridge with 3 enlarged scutes. *Caretta caretta caretta* — Atlantic Loggerhead_____(p. 261).

9b. Bridge with 4 enlarged scutes. *Lepidochelys kempi* — Atlantic Ridley_____(p. 263).

10a. Scutes of carapace overlapping. *Eretmochelys imbricata imbricata* — Atlantic Hawksbill_____(p. 263).

10b. Scutes of carapace not overlapping. *Chelonia mydas* — Green Turtle_____ _____(p. 262)

11a. Terrestrial; hind feet elephantine; forelimbs shovel-like, adapted for

digging. (Family Testudinidae) *Gopherus polyphemus* — Gopher Tortoise_____(p. 307).

11b. Terrestrial or aquatic; hind feet not elephantine; forelimbs not shovel-like_____12

12a. Plastron small; tail long, at least half the length of the carapace (Family Chelydridae)_____13

12b. Plastron large; tail short, less than half the length of the carapace____14

13a. Carapace with a row of supramarginals between the marginals and pleurals; beak strongly hooked. *Macroclemys temmincki* — Alligator Snapping Turtle_____ (p. 265).

13b. Carapace without a row of supramarginals; beak moderately hooked. *Chelydra serpentina serpentina* — Common Snapping Turtle (p. 264).

14a. Plastron with 10 or 11 scutes; pectorals of plastron not in contact with the marginals. (Family Kinosternidae)_____15

14b. Plastron with 12 scutes; pectorals touching the marginals_____21

15a. Pectoral scutes triangular. *Kinosternon subrubrum* ssp._____16

15b. Pectoral scutes squarish or quadrangular. (Genus *Sternotherus*)__17

16a. Side of head with 2 conspicuous light stripes. *Kinosternon subrubrum hippocrepis* — Mississippi Mud Turtle_____(p. 301).

16b. Side of head variously marked, but lacking the 2 conspicuous light stripes. *Kinosternon subrubrum subrubrum* — Eastern Mud Turtle _____(p. 299).

17a. Barbels on chin and neck; side of head usually with 2 conspicuous light stripes. *Sternotherus odoratus* — Common Musk Turtle____(p. 304).

17b. Barbels on chin only; side of head variously marked, but lacking 2 conspicuous light stripes_____18

18a. Plastron lacking gular scute; carapace high-keeled. *Sternotherus carinatus* — Keeled Musk Turtle (occurrence in Alabama problematical) _____(p. 24).

18b. Plastron with gular scute, carapace flattened to moderately high-keeled. *Sternotherus minor* ssp.__19

19a. Shell strongly flattened; top of head greenish with a dark reticulum; top of snout spotted or blotched. *Sternotherus minor depressus* — Flattened Musk Turtle_____(p. 303).

19b. Shell not strongly flattened; head and snout not pigmented as above _____20

20a. Top and sides of head and neck dark-spotted. *Sternotherus minor minor* — Loggerhead Musk Turtle _____(p. 301).

20b. Top and sides of head mottled or striped; top and sides of neck striped. *Sternotherus minor peltifer* — Stripe-Necked Musk Turtle_____ _____(p. 304).

21a. Plastron hinged. *Terrapene carolina* ssp._____22

21b. Plastron rigid_____24

22a. Carapace horn-color with inconspicuous markings, hind feet with 3 toes. *Terrapene carolina triunguis* — Three-toed Box Turtle_(p. 299).

22b. Carapace variously colored, its markings usually conspicuous except in very old individuals_____23

23a. Size large, exceeding 200 mm in carapace length; posterior marginals usually flaring strongly; fifth vertebral scute often strongly convex. *Terrapene carolina major* — Gulf Coast Box Turtle_____(p. 298).

23b. Size moderate, up to about 170 mm in carapace length; posterior marginals usually not flaring strongly; fifth vertebral scute flat or only slightly convex. *Terrapene carolina carolina* — Eastern Box Turtle_____ _____(p. 297).

24a. Head and neck without longitudinal light stripes; restricted to habitats associated with salt and brackish water. *Malaclemys terrapin pileata* — Mississippi Diamondback Terrapin_____(p. 283).

24b. Head and neck with longitudinal light stripes (except in some old melanistic individuals); found typically in freshwater habitats_____25

25a. Carapace smooth; pleurals olive to black, plain or light-rimmed. *Chrysemys picta* ssp._____26

25b. Carapace rough or, if smooth, pleurals with light stripes or reticulations._____28

26a. Carapace with a prominent yellow, orange, or red mid-dorsal stripe. *Chrysemys picta dorsalis* — Southern Painted Turtle_____(p. 269).

26b. Carapace without a prominent mid-dorsal light stripe_____27

27a. Pleural scutes alternating with vertebrals; plastron often with a central dark blotch. *Chrysemys picta marginata* — Midland Painted Turtle____ _____(p. 270).

27b. Pleurals and vertebrals not alternating, their transverse seams aligned; plastron usually plain.

Chrysemys picta picta — Eastern Painted Turtle_____(p. 267).

28a. Neck long; when extended, the distance from the shoulder to the snout tip approximately equals the length of the plastron. *Deirochelys reticularia reticularia* — Eastern Chicken Turtle_____(p. 270).

28b. Neck of moderate length; when neck is extended, the distance from the shoulder to the snout tip about one-half the length of the plastron _____29

29a. Head with an isolated yellow temporal spot. *Graptemys geographica* — Map Turtle_____(p. 273).

29b. Head variously marked, but lacking an isolated yellow temporal spot (except occasionally in *Graptemys pseudogeographica ouachitensis*)_____ _____30

30a. Side of head and cheek with large yellow or greenish blotch (obscure in old females); upper jaw without a terminal notch_____ 31

30b. Side of head and cheek lacking a large, light blotch on side or, if blotch is present, upper jaw with a terminal notch_____32

31a. Chin with a curved light bar following its outline, this bar not connected to a median longitudinal light chin stripe. *Graptemys barbouri* — Barbour's Map Turtle_____ _____(p. 272).

31b. Chin without a curved light bar or, if present, the bar usually connected to a median longitudinal light chin stripe. *Graptemys pulchra* — Alabama Map Turtle____(p. 280).

32a. Carapace with keel; keel accentuated by spines, knobs, or tubercles (carapacial prominences may be eroded and inconspicuous in old females)_____33

32b. Carapace with or without keel; if present, keel not accentuated by prominences _____ 36

33a. Chin with 3 conspicuous isolated light spots. *Graptemys pseudogeographica ouachitensis* — Ouachita (False) Map Turtle (in Alabama) _____(p. 278).

33b. Chin variously marked, but without 3 conspicuous isolated light spots ___ _____34

34a. Pleural and vertebral scutes of carapace with conspicuous yellow blotches. *Graptemys flavimaculata* — Yellow-blotched Sawback (occurrence in Alabama problematical)____ _____(p. 24).

34b. Carapace scutes without conspicuous yellow blotches. *Graptemys nigrinoda* ssp._____35

35a. Plastron plain or with a pattern occupying less than 60 percent of its surface; light stripes on soft parts wider than dark ones. *Graptemys nigrinoda nigrinoda* — Northern Black-knobbed Sawback (p. 275).

35b. Plastron with a pattern occupying 70 percent or more of its surface; dark stripes on soft parts wider than light ones. *Graptemys nigrinoda delticola* — Southern Black-knobbed Sawback_____(p. 277).

36a. Upper jaw with a terminal notch, flanked on each side by a cusp. *Pseudemys alabamensis* — Alabama Red-bellied Turtle_____(p. 284).

36b. Upper jaw with or without a terminal notch; terminal notch, if present, not flanked on each side by a cusp_____37

37a. Plastron having 2 or more scutes marked in their centers with a dark smudge, blotch, or ocellate spot; plastron without dark markings following seams. *Pseudemys scripta* ssp._____38

37b. Plastron plain or, if marked, the markings following seams_____39

38a. Plastron with 12 dark spots or smudges; head with an orange or reddish temporal bar (obscure in some adults); stripes on pleural scutes relatively narrow. *Pseudemys scripta elegans* — Red-eared Pond Slider_____(p. 294).

38b. Plastron usually with only 2 dark smudges or spots (these on gulars); head with a yellow blotch on the side; stripes on pleural scutes relatively wide. *Pseudemys scripta*

scripta — Yellow-bellied Pond Slider_____(p. 293).

39a. Undersides of all posterior marginals (those in back of bridge) with at least some dark pigment; second pleural scute with a C-shaped light figure; plastron usually with some dark markings; iris of eye entire in many populations. *Pseudemys concinna concinna* — River Cooter_____(p. 287).

39b. Undersides of most or all of posterior marginals lacking dark pigment (Alabama populations); second pleural scute usually with a vertical mark, which may have upper or lower bifurcations; plastron unmarked (except in a few old adults); iris of eye bisected (or nearly bisected) by a transverse dark bar. *Pseudemys floridana* ssp. _____40

40a. Head stripes broken and twisted. *Pseudemys floridana hoyi* — Missouri Slider (occurrence in Alabama problematical)_____(p. 24).

40b. Head stripes not broken and twisted. *Pseudemys floridana floridana* — Florida Cooter_____(p. 291).

ORDER ANURA—FROGS AND TOADS

Although diverse taxonomically, the frogs and toads form a distinctive group whose members can hardly be mistaken for anything else. The life histories of frogs and toads vary tremendously in details, but a majority, including those of all Alabama species, share the following features: (1) the male moves to an aquatic breeding site and emits a call peculiar to his species, to which the female is attracted; (2) upon her arrival, the female is seized from the rear by the male, whereupon the two are said to be in amplexus; (3) following a period of amplexus, the female lays the eggs, an act accompanied by emission of sperm-containing seminal fluid by the male; (4) the fertilized eggs develop in the water and hatch into tadpoles, which eventually transform into froglets. The time required to complete the aquatic phase of the life cycle varies from 20 days or less for the eastern spadefoot toad to as much as 2 years or more for the common bullfrog in the northern portions of its range.

Adult female frogs and toads tend to be larger than adult males of the same species; other sexual differences vary among families. In Alabama the males within all families except Ranidae may be distinguished from their female counterparts by the loose skin under the throat, which is usually darker than the belly. In such forms the vocal pouch is gular in location. Males of ranid frogs have internal or laterally situated vocal pouches. The males of ranids tend to have relatively larger tympana than the females and, in addition, they often have swollen thumbs.

Adult toads and frogs are all carnivorous. Most are insectivorous and obviously beneficial to man. The fried legs of some ranid frogs, especially those of the bullfrog, are considered a delicacy. Frogs and toads and their tadpoles provide food for many fish and other wild animals. But to an increasing number of people, the most desirable attribute of frogs and toads is the fascinating variety of sounds they fill the night air with during their breeding seasons. The most recent comprehensive work on frogs and toads of the United States is a 1949 volume, *Frogs and Toads of the United States and Canada*, by Albert and Anna Wright. Although much of its contents are out of date, the book contains a wealth of valuable information.

Taxonomically, Anura is by far the most diverse group of amphibians, with 16 families, 218 genera, and about 2,600 species. It is also the most widespread, occurring on all continents except Antarctica and on most continental islands as well. The richest faunas are found in South America, Africa, and southern Asia.

Anura is fairly well represented in Alabama, especially in some parts of the Coastal Plain. Twenty-eight species, representing 7 genera and 5 families, constitute the state's fauna.

FAMILY BUFONIDAE — TOADS

This large family, with 16 genera and about 170 species, is essentially cosmopolitan in distribution except for its absence (excluding introduced species) in Australia, New Guinea, Madagasgar, and Polynesia. *Bufo* is the only genus native to the United States.

GENUS *BUFO* Laurenti

Bufo is by far the largest bufonid genus, containing more than 125 species. Its range is essentially that of the family. About 18 species occur in the United States, and 4 are found in Alabama.

Bufo americanus Holbrook

Three subspecies of this toad are recognized, 1 of which occurs in Alabama.

Bufo americanus americanus Holbrook American Toad

Description: (Fig. 41) A medium-to-large-sized toad attaining a maximum snout-vent length of about 110 mm. Skin warty; warts usually not spine-tipped except in large females; parotoids present; pupils of eyes horizontally elliptical; dorsal color variable, ranging from gray to brown or reddish, nearly plain or variously spotted and mottled; most large dorsal spots with only 1 or 2 warts in each; venter light, occasionally dark-spotted on breast. Cranial crests prominent on adults; interorbital crests not projecting well beyond their junction with the postorbital ridges, nor ending in knoblike protuberances, as in *B. terrestris;* postorbital ridges not in contact with parotoids, as in *B. w. fowleri,* but connecting to them by backward-projecting spurs (Fig. 17B).

Remarks: This species reportedly hybridizes with *B. woodhousei fowleri* in some parts of its range, but I have found no obvious indications of such hybridization in Alabama. There is considerable evidence, however, of gene exchange between *B. americanus* and *B. terrestris,*

FIG. 41. *Bufo americanus americanus,* the American toad. (Calhoun County.) In this form the postorbital ridges do not contact the parotoids, and the head lacks knoblike protuberances.

the third large toad of our area. (See below.)

Alabama distribution: (Fig. 42) The distribution of *B. americanus* in Alabama appears to be inconsistent with previous interpretations. The species definitely occurs throughout the Piedmont and Blue Ridge. It is found locally in the Ridge and Valley region southwestward at least to northern Shelby County. The range includes that portion of the Appalachian Plateaus region above the Tennessee River in Madison and Jackson counties and the northeasternmost portion and eastern edges of that region below the Tennessee River. I have been

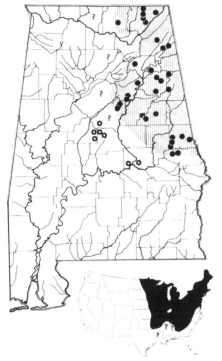

FIG. 42. Distribution of *Bufo americanus americanus,* the American toad. The hatched area contains populations clearly referable to this form. Solid symbols indicate localities from which the author examined specimens. Starred symbols indicate localities from which specimens intermediate between *B. a. americanus* and *B. terrestris* were examined. The areas questioned are those in need of further investigation with respect to toad populations. The small map depicts approximately the known range of the species *B. americanus* in the United States.

unable to find *B. americanus* in the central or western portions of the Appalachian Plateaus region or in the Tennessee Valley. Much of the land in those areas is intensively farmed and suitable habitat is often scarce. Specimens are also lacking from the Chert Belt, but that region has not been intensively collected.

The relationships between *B. americanus* and *B. terrestris* in Alabama are not clear. In Lee County, in the extreme eastern portion of the state, the Fall Line rather clearly separates the ranges of the 2, and I have found no evidence of interbreeding. Westward, distinctions between the 2 forms break down. In samples taken from breeding sites in central Alabama in the Fall Line Hills (in Bibb, Elmore, and Chilton counties) and in the lower portion of the Ridge and Valley region in Shelby County, the range of morphological variation virtually spans the spectrum from one phenotype to the other. Furthermore, whereas the period of intensive breeding activity in genetically pure *B. americanus* in Alabama is 4 to 6 weeks earlier than in *B. terrestris,* those of the problematical populations are unpredictable and apparently cover a longer time span in most years than that of either *B. americanus* or *B. terrestris.* These observations suggest that extensive interbreeding between *B. americanus* and *B. terrestris* is occurring in central Alabama.

Bufo terrestris, with no indication of *B. americanus* influence, inhabits the remainder of the Coastal Plain; in northwestern Alabama its range extends onto the western portion of Sand Mountain in the Appalachian Plateaus region. No evidence of interaction between *B. terrestris* and *B. americanus* has been found in the Plateaus region, and it is possible that their ranges there are separated by a hiatus.

Habits: The American toad is the first *Bufo* to emerge from hibernation in Alabama, and it may be seen on the roads on warm, rainy nights as early as mid-January, along with *Rana pipiens, Hyla crucifer,* and the 2 species of *Pseudacris* with which it is sympatric. Breeding activity usually gets underway in late January or February, with the peak of the season occurring in mid-March or, in extreme northern Alabama, mid-April. The latest I have found American toads breeding in Alabama is May 10 (Jackson County). Breeding sites include farm ponds, floodplain pools, and flooded roadside ditches. The male calls from the bank near the edge of the water, emitting a resonant, drawn-out trill, about half an octave lower than that of *B. terrestris* and having a slower pulse-rate. The eggs are laid in strings.

Bufo americanus appears to be greatly outnumbered within most of its Alabama range by *B. woodhousei fowleri*, and whereas the former is limited chiefly to rural areas with some forest land, the latter is practically ubiquitous. After mid-June, *B. americanus* is encountered only occasionally. I assume that it estivates during much of the summer. In contrast, both *B. w. fowleri* and *B. terrestris* are active, at least at night, throughout the summer. A comparative study of the natural history of these 3 toad species is needed to elucidate their ecological relationships.

Bufo quercicus Holbrook

Oak Toad

Description: (Fig. 43) The smallest member of its family, this species attains

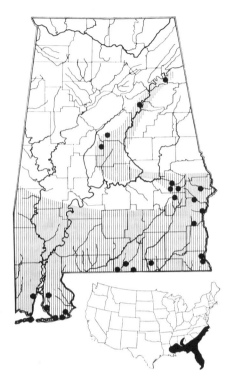

FIG. 44. Distribution of *Bufo quercicus,* the oak toad. The presumed range in Alabama is indicated by hatching. Symbols indicate localities from which the author examined specimens. The small map depicts approximately the known range of the species in the United States.

FIG. 43. *Bufo quercicus,* the oak toad (Barbour County). A light mid-dorsal stripe is an outstanding, though not an exclusive characteristic of this diminutive toad.

a maximum snout-vent length of about 35 mm. Cranial crests low; parotoids somewhat divergent posteriorly instead of parallel; dorsum gray or brown to almost black with a narrow, light median stripe; 2 dark dorsal blotches, each bisected by the median stripe, usually visible; dorsum rather evenly warty.

Alabama distribution: (Fig. 44) Generally distributed in the Lower Coastal Plain; found elsewhere in the Coastal Plain in areas where the soil is relatively sandy. The range extends across the Fall Line into the Ridge and Valley region northeastward at least to eastern Etowah County.

Habits: This miniature toad tends to

be fossorial, and in Alabama it is seldom encountered except during the breeding season. The call, a high pitched "peep-peep . . . peep," with each note slurred downward slightly at the end, closely resembles the peeping of a baby chicken. It is usually issued from a clump of grass or other sheltered situation around the edge of a flooded roadside ditch, borrow pit, or other small pond or pool. Breeding is associated with warm, rainy weather from April to July. During such periods the call is often heard during the day. The eggs are laid in small strands or bars, with 3 to 6 eggs per bar. Up to 500 eggs are laid per female (Volpe and Dobie, 1959). Breeding associates often include *Gastrophryne carolinensis*, *Hyla squirella*, and *H. femoralis*.

Bufo terrestris (Bonnaterre)
Southern Toad

Description: (Fig. 45) Typically a medium-sized toad attaining a maximum snout-vent length of about 80 mm, although individuals much larger than this have been collected on islands along the coasts of Georgia, Florida, and South Carolina. Skin warty, warts often spine-tipped; parotoids present; pupil of eye horizontally elliptical; dorsal coloration extremely variable, ranging from various shades of gray to brick red, variously spotted and mottled; venter light. Cranial crests prominent; interorbital crests projecting beyond their junction with the postorbital ridge and ending in prominent knoblike protuberances; postorbital

FIG. 45. *Bufo terrestris*, the southern toad (Barbour County). In this species the postorbital ridges do not contact the parotoids, and the head has knoblike protuberances posteriorly

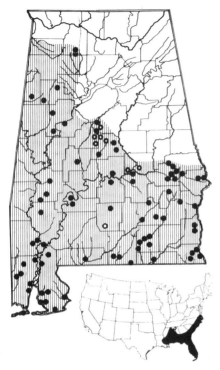

FIG. 46. Distribution of *Bufo terrestris*, the southern toad. The presumed range in Alabama is indicated by hatching. Solid symbols are localities from which the author examined specimens referable to *B. terrestris*. Starred symbols indicate localities from which specimens intermediate between *B. terrestris* and *B. a. americanus* were collected. The circle is a literature record for *B. terrestris*. The small map depicts the approximate known range of *B. terrestris* in the United States.

ridges not in contact with parotids, but connecting to them by a backward projecting spur (Fig. 17).

Remarks: The range of *B. terrestris* in Alabama is overlapped completely by that of *B. woodhousei fowleri*, and the 2 forms often hybridize (see Brown, 1970). There is also evidence of its interbreeding with *B. americanus*, in central Alabama. (See "Alabama distribution" below and in account of *B. americanus*.)

Alabama distribution: (Fig. 46) The Coastal Plain and westernmost portion of Sand Mountain in the Appalachian

Plateaus region; apparently interbreeds extensively with *B. americanus* in the central Fall Line Hills and in lower Shelby County in the southern portion of the Ridge and Valley region. (See account of *B. americanus*.)

Habits: This is the most common toad in the Lower Coastal Plain and is found in approximately equal numbers with Fowler's toad, *B. w. fowleri*, in other Coastal Plain provinces. It seems especially abundant in areas with friable soil. The fact that the range of *B. terrestris* crosses the Fall Line from the Coastal Plain into the Ridge and Valley region and Appalachian Plateaus but stops at the edge of the Piedmont may be related to substrate requirements.

Breeding in this species usually begins somewhat later than in *B. americanus* or *B. w. fowleri* and is confined mostly to wet-weather periods from mid-March to late May. Breeding may occur in small permanent ponds, woodland pools, or flooded depressions. I have never found the southern toad breeding in creeks or rivers, as Fowler's toad often does. The call is a high-pitched, drawn-out trill, about half an octave higher than that of *B. americanus*. The eggs are laid in strings.

Bufo woodhousei Girard

Three subspecies of this widely distributed toad are recognized, one of which occurs in Alabama.

Bufo woodhousei fowleri Hinckley
Fowler's Toad

Description: (Fig. 47) A medium-sized toad attaining a maximum snout-vent length of about 85 mm. Skin warty; parotoids present; pupil of eye horizontally elliptical; dorsal coloration extremely variable, ranging from light gray to brick red, variously spotted and mottled; large dorsal spots usually with 3 or more warts each; venter light except for an occasional dark breast spot. Cranial crests not prominent; interorbital crests not ending in knoblike protuberances; postorbital ridges in contact with the parotoids (Fig. 17).

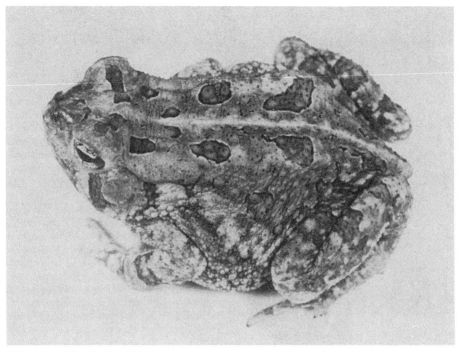

FIG. 47. *Bufo woodhousei fowleri,* Fowler's toad (Lee County). In this toad the postorbital ridges are low and contact the parotoids. The head lacks knoblike protuberances.

Remarks: This toad hybridizes frequently with *Bufo terrestris.* I have seen no hybrids between it and *B. americanus* in Alabama. The presence of hybrids often complicates the task of correctly assigning individual toads to species. Moreover, many of the taxonomic characters useful in identifying toads to species are poorly developed in the young, adding an additional complication.

Alabama distribution: (Fig. 48) Statewide, but not common in the Lower Coastal Plain.

Habits: Fowler's toad occurs in most, if not all, of our terrestrial habitat types. It thrives in the residential areas of most cities and towns, as well as in rural districts. It is active mostly at night but forages during the day during humid, cloudy weather.

Fowler's toad appears later in the season than does *Bufo americanus* and slightly earlier than *B. terrestris.* Breeding activity begins in March or April, peaks in May, and continues until sometime in August. It breeds during both dry and wet weather. The breeding sites selected by Fowler's toad are typically of a more permanent nature than those used by *B. terrestris* and *B. americanus.* They include lakes, farm ponds, rivers, creeks, and drainage ditches. The call note is a short, nasal "waah," issued from a spot near the water's edge. The eggs, up to 10,000 in number, are laid in strings. Fowler's toad feeds almost exclusively on insects and other arthropods.

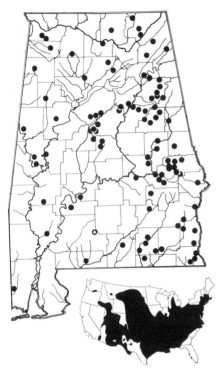

FIG. 48. Distribution of *Bufo woodhousei fowleri*, Fowler's toad. This form is believed to occur statewide, or essentially so, in Alabama. Solid symbols indicate localities from which the author examined specimens. The circle is a literature record believed to be valid. The small map depicts the approximate known range of the species *B. woodhousei* in the United States.

FAMILY HYLIDAE – HYLID FROGS

Hylidae is one of the largest anuran families. It includes about 32 genera and more than 500 species. Hylids occur in North and South America, northern Africa, Australia, New Guinea, and in portions of Europe and Asia. Four genera with 14 species are found in Alabama.

GENUS *ACRIS* Duméril and Bibron

This genus contains 2 species and occurs in much of the United States and northern Mexico east of the Rocky Mountains. Both species are found in Alabama.

Acris crepitans Baird

Two subspecies of this frog are recognized, 1 of which occurs in Alabama.

Acris crepitans crepitans Baird
Northern Cricket Frog

Description: (Fig. 49) A small frog attaining a maximum snout-vent length of about 35 mm. Tips of digits slightly rounded, not expanded as in *Limnaoedus ocularis, Hyla* spp., and most *Pseudacris;* longest (4th) toe on hind foot usually with only 1½ to 2 phalanges free of webbing.

Dorsum warty; ground color of dorsum gray to dark brown; head with a dark triangle between the eyes; dorsum and sides with variable dark spots or blotches; dorsum of some individuals with a median green stripe; front of snout with narrow, vertical light lines. Rear of thigh usually with a rough-edged longitudinal stripe; a prominent light wart usually present on each side of vent (Fig. 20A).

Remarks: *Acris c. crepitans* is quite similar in appearance to the more southerly distributed *A. gryllus* ssp. Some workers have on occasion considered the 2 conspecific. Studies during the past 2 decades have indicated, however, that

FIG. 49. *Acris crepitans crepitans,* the northern cricket frog (Tallapoosa County). In this form the body is fairly stout, the snout tends to be rounded, and the insides of the thighs lack smooth-edged dark stripes.

despite confusing similarities, they are distinct species, and that, except for occasional hybridization, they maintain their integrity in the areas where they overlap. (See Neill, 1950; Mecham, 1964; Boyd, 1964; and Bayless, 1969.)

My observations of *Acris* in Alabama lead me to believe that hybridization between the 2 forms is occurring to an extent much greater than has hitherto been realized. I have had no difficulty in distinguishing between the 2 where they occur together at localities in the Red Hills and Lower Coastal Plain. In fact, many of the *A. c. crepitans* from those regions resemble *A. c. blanchardi* and differ more from "typical" *A. g. gryllus* than do those from areas of extreme northern Alabama where the latter does not occur.

On the other hand, many populations of *Acris* from localities in the Coastal Plain north of the Red Hills are confusing, having a large proportion of their members intermediate between the 2 forms. Individuals easily identifiable as *A. g. gryllus* are fairly common in some samples from that area; individuals of *A. crepitans* are encountered but usually in fewer numbers. I suspect that these confusing populations are hybrid in origin. Sizable samples from such populations have been examined from Macon, Shelby, Dallas, and Marengo counties, as have smaller samples of apparently similar populations from several other areas of central Alabama.

Alabama distribution: (Fig. 50) *Acris c. crepitans*, or its influence in apparently hybrid populations, occurs essentially statewide, except perhaps in extreme southeastern Alabama. The species is widespread and abundant in most areas above the Fall Line and is locally common in portions of the Coastal Plain.

Habits: The northern cricket frog occurs in a wide variety of aquatic habitats, including streams, ponds, lakes, and floodplain pools. Unlike *A. gryllus*, it shuns places that dry up periodically and is not usually common at sites where the substrate is covered by dense, low vegetation. Mudflats and sparsely vegetated or barren shorelines are preferred micro-

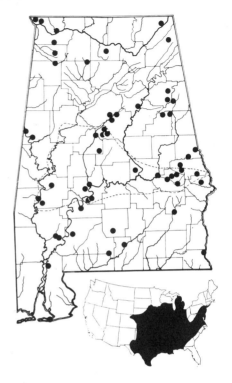

FIG. 50. Distribution of *Acris crepitans crepitans,* the northern cricket frog. This frog is presumed to occur statewide in Alabama. Symbols indicate localities from which the author examined specimens. The broken line encloses an area within which many cricket frog populations appear intermediate between *A. c. crepitans* and *A. g. gryllus,* the southern cricket frog. The small map depicts approximately the known range of the species *A. crepitans* in the United States.

habitats.

This form is decidedly less wary and less active than *A. gryllus* and is thus more easily captured. Breeding occurs from March through July or August. The call is a clicking "gik-gik . . . . . gik," usually said to resemble the sound made by striking 2 pebbles together. The eggs are laid singly or in small clusters, which float or are attached to objects in the water. The tadpoles typically have black-tipped tails, as do those of *A. gryllus.* Northern cricket frogs are cold-hardy and may be seen during any month of the year.

Acris gryllus (Le Conte)

Two subspecies of this frog, 1 of which is predominantly Floridian, are recognized. Populations with some characteristics intermediate between the 2 occur over a rather broad area, and the overall pattern of geographic variation within the species awaits accurate assessment. Populations in Alabama until now have all been assigned to the more northerly distributed, nominate subspecies. My studies indicate that the *A. gryllus* in extreme southern portions of Houston and Baldwin counties should be considered intergradient. *Acris gryllus* apparently hybridizes rather extensively in portions of Alabama with *A. c. crepitans*. (See "Remarks" under the latter.)

Acris gryllus gryllus (Le Conte)
Southern Cricket Frog

Description: (Fig. 51) A small, extremely variable frog attaining a maximum snout-vent length of about 30 mm. Body slender, snout pointed (see description of *A. c. crepitans*); tips of digits slightly rounded, not expanded to form discs; longest (4th) toe on hind foot relatively long, usually with at least 2½ phalanges free of webbing (as opposed to 1½ to 2 in *A. c. crepitans*).

Dorsum somewhat rugose, but rarely warty; anal region with a few scattered warts, but usually lacking the 2 prominent ones characteristic of most *A. crepitans*. Dorsal color extremely variable; ground color gray, brown, or black; a yellow, green, or red mid-dorsal stripe usually present, this sometimes bifurcating anteriorly, with a fork extending to each eye; head with a dark triangle between the eyes; sides with variable dark spots or blotches; front of snout with narrow, vertical light lines. Rear of thigh with a distinct median dark stripe on a light background, and frequently with a less distinct dark stripe below it (Fig. 20B).

Remarks: Positive identification of cricket frogs to species in Alabama is often difficult. *A. g. gryllus* and *A. c. crepitans* are not only similar, but they apparently hybridize, further complicating the task. (See "Remarks" under *A. c. crepitans*.)

Alabama distribution: (Fig. 52) Generally distributed below the Fall Line and local in the Tennessee Valley and Appalachian Plateaus. One sample is available from the Coosa Valley (Talladega County). Populations of *A. gryllus* near the Florida boundary in Houston County and in southern Baldwin County are intergradient between *A. g. gryllus* and *A. g. dorsalis*. *A. g. gryllus* hybridizes with *A. c. crepitans* in portions of the Coastal Plain above the Red Hills region.

FIG. 51. *Acris gryllus gryllus*, the southern cricket frog (Barbour County). In the species *A. gryllus* the body is relatively slender, the snout tends to be pointed, and the insides of the thighs usually have distinct, straight-edged stripes. Dorsal coloration is extremely variable.

Habits: The southern cricket frog may be found virtually year-round in Alabama. It occurs around most kinds of permanently aquatic habitats as well as around nearby temporary accumulations of water.

This form, in contrast to *A. c. crepitans*, thrives in densely vegetated places with little or no exposed substrate, such

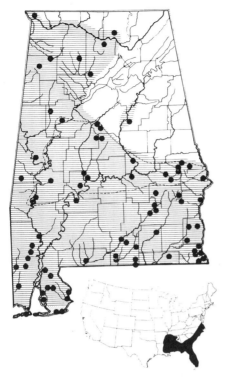

FIG. 52. Distribution of *Acris gryllus*. The hatched area indicates the presumed range of *A. g. gryllus,* the southern cricket frog, in Alabama. The stippled areas are zones of intergradation between *A. g. gryllus* and *A. g. dorsalis,* the Florida cricket frog. The broken line encloses an area within which many cricket frog populations appear intermediate between *A. g. gryllus* and *A. c. crepitans,* the northern cricket frog. Symbols indicate localities from which the author examined specimens. The small map depicts approximately the known range of the species *A. gryllus* in the United States.

somewhat more rasping or grating. The eggs are deposited singly or in small clusters; the tadpole, like that of *A. c. crepitans,* usually has a black tail-tip.

Acris g. gryllus is an excellent jumper and is considerably more active and elusive than *A. c. crepitans.* It avoids open water when attempting to escape, and if forced to jump into open water will usually jump immediately back onto land or into concealing vegetation.

Acris gryllus dorsalis (Harlan)
Florida Cricket Frog

Description: Similar to *A. g. gryllus* except as follows: size smaller, seldom exceeding 25 mm from snout to vent; rear of thigh with 2 distinct dark stripes, instead of only 1 as is usual in *A. g. gryllus* (Fig. 20B); anal warts lacking; mid-dorsal green or red stripe almost always bifurcating anteriorly.

Alabama distribution: (Fig. 52) See "Alabama distribution" under *A. g. gryllus.*

Habits: Generally similar to those of *A. g. gryllus.*

GENUS *HYLA* Laurenti

This large genus contains about 400 species, whose collective range is that of the family. It includes all but 2 of the species of "treefrogs" of the United States. Eight species of *Hyla* are known to occur in Alabama.

Hyla avivoca Vioscai
Bird-voiced Treefrog

Description: (Fig. 53) A fairly small treefrog, attaining a maximum snout-vent length of about 50 mm. Tips of digits with adhesive discs; dorsum of adults gray to green or brown, usually with an irregularly shaped, large dark blotch; dorsum of young green, lacking the blotch. A prominent light spot present under the eye; inner surfaces of thighs, and to a lesser extent those of the tibiae, light green to greenish, or rarely off-white with dark spots and reticulations.

as are provided by the edges of shallow sinkhole ponds and grassy bogs and marshes. In regions above the Fall Line, the southern chorus frog will more likely be found in areas where the soil is relatively sandy than in heavy-soil areas.

The males call from mats of floating or emergent vegetation in the water or from protected places along the shore. The call, which may be heard day or night from March through August, is similar to that of *A. c. crepitans* but is

FIG. 53. *Hyla avivoca,* the bird-voiced treefrog (Macon County). The dorsal ground color varies from green to gray or brownish. The light markings on the insides of the thighs are greenish or yellow-green. There is a light spot beneath the eye.

Remarks: Preserved large specimens of this species are often difficult to distinguish from similarly sized *H. versicolor.* The skin, which usually is somewhat smoother in the former, may provide a clue. Also, in *H. avivoca* the subarticular tubercle on the outer finger of the front foot is more often divided (66 percent) than in *H. versicolor* (19 percent).

Two subspecies of *H. avivoca* have been recognized on the basis of a study by Neill (1948). Neill's separation was based on differences in size, coloration, and relative size of the tympanum. The form he described, *H. a. ogechiensis,* was said to inhabit an area in eastern Georgia and adjacent South Carolina.

Neill stated in the description of *ogechiensis* that the wash on the hind leg varies from egg shell white to pale yellowish green, as opposed to green or yellowish green in *H. a. avivoca.* Among Alabama specimens I have examined alive, I have seen all these colors, and could detect no geographic significance in the variation displayed. The color least frequently encountered is grass green, which was reportedly common in *H. a. avicoca.* Egg shell white is also uncommon, with nearly every individual showing at least faint but definite traces of green or yellow.

The diameter of the tympanum as a proportion of eye diameter was said to average 52.5 percent in *H. a. ogechiensis*

and 49 percent in the nominate form. In forty-eight specimens from Alabama, the average was 55.2, higher than either of the reported figures. I could detect no geographic pattern of variation in this character among the Alabama specimens.

Finally, the Atlantic Coastal Plain form, *H. a. ogechiensis,* was said to exceed *H. a. avivoca* in maximum snout-vent length by from 2 to 3 mm, with males of the former reaching 38.5 mm and females 52.5 mm. Seven of forty-one Alabama males exceeded 37 mm in snout-vent length and two exceeded 40 mm. The largest female was only 42 mm, but there were only seven in the sample. It may be concluded that if *H. a. ogechiensis* is a valid subspecies, then

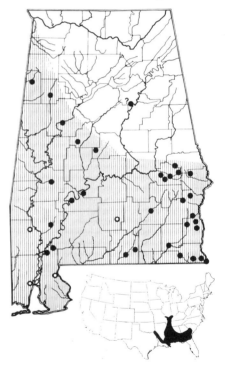

FIG. 54. Distribution of *Hyla avivoca,* the bird-voiced treefrog. The presumed range in Alabama is indicated by hatching. Solid symbols indicate localities from which the author examined specimens. The circles are literature records believed to be valid. The small map depicts approximately the known range in the United States.

most, if not all, of the Alabama range would be within a zone of intergradation, and the character involving the tympanum would be of no diagnostic value. I think it best to consider *H. avivoca* monotypic until a stronger argument is presented for recognizing *H. a. ogechiensis* than has hitherto been advanced. The validity of *ogechiensis* has also been questioned by P. Smith. (See Smith's (1966) review of the literature on *H. avivoca*.)

Alabama distribution: (Fig. 54) Found in every Coastal Plain subdivision and possibly above the Fall Line in the Ridge and Valley region. The latter is indicated by a single specimen in the Auburn Museum bearing the locality datum "St. Clair County, 3 mi. SW of Pell City." While this record has not been verified by the collection of additional specimens, the presence of the species at that locality would not be surprising. The ranges of a number of other forms usually associated with the Coastal Plain extend above the Fall Line into the Ridge and Valley region and are found nearby.

Habits: The bird-voiced treefrog is seldom encountered except during the breeding season, when the males emit their distinctive calls and announce their presence. The call is a series of clear, whistling notes, given at a rate of 2 to 5 per second. The oak toad and spring peeper also have whistling notes, but theirs are not so rapidly enunciated.

Breeding sites include semi-permanent and permanent pools in wooded and partially wooded situations. Floodplain pools are especially favored, particularly those with an abundance of shrubs and other low, woody vegetation growing in them. The calling male usually perches on a limb or vine 2 to 8 feet above the water. The eggs are laid in submerged packets (Hellman, 1953). The tadpoles have a series of red saddles on the dorsum and are thus easily recognized. Breeding takes place in spring and summer and is greatly enhanced by heavy rains. I have Alabama records for the period April through July.

Hyla cinerea (Schneider)
Green Treefrog

Description: (Fig. 55) A rather large, but slender treefrog attaining a maximum snout-vent length of about 65 mm. Tips of digits expanded into adhesive discs; dorsum light green to dark green, usually with a few randomly dispersed

FIG. 55. *Hyla cinerea*, the green treefrog (Macon County). The dorsum is green and lacks dark spots. The conspicuous straight, lateral light stripe is distinctive.

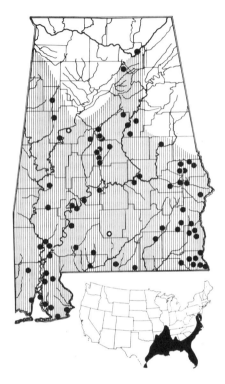

FIG. 56. Distribution of *Hyla cinerea*, the green treefrog. The presumed range in Alabama is indicated by hatching. Solid symbols indicate localities from which the author examined specimens. The circles are literature records believed to be valid. The small map depicts approximately the known range in the United States.

gold flecks or small gold spots; dorsum never with dark spots or blotches; side with a sharply delineated, straight, yellow or white stripe beginning on the upper lip and extending usually at least halfway back (*H. squirella* and *H. gratiosa* sometimes have a light lateral stripe, but in these the stripe is never sharply delineated); tibia-tarsus with a longitudinal light stripe; skin of dorsum relatively smooth.

Remarks: The length of the lateral light stripe has been used as a taxonomic character in efforts to describe subspecies in *Hyla cinerea*. A relatively short stripe (not reaching mid-body) occurs rather sporadically in Alabama populations and was noted in about 5 percent of the specimens examined.

Alabama distribution: (Fig. 56) Common to abundant throughout the Coastal Plain; occurs locally in adjacent portions of adjoining regions and at least as far northward as Talladega County in the Ridge and Valley region. One specimen from Sand Mountain in Marshall County and one from Blount County suggest the presence of apparently isolated populations in the Appalachian Plateaus region.

Habits: The familiar green treefrog is found in a variety of permanently aquatic situations, including lakes, ponds, swamps, and some streams. Sites with abundant emergent vegetation are favored. During the day the frogs sit quietly on green leaves or stems, with their legs folded beneath them.

The call note, a "quank" or "quonk," is issued at the rate of 30 to 60 per minute, usually from a perch 1 to 7 feet above the water. The bicolored brown-and-cream eggs are deposited 10 to 20 at a time in small, surface-floating packets (Brown, 1956). In Alabama, breeding usually begins in April and extends into August. Rainy weather is not necessary to initiate breeding in this species.

Hyla crucifer Wied

Two subspecies of this common frog are recognized, 1 of which occurs in Alabama.

Hyla crucifer crucifer Wied
Northern Spring Peeper

Description: (Fig. 57) A small frog attaining a maximum snout-vent length of about 35 mm. Tips of digits expanded into adhesive discs; dorsum with an X-shaped dark mark; a transverse interorbital bar usually present, but sometimes reduced to a medial blotch. Ground color tan or light brown; contrasting light markings absent. Skin relatively smooth.

Remarks: Significant geographic variation seems to be lacking among Alabama populations of this frog. Dark ventral flecking suggestive of *H. c. bartramiana*, the other, predominantly Floridian subspecies, is seen on an occasional individual, but such individuals may be found in almost every part of the

FIG. 57. *Hyla crucifer crucifer,* the northern spring peeper (Escambia County). The dark X-shaped mark on the dorsum is distinctive.

state and do not seem to indicate influence from that form.

Alabama distribution: (Fig. 58) Common to abundant in every part of the state.

Habits: In the seasonal progress of anuran reproductive activity in Alabama, breeding of the spring peeper gets underway a few weeks later than the earliest *Pseudacris* (except for *P. nigrita,* which it precedes). The males' clear, high-pitched whistles or peeps, rising slightly at the end and issued at the rate of about 1 per second, usually begin in late December in southern Alabama and in January or February in northern Alabama.

The breeding site is most frequently a temporary or semi-permanent pond or pool, preferably one with abundant emergent vegetation. The male perches from a few inches to several feet above the water on sticks, bushes, vines, or in a clump of grass. The female deposits several hundred eggs at a time, sticking them to vegetation in the water. The breeding season lasts until late April or into May. Frequently, the peeper breeds in company with 1 or more species of *Pseudacris.* Following breeding, the adults move to damp places in wooded areas, where they become secretive and difficult to find.

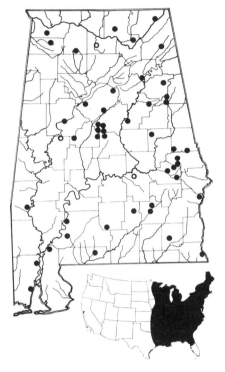

FIG. 58. Distribution of *Hyla crucifer crucifer,* the northern spring peeper. This form is believed to occur statewide, or nearly so, in Alabama. Solid symbols indicate localities from which the author examined specimens. Circles are literature records believed to be valid. The small map depicts approximately the known range of the species *H. crucifer* in the United States.

Hyla femoralis Sonnini and Latreille
Pine Woods Treefrog

Description: (Fig. 59) A small treefrog attaining a maximum snout-vent length of about 40 mm. Tips of digits expanded into adhesive discs; dorsum gray or brown with 1 or more dark, irregularly shaped blotches or, rarely, unicolorous; backs of thighs with rounded

FIG. 59. *Hyla femoralis,* the pine woods treefrog (both Russell County). The insides of the thighs of this small treefrog have rounded orange spots. Dorsal markings are variable. In many species of frogs, such as this one, the color of an individual varies with the ambient temperature. The frog on the left was photographed when the temperature was about 85°F, the one at the right, at about 75°F.

orange or yellow spots; light spots below eyes lacking; skin smooth to somewhat granular, the latter condition more prevalent in individuals from the northern portion of the range in Alabama.

Alabama distribution: (Fig. 60) Common to abundant in the Lower Coastal Plain; local in the other Coastal Plain provinces, where it occurs mostly in areas where the soil is sandy. In the Ridge and Valley region the range extends above the Fall Line at least as far northward as central Shelby County.

Habits: This treefrog reportedly spends most of its time during the warm months high up in pine trees. Occasionally it is collected from under the bark of rotting pine stumps and logs and in the foliage of shrubs and bushes. In the winter months and during hot, dry spells in summer, aggregations of pine woods treefrogs are sometimes found in damp

places under logs and in rotting stumps.

The breeding season in Alabama usually begins in April and extends into August. Rainy weather conjoined with warm temperatures elicit the breeding

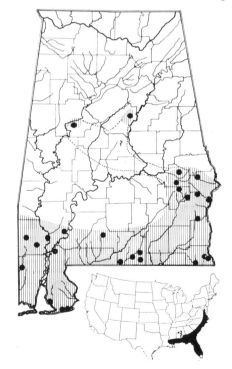

FIG. 60. Distribution of *Hyla femoralis,* the pine woods treefrog. The known range of this species in Alabama is indicated by hatching. The area outlined by the broken line likely contains widely scattered populations, but documentation is lacking. Symbols indicate localities from which the author examined specimens. The small map depicts approximately the known range of the species in the United States.

response. The usual sites are flooded roadside ditches and other transient pools and ponds. Typically, the male calls from a perch in a tuft of grass or on a stick or limb from 2 inches to 5 feet above the water. The call is a prolonged, monotonous "kek-kek-kek ... kek," the notes given in rapid succession. Frequently the pine woods treefrog shares a breeding site with *Hyla squirella, Bufo quercicus,* and *Gastrophryne carolinensis.*

The eggs are bicolored, brown and yellowish, and are laid in groups of about 100. They may be attached to vegetation or roots just beneath the surface or may form a surface film (Wright and Wright, 1949).

Hyla gratiosa Le Conte
Barking Treefrog

Description: (Fig. 61) A large, plump treefrog attaining a maximum snout-vent length of around 70 mm. Toes ending in adhesive discs; dorsal surface granular; color variable; usually green or greenish, but often brown; dorsum marked with rounded dark spots, these sometimes only faintly discernible; each side with a ragged light stripe or longitudinal series of irregular light markings and occasionally with some irregular purplish or maroon markings.

Remarks: Mecham (1960a) reported on introgressive hybridization between this species and the green treefrog, *Hyla cinerea,* in Lee County. The hybrids show various degrees of intermediacy between the 2 species, both in behavior and morphology. Evidence of hybridization can also be seen in specimens collected more recently in Covington, Shelby, and Macon counties. The construction of farm ponds and the ecological disturbances associated with their maintenance are probably causing breakdown of the biological isolating mechanisms that served to keep these species from hybridizing in their unaltered natural habitats.

Alabama distribution: (Fig. 62) Fairly generally distributed in the southeastern quadrant of the state, locally so else-

FIG. 61. *Hyla gratiosa,* the barking treefrog (Monroe County). The dorsal ground color of this large treefrog varies from bright green to brownish. Dark spots or blotches on the dorsum are usually visible.

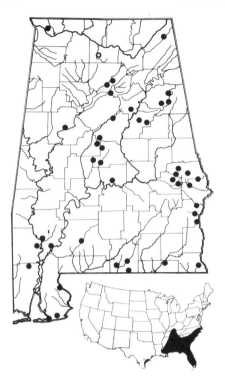

FIG. 62. Distribution of *Hyla gratiosa*, the barking treefrog. This species is believed to occur statewide, or essentially so, in Alabama. Solid symbols indicate localities from which the author examined specimens. The circle is a literature record believed to be valid. The small map depicts approximately the known range in the United States.

where. Records are lacking from much of western Alabama.

Habits: Shallow, semi-permanent ponds with at least some open water are the habitats most suitable for the breeding of *H. gratiosa*, which occurs mostly from April through July. Permanent ponds and lakes are used occasionally, but the presence of fish in such habitats may make them unsuitable. The male issues its call, a hollow "boonk" or "moonk," repeated every second or so, while floating on the water or sitting at the water's edge. The eggs are laid singly, on the bottom.

If kept in a humid terrarium and supplied with insects, the barking treefrog

makes an excellent pet. It is not nearly as skittish as our other treefrogs and has a generally pleasing "personality."

Hyla squirella Sonnini and Latreille
Squirrel Treefrog

Description: (Fig. 63) A fairly small frog attaining a maximum snout-vent length of around 45 mm. Digits ending in adhesive discs; color variable, ranging from green to brown, but without any sharply defined markings; a light lateral stripe, or indication thereof, often present but never as distinct as in *H. cinerea;* dorsum often with inconspicuous dark flecks or small spots; rear of thighs usually without marks or contrasting colors (98 percent).

Alabama distribution: (Fig. 64) The Coastal Plain, except possibly for the northwesternmost portion, and extending across the Fall Line into the Ridge and Valley region as far northeastward as Etowah County. Further investigation will probably reveal the presence of this species in Cherokee County, which lies east of Etowah County, and in the adjacent portion of Georgia as well.

Habits: In some of the low country of southern Alabama, the squirrel treefrog is exceedingly abundant. On warm nights following heavy rains it is often seen in large numbers hopping on the highways and around dwellings, service stations, restaurants, and other well-lit places. During the day *H. squirella* often heralds

FIG. 63. *Hyla squirella*, the squirrel treefrog (Houston County). The color of this small treefrog varies from light green to gray or brown. The dorsum may be plain or spotted or flecked with dark pigment. The insides of the thighs are usually unmarked.

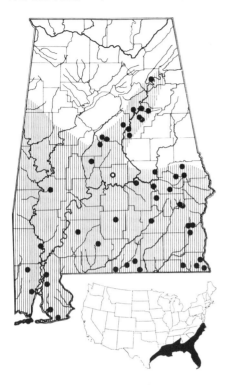

FIG. 64. Distribution of *Hyla squirella*, the squirrel treefrog. The presumed range in Alabama is indicated by hatching. Solid symbols indicate localities from which the author examined specimens. The circle is a literature record believed to be valid. The small map depicts approximately the known range in the United States.

the approach of wet weather by calling intermittently from a perch in a tree or shrub. The colloquial name "rain frog," frequently applied to this species, seems appropriate.

In Alabama this species usually breeds from about mid-April to mid-August, usually following rains. I have one record of males calling in chorus on October 15, apparently an unusual occurrence. On that date in 1966 there was a vigorous chorus of 10 to 15 individuals, accompanied by a chorus of *Pseudacris nigrita*, in a rainwater pool at Robertsdale, Baldwin County. The air temperature was 70°F. It is unlikely that either species bred at that time. Breeding sites for *H. squirella* include flooded roadside ditches,

flatwoods ponds, and small, semi-permanent stock-watering ponds. The males usually call from a perch a foot or two above the water or from the bank near the water's edge. The call note is a harsh, somewhat nasal rasp or "quack," repeated at the rate of about 100 times per minute. The eggs are deposited singly and sink to the bottom (Wright and Wright, 1949).

Hyla versicolor complex
(*Hyla versicolor* Le Conte and *Hyla chrysoscelis* Cope)
Gray Treefrogs

Description: (Fig. 65) Fairly large treefrogs attaining a maximum snout-vent length of about 60 mm. Tips of digits expanded into adhesive discs; dorsum light gray to dark gray or brownish (occasionally greenish) with 1 or 2 large, centrally located dark figures of varying shape usually visible. A prominent light spot usually present below the eye. Inner surface of thighs, and to a lesser extent those of the tibias, bright yellow or orange with dark spots and reticulations or, in some individuals, brownish with golden yellow spots. Skin roughly granular to somewhat warty. Subarticular tubercle on outer finger of front foot

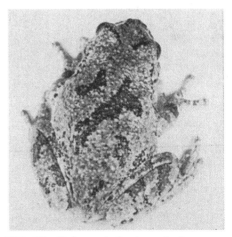

FIG. 65. *Hyla versicolor* (complex), a gray treefrog (Macon County). Gray treefrogs range in color from greenish gray to brownish. The light markings on the insides of the thighs are yellow or orange.

usually undivided (80 percent among Alabama specimens). (See "Remarks" under *H. avivoca*.)

Remarks: The 2 species within this complex are separable only on the basis of call characteristics and chromosome number. *Hyla versicolor* is said to have twice the number of chromosomes that *H. chrysoscelis* has. The trill rate in the call of *H. versicolor* reportedly ranges from about 17 to 35 notes per second, depending on temperature, whereas that of *H. chrysoscelis* is said to range from 34 to 69 notes per second.

To date there has been no concerted effort to determine the species composition of Alabama populations of gray treefrogs. An Auburn graduate student, Tom French, recorded and analyzed calls of gray treefrogs from several localities in the state but reached no firm conclusions with respect to the identity of the populations sampled (personal communication).

Alabama distribution: (Fig. 66) Gray treefrogs are found statewide.

Habits: Gray treefrogs are common throughout the state but are seldom encountered in abundance except during breeding. The breeding period extends from April to August, with the greatest activity occurring during warm, rainy periods. The mating call is a short trill, repeated at regular intervals. Gray treefrogs use a variety of aquatic sites for breeding, but streams and large bodies of water are usually shunned. The ideal breeding site appears to be a temporary or semi-permanent pool or pond, such as a flooded borrow pit.

Ralin (1968) studied *H. versicolor* and *H. chrysoscelis* in Texas and reported that the former tended to issue the mating call from the ground, while the latter usually called from trees or bushes. He also reported that during the breeding season the 2 differed in food habits, with proportionately more *H. versicolor* eating terrestrial insects and proportionately more *H. chrysoscelis* eating arboreal insects.

During dry periods gray treefrogs are likely to be found well away from water

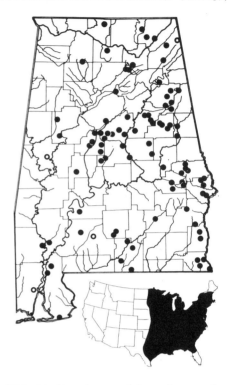

FIG. 66. Distribution of the *Hyla versicolor* complex, the gray treefrogs. Gray treefrogs occur statewide in Alabama, and more than 1 species may be present (see text, p. 74). Solid symbols indicate localities from which the author examined specimens. The circles are literature records believed to be valid. The small map denotes the approximate range of the complex in the United States.

and may take shelter in knotholes in trees and in other such protected arboreal microhabitats. They often announce their presence by sporadic calling. At night they may leave the trees and move to the ground to feed.

GENUS *LIMNAOEDUS* Mittleman and List

This genus contains only 1 species, which is confined to the southeastern United States. It has been included previously within *Hyla* and *Pseudacris*.

Limnaoedus ocularis (Bosc and Daudin)

Little Grass Frog (Least Treefrog)

Description: (Fig. 67) The smallest of North American frogs, attaining a

FIG. 67. *Limnaoedus ocularis,* the little grass frog (Houston County). This is the smallest frog in North America.

maximum snout-vent length of about 18 mm. Tips of digits expanded; color tan or grayish tan; a dark lateral stripe beginning on the snout, passing through the eye, continuing in undiminished intensity to the level of the forelimbs, and gradually blending with the ground color before reaching the groin. Dorsum with a less prominent median stripe, and on most individuals with 2 obscure dorsolateral stripes; skin of dorsum relatively smooth.

Alabama distribution: (Fig. 68) Known only from the lower half of Houston County, in extreme southeastern Alabama.

Habits: This tiny frog prefers low pine flatwoods areas. During the day it frequents damp, grassy swales and the edges of cypress ponds, where it clings to grass blades and low shrubs. Favored breeding sites are grassy, rain-filled depressions and semi-permanent ponds. The males usually perch 3 inches to 3 feet above the water on a grass stem or leaf. The call is an insect-like, high-pitched tinkling or chirping, resembling the calls of some of the long-horned grasshoppers. The eggs are laid singly, on the bottom or among submerged vegetation (Wright and Wright, 1949).

Breeding congregations in Houston County were recorded on March 11 and July 29. Sporadic calling by a few indi-

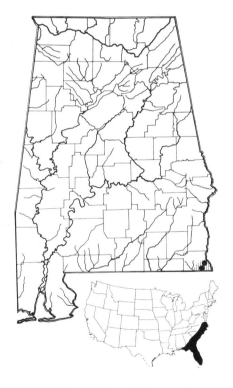

FIG. 68. Distribution of *Limnaoedus ocularis,* the little grass frog. The presumed range in Alabama is indicated by hatching. Symbols indicate localities from which the author examined specimens. The small map depicts approximately the known range in the United States.

viduals, in the midst of a congress of *Pseudacris ornata,* was heard on January 2. According to Harper (1939), breeding occurs in Georgia from January to September.

GENUS *PSEUDACRIS* Fitzinger

This genus occurs throughout much of the United States east of the Rocky Mountains and over a fairly large portion of Canada. Seven species are included, 4 of which are native to Alabama.

Pseudacris brachyphona (Cope)
Mountain Chorus Frog

Description: (Fig. 69) A small frog attaining a maximum snout-vent length of around 35 mm. Tips of digits moderately expanded; dorsum brown to grayish; a dark triangle between the eyes and, typically, a pair of outward-curving dorsolateral dark bars on the back, these often inconspicuous and frequently irregular in shape (Fig. 21C); dorsolateral bars occasionally absent and replaced by small, irregularly shaped dark spots or flecks; upper lip with a light stripe; skin somewhat rough. Tibia length as a percentage of snout-vent length in sixteen Alabama specimens: range 47.9 to 57.1; mean, 53.4.

Alabama distribution: (Fig. 70) Local north of the Black Belt. More common above the Fall Line than below.

Habits: This frog, as with other members of its genus in Alabama, is seldom collected except during its breeding season, which usually begins in December or January, depending on the weather, and lasts until mid- or late April. The earliest I have recorded males calling is December 9 (Macon County).

The breeding sites are usually in hilly, wooded, or partially wooded areas and include seepages at the base of hills or mountains, flooded roadside ditches, and other shallow pools and puddles.

During the height of the breeding season the mating call, a rasping "wrrink-wrrink.....wrrink," may be heard both

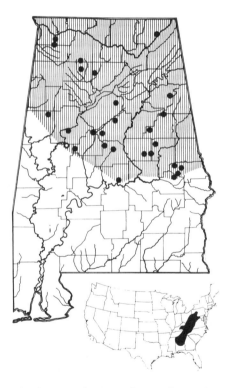

FIG. 70. Distribution of *Pseudacris brachyphona,* the mountain chorus frog. The presumed range in Alabama is indicated by hatching. Solid symbols indicate localities from which the author examined specimens. The circle is a literature record believed to be valid. The small map depicts approximately the known range in the United States.

FIG. 69. *Pseudacris brachyphona,* the mountain chorus frog (Macon County). The "reversed parentheses" on the dorsum are usually present on this small frog, which is seldom encountered except during the winter.

day and night. The frogs are shy, and they usually cease calling abruptly at the slightest disturbance. If approached, they will frequently dive to the bottom of the pool and take shelter under debris until the intruder has left.

Small clumps of 10 to 30 eggs are deposited under water. Usually the clumps are attached to vegetation or sticks, but occasionally they are free and sink to the bottom (Brown, 1956).

Pseudacris nigrita (Le Conte)

Two subspecies of this frog are currently recognized, 1 of which occurs in Alabama.

Pseudacris nigrita nigrita (Le Conte)
Southern Chorus Frog

Description: (Fig. 71) A small frog attaining a maximum snout-vent length of around 32 mm. Tips of digits moderately expanded; upper lip with a light stripe bordered above by a dark stripe that passes through the eye and extends onto the side. Dorsum smooth to slightly pustulate, gray to brown with 3 dark stripes or longitudinal series of dark spots; median stripe terminating anteriorly in a point between the eyes or on the snout. Often confused with *P. triseriata feriarum*, from which it differs in lacking an expanded dark area between the eyes, having a narrower head and more pointed snout, and in being generally less robust and more *Acris*-like (Fig. 21A).

Alabama distribution: (Fig. 72) Restricted to the Lower Coastal Plain except in the area east of the Conecuh River where the range extends northward to southern Russell County.

Habits: In Alabama this frog is the Lower Coastal Plain counterpart of the

FIG. 71. *Pseudacris nigrita nigrita,* the southern chorus frog (Barbour County). This small, winter-breeding frog lacks the expanded dark area between the eyes characteristic of *P. triseriata feriarum*.

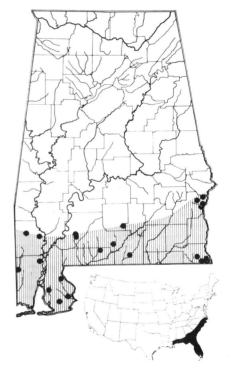

FIG. 72. Distribution of *Pseudacris nigrita nigrita*, the southern chorus frog. The presumed range in Alabama is indicated by hatching. Symbols indicate localities from which the author examined specimens. The small map depicts approximately the known range of the species *P. nigrita* in the United States.

upland chorus frog, *Pseudacris triseriata feriarum*, except in the area east of the Conecuh River where the ranges of the 2 species broadly overlap.

The ecological and temporal relationships between the 2 closely related frogs are not well known. Schwartz (1957) noted that in South Carolina *P. t. feriarum* begins breeding earlier than *P. n. nigrita*, and that the major choruses of *P. t. feriarum* have waned by the time the major choruses of *P. n. nigrita* begin. This relationship also holds in Alabama in most years. Major choruses of *P. t. feriarum* usually begin in December in central and southern Alabama, whereas those of *P. n. nigrita* are seldom underway before late January or early February. Breeding in *P. n. nigrita* apparently extends well into April and possibly into May. Heavy thundershower activity may initiate vigorous calling by a group of males almost anytime during the summer and, on rare occasions, during the fall. One large chorus was heard in Robertsdale, Baldwin County, on October 14 following a heavy rain. It is doubtful that any breeding occurs during summer and fall, however.

Differences in habitat preference between *P. t. feriarum* and *P. n. nigrita* are significant, if breeding sites are any indication. In the area where the 2 are sympatric, *P. n. nigrita* is likely to be found where the soil is sandy and friable, whereas *P. t. feriarum* occurs mostly in places where the soil is heavier. Flooded fields and roadside ditches, the weedy margins of shallow flatwoods ponds, and temporary woodland pools serve as breeding sites for *P. n. nigrita*.

Where grassy vegetation is abundant, the calling males are usually well concealed and positioned vertically, with only the head protruding above the water. They are considerably more difficult to locate and are more elusive than *P. t. feriarum* males. In places where vegetation is scarce or absent, the males may call while sitting on the bank or in the edge of the water, or while clinging to sticks or detritus floating in the water. Crenshaw and Blair (1959) reported on differences in breeding behavior between *P. t. feriarum* and *P. n. nigrita* in southwestern Georgia.

The call of *P. n. nigrita* is similar to that of *P. t. feriarum* except for its slower pulse rate. At temperatures between 60 and 70°F, the pulse rate for *P. n. nigrita* is usually 3 to 4 times slower, a difference that is readily detectable by ear. There is virtually no information available on the eggs or tadpoles of *P. n. nigrita*.

Pseudacris ornata (Holbrook)
Ornate Chorus Frog

Description: (Fig. 73) A moderately small, stout frog attaining a maximum

FIG. 73. *Pseudacris ornata*, the ornate chorus frog (Escambia County). This boldly marked, small frog breeds during the winter. Ground color varies from tan or pink to greenish.

snout-vent length of about 35 mm. Tips of digits somewhat rounded, not obviously expanded; head with a dark triangular mark between the eyes; dorsum usually with 2 rather irregular wide, longitudinal dark stripes; side with a sharply defined, dark stripe or blotch about midway and a dark blotch or spot anterodorsal to the groin, the latter sometimes connected to the dorsal stripe. Ground color variable, ranging from green to pink or pinkish brown; groin washed with yellow or orange; skin on dorsum smooth. Tibia length as a percentage of snout-vent length in seventy-seven Alabama specimens: range, 39.8 (Houston County) to 51.9 (Russell County); average, 45.2.

Alabama distribution: (Fig. 74) Re-

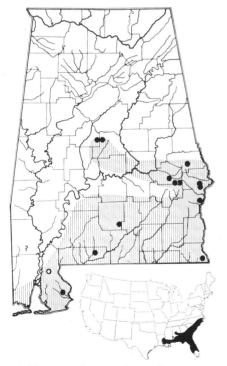

FIG. 74. Distribution of *Pseudacris ornata*, the ornate chorus frog. The presumed range in Alabama is indicated by hatching. Solid symbols indicate localities from which the author examined specimens. The circle is a literature record believed to be valid. The small map depicts approximately the known range in the United States.

stricted to the Coastal Plain, this frog is most common in sandy areas in the southeastern quadrant of the state. The range extends westward into Mississippi, but the northern range limit in western Alabama has not been determined.

Habits: This frog is seldom encountered except during the breeding season, which extends from December or January, depending on rainfall, to March. The earliest record of males calling in Alabama is December 1, in Russell County. Shallow, transient pools and ponds, particularly those with abundant emergent vegetation, are the chief breeding sites of the ornate chorus frog. Although *P. ornata* often shares breeding sites with other *Pseudacris*, it is less likely to breed in shallow roadside ditches and seepage areas than other Alabama chorus frogs. The calling male usually sits 1 to 10 inches above the water in clumps of grass or on floating debris. The call note, given at the rate of 65 to 80 per minute, is a high pitched "peep" or "peet," somewhat similar to the notes of *Hyla crucifer* and *Bufo quercicus* but more sharply abbreviated. The note has appropriately been likened to the sound made when a steel chisel is struck with a hammer.

Reportedly the eggs are laid in loose clusters attached to vegetation and debris in the water (Wright and Wright, 1949). Brown (1956) reported a cluster containing 25 eggs in Macon County.

Pseudacris triseriata (Weid)

Three subspecies of this frog are recognized, 1 of which occurs in Alabama.

Pseudacris triseriata feriarum (Baird)
Upland Chorus Frog

Description: (Fig. 75) A small frog attaining a maximum snout-vent length of about 35 mm. Upper lip with a light stripe; a dark stripe begins on snout, passes through eye, and continues onto side; top of head with an expanded dark area between eyes; dorsal ground color light gray, tan, or brown; dorsal markings on body variable, but usually consisting of 3 dark stripes or series of longitudinal dark spots, these sometimes re-

FIG. 75. *Pseudacris triseriata feriarum*, the upland chorus frog (Choctaw County). The 3 dorsal stripes and the expanded dark area between the eyes are usually evident on this small, winter-breeding frog.

duced to scattered flecks or dots. Head relatively wider, snout less pointed, and body more robust than in *P. n. nigrita;* general appearance not *Acris*-like as in *P. n. nigrita* (Fig. 21B).

Remarks: In this subspecies the ratio of tibia length to body length is usually 47 percent or greater. In the other 2 subspecies the tibia is relatively shorter. Also, the longitudinal dark stripes tend to be narrower and show a greater tendency to break up in *P. t. feriarum* than in the others.

In populations of *P. t. feriarum* west of the Tombigbee River in Alabama, the dorsal stripes tend to be distinctly wider and are more frequently unbroken than in other populations sampled in the state. In this character they approach *P. t. triseriata*. In tibia length, however, which has been accepted as the most important taxonomic character, all Alabama populations are referable to *P. t. feriarum*. Variation in this character is rather chaotic in Alabama, with average ratios of tibia length to body length ranging from 48.5 percent (Russell County) to 54.0 percent in an area around Centreville (Bibb County).

Statewide, the average is approximately 50.0 percent.

Alabama distribution: (Fig. 76) The upland chorus frog is common to abundant in all areas of the state southward to the southern boundary of the Red Hills region. In the Lower Coastal Plain it is local from the Conecuh River eastward and apparently absent from the Conecuh River westward.

Habits: The cheery sounds of this little frog, along with those of the other members of its genus, are heard in Alabama during wet weather in winter and early spring. In some years as early as October or November, but more often around the middle of December, the males begin calling from rainwater pools in ditches, fields, and open woods. The

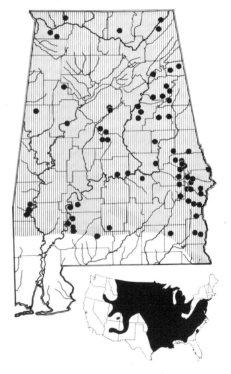

FIG. 76. Distribution of *Pseudacris triseriata feriarum*, the upland chorus frog. The presumed range in Alabama is indicated by hatching. Symbols indicate localities from which the author examined specimens. The small map depicts approximately the known range of the species *P. triseriata* in the United States.

call consists of a continuous series of short trills, "prreep-prreep....preep," resembling the sound produced when the thumbnail is run along the teeth of a plastic comb, but somewhat more ringing. Each trill rises at the end; the pulse rate is typically faster than in the call of *P. n. nigrita.* The call is issued as the male sits in shallow, open water, on the bank, or amid clumps of grass or debris in the water. During cloudy weather calling may continue day and night.

The eggs are laid in clusters ranging in number from about 20 to 100 each. The clusters adhere to sticks and grass. Breeding activity in Alabama usually ends by late April, although a cool, rainy spell in the summer may produce sporadic calling. During the non-breeding season, upland chorus frogs are rarely seen abroad except at night during damp weather. Whitaker (1971) reported the results of an intensive study of the life history and habits of *P. triseriata* in Indiana.

FAMILY MICROHYLIDAE — NARROW-MOUTHED TOADS

A large family of predominantly tropical frogs, Microhylidae contains 55 genera with about 215 species. Microhylids are widely distributed in both the New World and the Old World, but only 2 genera reach the United States. One of these is represented in Alabama.

GENUS *GASTROPHRYNE* Fitzinger

Members of this genus occur from the eastern United States to Nicaragua. Five species are included, 1 of which is found in Alabama.

Gastrophryne carolinensis (Holbrook) Eastern Narrow-mouthed Toad

Description: (Fig. 77) A small frog attaining a maximum snout-vent length of about 35 mm. Head tiny; snout pointed; legs short (tibia length usually around 40 percent of snout-vent length); skin on back of neck usually with a transverse fold (in life); toes free of webbing; tympanum concealed; skin usually smooth; dorsum brown, yellowish brown, or gray, usually with a large, dark figure oriented longitudinally; venter heavily mottled.

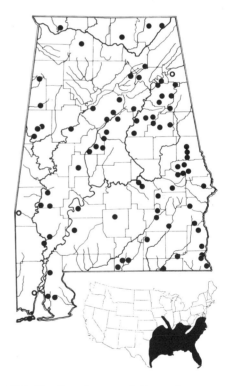

FIG. 78. Distribution of *Gastrophryne carolinensis,* the eastern narrow-mouthed toad. This species is believed to occur statewide, or essentially so, in Alabama. Solid symbols indicate localities from which the author examined specimens. The circles are literature records believed to be valid. The small map depicts approximately the known range in the United States.

FIG. 77. *Gastrophryne carolinensis,* the eastern narrow-mouthed toad (Lawrence County). This small, "pointy-headed" frog is brown or yellowish brown in color and is common throughout Alabama.

Remarks: There is an apparent lack of significant geographic variation in this species in Alabama. About 10 percent of the males have chin papillae; specimens so characterized were found in Calhoun, Russell, Houston, and Marengo counties.

Alabama distribution: (Fig. 78) Abundant throughout the state.

Habits: The narrow-mouthed toad is secretive and spends most of its time in subterranean burrows, in decaying logs and stumps, and under rocks. When exposed it may hop away quickly or attempt to burrow into rotting wood or debris.

Breeding activity in Alabama occurs from April to September and is elicited by heavy rains. Breeding sites include lakes, ponds, sloughs, and flooded roadside ditches. The calling males are typically well hidden beneath clumps of grass or debris at the water's edge and

are surprisingly difficult to locate. The call is a nasal, sheeplike bleat. After initial amplexus, which is axillary, the male may become attached to the female's back by an adhesive substance secreted by special breeding glands on his chest (Conway and Metter, 1967).

The eggs are laid in groups of 10 to 90 as a surface film one egg-layer deep (Wright and Wright, 1949). The tadpole's mouth is a sucking disk and lacks mandibles and labial teeth. Anderson (1954) provided a detailed study of the ecology of this species.

FAMILY PELOBATIDAE — SPADEFOOT TOADS

The spadefoot toads include 8 genera with about 60 species. Representatives are found in North America, Eurasia, and the East Indies. Only 1 genus occurs in the United States.

FIG. 79. *Scaphiopus holbrooki holbrooki,* the eastern spadefoot (Greene County). This frog breeds following heavy rain. The dorsal ground color is brownish and the light markings are yellow. The pupils of the eye are vertically elliptical.

GENUS *SCAPHIOPUS* Holbrook

This genus occurs in the United States and Mexico and includes 6 species. Most are inhabitants of dry regions, and only 1 occurs in Alabama.

Scaphiopus holbrooki (Harlan)

Two subspecies are recognized, 1 of which occurs in Alabama.

Scaphiopus holbrooki holbrooki (Harlan)
Eastern Spadefoot Toad

Description: (Fig. 79) A medium-sized frog attaining a maximum snout-vent length of about 70 mm. Skin warty; hind feet completely webbed; pectoral glands present and rather distinct; pupil of eye vertically elliptical; back with a lyre-shaped figure formed by a pair of yellowish or greenish yellow stripes extending from behind eye to region of vent; ground color olive to brownish. Cranial crests absent; hind foot with a horny, black "spade" on inner surface of inner toe.

Remarks: In this subspecies, the head is wider than long at the angle of the mouth; and the interorbital region is not raised above the postorbital region.

Alabama distribution: (Fig. 80) Apparently statewide but somewhat local.

Habits: The eastern spadefoot toad is a secretive, burrowing form, emerging from its burrow only at night or on heavily overcast days. Breeding is confined to temporary pools and ponds resulting from heavy rain. In Alabama a minimum of 2 to 3 inches of rain coinciding with a temperature of 60°F or above is usually necessary to elicit the breeding response. Such conditions usually occur during the spring and summer, but breeding may take place in any month of the year.

The call is an explosive, nasal "quank" or "quonk," issued while the male sits or floats in the water. A large chorus can be heard from a distance of a mile or more and is one of nature's oddest sounds.

Stringy masses of 1,000 to 2,500 eggs are laid. These hatch in 1½ to 15 days, depending on temperature, and the tad-

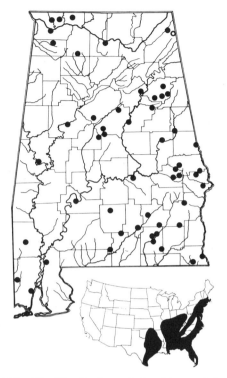

FIG. 80. Distribution of *Scaphiopus holbrooki holbrooki*, the eastern spadefoot. This form is believed to occur statewide, or nearly so, in Alabama. Solid symbols indicate localities from which the author examined specimens. The circle is a literature record believed to be valid. The small map depicts approximately the known range of the species *S. holbrooki* in the United States.

poles transform 14 to 25 days later. Wasserman (1968) reviewed the literature on *S. holbrooki.*

FAMILY RANIDAE – TRUE FROGS

With more than 700 species representing about 37 genera, Ranidae is the largest anuran family. It is widely distributed throughout the world, with representatives on almost every major land mass with the exception of Antarctica. Only one genus occurs within the United States.

GENUS *RANA* Bonaparte

The genus *Rana* is essentially cosmopolitan in distribution, although relatively few of its 400 species are found in the New World. Of the 15 species found in the United States, 8 occur in Alabama.

Rana areolata Baird and Girard

Currently, this species is considered to include 5 subspecies, at least 1 of which occurs in Alabama. (See also *R. a. circulosa* under "Problematical Forms.")

Rana areolata sevosa Goin and Netting
Dusky Gopher Frog

Description: (Fig. 81) A rather large, stout-bodied frog attaining a maximum snout-vent length of about 100 mm. Hind feet with extensive webbing between toes; toes pointed; vocal sacs lateral; dorsolateral ridges present, but often inconspicuous due to roughness of skin; tympanum and eye about the same size; dorsum roughened to rugose or warty; color gray or light brown with dark blotches and interspersed smaller dark markings of varying shape; venter light with numerous small spots, many of which coalesce; groin and inner surfaces of thighs tinged with yellow in live animals.

Alabama distribution: (Fig. 82) Local in the Lower Coastal Plain and Red Hills where suitable breeding sites occur in the vicinity of gopher tortoise burrows (or, perhaps, other suitable shelters?). Known from the following counties: Covington, Mobile, Baldwin, Escambia, and Barbour. A single specimen reported by me in 1964 from Shelby County in central Alabama is almost 200 miles from the nearest of the other localities. I am still unable to explain the significance of that occurrence.

Habits: There is little information on the habits of this shy frog. It is reported to take shelter during the day in the burrows of gopher tortoises, and in this respect may be similar to the Florida gopher frog (*R. a. aesopus*) and to some populations of the Carolina gopher frog (*R. a. capito*). Except for the Shelby County record, all Alabama localities for the dusky gopher frog are within the

FIG. 81. *Rana areolata sevosa,* the dusky gopher frog (Covington County). This shy frog relies on the burrows of gopher tortoises for shelter and is exceedingly scarce. Only a few populations are known to exist in Alabama.

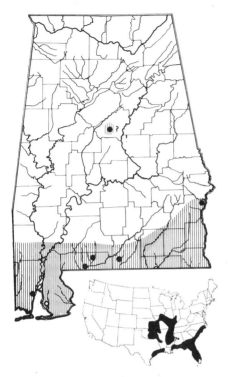

FIG. 82. Distribution of *Rana areolata sevosa*, the dusky gopher frog. The presumed range in Alabama is indicated by hatching. Solid symbols indicate localities from which the author examined specimens. The Shelby County record, questioned on the Alabama map, is based on only 1 specimen and needs further documentation. The circle is a literature record believed to be valid. The small map denotes the approximate known range of the species *R. areolata* in the United States.

range of the gopher tortoise. The Shelby County frog was collected during heavy rain along a road near a low, weedy pasture. Crawfish burrows were common in the vicinity, and the frog may represent a population whose members live in crawfish burrows. Repeated attempts to find other specimens there or to find evidence of breeding in nearby ponds failed, however.

Dusky gopher frogs breed during the winter following heavy rains. The call has a snorelike quality, essentially similar to those I have heard of *R. a. aesopus* in Florida and *R. a. capito* in western Geor-

gia. The call may be heard from a distance of at least ¼ mile. At the breeding site, it is possible to ascertain the direction of a calling individual, but exceedingly difficult to judge its distance. Usually the male calls while floating on the surface of water where the depth ranges from 2 to 4 feet. The slightest disturbance will cause it to pull its head under and swim to the bottom. In Alabama, breeding has been recorded in Barbour County in February and March, and in Escambia County in early March.

The Barbour County population, extant at the time of this writing, breeds in 3 shallow ponds. One is semipermanent, grassy and rather small, about 1 acre in size. One of the others has a fairly dense growth of shrubs covering most of its area, while the remaining one is relatively open with predominantly grassy vegetation. Amphibian breeding associates of the dusky gopher frog in these ponds are the frogs *Pseudacris ornata*, *P. nigrita*, *Hyla crucifer*, *Rana pipiens*, and the salamander *Ambystoma tigrinum*. The soil in the area is sandy loam. It is not known whether gopher tortoises occur in the vicinity.

The Escambia County frogs were breeding in an isolated, saucer-shaped, sink-hole depression surrounded by rolling, sandy pine hills. Gopher tortoise burrows were present nearby. This depression holds water for about 8 or 9 months during most years. *Pseudacris nigrita*, *P. ornata*, and *Ambystoma tigrinum* also breed there. Several chicken turtles, *Deirochelys reticularia*, have been collected at the site along with 1 yellow-bellied pond slider, *Pseudemys s. scripta*. Aquatic vegetation is abundant. At 1 other site in Escambia County, tadpoles of *R. areolata sevosa* were found (Mount and Folkerts, 1968). That site, which has not been revisited, was a weedy, flooded borrow pit. Tadpoles of several other frogs, mostly hylids, were found. One end of the pit had been deepened and contained several large channel catfish. No other fish were seen. The Covington County record is based on a single specimen collected on a highway near Open Pond, Conecuh National Forest.

Rana catesbeiana Shaw
Bullfrog

Description: (Fig. 83) A widely distributed, large frog attaining a maximum snout-vent length of about 200 mm. Hind foot with extensive webbing between toes, but with the longest toe projecting well beyond the limit of the webbing; toes pointed; vocal pouch mostly internal; dorsolateral ridges lacking; tympanum larger than eye; chin and lips usually without white spots (90 percent); dorsum green to brown, usually with obscure dark markings; venter light, usually with dark markings of varying shape and intensity; rear of thigh spotted or mottled, the white ground color not forming a longitudinal stripe or suggestion thereof, as in R. grylio; snout less pointed than in R. grylio; integument fairly smooth to slightly rough.

Alabama distribution: (Fig. 84) Statewide.

Habits: This familiar frog is a common inhabitant of nearly all of our lakes and permanent ponds, and many medium and large-sized streams. Its deep, throaty, honking call can be heard at night from March to August. Calling during the day is not uncommon. While calling, the male usually sits on the bank near the water.

The eggs are deposited as surface masses or films, varying in diameter from 150 mm to 900 mm and containing up to 20,000 eggs each. In Alabama the tadpoles usually transform during the second season. On warm, rainy nights small, newly transformed bullfrogs are often seen in abundance on the highways as they disperse from the sites of their origin.

The bullfrog is a voracious feeder, capturing and swallowing almost anything of appropriate size that crosses its path. Invertebrates constitute the bulk of the

FIG. 83. *Rana catesbeiana*, the bullfrog (Lee County). The largest frog in Alabama, the bullfrog is particularly common around ponds and lakes. It lacks the dorsolateral ridges characteristic of several of the other common ranid frogs in Alabama.

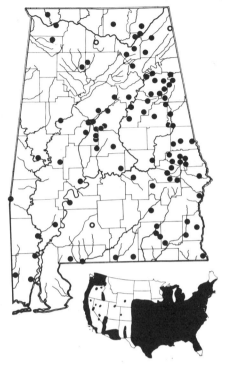

FIG. 84. Distribution of *Rana catesbeiana,* the bullfrog. This species is believed to occur statewide, or essentially so, in Alabama. Solid symbols indicate localities from which the author examined specimens. The circles are literature records believed to be valid. The small map depicts approximately the known range in the United States.

diet, but birds, snakes, turtles, mice, and other frogs, including members of its own species, may also be included.

A rare albino adult bullfrog is shown in Fig. 85. This frog was found in Lee County in the bottom of an abandoned well, one of the few microhabitats in which an albino bullfrog might be expected to survive to adulthood. Most such individuals are taken by predators at a relatively early age.

Rana clamitans Latreille

Two somewhat poorly defined subspecies of this common species are recognized, both of which occur in Alabama.

FIG. 85. An albino adult bullfrog, *Rana catesbeiana,* collected from an abandoned well in Lee County. Albino amphibians occur only rarely and seldom survive to adulthood.

Rana clamitans clamitans Latreille
Bronze Frog

Description: (Fig. 86) A medium-sized ranid frog attaining a maximum snout-vent length of about 85 mm. Hind foot with extensive webbing between toes; tympanum about the same size as eye; back with dorsolateral ridges; skin of dorsum somewhat rough, but not rugose; edge of jaw with alternating dark and light spots; color of dorsum of adults brown or bronze, lacking distinct spots; undersurfaces light with wormlike dark markings, these sometimes confined to the legs and throat.

Alabama distribution: (Fig. 87) The Lower Coastal Plain. Specimens of *R. clamitans* seemingly referable to this subspecies often occur in other Coastal Plain provinces, but a study of the populations to which they belong will reveal their intergradient nature.

Habits: Swamps, floodplain pools, and small streams are the favored habitats of this common frog, although it may occur in other types of aquatic situations. It tends to be less wary than *R. pipiens,* another Alabama ranid of about the same size, and is thus more easily captured. Breeding of *R. clamitans* in Alabama apparently begins in April and lasts into August or September. Most of my records are for May, June, and July. The call note in an explosive "twang" or "clung," resembling the sound made by plucking a banjo string. It is issued from 1 to 3 times. Several thousand eggs are laid, as a surface film.

Rana clamitans melanota (Rafinesque)
Green Frog

Description: Differs from *R. c. clamitans* in the following: size larger, up to about 100 mm in snout-vent length; dorsum of adults often rugose, predominantly green in color with dark spots; dark vermiculations on undersurface usually scant or, in some individuals, lacking altogether; throat of male bright yellow.

FIG. 86. *Rana clamitans clamitans* x *melanota,* intergrade between the bronze frog and the green frog (Lee County). Although belonging to a population with characteristics intermediate between the 2 subspecies, this individual is in most respects similar to *R. c. clamitans.* The dorsolateral ridges and spotted lips are characteristic of the species *R. clamitans.*

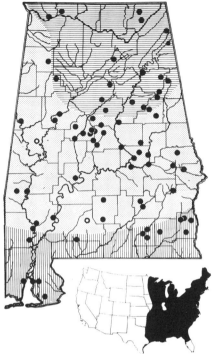

FIG. 87. Distribution of *Rana clamitans* and subspecific variation in Alabama. Horizontal hatching indicates the presumed range of *R. c. melanota,* the green frog, and vertical hatching, the range of *R. c. clamitans,* the bronze frog. The zone of intergradation is indicated by stippling. Solid symbols indicate localities from which the author examined specimens. The circles are literature records believed to be valid. The small map depicts approximately the known range of the species *R. clamitans* in the United States.

Alabama distribution: (Fig. 87) Northern Alabama, southward approximately to Randolph County in the eastern portion of the state; to Shelby County in the central portion; and to the Fall Line in the western portion. Intergrades with *R. c. clamitans* southward to the range of that subspecies.

Habits: The habits of this subspecies in Alabama are apparently similar in most respects to those of *R. c. clamitans.* (See "Habits" under the latter.)

FIG. 88. *Rana grylio,* the pig frog (Dauphin Island, Mobile County). This large, deep southern frog resembles the bullfrog but has a more pointed snout. Also the light markings on the backs of the thighs usually tend to form single, longitudinal stripes, whereas in the bullfrog they do not.

Rana grylio Stejneger
Pig Frog

Description: (Fig. 88) A large frog attaining a maximum snout-vent length of about 165 mm. Hind foot with extensive webbing between toes, with webbing extending to near the tip of the longest toe; toes pointed; vocal pouch mostly internal; dorsolateral ridges lacking; tympanum larger than eye; chin and lips without conspicuous white spots; dorsum brownish to green, occasionally with obscure dark markings; venter light with dark spots or mottling (occasionally unmarked); rear of thigh usually with a longitudinal light stripe or longitudinally oriented series of light spots; snout more pointed than in *R. catesbe-*

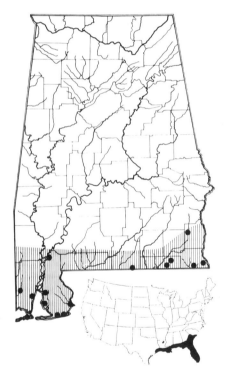

FIG. 89. Distribution of *Rana grylio*, the pig frog. The presumed range in Alabama is indicated by hatching. Symbols indicate localities from which the author examined specimens. The small map depicts approximately the known range in the United States.

iana; integument smooth to slightly rough.

Alabama distribution: (Fig. 89) Local in the Lower Coastal Plain.

Habits: Permanent, open bodies of water with emergent herbaceous vegetation are favored by this frog. In places where it is abundant, such as the large lake at Gulf State Park in Baldwin County, calling can be heard both day and night. The call, a loud, resonant grunting, is unmistakable, and is issued as the male floats in the water or sits among a mass of aquatic vegetation.

The breeding season as given by Wright and Wright (1949) is "March 1 through September." I have Alabama records for May 26 (Mobile County) and June 28 (Houston County). On the night of June 17, 1967, I was driving through Houston County near Grangeburg and heard calls of *R. grylio*, apparently from some distant locality. Stopping to investigate, I was surprised to find that the calls were coming from a small pond less than 20 feet from the highway, and that the calling individuals were two males measuring only 52 mm and 59 mm in snout-vent length. Superficial examination of the testes of one of these frogs indicated that it was sexually mature.

The eggs of *R. grylio* are laid as a surface film, attached to vegetation, up to about 500 mm in diameter. (Wright and Wright, 1949.)

Rana heckscheri Wright
River Frog

Description: (Fig. 90) A large southeastern frog attaining a maximum snout-vent length of about 140 mm. Hind foot with extensive webbing between toes; toes pointed; vocal pouch mostly internal; dorsolateral ridges absent or poorly defined; tympanum larger than eye; dorsum dark brown to greenish brown, mottled; venter gray to grayish brown with light markings (as opposed to light with dark markings as in *R. catesbeiana* and *R. grylio*); lower lip dark with light spots; upper lip trimmed with dark pigment on lower edge and usually light-

FIG. 90. *Rana heckscheri,* the river frog (Escambia County). This large, swamp-dwelling frog resembles the bullfrog but can be distinguished from it by the coloration of the venter, which is gray with white markings. The venter of the bullfrog is white with dark markings or, rarely, plain white.

spotted; integument somewhat more roughened than in *R. catesbeiana* and *R. grylio.*

Alabama distribution: (Fig. 91) Extremely local in the lower portion of the Lower Coastal Plain.

Habits: This frog is known from only 3 localities in Alabama, 1 each in Mobile, Baldwin, and Escambia counties. Its common name is somewhat misleading in as much as the preferred habitat, at least in Alabama, seems to be not along rivers but along the swampy margins of smaller streams and around the edges of shallow impoundments, such as beaver ponds, where the growth of titi, bay, and cypress is favored.

The river frog, a nocturnal species, is remarkably less wary than our other ranid frogs. When captured and held in the hand, it usually becomes limp and does not struggle to free itself. Indeed, this characteristic can be used with a fair amount of confidence to identify the species.

There are no data on river frog reproduction from Alabama, and data from other portions of the range are scarce. Carr (1940) indicates that breeding begins in Florida in April and continues spasmodically throughout the summer. The call is variable and has been variously described as a snort, snarl, grunt, and gutteral roll. Apparently the eggs are laid as a surface film (Wright and Wright, 1932). The tadpoles move about in schools and are notable for the exceptionally large size they attain (up to about 160 mm in length). Transformation takes place at about 1 year of age (Allen, 1938).

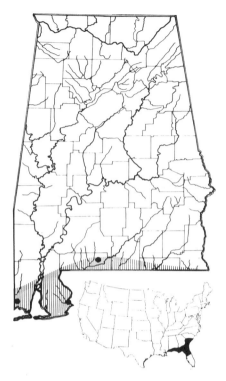

FIG. 91. Distribution of *Rana heckscheri*, the river frog. The presumed range in Alabama is indicated by hatching. Symbols indicate localities from which the author examined specimens. The small map depicts approximately the known range in the United States.

Rana palustris Le Conte
Pickerel Frog

Description: (Fig. 92) A medium-sized ranid frog attaining a maximum snout-vent length of about 80 mm. Hind foot with extensive webbing between toes; tympanum and eye about the same size; dorsum grayish with dorsolateral ridges, between which are about 14 bold, squarish dark spots in 2 rows, some of which may be fused; a small spot present above each eye and often one on the snout. Sides with scattered dark spots; dorsal surfaces of legs barred, their inner surfaces, along with the posterior portion of the venter, suffused with yellow (in live individuals).

Remarks: Hardy (1964) described *R. p. mansuetii* from the Coastal Plain of North Carolina as a form with a small number of dorsal spots, often fused to form longitudinal stripes; dark mottling on the venter; and melanophore stippling on the vomerine teeth. Schaaf and Smith (1970) reported that the *mansuetii* phenotype occurs in 3 widely separated areas: the Carolina Coastal Plain, the Del.-Mar.-Va. Peninsula, and the lowlands of the Western Gulf Coastal Plain. Zones of intermediacy between it and the nominate form are broad, and it seems possible that the *mansuetii* characteristics have arisen independently in the 3 groups. Schaaf and Smith recommended that *mansuetii* not be accorded subspecific recognition, and I am following their recommendation.

The 24 Alabama specimens I examined were predominately of the *R. p. palustris* phenotype, although about one-half showed 1 or more *mansuetii*-like tendencies. I detected no concordant geographic variation among the specimens of the sample. Schaaf and Smith (1971) reviewed the literature on *R. palustris*.

Alabama distribution: (Fig. 93) Local north of the Fall Line, except in the lower Piedmont and lower reaches of the Ridge and Valley region where it is apparently absent. Also occurs locally in the Coastal Plain in the western segment of the Red Hills, and is recorded from a cave near Brooklyn, Covington County, in the upper edge of the Lower Coastal Plain.

Habits: Throughout most of its range the pickerel frog tends to be associated with cool, clear water in upland forests and meadows. Its habits and distribution in Alabama reflect this tendency. In Texas and in the coastal region of the Carolinas, however, the pickerel frog is associated with "relatively warm, turbid waters of the coastal plain and floodplain swamps" (Schaaf and Smith, 1970). Inexplicably, in Georgia and Alabama such habitats appear to be shunned.

Breeding occurs during winter and early spring. The call is a variable, low-

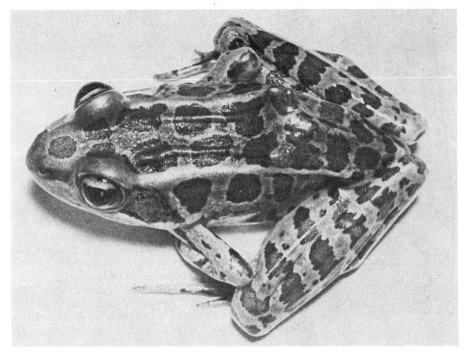

FIG. 92. *Rana palustris,* the pickerel frog (Limestone County). This medium-sized frog has dorsolateral ridges and large rectangular blotches on the back (usually).

pitched croaking which often has a snore-like quality. The eggs are laid in globular masses of up to about 3,000 per mass. The breeding site is usually a woodland pool or a quiet pocket in a small stream.

Pickerel frogs produce a secretion that is toxic to many reptiles and other amphibians and should not be confined closely with other forms.

Rana pipiens Schreber

This taxon consists of a complex of forms whose range extends from border to border and from the Atlantic Coast to the Sierras and Cascades. It has long been a subject of disagreement among herpetologists. Most of the dispute initially centered around the validity of various subspecies. Recently, Littlejohn and Oldham (1968) found evidence that the complex consists of 4 major call types, which, though largely allopatric, have zones of contact where they appar-

ently do not intergrade. Mecham (1968) reported still another call type in southern Arizona. One type, termed the "eastern call type," may correspond to *R. p. sphenocephala,* and another, the "northern call type," to *R. p. pipiens.* Research continues in an effort to elucidate the nature of the relationships among the "call types" within the complex and to determine the closeness of correspondence between the call types and the currently recognized morphological subspecies. (See Mecham, 1969, 1971; Mecham, *et al.,* 1973.) Meanwhile, it seems appropriate, for the time being at least, to continue the usage of traditional subspecific designations for populations of our region.

Brown (1956) referred all Alabama populations of *R. pipiens* to *R. p. sphenocephala* except for those in some mountainous areas of northeastern Alabama. He reported *R. p. pipiens* from Madison County (Monte Sano Mountain) and

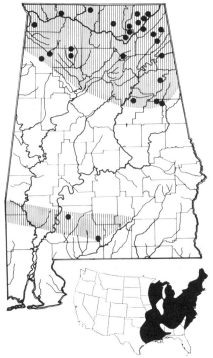

FIG. 93. Distribution of *Rana palustris*, the pickerel frog. The presumed range in Alabama is indicated by hatching. Symbols indicate localities from which the author examined specimens. The small map depicts approximately the known range in the United States.

from Talladega County (Mt. Cheaha). I have examined specimens from Madison County and from Mt. Cheaha, as well as from DeKalb, Marshall, and Calhoun counties in northeastern Alabama, and have yet to find a frog that I consider *R. p. pipiens*. Furthermore, I have found nothing to indicate to my satisfaction that there is any influence of that form in northeastern Alabama. I have not, however, examined specimens from northern Jackson County. The possibility that the 2 forms occurs in sympatry in northeastern Alabama as distinct "call types" should be explored.

FIG. 94. *Rana pipiens sphenocephala*, the southern leopard frog (Covington County). A medium-sized frog with dorsolateral ridges, this frog is common in nearly all of our aquatic habitats. The specimen shown here is somewhat unusual in having a spot on the center of the snout, a feature typically associated with another subspecies, *R. p. pipiens*.

Rana pipiens sphenocephala Cope
Southern Leopard Frog

Description: (Fig. 94) A medium-sized frog attaining a maximum snout-vent length of around 130 mm. Hind foot extensively webbed; tips of digits not expanded; vocal sacs lateral; dorsum with dorsolateral folds; upper jaw with a light line; dorsal color green to brownish with elongate or rounded dark spots, these mostly light-bordered; sides variously spotted; tibiae marked with interrupted bars; back of thigh with a dark reticulum; venter light, unmarked; tympanum with a light spot in the center.

Remarks: The *burnsi* mutant appears occasionally in Alabama, as do other variants that do not conform to the generalized description given above. The *burnsi* mutant, which is bronze and lacks the dark spots, is easily confused with the bronze frog, *R. c. clamitans.*

Rana p. pipiens, which may be referable to the "northern call type" of Littlejohn and Oldham (1968), may occur in parts of extreme northeastern Alabama (see above). In this form the snout is less pointed and has a medial spot which is usually lacking in *R. p. sphenocephala.* The tympanum usually lacks the conspicuous light spot. Where the 2 come together in Texas, the males of the "northern call type" (*R. p. pipiens*) are reported to possess vestigial ovaries, whereas the males of the "eastern call type" (*R. p. sphenocephala*) do not.

Alabama distribution: (Fig. 95) Leopard frogs are found throughout the state.

Habits: Probably the most nearly ubiquitous of our ranids, this frog can be found around most types of aquatic habitats. On rainy nights leopard frogs are often seen on highways. Preferred breeding sites include permanent and semi-permanent woodland pools, but breeding also occurs in flooded roadside ditches, ponds, lakes, and beaver swamps.

The breeding call is a series of guttural croaks and clucks. Smith (1961) aptly states that the call can be roughly simulated by rubbing the thumb across an inflated balloon. Littlejohn and Old-

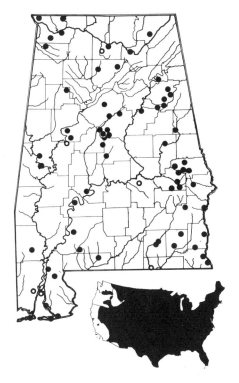

FIG. 95. Distribution of *Rana pipiens sphenocephala,* the southern leopard frog. This form is believed to occur statewide, or nearly so, in Alabama. Solid symbols indicate localities from which the author examined specimens. Circles are literature records believed to be valid. The small map depicts approximately the known range of the species *R. pipiens* in the United States.

ham (1968) and Mecham (1971) have elaborated on the differences in mating calls among "call types" of *R. pipiens.* Leopard frogs may breed at any time of the year in Alabama when heavy rains coincide with temperatures above 50°F. Most breeding occurs from December through March. The eggs are laid in shallow water in masses of from a few hundred to several thousand per mass. Brown (1956) states that *R. p. sphenocephala* lays smaller eggs than *R. p. pipiens* and that masses laid by the former usually contain less than one thousand eggs each.

During the day the leopard frog is frequently flushed from around the margins of aquatic situations. It is alert and active and is a strong jumper. The hind legs of this species and those of our other ranid frogs are relished by many people.

Rana sylvatica Le Conte
Wood Frog

Description; (Fig. 96) A medium-sized frog attaining a maximum snout-vent length of about 85 mm. Hind feet extensively webbed; vocal sacs dorsolateral; tips of digits not expanded; dorsum with dorsolateral folds. Dorsal ground color tan to brown; face with a dark brown to blackish mask extending from snout to behind tympanum; upper jaw with a light stripe bordering facial mask; back and sides of body with or without scattered dark markings. Venter white, plain or with dark mottling under throat and breast; undersides of femurs often tinged with yellow.

Alabama distribution: (Fig. 97) A species best adapted to climates cooler than ours, the wood frog is found in Alabama only at higher elevations in the Blue Ridge region and possibly in the Appalachian Plateaus region in DeKalb and Jackson counties. The presence of this species in Alabama is documented by 3 specimens, 1 collected by Ruben McCullers in Cleburne County, on the northeastern slope of Mt. Cheaha, and the other 2 by Tom Yarbrough on the western slope of Mt. Cheaha. L. G. Sanford, of Jacksonville State University, told me of a specimen of R. sylvatica reportedly collected in Calhoun County by one of his students. The specimen, retained by the student, apparently was lost.

Habits: The wood frog is a terrestrial form, inhabiting mesic woodlands. Its color camouflages it well on a leafy forest floor, and unless it jumps, it is not likely to be noticed.

FIG. 96. *Rana sylvatica*, the wood frog (Cleburne County). A medium-sized frog of northern affinity, this species is easily recognizable by its dark mask. In Alabama it is known only from Mt. Cheaha and vicinity.

FIG. 97. Distribution of *Rana sylvatica*, the wood frog. The presumed range in Alabama is indicated by hatching. Symbols indicate localities from which the author examined specimens. The small map depicts approximately the known range in the coterminous United States.

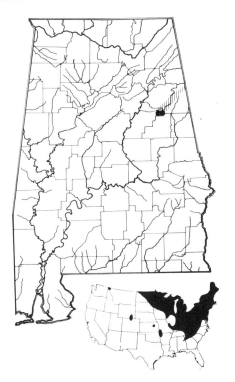

Breeding has not been reported in Alabama, but on the basis of breeding records from other parts of the range, the breeding season here is assumed to be in January or February. It is reportedly an "explosive" breeder, spending only a few days at the breeding site, usually a woodland pond or pool.

The mating call has been described as a rasping "craw-aw-auk," suggesting the quacking of a duck, and as having little carrying power. The eggs are deposited in globular masses, 2.5 to 6.0 inches in diameter. The masses are attached to submerged vegetation and contain an average of 2,500 eggs each. Martof (1970) reviewed the literature on *R. sylvatica*.

ORDER CAUDATA (URODELA)—SALAMANDERS

Commonly called spring lizards, puppy dogs, water dogs, and any one of several other colorful names, the salamanders are a diverse assemblage of amphibians that have tails; moist, scaleless skins; and 2 pairs of limbs. In southern Alabama, as well as in some areas of Georgia and Florida, the name "salamander" is frequently applied to an altogether different animal, the eastern pocket gopher, *Geomys pinetis*, a rat-like mammal. This animal burrows in sandy soil and at intervals pushes excess soil to the surface in piles, perhaps giving rise to the name "sandy mounder," which in turn may have been corrupted to "salamander."

Salamanders of the amphibian variety are secretive in habit and are most often found in damp places under logs, rocks, or in piles of debris. On wet nights they move about in the open and may be spotted with a light. Some forms are aquatic throughout life, and a few are arboreal.

Most species of salamanders, including, apparently, all those found in North America, lay eggs. Typically, fertilization in salamanders is accomplished by means of a spermatophore. The spermatophore is a stalked capsule of sperm deposited by the male during courtship. The capsular portion is picked up by the female with the cloacal lips, and sperm thus gain entrance to the cloaca. External fertilization in salamanders is limited to forms within the Asian family Hynobiidae and the family Cryptobranchidae. The latter is represented in Alabama by 1 species, the hellbender, *Cryptobranchus alleganiensis*.

In the life cycle of most Alabama salamanders there is a gilled, aquatic or semi-aquatic larval stage. The exceptions, in which development is completely terrestrial, are the green salamander

(*Aneides aeneus*) and the 3 species of *Plethodon*. The Red Hills salamander, *Phaeognathus hubrichti*, is thought to lack an aquatic larval stage, but this has not been established with absolute certainty.

Neoteny occurs in some species of Alabama salamanders. This phenomenon, in which 1 or more members of a population attain adulthood but retain many larval features, such as gills, has been found in Alabama populations of *Ambystoma talpoideum*, *Eurycea bislineata*, *Pseudotriton ruber*, and *Notopthalmus viridescens*.

All salamanders are carnivorous, with arthropods constituting the bulk of the diet of most species. Some forms are cannibalistic, particularly *Pseudotriton ruber*, *Gyrinophilus porphyriticus*, and the larvae of several *Ambystoma* species.

Salamanders occur in the North Temperate Zone of the Old World, in South America, and in North America, where they attain greatest overall diversity. Approximately 312 living species are recognized; they are contained within 52 genera and 7 families. The sirens, treated separately herein as the order Trachystomata, are considered salamanders by many workers. The salamander fauna of Alabama consists of 31 species, belonging to 15 genera, 1 of which is endemic. Six families are represented. Bishop (1943) wrote *Handbook of Salamanders* (Comstock Publishing Co.), which, though badly in need of revision, remains the one best source of information on the natural history of salamanders of the United States.

FAMILY AMBYSTOMATIDAE — MOLE SALAMANDERS

This exclusively North American family contains 4 extant genera, 1 of which occurs in Alabama.

GENUS *AMBYSTOMA* Strauch

This genus, whose range extends from coast to coast, consists of about 15 species, most of which occur in the eastern half of the country. Most are fairly stout-bodied, and all lack the nasolabial groove characteristic of plethodontid salamanders. Six species occur in Alabama.

Ambystoma cingulatum (Cope)
Flatwoods Salamander

Martof and Gerhardt (1965) studied variation in this species and recommended that subspecies not be recognized.

Description: (Fig. 98) A fairly small but somewhat stocky salamander attaining a maximum total length of about 130 mm. (Individuals from our area tend to be smaller than those from farther east in the range.) Nasolabial grooves absent; tongue fleshy, free at sides; head small. Color blackish, with a reticulum of gray markings on about 95 percent of individuals; costal grooves 13 to 16.

Alabama distribution: (Fig. 99) Local in the Lower Coastal Plain, recorded only from Baldwin, Mobile, and Covington counties.

Habits: This salamander inhabits damp places in pine flatwoods areas, where it hides beneath logs, piles of debris, or in

FIG. 98. *Ambystoma cingulatum*, the flatwoods salamander (Covington County). This salamander is rarely found in Alabama. It is black with a reticulum of light gray or white markings. (Photo by Kelly Thomas.)

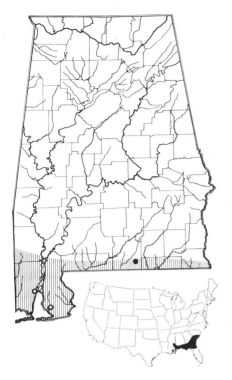

FIG. 99. Distribution of *Ambystoma cingulatum,* the flatwoods salamander. The presumed range in Alabama is indicated by hatching. Solid symbols indicate localities from which the author examined specimens. The circles are literature records believed to be valid. The small map depicts approximately the known range in the United States.

its burrows. Breeding occurs in late fall or winter. Breeding sites are usually cypress ponds, swamps, or flooded roadside ditches. The aquatic larvae, which are easily identified by the conspicuous stripes on their sides, transform in March or April.

The flatwoods salamander is fairly common in parts of the Florida Panhandle but is scarce in Alabama. Bruce Means, of Tall Timbers Research Station, stated (oral communication) that the eggs may be laid at the bases of clumps of wiregrass in depressions prior to flooding by winter rains. In Alabama, much of the formerly suitable habitat has been destroyed by drainage and clearing. Also, many natural depressions that could pro-

vide suitable breeding sites have been deepened and converted into permanent stock-watering ponds. Kelly Thomas, a former student at Auburn University, found newly hatched larvae of *A. cingulatum* on December 24, 1970, in southern Covington County, constituting the first state record since 1922.

Ambystoma maculatum (Shaw)
Spotted Salamander

Description: (Fig. 100, 101) A large, stout salamander attaining a maximum total length of about 230 mm. Nasolabial grooves absent; tongue fleshy, free at sides; gular fold present. Dorsum dark gray to black; head, body, and tail with 2 irregular rows of distinct, more or less rounded, yellow or orange spots (rarely, spots are lacking; one such individual has been collected in Calhoun County); costal grooves typically 12.

Alabama distribution: (Fig. 102) Apparently statewide or essentially so, although records are lacking from some large areas of southern and western Alabama.

Habits: In Alabama the spotted salamander inhabits low areas where hardwood trees predominate in the vicinity of suitable breeding sites. Temporary woodland ponds and pools and other such flooded depressions are required for breeding.

Breeding takes place during the winter at times when heavy rains coincide with relatively warm temperatures. The eggs are deposited in compact masses, which are attached to submerged sticks or twigs. The female may deposit her complement in 1 or 2 large masses or in several small ones. A mass may contain 200 or more eggs. Each egg is individually enclosed in membranes, and the entire mass is surrounded by a firm, gelatinous common covering. A symbiotic green alga usually develops within the inner egg capsules of this salamander. I have recorded breeding activity on January 2 (Houston County), January 25 and February 6 (separate years, in Shelby County), and February 10 (Houston County). Two periods of breeding occurred

FIG. 100. *Ambystoma maculatum,* the spotted salamander (Calhoun County). This large salamander typically has round, yellow or orange spots in 2 rows down the back.

in Macon County during the winter of 1970-71, December 29 to January 5, and February 1 to February 6.

The eggs hatch in 1 to 2 months, depending on temperatures, and the larval stage lasts 2 to 4 months. The larvae of *A. maculatum* are often found in company with those of *A. opacum.* Some question has arisen as to whether *A. maculatum* will breed successfully in the same ponds with *A. tigrinum.* Once, after a heavy winter rain, James Dobie and I visited a site in Chilton County, expecting to find the flooded depression I had

FIG. 101. An unusual, unmarked variant of the spotted salamander, *Ambystoma maculatum.* This specimen was collected in Calhoun County by Thomas Yarbrough and is the only one of its kind from Alabama that I have seen.

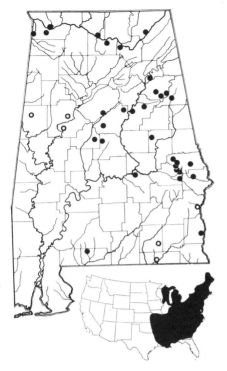

FIG. 102. Distribution of *Ambystoma maculatum*, the spotted salamander. This species is believed to occur statewide, or essentially so, in Alabama. Solid symbols indicate localities from which the author examined specimens. The circles are literature records believed to be valid. The small map depicts approximately the known range in the United States.

noticed there previously during rainy periods. Drainage operations had been underway, and instead of a pool, we found a ditch containing shallow, running water. In the ditch were 16 adult *A. maculatum* and 13 adult *A. tigrinum*, all in breeding condition. I assume that both these species had bred at this site in previous years.

The literature on *A. maculatum* was summarized by Anderson (1967c).

Ambystoma opacum (Gravenhorst)
Marbled Salamander

Description: (Fig. 103) A medium-sized, stout salamander attaining a total length of up to about 120 mm. Nasolabial grooves absent; tongue fleshy, free at sides; gular fold present. Tail and limbs short; ground color dark gray to black; back and tail with bold white or silvery markings, these usually brightest in males, typically forming crossbands (light markings extremely variable, occasionally forming dorsolateral stripes or other patterns). Costal grooves 11 or 12. Newly transformed individuals dark gray to brown with light flecks, bearing only slight resemblance to adults.

Alabama distribution: (Fig. 104) Statewide.

Habits: The marbled salamander is by far the most commonly encountered member of its family in Alabama. Flood-

FIG. 103. *Ambystoma opacum*, the marbled salamander (Lee County). A dark ground color with silvery markings is characteristic of this salamander, the most abundant member of its family in Alabama.

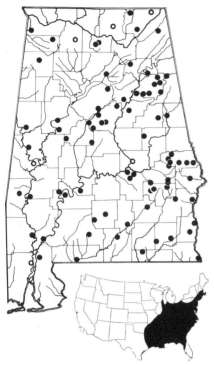

FIG. 104. Distribution of *Ambystoma opacum*, the marbled salamander. This species is believed to occur statewide, or essentially so, in Alabama. Solid symbols indicate localities from which the author examined specimens. The circles are literature records believed to be valid. The small map depicts approximately the known range in the United States.

plains and low hammocks are its usual habitats, but not infrequently it turns up in drier situations. In contrast to our other ambystomatid salamanders, *A. opacum* mates and oviposits on land, usually during the months of October and November in Alabama. The adults gather in forest-floor depressions beneath logs, leaf litter, or other debris, where they engage in courtship and mating. The eggs are laid singly in protected places in the depressions and are attended by the females until rains in late fall or winter flood the sites. The embryos are often in an advanced stage of development by that time, and hatching may occur within a day or two following inundation. The larval stage lasts 4 to 6 months.

Anderson and Graham (1967) found that the intermediate-sized larvae usually feed at night, in the upper stratum of water. They also found that when more than 1 species of *Ambystoma* occur in the same pond, there is often a temporal sequence of stratification. They suggest that this may be a factor in minimizing competition for food between the different species. In Alabama, the larvae of *A. opacum* are often found in the same ponds with those of *A. tigrinum, A. maculatum,* and *A. talpoideum,* as well as with adults and larvae of *Notopthalmus viridescens.* Anderson (1967b) reviewed the literature on *A. opacum.*

FIG. 105. *Ambystoma talpoideum,* the mole salamander (Macon County). A particularly stout-bodied salamander, this species is dark gray to nearly black with light flecks or lichen-like markings. (Photo by Robert Shealy.)

Ambystoma talpoideum (Holbrook)
Mole Salamander

Description: (Fig. 105) A stout-bodied salamander of medium length (up to about 120 mm total). Nasolabial grooves absent; tongue fleshy, free at sides; gular fold present; head broad. Dorsum dark gray to blackish with flecks or lichen-like markings of lighter intensity. Venter usually with a dark median stripe in larvae, newly transformed individuals, and neotenic adults. Costal grooves usually 11.

Alabama distribution: (Fig. 106) Local in the Coastal Plain and in the eastern portion of the Tennessee Valley. Possibly occurs in the western portion of the Tennessee Valley, but records are lacking.

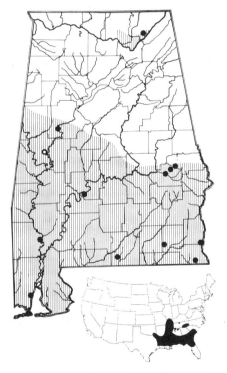

FIG. 106. Distribution of Ambystoma talpoideum, the mole salamander. The presumed range in Alabama is indicated by hatching. Solid symbols indicate localities from which the author examined specimens. The circle is a literature record believed to be valid. The small map depicts approximately the known range in the United States.

Habits: The mole salamander lives in burrows in or near floodplains or other low-lying areas. In Alabama it is seldom encountered except at its breeding sites. Larvae have been collected in flooded ditches and ponds in Mobile County (Dauphin Island) and Barbour County and in flooded borrow pits in Macon County. Kelly Thomas, formerly of Auburn University, found adults in breeding condition on January 11 in a flooded depression in a hardwood bottom in Macon County, but found no eggs until after a rain on January 23, one day following a seasonal low temperature reading of 17°F. Several loose egg clusters containing 15 to 40 eggs were noted. The same site also provided breeding habitat for A. opacum and A. maculatum.

Shoop (1960) observed that in Louisiana breeding occurs during a 6- to 16-day period each winter when heavy rains occur simultaneously with low temperatures. Shoop noted that eggs may be laid singly as well as in small clusters. His counts of ripe ovarian eggs in 33 females ranged from 226 to 401. Shoop (1964) provided a review of the literature on this species.

Ambystoma texanum (Matthes)
Small-mouthed Salamander

Description: (Fig. 107) A medium-sized salamander, attaining a total length of up to about 150 mm. Nasolabial grooves absent, tongue fleshy, free at sides; head and mouth noticeably small, particularly when viewed in profile; color dark brown to dark gray, plain or with lichen-like light blotches. Costal grooves 13 to 15.

Alabama distribution: (Fig. 108) Occurs locally in the Tennessee Valley and in the western two-thirds of the Coastal Plain. The species possibly occurs in the Ridge and Valley region, a speculation based on a sight record, unconfirmed by me, from Calhoun County.

Habits: The small-mouthed salamander inhabits floodplains and other low, damp places. Little is known of its habits in Alabama. The only record of breeding is that by Brandon (1966), who found

FIG. 107. *Ambystoma texanum,* the small-mouthed salamander (Marengo County). This salamander, infrequently encountered in Alabama, has a noticeably small head and dark gray to brownish body. Obscure light markings are usually present on the dorsum. (Photo by Robert Shealy.)

clusters of nearly full-term eggs in a flooded roadside ditch in Greene County on February 28, 1963. The clusters con-

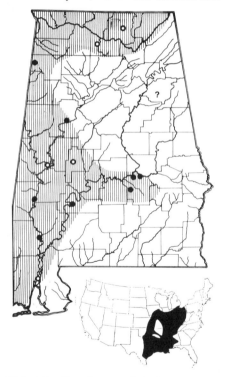

FIG. 108. Distribution of *Ambystoma texanum,* the small-mouthed salamander. The presumed range in Alabama is indicated by hatching. Solid symbols indicate localities from which the author examined specimens. The circles are literature records believed to be valid. The small map depicts approximately the known range in the United States.

tained 15 to 20 eggs each. In some areas of its range outside Alabama, *A. texanum* is known to breed in small streams, attaching its eggs singly on the undersurfaces of rocks. The literature on this species was summarized by Anderson (1967a).

Ambystoma tigrinum (Green)
Tiger Salamander

Seven subspecies of this wide-ranging form are currently recognized, 1 of which occurs in Alabama.

Ambystoma tigrinum tigrinum (Green)
Eastern Tiger Salamander

Description: (Fig. 109) A large salamander attaining a maximum total length of about 330 mm. Head broad, flattened; eyes relatively small; nasolabial grooves absent; tongue large, fleshy, free at sides; gular fold present; costal grooves well defined; tail compressed. Dorsum dark gray to black with variously shaped, somewhat obscure yellowish spots or blotches, these typically larger and less distinct than those on *A. maculatum;* venter yellowish, sometimes with dark smudges.

Alabama distribution: (Fig. 110) Statewide, but limited by availability of suitable breeding sites and possibly other factors.

Habits: Tiger salamanders seldom leave their subterranean retreats except during breeding periods. The breeding site is a fishless pool or pond, often in relatively open terrain. I have found

FIG. 109. *Ambystoma tigrinum tigrinum,* the eastern tiger salamander (Calhoun County). This large salamander is dark gray or brownish with irregularly-shaped yellowish blotches.

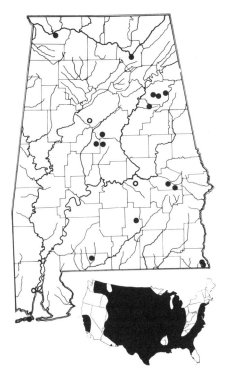

them breeding in a 20-inch-deep rainwater pool in a pasture in Macon County and have found larvae in a small farm pond in Bibb County. The latter contained water up to 5 feet deep. Larvae were found in a temporary flatwoods pond approximately 3 feet in maximum depth in Escambia County. On Dauphin Island, Mobile County, a flooded roadside ditch served as a breeding site. Dates of breeding congregations in Alabama include February 10, 1966 (Chilton County; see also account of *A. maculatum*), December 18, 1967, and January 19, 1969 (both Macon County).

The eggs are laid in loose clusters of

FIG. 110. Distribution of *Ambystoma tigrinum tigrinum,* the eastern tiger salamander. This form is believed to occur statewide, or nearly so, in Alabama. Solid symbols indicate localities from which the author examined specimens. Circles are literature records believed to be valid. The small map depicts approximately the known range of the species *A. tigrinum* in the United States.

10 to 100 per cluster. The gelatinous outer covering does not become firm as it does in *A. maculatum* egg masses. The eggs hatch in about 20 to 40 days, depending on water temperature. The larvae require about 4½ to 5 months to complete development. They are extremely voracious and will eat almost any animal they can swallow. Captives thrive on a diet of mosquito larvae and tadpoles. The adults do nicely in captivity, as do those of other *Ambystoma*, if kept in a fairly cool place and provided with moist soil for burrowing. They will feed on earthworms, mealworms, and spiders, and often can be induced to take small pieces of raw meat. The literature on *A. tigrinum* was reviewed by Gehlback (1967).

FAMILY AMPHIUMIDAE – AMPHIUMAS

This family of large, eel-like salamanders is restricted to the southeastern quadrant of the United States. Three forms are recognized and are included within a single genus.

GENUS *AMPHIUMA* Garden

Three species are included within this genus. Two, *A. means* and *A. tridactylum*, are known to occur in Alabama, and the third, *A. pholeter*, has been collected within a few miles of the Alabama boundary in the Florida Panhandle. (See Problematical Forms, p. 24.)

Amphiuma means Garden
Two-toed Amphiuma

Description: (Fig. 111) A large, eel-like, aquatic salamander attaining a maximum total length of about 1,015 mm. Snout pointed; eyes small, lidless; external gills lacking; limbs 4, tiny, each with 2 toes; body elongate, rounded in cross-section; dorsum dark gray to grayish brown; ventral color somewhat paler but not sharply set off from dorsal color.

Alabama distribution: (Fig. 112) Locally distributed throughout most of the Coastal Plain, but most abundant in the Lower Coastal Plain.

Habits: The two-toed amphiuma occurs in a wide variety of aquatic and

FIG. 111. *Amphiuma means*, the two-toed amphiuma (Baldwin County). This eel-like aquatic salamander has 4 tiny legs with 2 toes on each foot.

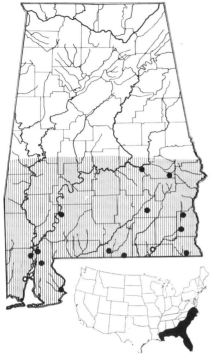

FIG. 112. Distribution of *Amphiuma means*, the two-toed amphiuma. The presumed range in Alabama is indicated by hatching. Solid symbols indicate localities from which the author examined specimens. The circles are literature records believed to be valid. The small map depicts approximately the known range in the United States.

semi-aquatic habitats where the substrate permits burrowing or where an abundance of aquatic vegetation or debris provides necessary shelter. Shallow, weedy ponds and lakes, floodplain pools, and swamps provide optimal living conditions. Occasionally an individual is found under a rock or log in a small stream or in an accumulation of leaf litter or organic debris along the stream edge. The main channels of large rivers with substantial current are usually devoid of amphiumas.

Amphiumas, called "ditch eels" and "congo eels" by some, are active mostly at night, especially during rainy weather. They feed on earthworms, crawfish, and other forms of small animal life and are occasionally caught by fishermen. They are capable of delivering a painful, though inconsequential, bite and will do so if handled carelessly.

Amphiumas, like sirens, are able to survive droughty periods during which their habitats dry up by burrowing into the substrate or, perhaps, by taking shelter in crawfish burrows. For several consecutive years I observed amphiumas during the winter in an isolated, small flooded depression that often dries up completely during the summer. Unquestionably, at least some of these animals spend a portion of the summer underground, probably in crawfish burrows.

Relatively little is known of the breeding habits of this species. The few reports available indicate that the eggs are laid in a damp place or possibly in shallow water in a depression under some sheltering object, such as a rock or a log, or are laid in a cavity beneath the ground surface. An extended incubation period of up to 5 months has been postulated. The breeding season apparently begins in winter or spring, depending on latitude. The female apparently guards the nest following oviposition. The larvae are about 55 mm long at hatching and possess light-colored gills, which they lose at a relatively early age.

Amphiumas thrive in captivity if kept in fairly clean water and fed regularly. The captives I have maintained have done well on a diet of beef liver supplemented with minnows and crawfish. Salthe (1973a) summarized the literature on *A. means*.

Amphiuma tridactylum Cuvier
Three-toed Amphiuma

Description: (Fig. 113) Similar to *A. means* except in having 3 instead of 2 toes on each foot and in being distinctly bicolored. The dorsum of *A. tridactylum* is dark brown and rather sharply set off from the light gray venter.

Alabama distribution: (Fig. 114) Western Alabama, but recorded only from Tuscaloosa, Hale, Dallas, Sumter, Washington, and Escambia counties. The Escambia County record indicated by Conant (1958) is questionable.

FIG. 113. *Amphiuma tridactylum*, three-toed amphiuma (Washington County). This amphiuma has 3 toes on each foot and rather sharply contrasting dorsal and ventral colors.

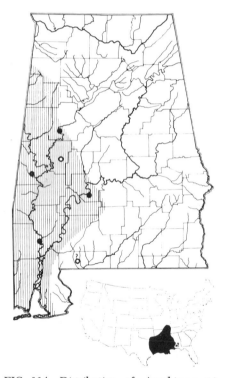

FIG. 114. Distribution of *Amphiuma tridactylum*, the three-toed amphiuma. The presumed range in Alabama is indicated by hatching. Solid symbols indicate localities from which the author examined specimens. The circles are literature records believed to be valid. The small map depicts approximately the known range in the United States.

Habits: Apparently similar to those of *A. means*, although the egg-laying period may be longer. Salthe (1973b) reviewed the literature on this species.

FAMILY CRYPTOBRANCHIDAE — GIANT SALAMANDERS

This family consists of 2 genera, both of which are outstanding because of the large size and grotesque appearance of their members. One genus, *Andrias*, has 2 species which inhabit streams in eastern Asia. The largest of these, *A. japonicus*, attains a length of up to 150 cm (nearly 5 feet) and is the world's largest salamander. The other genus, *Cryptobranchus*, with 1 species, is confined to eastern North America, and although smaller, is nonetheless spectacular.

GENUS *CRYPTOBRANCHUS* Leukart
Cryptobranchus alleganiensis (Daudin)

Two subspecies of this salamander are recognized, 1 of which occurs in Alabama.

Cryptobranchus alleganiensis alleganiensis (Daudin)
Hellbender

Description: (Fig. 115) An exceptionally large aquatic salamander attaining a maximum total length of around 750 mm. Body and head flattened, the latter

FIG. 115. *Cryptobranchus alleganiensis alleganiensis,* the hellbender (Lauderdale County). This spectacular aquatic salamander is unmistakable. Unfortunately, it appears to be declining in most parts of its range, which includes only the northernmost portion of our state.

especially so; skin along lower sides of body loose and folded; both pairs of limbs well developed; hind foot with 5 toes; tail strongly compressed, with a deep dorsal keel; gills lacking; neck with an opening, the spiracle, on each side. Dorsum brownish to gray, with or without irregular dark gray, brown, or black spots or blotches.

In this subspecies, spiracular opening is relatively large, its diameter contained in internarial distance (distance between nostrils) an average of 2.0 times, compared to an average of 3.8 times in *C. a. bishopi,* the other subspecies; skin above the lateral-line canals in pectoral region with papillate elevations (these are lacking in *C. a. bishopi*).

Remarks: The Alabama specimens vary considerably in color. A few are relatively uniform gray or brown but most are spotted or blotched. On one, the ground color is almost obliterated by the invasion of darker pigment. In relative size of the spiracular opening, all fall

clearly within the range of the nominate subspecies.

Alabama distribution: (Fig. 116) Confined to the Tennessee River drainage. Most records are from north of the river and include Butler Creek, Cypress Creek, and Little Cypress Creek in Lauderdale County and Flint River and Walker Creek in Madison County. It is likely that Shoal Creek in Lauderdale County and some of the streams in Limestone County also support populations of *Cryptobranchus.* The sole record from south of the Tennessee River in Alabama is from Bear Creek in Marion County.

Several streams within the Tennessee River drainage in Alabama, including the Tennessee River itself, have been polluted, impounded, or otherwise modified to the extent that they are, from all indications, incapable of supporting hellbender populations. A continuation of this trend ultimately may eliminate the hellbender from Alabama.

Habits: This spectacular salamander

FIG. 116. Distribution of *Cryptobranchus alleganiensis alleganiensis*, the hellbender. The presumed range in Alabama is indicated by hatching. Symbols indicate localities from which the author examined specimens. The small map depicts approximately the known range of the species *C. alleganiensis* in the United States.

virtually never leaves the water and is found exclusively in creeks and rivers. Medium-sized and large rock-bottomed streams with relatively clear water provide the most suitable habitats; small creeks are occasionally inhabited, especially during the months of September through April.

Hellbenders are active mostly at night, taking shelter during the day under rocks, rock overhangs, and logs. Crawfish constitute the bulk of the diet, but other forms of animal life may also be eaten. Fishermen report catching hellbenders on minnows and earthworms, and Tom Yarbrough informed me that a freshly captured individual in his possession ate a live mudpuppy (*Necturus*

maculosus). Some fishermen are afraid of hellbenders and have the mistaken idea that they are venomous. They can bite, but are not inclined to. They move rather slowly and are easily collected with a dipnet in relatively still, clear water.

Breeding occurs from August to October. Specimens in breeding condition have been collected in Alabama in late September and early October, and freshly laid eggs have been seen in October. The eggs are laid in rosary-like strings in depressions under rocks. Each female may deposit several hundred eggs, and several females may oviposit in the same nest. The male fertilizes the eggs externally and guards the nest until hatching, which occurs in 2 to 3 months. The larvae have external gills, which they keep until they are about 18 months old. Nickerson and Mays (1972) published a complete review of the literature on hellbenders along with the results of an intensive study they made on the natural history of a hellbender population in the Ozarks region.

FAMILY PLETHODONTIDAE — WOODLAND SALAMANDERS

This family is by far the largest and most diverse of the order. It has about 185 species contained within 23 genera. All but 2 species are New World in distribution. Nine genera occur in Alabama; one of these, *Phaeognathus*, is endemic to the state.

GENUS *ANEIDES* Baird

Five species are included within this genus. One of these occurs in eastern United States, including a portion of Alabama; the other 4 are western in distribution.

Aneides aeneus (Cope and Packard) Green Salamander

Description: (Fig. 117) A small to medium-sized salamander attaining a maximum total length of about 140 mm. Nasolabial grooves present; body flattened; dorsal color blackish with lichen-like yellowish green patches on body,

FIG. 117. *Aneides aeneus,* the green salamander (Jackson County). Our only salamander with expanded toe-tips and greenish markings, this species inhabits rock-face habitats.

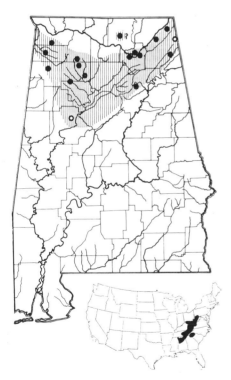

FIG. 118. Distribution of *Aneides aeneus,* the green salamander. The presumed range in Alabama is indicated by hatching. Solid symbols indicate localities from which the author examined specimens. The circles are literature records believed to be valid. The small map depicts approximately the known range in the United States.

legs, and tail; venter light. Costal grooves 14 or 15; tips of digits expanded.

Alabama distribution: (Fig. 118) Locally common in the Appalachian Plateaus region and at scattered localities in the Fall Line Hills region in northwestern Alabama.

Habits: The usual habitat of the green salamander is a narrow crevice in a sandstone ledge, bluff, or outcrop. Shaded sites are preferred; permanently wet substrates are shunned. In the vicinity of optimal habitats, the salamanders may be found under the bark of rotting trees or stumps. At night green salamanders leave the crevices and climb about on the vertical rock faces, their climbing ability enhanced by the disclike expansions on the tips of the toes. During the day, while secluded in the crevices, they can often be induced to crawl out if prodded gently from behind with a slender stick or switch. The eggs are deposited in the rock crevices, in rotting stumps, or in other sheltered, moist places. They are attended by the female until they hatch. There is no aquatic larval stage. Nests were observed in Marshall County in July. The eggs were suspended from the roof of a crevice about ½-inch wide. Gordon (1952) studied the life history and ecology of this species and reviewed the literature in 1967.

GENUS *DESMOGNATHUS* Baird

One of the most perplexing and frustrating unsolved problems in North American herpetology is that of determining relationships among the forms within the genus *Desmognathus*. There is little agreement on the number of species involved and even less on the number of subspecies.

The most recent work which contributes significantly to solving the problems concerning this genus in Alabama is that by Folkerts (1968). He collected and examined specimens from every county in the state and, in my opinion, his study goes farther than any yet made toward bringing about an understanding of some of the more complex relationships within the group. I have, therefore, based my treatment of the genus and its contained forms chiefly on Folkerts' work. Four species are considered to occur in Alabama.

Desmognathus aeneus Bishop and Brown Seepage Salamander

Description: (Fig. 119) A small salamander attaining a maximum total length of about 57 mm. Nasolabial grooves present; face with a light line extending from the eye to the angle of the jaw; costal grooves usually 14; tail rounded in cross-section, never keeled; dorsum with a longitudinal stripe from head to near tail tip; dorsal stripe yellow to reddish brown, jagged or wavy, usually with a dark midline. Sides with irregular mottling or reticulations, often with 1 to 6 light ovals; top of thigh with a conspicuous light oval spot (at least in all Alabama populations). Undersurfaces light with variable dark pigmentation. Juvenile pattern similar to adults but more vivid.

Remarks: The pattern of geographic variation in this form, while involving a cline in at least one character, is mostly chaotic. The form *chermocki*, described by Bishop and Valentine (1950) from Tuscaloosa County, Alabama, has until recently been considered a subspecies of *D. aeneus*. On the basis of the material now available, especially from Alabama, it appears that the *"chermocki* type" is indeed a variant of *D. aeneus*, but not a distinct geographic entity entitled to subspecific recognition. Therefore, *chermocki* is considered here to belong to the synonymy of *D. aeneus*.

Alabama distribution: (Fig. 120) Local in the Blue Ridge, adjacent portion of the Piedmont, and in a portion of the Fall Line Hills region paralleling the Fall Line from northern Hale County to southern Marion County.

Habits: Folkerts (1968) characterized the habitat of this small salamander in Alabama as "shaded seepage areas in moist deciduous or semideciduous ravines." He stated that it never appears in the open, but remains beneath the leaf litter and among spongy masses of entangled roots. *Desmognathus aeneus* is wholly terrestrial and never voluntarily takes to water. Donovan and Folkerts (1972) studied the habits of this species in Alabama.

The eggs are laid in small depressions in protected places and are attended by

FIG. 119. *Desmognathus aeneus,* the seepage salamander (Cleburne County). This diminutive salamander usually has a light spot on the top of the thigh and a longitudinal light stripe on the dorsum.

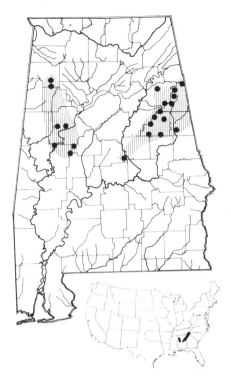

FIG. 120. Distribution of *Desmognathus aeneus,* the seepage salamander. The presumed range in Alabama is indicated by hatching. Symbols indicate localities from which the author examined specimens. The small map depicts approximately the known range in the United States.

the female. In some areas of the range, there may be 2 nesting periods each year. In eastern Alabama, Folkerts found nests in the spring and in each of the months from July through October; in western Alabama nesting is known to occur only in late winter and spring, with most of the dates reported in February and March. Valentine (1963) described the nest, eggs, and hatching of *D. aeneus* in Tuscaloosa County. Clutch size in this species varies from 5 to 17. Apparently this salamander is easily eliminated by alterations of its habitat, which may account in part for its spotty distribution.

Desmognathus fuscus (Green)

As many as 6 forms have, at one time or another, been included within *D.*

fuscus. Folkerts (1968) recognizes 2 subspecies, *D. f. fuscus* and *D. f. auriculatus,* both of which occur in Alabama. The form *conanti* was described by Rossman (1958) as a subspecies of *D. fuscus* that was distinguishable from other subspecies primarily on the basis of color. It was described as having "six to eight pairs of golden or reddish gold spots, usually separate, but occasionally partially fused to form a dorsal band with deeply serrate margins; prominent postocular bar yellow or orange." Folkerts has shown that individuals fitting this description, along with several other pattern types, occur sporadically throughout most of Alabama above the Lower Coastal Plain. He further noted that when the *"conanti* type" predominates in a population, the population is usually small, and that nowhere does the type dominate any of the large populations. It seems, therefore, that the continued recognition of *conanti* as a subspecies only adds to the confused state of *Desmognathus* taxonomy, and that it should be regarded as but one of several variants within the subspecies *D. f. fuscus.*

Desmognathus fuscus fuscus (Green) Northern Dusky Salamander

Description: (Fig. 121) A medium-sized salamander attaining a maximum length of about 135 mm. Nasolabial grooves present; face with a light line from the eye to the angle of the jaw (except in a few extremely melanistic individuals); costal grooves usually 14; 2 to 5, usually less than 4, intercostal folds between adpressed limbs; tail trigonal, conspicuously keeled in cross-section, tip not attenuate; width of tail behind vent less than its height; commissure of jaw not markedly sinuate. Dorsal pigmentation extremely variable; dorsum tan to dark brown usually patterned but sometimes plain; pattern, if present, consisting of 6 or 7 pairs of alternating rhombic to oval blotches, these often fused to form a longitudinal stripe with jagged, smooth, or wavy edges; dorsal pattern continuing onto tail as a narrow, irregularly edged stripe, usually lighter than pattern on dorsum.

FIG. 121. *Desmognathus fuscus fuscus,* the northern dusky salamander (Lauderdale County). This abundant salamander is extremely variable and is found in a wide variety of damp habitats.

Pigmentation on upper sides not sharply delineated from that below, but blending irregularly with the latter; a row of inconspicuous light lateral spots often present; head lighter in front of eyes than behind them; inner linings of mouth often with conspicuous melanophores; venter cream with brown blotches or spots; cheek length of males entering jaw length more than 1.4 times.

Remarks: In portions of the Appalachian Plateaus and Chert Belt, some populations of *D. f. fuscus* are easily mistaken for *D. monticola.* Such populations are most often those inhabiting small, clear, fast-flowing rocky streams in areas of cave topography. Individuals of such populations tend to be stouter and darker than others.

Alabama distribution: (Fig. 122) Generally, the northern half of the state, intergrading irregularly with *D. f. auriculatus* southward to the lower portion of the Lower Coastal Plain.

Habits: This salamander, one of the most abundant in its range, is found in a variety of damp situations. Swamps, seepage areas, and the edges of springs and small rocky or muddy streams are preferred habitats. It is active mostly at night and hides during the day under rocks, damp leaf litter, or in burrows or rotting logs. When pursued it is quick and elusive and often jumps into the water to avoid capture, although it is

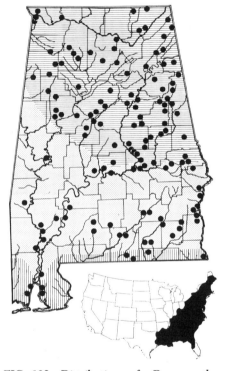

FIG. 122. Distribution of *Desmognathus fuscus* and subspecific variation in Alabama. Horizontal hatching indicates the presumed range of *D. f. fuscus,* the northern dusky salamander, and vertical hatching, the range of *D. f. auriculatus,* the southern dusky salamander. The zone of intergradation is indicated by stippling. Symbols indicate localities from which the author examined specimens. The small map depicts approximately the known range of the species *D. fuscus* in the United States.

not as adept at swimming as is *D. monticola.*

Folkerts (op. cit.) studied the life history of this salamander in Alabama and found nests with eggs from mid-July until mid-October. The nests, attended by the females, were in sheltered, damp places and contained clutches of 13 to 24 eggs each. Usually, the eggs hatch in 5 to 7 weeks. Larval development may take up to 13 months if the larvae are in water. If the larval habitat is merely a damp place on land, larval development is greatly accelerated.

Desmognathus fuscus auriculatus (Holbrook)
Southern Dusky Salamander

Description: (Fig. 123) Generally similar to *D. f. fuscus* except as follows: size smaller, up to about 120 mm in total length; overall color darker; dorsum suffused with black, patternless or with traces of spots; sides dark with 1 or 2 rows of conspicuous light oval spots; venter dark brown or black with white specks; intercostal folds between adpressed limbs 3 to 6, but usually more than 4.

Juveniles wtih dorsal pattern of 6 to 7 pairs of pale spots, often fused to form an indistinct dorsal stripe with irregular edges, or with pattern obliterated entirely by dark pigment.

Remarks: Valentine (1963a) proposed that *D. f. auriculatus* be assigned full species status on the basis of studies he conducted in the South. Several authorities accepted the proposal. Folkerts (1968) presented evidence of intergradation between *D. f. fuscus* and *auriculatus* and explained the apparent sympatry on the basis of ecotypic selection. In the most recent study of the problem, Means (1974) concurred in Valentine's opinion.

Alabama distribution: (Fig. 122) The lower portion of the Lower Coastal Plain. *Desmognathus f. auriculatus* intergrades with *D. f. fuscus* northward to the range of that subspecies. Intergradient populations may also occur in some of the mesic, hardwood forest habitats in the Florida Panhandle.

Habits: The southern dusky salamander is usually found around springs, swamps, cypress heads, mud-bottomed streams, and pools in floodplains. Sandy places are shunned. It spends less time in the water and more time in burrows than the northern dusky salamander. Areas devoid of hardwood trees are seldom inhabited.

Data on nesting are rather scarce. In Alabama, nests have been found from September 4 to October 12. They were located in depressions under logs or other protective cover and were being guarded by the female.

Desmognathus monticola ssp. Dunn
Seal Salamander

Two subspecies of this salamander are generally recognized. The nominate form has been considered to be that inhabiting the bulk of the range, including Alabama. The other subspecies, *D. m. jef-*

FIG. 123. *Desmognathus fuscus auriculatus,* the southern dusky salamander (Covington County). In this subspecies the ground color is dark, and light "portholes" on the sides are conspicuous.

FIG. 124. *Desmognathus monticola* ssp., the seal salamander (Talladega County). In this salamander, which closely resembles *D. fuscus,* the dorsal and ventral colors meet abruptly, with little or no blending.

fersoni, has been thought to be confined to the Blue Ridge Mountains of Virginia. Folkerts (1968) noted several indications of intermediacy between the 2 described forms in Alabama populations, thus casting doubt on the validity of the subspecific breakdown. The problem is currently under investigation, and, until a clearer picture emerges, I shall defer assigning Alabama populations to subspecies.

Description: (Fig. 124) A medium-sized to rather large salamander attaining a maximum total length of around 145 mm. Nasolabial grooves present; face with a light line or stripe extending from the eye to the angle of the jaw; costal grooves usually 14; intercostal folds between adpressed limbs 2 to 4, usually 3; tail trigonal, sharply keeled in cross-section; tip of tail pointed; dorsal coloration variable, but most often with numerous heavy, dark brown lines or small blotches on a lighter brown background; dark markings on dorsum sometimes surrounding 5 or 6 pairs of light brown or yellowish spots; dorsum becoming plain dark brown in large adults of many populations; dorsum never with a distinct longitudinal light stripe.

Tail often with a median yellowish brown line bordered on each side by alternating, dark-margined, light brown spots; sides of body dark above, light-speckled below, the transition abrupt, producing a rather well-defined line of demarcation; venter cream-colored with large light brown patches; head usually darker in front of eyes than behind them.

Juveniles with a dorsal pattern of 5

to 7 pairs of circular, light yellow spots, heavily ringed or margined with dark brown; venter light.

Remarks: The cheeks of old males of this species are often conspicuously swollen behind the jaws. While this tendency is also noted in some populations of *D. fuscus,* it is usually much less pronounced in that species.

A confusing aspect of variation in *D. monticola* in Alabama is the sporadic occurrence of large, dark individuals in certain populations. In a study of the salamanders of Mt. Cheaha, Cleburne County, Rubenstein (1969) stated that the population there which was being referred to as *D. monticola* was an undescribed form. He gave no specifics, but stated that the "new form" would be described by him and Dr. Barry Valentine "shortly." The description has not yet appeared nor has any evidence been presented to support Rubenstein's contention. It is possible that Rubenstein's initial assessment was influenced by the large, dark *Desmognathus* that occur on Mt. Cheaha, which Folkerts (op. cit.) assigns to *D. monticola.*

Alabama distribution: (Fig. 125) The seal salamander is discontinuously distributed in Alabama. In the northeastern quadrant of the state, it inhabits the Blue Ridge and Piedmont regions as well as the middle and lower reaches of the Ridge and Valley region. Specimens have also been collected in the Appalachian Plateaus region north of the Tennessee River in Jackson County. Seal salamanders are apparently absent from

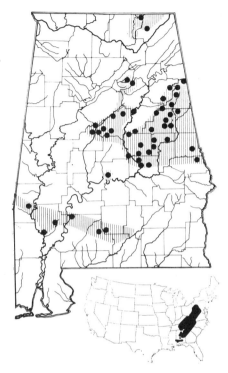

FIG. 125. Distribution of *Desmognathus monticola* ssp., the seal salamander. The presumed range in Alabama is indicated by hatching. Solid symbols indicate localities from which the author examined specimens. The circles are literature records believed to be valid. The small map depicts approximately the known range in the United States.

the Appalachian Plateaus region below the Tennessee River, although a specimen in the Auburn Museum bears the locality datum "Bankhead National Forest." Repeated attempts to confirm this record by finding additional specimens have failed. There are no records of the species from the Chert Belt or Tennessee Valley.

Below the Fall Line, seal salamanders occur in the western segment of the Red Hills, where they were first reported by Rose and Dobie (1963). Aside from the Red Hills records, there is one other from the Alabama Coastal Plain, from Ivy Creek in Autauga County. The site lies in central Alabama north of the Alabama River, in an area of ·complex physiog-raphy where the Black Belt interdigitates with the Fall Line Hills.

Habits: In Alabama the seal salamander is associated almost exclusively with rocky, highly aerated brooks and creeks. Optimum conditions occur along many of the small streams in the hilly terrain of the Blue Ridge region. In the Piedmont, the salamander's occurrence is much more local, due apparently to the scarcity of suitable habitats. The Red Hills populations inhabit small, rocky brooks in the bottoms of mesic, hardwood forested ravines. In these ravine-area habitats, *D. monticola* is often associated with other forms of northern affinity, such as *Rana palustris, Plethodon dorsalis,* and *Carphophis amoenus,* as well as with the endemic Red Hills salamander, *Phaeognathus hubrichti.*

The seal salamander is more aquatic than other members of its genus in Alabama and readily takes to the water when disturbed. During the day it may be found under rocks, in burrows, or occasionally basking on a wet rock.

Folkerts (op. cit.) found nests of *D. monticola* from August to October. The eggs were attached to the undersurfaces of rocks that were lying in seepages or in shallow water. The female attends the eggs during the 4- to 8-week developmental period. Clutch size ranges from 13 to 31. The length of time for larval development varies from a few weeks to several months and may be influenced by certain conditions of the habitat, such as substrate and moisture.

Desmognathus ochrophaeus Cope
Mountain Dusky Salamander

Desmognathus ochrophaeus shows extensive geographic variation of a rather chaotic nature and is not appropriately divisible into subspecies (Martof and Rose, 1963). The species was first reported in Alabama by Valentine (1961). The form discovered was the "cliff-face phenotype," which was then known as *Desmognathus ocoee* (also see Valentine, 1964). Martof and Rose (op. cit.) showed *D. ocoee* to be a form of *D. ochrophaeus.* There is some evidence of genetic interchange between *D. ochrophaeus* and *D.*

FIG. 126. *Desmognathus ochrophaeus,* the mountain dusky salamander (DeKalb County). This species is usually distinguishable from *D. f. fuscus* by its flattened body and attenuate tail-tip.

fuscus in the Sand Mountain area of northeastern Alabama, but the nature and extent is undetermined.

Description: (Fig. 126) A medium-sized salamander attaining a maximum total length of about 110 mm. (Alabama specimens seldom exceed 85 mm.) Nasolabial grooves present; face with a light line extending from the eye to the angle of the jaw; costal grooves usually 14; intercostal folds between adpressed limbs 2 to 4 (usually 3); tail trigonal in cross-section but rounded above, lacking a prominent dorsal keel; tip of tail attenuate; body somewhat flattened. Dorsal coloration variable; dorsum typically brownish with 5 or 6 pairs of alternating spots, these sometimes fused to form a broad stripe with zig-zag edges, bordered on the sides by heavy dark brown or black pigment; entire dorsum often becoming suffused with brown pigment which largely obliterates the pattern; top of tail with a narrow jagged-edged stripe representing a continuation of the body pattern; dorsum of body and tail becoming dark brown or black in very old individuals. Sides of body suffused or speckled with dark pigment; dorsal and ventral colors not separated by a sharp line; lateral rows of light oval spots usually absent. Venter light gray or light brown to nearly black, mottled; head lighter in front of eyes than behind them; commissure of jaws markedly sinuate. Juveniles usually with the spotted dorsal pattern.

Alabama distribution: (Fig. 127) Extreme northeastern portion of the Ap-

palachian Plateaus region below the Tennessee River. Populations of *D. fuscus* with a relatively high frequency of individuals with *D. ochrophaeus*-like characteristics occur in the vicinity of the

FIG. 127. Distribution of *Desmognathus ochrophaeus,* the mountain dusky salamander. The presumed range in Alabama is indicated by hatching. Symbols indicate localities from which the author examined specimens. The small map depicts approximately the known range in the United States.

recorded localities, suggesting the possibility of genetic interchange.

Habits: Folkerts (1968) indicated that within its range in Alabama, the mountain dusky salamander inhabits moist cliff faces and talus areas beneath waterfalls. He rates it intermediate in aquatic tendency among the Alabama *Desmognathus* and states that it is often found considerable distances from water. The flattened body enhances its ability to move about on wet cliff faces and to take refuge in crevices and under mats of vegetation that adhere to these faces. Where *D. ochrophaeus* is found, it is usually extremely abundant, and in such places *Desmognathus fuscus* is usually absent.

Nests of this species were found in Alabama in August and September. The nesting sites were on land under sheltering objects and inside water-soaked logs. The nests were attended by the females and contained 5 to 18 eggs each. Hatching required 5 to 9 weeks. Nothing is known of the time required for larval development in Alabama. Folkerts surmises that the aquatic stage may possibly be omitted.

GENUS *EURYCEA* Rafinesque

This genus contains 8 species, 3 of which are found in Alabama. *Eurycea aquatica* is considered herein to belong to *E. bislineata* and is discussed under the latter.

Eurycea bislineata (Green)
Two-lined Salamander

Description: (Fig. 128, 129) A small salamander attaining a maximum total length of about 115 mm. Fairly slender; nasolabial grooves present. Color extremely variable, but almost always with a broad light dorsal stripe extending from the snout to near the tail tip. Dorsal stripe clear or with small dark spots or flecks, most of which are arranged in a longitudinal series along the midline; light dorsal stripe bordered on each side by a dark line, stripe, or band, which usually begins at the eye, or slightly in front of the eye, and extends well onto the tail, or all the way to the tail tip.

Ground color usually yellow or orange-yellow, but occasionally orange or light brownish. Darkest markings black to brownish. Sides of body and tail light, dark, or mottled; sides of tail never with dark vertical bars as in *E. l. longicauda*; belly yellowish, unmarked.

Hind feet with 5 toes; costal grooves 13 to 16 (or rarely 17). Sexually active males of some populations with 2 fleshy protuberances ("cirri") projecting downward from front of upper lip.

Remarks: Until recently, 4 subspecies of *E. bislineata* were recognized. Characters used to separate them included number of costal grooves, counts of teeth, presence or absence of cirri on sexually

FIG. 128. *Eurycea bislineata*, the two-lined salamander (Lee County). This variable species is yellow to orange-brown with dorsolateral dark stripes or lateral bands.

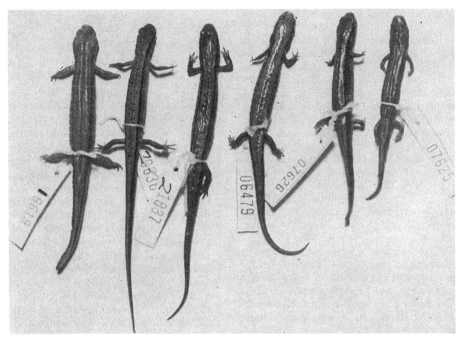

FIG. 129. Some variation among Alabama *Eurycea bislineata*. L to R, (1) Morgan County (the "Cole Springs morphotype"); (2) Clay County; (3) Shelby County; (4) St. Clair County (the *"aquatica* morphotype"); (5, 6) Jefferson County (the *"aquatica* morphotype").

active males, and color pattern (Mittleman, 1966). Two of the 4 subspecies, *E. b. cirrigera* (Green) and *E. b. wilderae* Dunn, were presumed to occur in Alabama, with the latter confined to the northeastern portion (Conant, 1958). In 1965 Rossman reported *E. b. wilderae* from southern central Alabama in the Coastal Plain Red Hills, an area thought to be inhabited exclusively by *E. b. cirrigera*. Mittleman (op. cit.) indicated that Rossman's specimens "were intergrades with *E. b. cirrigera*," although he failed to give any such indication on his subspecies range map.

Sever (1972) studied variation in *E. bislineata* and called attention to inconsistencies in interpretation of range relationships and presumed phenotypic differences among the described subspecies. He concluded that *E. b. rivicola*, a form with which he was especially concerned, should be placed in the synonymy of *E. b. bislineata*. He implied somewhat

subtly that the other subspecies may likewise be invalid.

Variation among Alabama populations of *E. bislineata* is complex and in need of comprehensive study. Even a cursory examination, however, such as I was able to undertake, will reveal the futility of attempting to describe it in terms of taxa now established. Adding to the complexity is the sporadic occurrence of populations referable to *Eurycea aquatica* Rose and Bush (Fig. 129), a form which appears to be conspecific with *E. bislineata*. (See account of *E. aquatica* under "Problematical Forms," p. 25.)

In 1970 Tom Yarbrough brought me specimens of a large, orange-to-brownish *E. bislineata*, which I had not seen before (Fig. 129). This form, which we call the Cole Springs phenotype, was found originally at Cole Springs in Morgan County, on the edge of Sand Mountain. Similar specimens have since been collected at another locality in the vicinity, as well as in Lawrence County.

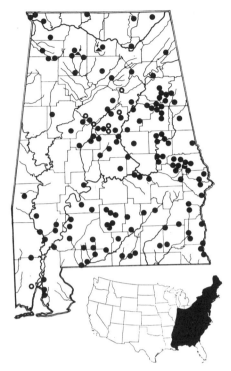

FIG. 130. Distribution of *Eurycea bislineata*, the two-lined salamander. This species occurs statewide, or essentially so, in Alabama. Solid round symbols indicate localities from which the author examined specimens with characteristics traditionally associated with *E. bislineata*. The circle is a literature record believed to be valid. The 2 triangles indicate localities from which the Cole Springs morphotype was collected, and the starred symbols are localities for the *aquatica* morphotype (see text, pp. 25, 119-121). The small map depicts approximately the known range of the species *E. bislineata* in the United States.

As in the case of *aquatica*, however, there are in the same areas individuals intermediate between it and the "typical" form, a small, slender, yellow or yellowish animal.

Folkerts (1971) commented on the complexity of variation in *E. bislineata* in Alabama, compared it with that found in Alabama *Desmognathus fuscus*, and suggested that strong ecotypic selection may be the causative factor in both cases.

Alabama distribution: (Fig. 130) Statewide.

Habits: The two-lined salamander is one of the most abundant amphibians in Alabama, occurring in a wide variety of damp and wet habitats. In many parts of the state optimal habitat is the edge of a small, rock-bottomed brook. In the Coastal Plain, forested floodplain bottoms with occasional pools of stagnant water often provide favorable habitat, with the adults taking shelter in and under rotting logs and beneath piles of flood-washed debris.

The environments around springs and spring runs are nearly always inhabited by two-lined salamanders, where they may be found in the water among the submerged portions of emergent aquatic vegetation or under rocks and debris along the edge. The *aquatica* form of *E. bislineata*, accorded specific rank by some workers, occurs most frequently in and around watercress-choked springs in limestone areas of the Ridge and Valley region.

In most parts of Alabama the two-lined salamander breeds during the winter. The white eggs are attached to the undersurfaces of submerged rocks or logs or to submerged parts of aquatic plants. The female attends the eggs until they hatch. Egg number, based on counts of enlarged ova in gravid females, averages about 50, with a range among Alabama specimens examined of from 15 to 114. Reproductive potential in the *aquatica* form is higher than in other populations sampled by an average of about 30 eggs. The larvae of *E. bislineata* transform in 1 to 3 years; neotenic individuals are not uncommon.

Eurycea longicauda (Green)

Three subspecies of this species are recognized, 2 of which occur in Alabama.

Eurycea longicauda longicauda (Green) Long-tailed Salamander

Description: (Fig. 131) A slender, long-tailed salamander attaining a maximum total length of about 185 mm. Nasolabial grooves present. Ground color yellow to yellowish orange; back and sides with black or dark brown spots or

FIG. 131. *Eurycea longicauda longicauda,* the long-tailed salamander (Limestone County). This form is yellow or orange-yellow in ground color. The tail has a pattern of vertical dark bars on the sides.

vermiculations, occasionally absent on the former and always more numerous on the latter. Sides of tail with vertical dark bars, producing a "herringbone" effect; venter immaculate. Costal grooves 13 or 14.

Alabama distribution: (Fig. 132) Occurs in that portion of the state above the Tennessee River except for the western three-fourths of Lauderdale County. Valentine (1962) determined the De-Kalb County population referred to by Penn (1940) as *E. l. longicauda* to be intergradient with *E. l. guttolineata,* the form inhabiting the southern three-fourths of the state.

The zone of intergradation between *E. l. longicauda* and *E. l. guttolineata* in Alabama is a semi-circular belt varying in width from 30 to 70 miles. Intergradation within the zone occurs in predictable fashion except in extreme northwestern Alabama in the western portions of Lauderdale and Colbert counties. There the populations are characterized by a high frequency of individuals with a greater profusion of dark markings than are seen in either of the 2 intergrading subspecies in Alabama. Whether this is a local phenomenon or one that involves populations in adjacent portions of Tennessee and Mississippi has not been determined.

Habits: Long-tailed salamanders inhabit damp places around streams, seepages, and springs. Under rocks and piles of debris are favorite hiding places. The salamanders are active at night, especially during wet weather, and are easily observed with a light.

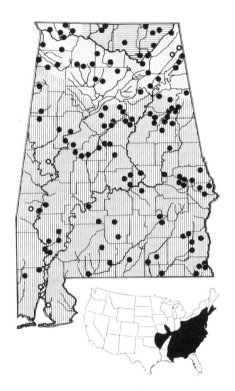

FIG. 132. Distribution of *Eurycea longicauda* and subspecific variation in Alabama. Horizontal hatching indicates the presumed range of *E. l. longicauda,* the long-tailed salamander, and vertical hatching, the range of *E. l. guttolineata,* the three-lined salamander. The zone of intergradation is indicated by stippling. Solid symbols indicate localities from which the author examined specimens. Circles are literature records believed to be valid. The small map depicts approximately the known range of the species *E. longicauda* in the United States.

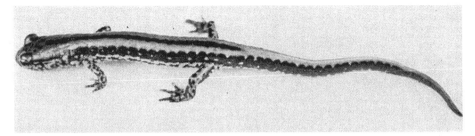

FIG. 133. *Eurycea longicauda guttolineata,* the three-lined salamander (Macon County). This common salamander is easily identified by its yellow ground color and conspicuous mid-dorsal black stripe.

The life history of the long-tailed sala-mader is poorly known. The larvae have been found in streams and woodland pools. Presumably, the eggs are laid under rocks.

Eurycea longicauda guttolineata (Holbrook)
Three-lined Salamander

Description: (Fig. 133) A moderately slender, long-tailed salamander attaining a maximum total length of about 185 mm. Nasolabial grooves present; ground color yellow to yellowish orange; back with a conspicuous black or dark brown mid-dorsal stripe and 2 dorsolateral ones, the latter often containing a row of widely separated, small yellow spots. Venter with a profusion of dark spots and vermiculations; tail with dark vertical bars which are often so expansive as to virtually obscure the ground color.

Alabama distribution: (Fig. 132) Generally, the southern three-fourths of the state, intergrading northward with *E. l. longicauda.*

Habits: The three-lined salamander is found in most kinds of shaded, moist natural habitats in Alabama. It is especially common in forested floodplains, where it spends its daylight hours under logs, in burrows, or in piles of damp debris deposited by floods. In such habitats, its most frequent salamander associates are usually *Plethodon glutinosus* and *Eurycea bislineata.*

Despite the abundance of the three-lined salamander, its reproductive habits remain poorly known. The few observations which have been made suggest that in many cases nesting and larval development take place below the ground in flooded underground passages or cavities. Darkness may be a requisite for breeding site selection. The only observation I have made was in early December in Shelby County, Alabama, where several adults with eggs were found in a reservoir in a shallow spring. The reservoir was a concrete cylinder about 2 feet in diameter. It rested on the floor of the spring, with a piece of tin covering its top. Inside the water stood to a depth of about 20 inches. The eggs, which had been attached individually to the sides of the reservoir at depths ranging from 2 to 10 inches, were in groups of 8 to 14 each.

The groups were in various stages of development, ranging from freshly laid to about midway to hatching. Several adult salamanders were clinging to the walls of the reservoir at the surface when I first lifted the top; upon being disturbed, they swam to the bottom and crawled beneath the sides. I was unable to make further observations at this site. Bruce (1970) published on larval development of *E. l. guttolineata* in North Carolina.

Eurycea lucifuga Rafinesque
Cave Salamander

Description: (Fig. 134) A medium-sized salamander attaining a maximum total length of about 180 mm. Body slender; tail long; eyes bulging; nasolabial

FIG. 134. *Eurycea lucifuga,* the cave salamander (Jackson County). Locally common around caves and similar types of habitats, this slender salamander has a yellow to reddish orange ground color and scattered black markings. It is sometimes confused with the long-tailed salamander.

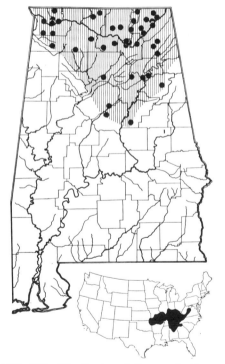

FIG. 135. Distribution of *Eurycea lucifuga,* the cave salamander. The presumed range in Alabama is indicated by hatching. Symbols indicate localities from which the author examined specimens. The small map depicts approximately the known range in the United States.

grooves present. Color orange-yellow to orange and orange-red, with irregular black spots scattered over tail and body; venter yellowish, typically unmarked.

Remarks: This species is easily confused with *E. longicauda longicauda,* but the black pigment on the tail does not form the "herringbone pattern" of vertically oriented bars as it does in *E. l. longicauda.*

Alabama distribution: (Fig. 135) Locally common in the Appalachian Plateaus and Chert Belt and known from a few localities in the Tennessee Valley and Ridge and Valley regions. The Piedmont and Blue Ridge are apparently uninhabited by this species.

Habits: Although caves seem to provide optimum living conditions for cave salamanders, they are by no means the only habitats exploited. When associated with caves, the salamanders most often occur around the mouths and in the twilight zones, forsaking the permanently dark recesses. They may be found crawling on the cave walls, secreted in crevices, or under rocks and litter.

Data on reproduction are somewhat scarce, although it is known that the eggs are laid from September to January. They may be attached or free. The breeding site may be a pool or sluggish stream in a cave or a pool associated with a small brook or seepage area in the open.

GENUS *GYRINOPHILUS* Cope

The forms within this genus are now considered to belong to 2 species, both of which occur in Alabama.

Gyrinophilus palleucus McCrady
Tennessee Cave Salamander

Three subspecies of this cave-dwelling, aquatic salamander are recognized (Brandon, 1966). The Alabama populations from which representative series have been obtained are considered intergradient between 2 of these. The subspecies have not been assigned common names. (Also see account of *Gyrinophilus porphyriticus.*)

Gryinophilus palleucus palleucus McCrady

Description: (Fig. 136) A rather large, permanently gilled aquatic salamander attaining a maximum total length of about 155 mm. Nasolabial grooves present; head broad; snout flattened and spatulate; eyes smaller than in larval *G. porphyriticus,* with which it is most easily confused (eye diameter entering distance from anterior corner of eye to snout tip from 4 to 5 times, as opposed to 1.5 to 3.5 times in latter); color pale pinkish or flesh-color except for the gills, which, in life, are bright red.

Alabama distribution: (Fig. 137) Influence of this subspecies is pronounced in most, if not all, of the Tennessee cave salamander populations in Alabama, all of which are considered intergradient. The species *G. palleucus* is known from several caves above the Tennessee River in Jackson County; it is thought to occur in Shelta Cave in Madison County and in Rockhouse Cave in Limestone County. It is known on the basis of 1 specimen from a cave below the Tennessee River in Colbert County (Cooper and Cooper, 1968). The Colbert County population, the last to be discovered, has not been subspecifically analyzed.

Habits: Aside from the fact that it is found in water in caves and feeds pre-

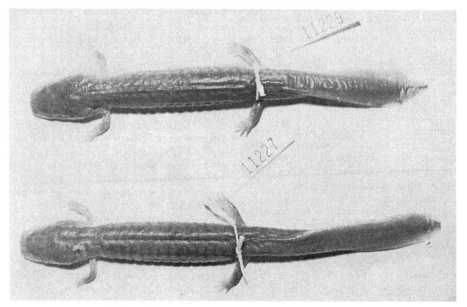

FIG. 136. *Gyrinophilus palleucus* ssp., the Tennessee cave salamander (Jackson County).

FIG. 137. Distribution of *Gyrinophilus pal-leucus* ssp., the Tennessee cave salamander. The presumed range of this species in Ala-bama is indicated by stippling. The solid symbol indicates the locality from which the author examined specimens. Circles are lit-erature records believed to be valid. The populations in Alabama are tentatively being considered intergradient between the sub-species *G. p. palleucus* and *G. p. necturo-ides*. The small map depicts approximately the known range of the species in the United States.

dominantly on arthropods, little is known of the habits of the Tennessee cave sala-mander. Notes on habitats and ecological associates are provided by Cooper (1968) and Cooper and Cooper (1968). These papers also provide information on the distributional relationships between that species and *G. porphyriticus*.

Gyrinophilus palleucus necturoides
Lazell and Brandon

Description: (Fig. 136) Differs from *G. p. palleucus* in having a dark-spotted dorsum in adults and a uniformly darker ground color in juveniles.

Alabama distribution: (Fig. 137) Ap-parently intergrades with *G. p. palleucus* throughout the species range in Alabama. (See "Alabama distribution" under *G. p. palleucus*.)

Habits: See "Habits" under *G. p. pal-leucus*.

Gyrinophilus porphyriticus (Green)

On the basis of a study of the genus *Gyrinophilus* by Brandon (1966d), 4 subspecies of *G. porphyriticus* are cur-rently recognized. Regarding Alabama populations, Brandon stated, "It is im-possible to assign a simple subspecific identification to the specimens from most parts of Alabama. Populations on Mt. Cheaha, in Talladega and Clay counties, closely resemble *p. dunni*. Those in ex-treme northern counties closely resemble *p. porphyriticus*. Other populations in Alabama appear to result primarily from *p. porphyriticus* with admixed genetic material from *p. dunni* to the east and from *p. duryi* to the north. The overlap in characteristics between *p. porphyriti-cus* and *p. duryi*, then, extends from east-ern Ohio to the Fall Line in Alabama."

Gyrinophilus porphyriticus porphyriticus
(Green)
Northern Spring Salamander

Description: (Fig. 138, 139) A large metamorphosing salamander attaining a maximum total length of about 220 mm. Nasolabial grooves present; snout with a feature on each side, the canthus ros-tralis, having the appearance of a slight ridge extending from the eye to the nos-tril; snout somewhat broadened and an-gular; color salmon to reddish brown or yellowish brown, with dark mottling or reticulations on dorsum, lacking distinct black spots (in our area). Belly of large individuals with or without melanophores (melanophores usually lacking in Ala-bama populations).

Eye of larva larger than that of *G. pal-leucus* ssp. (diameter entering distance from anterior corner of eye to snout tip from 1.5 to 3.5 times, as opposed to 4 to 5 times in *G. palleucus*). Head and

FIG. 138. *Gyrinophilus porphyriticus* ssp., the spring salamander (Cleburne County). A large salamander common in some of the mountainous areas of the state; the ground color of this species ranges from orange to dark brown. (See Fig. 139.)

snout of larva not as noticeably broad and spatulate as in *G. palleucus*.

Alabama distribution: (Fig. 140) Spring salamanders occur locally in the Blue Ridge, Ridge and Valley, and Appalachian Plateaus regions. All Alabama populations are considered intergradient, with *G. p. porphyriticus* influence predominating in all but those in the Blue Ridge. Cooper and Cooper (1968) postulated that *G. porphyriticus* and *G. palleucus* are allopatric.

Habits: Spring salamanders occur in

FIG. 139. Some variation among Alabama *Gyrinophilus porphyriticus*. L to R: Ridge and Valley region, Etowah County; Blue Ridge, Cleburne County; and Ridge and Valley region, Shelby County.

and around caves, springs, seepages, and small streams. Usually they are found under rocks or logs; on one occasion I unearthed a specimen in a burrow in a stream bank. Information on nesting is scarce. Organ's observations (1961) and those of others he summarizes indicate that the eggs are laid in summer and fall. Organ found one clutch of 41 eggs and another of 66; both were attached to the undersurfaces of partially submerged rocks and attended by the females. I know of no observations on reproduction of this species in Alabama.

Gyrinophilus porphyriticus dunni
Mittleman and Jopson
Carolina Spring Salamander

Description: (Fig. 139) Differs from *G. p. porphyriticus* and *G. p. duryi* in having a profusion of dark markings on the dorsum that are often arranged in chevronate fashion and in having the canthus rostralis bordered below by dark pigment.

Alabama distribution: (Fig. 140) Populations with characteristics of *G. p. dunni* occur virtually throughout the Blue Ridge. According to Brandon (1966), however, these populations also show influence from the subspecies *G. p. porphyriticus*.

Habits: See "Habits" under *G. p. porphyriticus*.

GENUS *HEMIDACTYLIUM* Tschudi

This is a monotypic genus, widely distributed in the eastern United States and the adjacent portion of Canada.

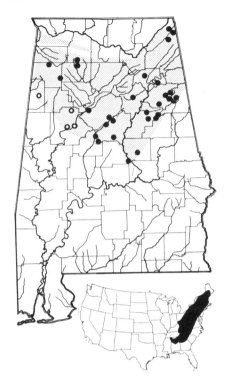

FIG. 140. Distribution of *Gyrinophilus porphyriticus* ssp., the spring salamander. The presumed range in Alabama is indicated by stippling. Solid symbols indicate localities from which the author examined specimens. Circles are literature records believed to be valid. Populations in Alabama are considered to be intergradient, with various combinations involving the subspecies, *G. p. porphyriticus*, *G. p. duryi*, and *G. p. dunni*. The small map depicts approximately the known range of the species in the United States.

Hemidactylium scutatum (Schlegel)
Four-toed Salamander

Description: (Fig. 141) A rather small salamander attaining a maximum total length of about 75 mm. Nasolabial grooves present; gular fold pronounced; tail with a basal constriction; hind foot with 4 toes. Dorsum grayish, brownish, or dull orange; venter white with distinct black flecks. Costal grooves 13 or 14.

Alabama distribution: (Fig. 142) Probably statewide, or nearly so, but very local.

Habits: The four-toed salamander is encountered infrequently in Alabama. The few specimens my colleagues and I have collected have come from floodplains, near the edges of floodplains, or other such low places. Most were found in wooded areas under logs in the vicinity of sloughs or other standing water. Investigators in several other states within the range report that sphagnum bogs offer optimal habitat.

The sluggish nature of this salamander is one of its noticeable attributes. Where-

FIG. 141. *Hemidactylium scutatum*, four-toed salamander (Lee County). This species, infrequently encountered in Alabama, can be distinguished by the bold black markings on the venter and the constriction of the tail near its base. In addition, it has only 4 toes on the hind foot.

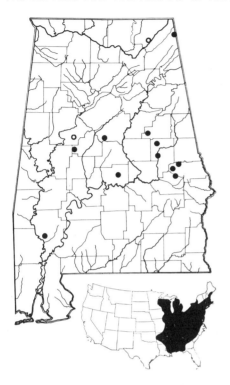

FIG. 142. Distribution of *Hemidactylium scutatum*, the four-toed salamander. This species is believed to occur statewide, or essentially so, in Alabama. Solid symbols indicate localities from which the author examined specimens. The circles are literature records believed to be valid. The small map depicts approximately the known range in the United States.

as most small salamanders that occur in Alabama are quite active when exposed or handled, *H. scutatum* moves slowly and often appears moribund.

Neill (1963) summarized the most important works dealing with this species. The reproductive habits have been studied by several investigators. Wood (1955) reported on 224 nests in Virginia. Most were found in crevices among the leaves and stems of mosses, sedges, and hepatics. All were near water, in which the larvae develop, usually consisting of sluggish bog streams, ponds, seepage springs, or brooks. The earliest date given was February 24. My only observation of nesting in Alabama was on February 23,

1962, in Bibb County. A nest with an undetermined number of eggs attended by 2 females was exposed in a small cavity in a rotting log. The log protruded from the bank into a shallow woodland pool, and the nest was situated about 12 inches above the water's surface.

GENUS *MANCULUS* Cope

The single species belonging to this genus occurs in Alabama. Some authorities favor placing it within the genus *Eurycea*.

Manculus quadridigitatus (Holbrook)
Dwarf Salamander

Description: (Fig. 143) A small, slender salamander attaining a maximum total length of about 90 mm. Nasolabial grooves present; hind foot with 4 toes; color yellowish to brown with dark dorsolateral stripes extending from snout to tip of tail. Costal grooves 14 to 17 .

Alabama distribution: (Fig. 144) Generally, the southern one-half of the state, extending into the lower edge of the Piedmont in eastern Alabama. The northern extent of the range in western Alabama is not known.

Habits: The dwarf salamander, resembling at first glance an undernourished, dark two-lined salamander, is found most frequently under logs, boards, and debris in low, damp places. It is often the most abundant salamander in low pine flatwoods habitats in extreme southern Alabama.

Data on egg laying are lacking for Alabama. Reports from other areas indicate that the eggs are laid during the late fall or winter, in or near the water, where they are usually attached singly to pine needles and various other objects. Hatching occurs in 3 to 4 weeks, and larval development requires 2 to 3 months. I have found larvae in March in southern Alabama in permanent and semi-permanent woodland pools and in flooded roadside ditches. Mittlemen (1967) reviewed the literature on this species, and Harrison (1973) provided an account of its natural history in South Carolina.

FIG. 143. *Manculus quadridigitatus,* the dwarf salamander (Macon County). This small, slender salamander is brown or yellowish brown with obscure dorsolateral dark stripes. It has only 4 toes on the hind foot.

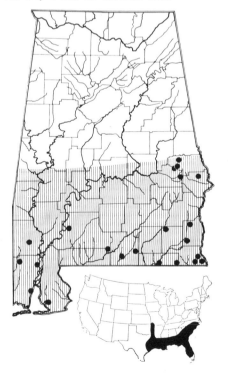

GENUS *PHAEOGNATHUS* Highton

Phaeognathus is a monotypic genus confined to Alabama.

Phaeognathus hubrichti Highton
Red Hills Salamander

Description: (Fig. 145) A fairly large, terrestrial salamander attaining a maximum total length of about 255 mm. Nasolabial grooves present; body elongate; limbs relatively short, intercostal folds between adpressed limbs more than 12. Color dark gray to brownish, unmarked. Costal grooves 20 to 22, the usual number 21.

Remarks: On preserved specimens a small, pale spot is visible on each side of

FIG. 144. Distribution of *Manculus quadridigitatus,* the dwarf salamander. The presumed range in Alabama is indicated by hatching. Symbols indicate localities from which the author examined specimens. The small map depicts approximately the known range in the United States.

FIG. 145. *Phaeognathus hubrichti,* the Red Hills salamander (Monroe County). The existence of this salamander, whose range is confined to Alabama, was unknown until 1960. The dorsal color is dark gray to brownish, and there are obvious markings.

the base of the tail. This spot is obscure on live animals. Sexual dimorphism is evident not only in the appearance of the vent walls (plicate in females, papillate in females), but also in the nature of the integument. Males have numerous tiny pigmentless glands, visible to the unaided eye, on the tail and on the ventral and lateral surfaces of the abdomen. These structures, absent on females, are apparently hedonic glands, similar to those on some other plethodontid salamanders (Jordan, 1973). Geographic variation in this species has not been detected.

Alabama distribution: (Fig. 146) The range of *P. hubrichti* is confined to a narrow belt of 2 geological formations (Tallahatta and Hatchetigbee) in the Red Hills. The range is limited to the east and west by the Conecuh River and Alabama River, respectively (Schwaner and Mount, 1970).

Habits: This remarkable salamander, whose existence was unknown until 1960, lives in burrows on the slopes of shaded, mesic ravines dominated by hardwood

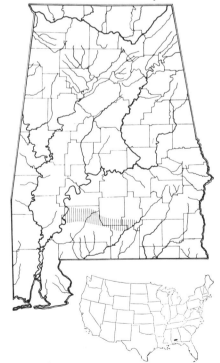

FIG. 146. Distribution of *Phaeognathus hubrichti,* the Red Hills salamander. The presumed range is indicated on the Alabama map by hatching and is blackened on the small United States map. Locality records are not indicated because of the scarcity of the species and its apparent susceptibility to overcollecting.

trees. At night it comes to the mouth of the burrow and feeds on insects and spiders, which usually abound in the salamander's habitat. The burrow mouth frequently opens on a slope steep enough to be relatively free of litter, is transversely oval in shape, and usually has a smoothly rounded rim. The burrow sometimes opens from near the base of a tree or from under an outcropping of siltstone.

Little is known of the reproduction of *P. hubrichti.* The nests have never been observed, although numerous attempts have been made to find them. Apparently breeding is wholly terrestrial and occurs largely during the spring.

Brandon in 1966 reviewed the literature on *P. hubrichti* and added some additional information. Subsequently, Mount and Schwaner (1970) published on a collecting technique; Schwaner and Mount (1970) added notes on its distribution, ecology, and life history; and Jordan and Mount (1975) reported on the current status of the species and on its prospects of continued survival.

GENUS *PLETHODON* Tschudi

This genus contains about 18 species. Five of these occur in the Pacific Northwest, 1 in New Mexico, and the remainder in the eastern portion of the United States and adjacent Canada. Three species occur in Alabama.

Plethodon cinereus (Green)

Three subspecies of *P. cinereus* are recognized, 1 of which occurs in Alabama.

Plethodon cinereus polycentratus
Highton and Grobman
Georgia Red-backed Salamander

Description: (Fig. 147) A small salamander, attaining a maximum total length of about 125 mm. Nasolabial grooves present; upper sides dark gray to nearly black; dorsum reddish, unstriped, or more often with an even-edged red stripe; stripe, when present, not widening at tail base as in *P. d. dorsalis,* a similar form with which *P. cinereus* is sympatric; stripe never with lateral lobes as in most *P. d. dorsalis.*

Lower sides and venter mottled with approximately equal amounts of light and dark pigments, producing a "salt-and-pepper" effect. Costal grooves usually 20 to 21. Mental gland on chin of sexually active males shelflike, situated near the apex of the lower jaw rami (mental gland in *P. dorsalis* is rounded or oblong, not contacting jaw rami laterally).

Alabama distribution: (Fig. 148) Known only from a few localities around Anniston, Calhoun County, in northeastern Alabama. Probably occurs in Cherokee and Cleburne counties as well, and possibly in DeKalb and Randolph counties. A record of *P. cinereus* for Lauderdale County, reported by Mount and Folkers (1968), was based on misidentified *P. d. dorsalis.*

FIG. 147. *Plethodon cinereus polycentratus,* the Georgia red-backed salamander (Calhoun County). This salamander is known in Alabama from a few localities in the northeastern portion. A straight-edged, reddish mid-dorsal stripe may or may not be present. This salamander is easily confused with the zigzag salamander, a form that is much more common and widespread in the state.

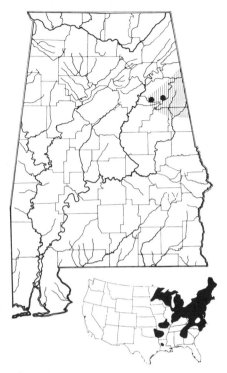

FIG. 148. Distribution of *Plethodon cinereus polycentratus*, the Georgia red-backed salamander. The presumed range in Alabama is indicated by hatching. Symbols indicate localities from which the author examined specimens. The small map depicts approximately the known range of the species *P. cinereus* in the United States.

Habits: This salamander inhabits mesic woodlands where it takes shelter under logs, rocks, and leaf litter. It is most frequently encountered during late winter and early spring. Tom Yarbrough, who first discovered its presence in Alabama, has collected a number of individuals as they were crossing the highway at night following warm rains.

Little is known of the habits of this form in Alabama. In its life history the aquatic larva is omitted. The nesting habits of *P. c. polycentratus* are presumably similar to those of *P. c. cinereus.* The latter nests during the summer in a cavity within a log or stump, beneath a rock, or in leaf litter. The eggs, 8 or 10 in number, are laid in a cluster and attached to the roof of the cavity by a pedicel. The nest is attended by the female until hatching. A survey of the literature on *P. cinereus* was provided by Smith (1963).

Plethodon dorsalis Cope

Two subspecies of *P. dorsalis* are recognized, 1 of which occurs in Alabama.

Plethodon dorsalis dorsalis Cope
Zigzag Salamander

Description: (Fig. 149) A small salamander attaining a maximum total length of about 110 mm. Nasolabial grooves present; dorsum usually brown to dark gray with a red or yellowish, laterally lobed stripe; stripe occasionally lacking lateral lobes or obscure or absent due to melanism. (Individuals with even-edged stripes are rare in Alabama and occur mostly in the extreme northwestern portion.) Stripe, when present, extending onto tail and widening at tail base

FIG. 149. *Plethodon dorsalis dorsalis,* the zigzag salamander (Lee County). A lobed, red or orange mid-dorsal stripe is usually present in this form, but the stripe may be straight-edged or lacking altogether.

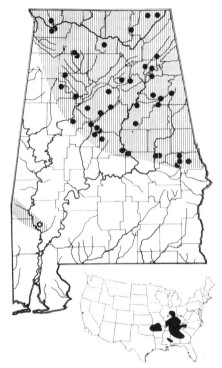

FIG. 150. Distribution of *Plethodon dorsalis dorsalis,* the zigzag salamander. The presumed range in Alabama is indicated by hatching. Solid symbols indicate localities from which the author examined specimens. The circle is a literature record believed to be valid. The small map depicts approximately the known range of the species *P. dorsalis* in the United States.

(stripe, when present, on *P. cinereus,* a closely related species, does not widen on tail base).

Belly light, mottled, suffused, or flecked with dark pigment of varying intensity; costal grooves usually 18. Mental gland under chin of sexually active males rounded or longitudinally oblong, failing to reach jaw rami laterally (mental gland of *P. cinereus* shelflike, in contact with jaw rami laterally).

Alabama distribution: (Fig. 150) Occurs in suitable habitats in the Upland Regions and in portions of the Fall Line Hills and Red Hills. The Red Hills population, reported by Blaney and Relyea (1967) from Clarke County, is apparently disjunct from those to the north. The extent of the range of this population is unknown.

Habits: The optimal habitat of *P. dorsalis* in Alabama is a mesic, rocky woodland dominated by hardwood trees. In such habitats it is often abundant and can be found during the fall, winter, and early spring under rocks and logs. The period from about mid-May through September is spent mostly underground.

Surprisingly little is known of the reproductive habits of this salamander. A completely terrestrial form, it omits the aquatic larval stage, as do other members of its genus. Nesting presumably takes place in subterranean passages or cavities, probably during the summer. A literature survey on *P. dorsalis* was provided by Thurow (1966).

Plethodon glutinosus (Green)

Two subspecies of this salamander are recognized, 1 of which occurs in Alabama.

Plethodon glutinosus glutinosus (Green) Slimy Salamander

Description: (Fig. 151) A rather large salamander attaining a maximum total length of about 190 mm. Body fairly slender; snout with nasolabial grooves; costal grooves usually 16. Color black or dark brown, usually with scattered yellow or white flecks or small spots, and occasionally with diffuse brassy mottling; sides sometimes white-frosted; venter usually uniformly dark.

Remarks: Slimy salamanders vary extensively in the number and size of the light markings. An occasional individual has none. Individuals with brassy mottling on the dorsum have been found in Jackson County. *Plethodon glutinosus* can be quickly distinguished from *Ambystoma texanum* by its nasolabial grooves, which are lacking in the latter, and from *Phaeognathus hubrichti* by its 16 costal grooves. *Phaeognathus* has 20 to 22.

FIG. 151. *Plethodon glutinosus glutinosus,* the slimy salamander (Lee County). This fairly large salamander is abundant in Alabama. It is black with white or yellow markings.

Alabama distribution: (Fig. 152) Statewide.

Habits: The slimy salamander is abundant throughout the state, and any predominantly black, terrestrial salamander with moderate body proportions will more than likely belong to this species. It exploits almost all of our terrestrial habitats and is especially abundant in wooded floodplains and shaded ravine slopes. Well rotted logs and stumps are favored microhabitats.

When handled, the slimy salamander produces a sticky skin secretion that is difficult to remove but otherwise innocuous. As with other members of the genus,

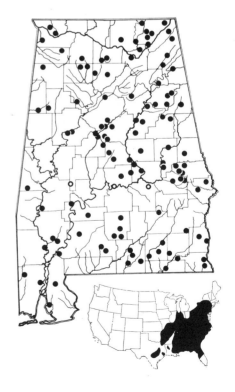

FIG. 152. Distribution of *Plethodon glutinosus glutinosus,* the slimy salamander. This form is believed to occur statewide, or nearly so, in Alabama. Solid symbols indicate localities from which the author examined specimens. Circles are literature records believed to be valid. The small map depicts approximately the known range of the species *P. glutinosus* in the United States.

the aquatic larval stage is omitted. In spite of its abundance, we know relatively little of this salamander's reproductive habits. Presumably, the eggs are laid mostly in underground burrows, and there are a few instances of nests having been found in caves.

GENUS *PSEUDOTRITON* Tschudi

Currently this genus is considered to contain 2 species, both of which are found in Alabama.

Pseudotriton montanus Baird

This species is represented in Alabama by *P. m. flavissimus*, 1 of the 4 subspecies now included within it. Another form, *P. m. diastictus*, has been reported, but its presence is not, to my knowledge, documented by available specimens. Intensive efforts during the course of this study to find *P. m. diastictus*, or its influence, in Alabama have failed. In the absence of more substantial evidence to the contrary, I consider the occurrence of *P. m. diastictus* in Alabama questionable and am listing it under "Problematical Forms" (p. 24).

Pseudotriton montanus flavissimus Hallowell

Gulf Coast Mud Salamander

Description: (Fig. 153) A salamander of moderate-to-slender body proportions attaining a maximum total length of about 119 mm. The individual on which this measurement was made (AM 9985, from Lee County, Alabama) is apparently a record-sized specimen for the subspecies. Nasolabial grooves present; color light orange-brown or reddish brown with small, dark spots scattered over the dorsum and along the sides; ground color darkening with age, spots becoming somewhat obscure; venter lighter than dorsum, unmarked. Costal grooves 16 to 18.

Remarks: *Pseudotriton ruber*, a form with which *P. m. flavissimus* may be confused, is generally stouter than the latter and has a brighter ground color, except in old individuals. Also, the spots on the dorsum of *P. ruber* are typically larger and closer together, except on some small individuals, than they are on *P. m. flavissimus*.

FIG. 153. *Pseudotriton montanus flavissimus,* the Gulf Coast mud salamander (Macon County). This species is salmon to brownish red in color and has small dark spots on the dorsum. It is infrequent in Alabama.

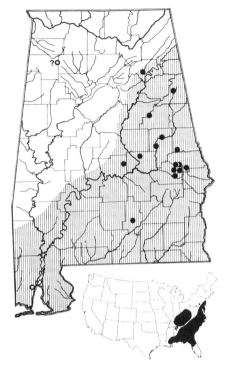

FIG. 154. Distribution of *Pseudotriton montanus flavissimus*, the Gulf Coast mud salamander. The presumed range in Alabama is indicated by hatching. Solid symbols indicate localities from which the author examined specimens. The circles are literature records; the one from northwestern Alabama is of questionable validity. The small map depicts approximately the range of the species *P. montanus* in the United States.

Alabama distribution: (Fig. 154) Gulf Coast mud salamanders have been collected in the Coastal Plain, Piedmont, Blue Ridge, and Ridge and Valley regions.

Habits: This salamander, described in 1856, remains one of our most poorly known forms. Nowhere does it seem to be abundant. The concentration of locality records for eastern Alabama indicated on the distribution map occurs within an area that has been searched intensively for salamanders for the past 15 years, and one which contains seemingly optimal habitat for *P. m. flavissimus*.

All the specimens of *P. m. flavissimus* from Alabama have, to my knowledge, been collected in low, wooded floodplains or similar situations. Nearly all have been found beneath logs. Whereas *P. ruber* is often found well away from water in fairly dry habitats, *P. m. flavissimus* seldom leaves the low ground. Larvae have been found in shallow, mud-bottomed, floodplain pools, but nesting habits are unknown. Presumably the eggs are attached to objects in the water, as are those of *P. ruber*.

Pseudotriton ruber (Sonnini)

Many aspects of variation within this species are poorly understood, and a comprehensive analysis is needed. The abundance of material that has accumulated within recent years would facilitate such an undertaking. Currently, 4 subspecies are recognized, 2 of which occur in Alabama.

Pseudotriton ruber ruber (Sonnini)
Northern Red Salamander

Description: (Fig. 155) A large salamander attaining a maximum total length of about 180 mm. Body stout, tail short; nasolabial grooves present; dorsum and sides orange to red with numerous bold dark spots that tend to coalesce in old individuals; old individuals occasionally almost uniform pinkish or purplish brown. Belly reddish to pink, clear in young, usually becoming sprinkled with small dark spots in adults. Differs from *P. r. vioscai* in lacking dark spots on the undersurfaces of the hind legs and white flecks on the head and jaws.

Alabama distribution: (Fig. 156) Upland provinces except for the lower Piedmont and western portion of the Appalachain Plateaus province. Intergrades *P. r. vioscai* southward and southwestward to the range of that subspecies.

Habits: This colorful salamander is most abundant around springs and small streams in forested areas, where it takes shelter under rocks, logs, and debris. In April and May it is often found consider-

FIG. 155. *Pseudotriton ruber ruber* x *vioscai,* the red salamander (Lee County). The specimens shown here are intergradient between the 2 subspecies that occur in Alabama. The ground color is orange to red or reddish brown.

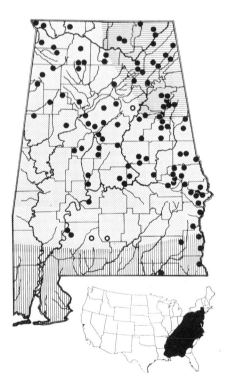

able distances from water in relatively dry habitats. In late fall or early winter, the white eggs are laid singly, in small clusters, on the undersurfaces of rocks or other sheltering objects in shallow water. Bruce (1972) reported on a detailed study of larval development in the species *P. ruber* in the Blue Ridge area of North Carolina and South Carolina. Red salamanders feed on a variety of invertebrate life and in captivity will eat other salamanders.

Pseudotriton ruber vioscai Bishop
Southern Red Salamander

Description: Differs from *P. ruber ruber* in having a somewhat darker, more

FIG. 156. Distribution of *Pseudotriton ruber* and subspecific variation in Alabama. Horizontal hatching indicates the presumed range of *P. r. ruber,* the northern red salamander, and vertical hatching, the range of *P. r. vioscai,* the southern red salamander. The zone of intergradation is indicated by stippling. Solid symbols indicate localities from which the author examined specimens. Circles are literature records believed to be valid. The small map depicts approximately the known range of the species *P. ruber* in the United States.

FIG. 157. *Necturus maculosus,* the mudpuppy (Lauderdale County). The larva of this permanently aquatic salamander is striped. Adults are virtually impossible to distinguish from some of *N. beyeri.* (Photo by Kelly Thomas.)

brownish ground color, white flecking about the head and jaws, dark spots on the undersurfaces of the hind limbs, and a strong tendency to develop a "herringbone" pattern on the dorsum. Maximum total length about 160 mm.

Distribution: (Fig. 156) Populations referable to this subspecies are confined to the Lower Coastal Plain. *P. r. vioscai* intergrades with *P. r. ruber* throughout the remainder of the Coastal Plain, in the lower Piedmont, and in the outer portion of the Appalachain Plateaus region.

Habits: Within the range of *P. r. vioscai,* red salamanders are encountered much less frequently than they are elsewhere in the state. They usually occur under logs and debris around springs and small creeks. The habits of this subspecies are presumably similar in most respects to those of *P. r. ruber.*

FAMILY PROTEIDAE — MUDPUPPIES, WATERDOGS, AND THE OLM

This family contains the polytypic genus *Necturus,* which is limited to eastern United States and adjacent portions of Canada, and the olm, *Proteus anquineus,* a blind, cave-dwelling form of Europe. All family members are permanently aquatic, and have external gills throughout life.

Genus *Necturus* Rafinesque

The members of this genus, called waterdogs and mudpuppies, are relatively large salamanders with conspicuous external gills and 2 pairs of well-developed limbs (Fig. 157, 158). Both front and hind feet have 4 toes. The only other 4-legged salamanders in Alabama with

FIG. 158. *Necturus beyeri,* Beyer's waterdog (Covington County). The specimen shown here is a subadult and is somewhat darker than usual for the species.

this condition are *Manculus quadridigitatus* and *Hemidactylium scutatum*. Except for *Amphiuma* spp., all others have 4 toes on front and 5 on back. Male *Necturus* have prominent papillae, one on each side, projecting posteriorly from the vent.

Variation among and within *Necturus* populations is marked and confusing. Dorsal color varies from plain brown or dark gray to brown, pink, reddish, or gray with dark spots or stripes. The venter may be immaculate, splotched, or spotted. Ontogenetic variation in color pattern is pronounced in most populations. Old individuals are likely to be darker dorsally and ventrally than young ones, although in some populations the reverse is true. Maximum size and size at the advent of sexual maturity are variables that have been used as taxonomic characters. Among numerous other variable characters that have been considered important are shape of head and body, ratio of jaw length to jaw width, and nature of the footplate of the columella of the ear.

Eight forms have been described within the genus, 7 of which have, at one time or another, been accorded the rank of species. A ninth form is being considered for subspecific recognition by one worker.

The interrelationships among the forms remain poorly understood, and the taxonomic validity of several has been questioned. Currently, estimates of the number of species involved range from 2 (Brode, 1969) to 5 (Porter, 1972).

One reason for the confused state of *Necturus* taxonomy, aside from the animals' extreme variability, is that representative series from critical areas are often lacking. Unfortunately, specimens from these areas are usually difficult to collect in sizable numbers or in representative age groups. Perhaps the most critical area of all is Alabama, from which 5 of the 9 forms in question have been reported. The type localities for 2 described forms are in Alabama, as is the proposed type locality for the undescribed "subspecies."

My efforts to develop an understanding of the variation and interrelationships among Alabama *Necturus* have so far met with little success. In the following discussion, I have attempted to summarize the pertinent aspects of the most recent taxonomic works on *Necturus* that deal with the problems in Alabama, and to relate my own observations thereto.

Hecht (1958) conducted a comprehensive study of the systematics of *Necturus* and recognized 4 species, with a total of 8 subspecies. Three forms were reported from Alabama: "*N. m. maculosus,*" a large form in which the dorsum of the adult is spotted and the larva is striped, which has a range in Alabama restricted to the Tennessee River system; "*N. beyeri alabamensis,*" an intermediate-sized form in which the dorsum of adults is sparsely spotted, the venter is immaculate (at least the medial portion), and the larva is unstriped, inhabiting stream systems from the Mobile Bay drainage eastward to the Apalachicola River drainage; and "*N. punctatus lodingi,*" a small *Necturus* in which the dorsum is usually unspotted and the larva is unstriped, occurring in streams within the Lower Coastal Plain from the Mobile Bay area eastward to the Apalachicola River drainage.

A fourth form, "*N. b. beyeri,*" said to be distinct from "*N. b. alabamensis*" in having a spotted or darkly pigmented venter in adults, was reported to range eastward in Mississippi to the Escatawpa River and, by implication, to southwestern Alabama in that stream.

Hecht's interpretation was generally accepted until 1963, when Neill (1963b) challenged listing *alabamensis* as a subspecies of *N. beyeri.* Neill contended that *beyeri* and *alabamensis* occur in sympatry in Alabama in the Mobile Bay drainage, and that the latter should be returned to its original status of full species. Neill stated further that *alabamensis* was most closely related not to *beyeri* but to *N. m. maculosus* in the Tennessee River system, as was indicated by the flattened habitus (as opposed to rounded or subcylindrical in *beyeri*), a reduced number of spots (about 100 on the entire animal as opposed to about 200), and a clear venter (as opposed to spotted, typically, in *beyeri*). Neill did not comment on Hecht's interpretation of *N. punctatus.*

Gunter and Brode (1964), after examining specimens from Mississippi, Louisiana, and Alabama, concluded that (1) Hecht was correct in considering *alabamensis* a subspecies of *N. beyeri,* (2) the subspecies *N. b. beyeri* does not occur in Alabama, and (3) *lodingi* should be listed as a synonym of "*N. b. alabamensis.*" In differentiating between *beyeri* and *alabamensis,* at the subspecific level, these workers emphasized the "squatty" form and spotted venter of *beyeri,* as opposed to the relatively slender form and clear venter (medial portion) of *alabamensis.*

The next, and most recent, work on *Necturus* that considered the taxonomy of Alabama populations was by Brode (1969). He considered the genus to be composed of 2 polytypic species: *N. maculosus,* containing the subspecies *maculosus, lewisi,* and an undescribed form; and *N. punctatus,* containing, in addition to the nominate form, *alabamensis* and *beyeri.* He stated that the 2 "species" were completely separable on the basis of the ratio of length-to-width of the "lower jawbone" and on the "shape and form of the footplate forming the basal section of the columella of the middle ear ossicles." According to Brode the "lower jawbone" of *N. maculosus* is much wider than long, while that of *N. punctatus* is equal in width and length, or longer than wide. The footplate of the columella of *N. maculosus* was described as rounded and cupshaped, in contrast to that of *N. punctatus* which is oval and flattened.

Brode considered the *Necturus* in the Tennessee River system to be *N. m. maculosus.* A population in the West Sipsey Fork, Black Warrior River system, in northwestern Alabama was considered to be an undescribed subspecies of *N. maculosus.* The population was characterized as having dark stripes extending from the nostrils onto the gills, thence backward, becoming progressively darker and wider to the tip of the tail. Flanking the dark stripes above were said to be light brown stripes that begin on the back of the head and converge along the upper keel of the tail.

The *Necturus* populations within the remainder of Alabama were all assigned to "*Necturus punctatus alabamensis.*" This form, according to Brode, is the intermediate one in a cline whose easternmost populations have characteristics traditionally associated with the *punctatus* phenotype and whose westernmost populations have those of the *beyeri* form.

I cannot agree entirely with any of the above interpretations of interrelationships among Alabama *Necturus.* Geographic variation in adult color pattern is rather chaotic and of limited utility as a practicable means of allocating individuals or populations to described taxa. Striking differences occur among some creek populations within the same river system, conjoined with remarkable homogeneity among the individuals within the populations themselves. Various combinations of characteristics are found among the populations, and general concordance appears to be lacking. I have not yet seen specimens of the striped form that Brode (op. cit.) reported from the West Sipsey Fork. However, the color characteristics ascribed to it also fit specimens in the Auburn Museum from the Cumberland River, Smith County, Tennessee, and appear to fit one pictured by Gunter and Brode (op. cit.) from the same locality. The pattern exhibited by these specimens is essentially the one possessed by the larvae of *N. maculosus.* In discussing the West Sipsey Fork population, Brode did not comment on the apparent similarity of the 2 widely separated groups, nor did he call attention to the striped form of the Cumberland River elsewhere in his work. The color pattern on a series of specimens, designated paratypes of *N. lodingi,* from the Dog River drainage in Mobile County, is not appreciably different from some on specimens representing other *Necturus* populations and, as nearly as I can determine, is not of taxonomic significance.

I have seen no adult *Necturus* from

Alabama that resembles the small, uni-colorus form that inhabits the extreme southeastern portion of the range of the genus. That form, described from South Carolina as the species *N. punctatus,* a taxon expanded later to include other taxa, apparently does not occur in Ala-bama. George Folkerts, who is familiar with the form, informed me that he had seen no *Necturus* in Alabama with which he believes it to be conspecific.

The larval color pattern may be, as Brode (op. cit.) has implied, a character that can be used to separate populations in the Tennessee River system from most others in Alabama. I am aware of no larval specimens from the Tennessee sys-tem in Alabama that do not have a striped pattern, nor of any from else-where in the state that do. Larvae are available from only a few localities in Alabama, however, and many more col-lections are needed to substantiate the validity of larval coloration as a taxo-nomic character. I have not seen larvae from the West Sispey Fork, nor, appar-ently, had Brode. Shoop (1965) sup-plied good photographs of striped and unstriped *Necturus* larvae.

I could detect among Alabama speci-mens no variation in habitus that ap-peared to be of taxonomic significance. The characteristics involving habitus re-ferred to by Neill (op. cit.) (rounded in *beyeri,* flattened in *alabamensis*) and those used by Gunter and Brode (op. cit.) ("squatty" in *beyeri,* slender in *ala-bamensis*) may be useful when compar-ing live animals of a similar nutritional state, but would be of greater value if expressed in objective terms.

Brode's (op. cit.) character involving relative jaw length is, at best, a poor one. I was unable to demonstrate its util-ity either by taking direct measurements on the specimens themselves or by using radiography. I did not attempt to eval-uate the character involving the foot-plate of the columella.

Size, both in terms of total length at-tained and of length at the advent of sexual maturity, is a geographic variable in *Necturus.* The largest adult specimens are from the Tennessee River system and

the smallest ones are from the Dog River drainage in Mobile County. Consider-ably more sampling must be done before this aspect of variation can be assessed and correlated with other variables.

In conclusion, my opinion is that firm taxonomic allocation of the *Necturus* in Alabama cannot be made with reason-able confidence on the basis of current knowledge. Until we arrive at a better understanding than has been reached thus far, I shall (1) refer to the popula-tions of large (over 300 mm maximum length) *Necturus* which have striped larva and occur in the Tennessee River system as *N. maculosus* (Rafinesque); (2) refer to the populations of the smal-ler (up to about 275 mm total length) form which has an unstriped larva and inhabits the remainder of the state as *N. beyeri* Viosca; and (3) consider *ala-bamensis* a problematical form. *N. p. lodingi* will be treated as a synonym of *N. beyeri.* The uncertainties of the re-lationships among described taxa in por-tions of the range outside Alabama, as well as of those within, make it unwise to attempt at this time to allocate popu-lations to subspecies.

Alabama distribution of *Necturus*: *N. maculosus,* the "mudpuppy," occurs in the Tennessee River and many of its tributaries (Fig. 159). The assignment of the population in the West Sipsey Fork, Warrior River system, to this spe-cies by Brode (op. cit.) is, in my opin-ion, questionable.

Necturus beyeri, "Beyer's waterdog," occurs above and below the Fall Line and is known from all drainages from the Mobile Bay to the Apalachicola except for Blackwater Creek (Fig. 160). *N. beyeri* also occurs in the drainage of Dog River, which empties into Mobile Bay from the west, and would be expected in Escatawpa River and Big Creek of the Pascagoula drainage. (See above.)

Habits of *Necturus*: In Alabama, *Nec-turus* inhabit permanent streams ranging in size from medium-sized creeks to large rivers. They are found in impound-ments of such streams, as well as in free-flowing segments. Streams with large rocks, logs, accumulations of bottom debris, and other hiding places are favored. Recesses beneath overhanging banks may provide necessary shelter in some streams.

Neill (op. cit.), who considered *beyeri* and *alabamensis* different species, apparently concurred in earlier reports that *beyeri* inhabits spring-fed, sand-bottomed streams. He gave the habitat of *alabamensis* as medium-sized to large streams with bottom deposits that include logs and leafy trash. Neill contended that *beyeri*, when inactive, lives in cylindrical holes in the stream banks, whereas *alabamensis* and *N. maculosus* dwell beneath bottom debris. Shoop and Gunning (1967) found no evidence in Louisiana that *N. beyeri* and *N. maculosus* differed in microhabitat preference, as Neill had stated. Both species, they re-

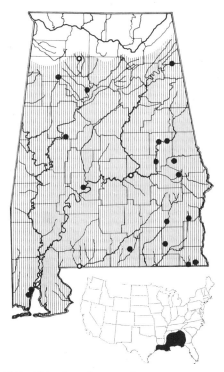

FIG. 160. Distribution of *Necturus beyeri*, Beyer's waterdog. The presumed range in Alabama is indicated by hatching. Solid symbols indicate localities from which the author examined specimens. The circles are literature records believed to be valid. The small map depicts approximately the known range in the United States.

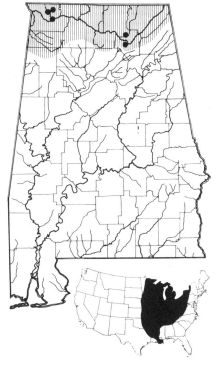

FIG. 159. Distribution of *Necturus maculosus*, the mudpuppy. The presumed range in Alabama is indicated by hatching. Symbols indicate localities from which the author examined specimens. The small map depicts approximately the known range in the United States.

ported, spend most of their time in pools near shelter.

There are no reports on the reproductive habits of *N. maculous* or *N. beyeri* from Alabama. Reports are available, however, from other portions of their ranges. Among the most important of these are the works by Harris (1961) and Shoop (1965). Courtship in *Necturus* occurs in fall and winter. Fertilization is accomplished by means of spermatophores. Nesting takes place from April to June, depending, apparently, on location. The nest is under a sheltering object, usually a flattened one, with the eggs being attached to the undersurface. Clutches of 37 to 67 eggs have been reported for *N. beyeri* and from 32 to 193 for *N. maculosus*.

Necturus are opportunistic feeders, with crawfish and annelid worms being dominant dietary items. Fish and other forms of vertebrate life are occasionally eaten. *Necturus* feed throughout the year, but venture from shelter mostly at night and during periods when the water is turbid, at which times they are less susceptible to being caught by large predatory fish. Hook-and-line fishermen occasionally catch *Necturus*, especially *N. maculosus*.

FAMILY SALAMANDRIDAE — NEWTS

The newts and their allies, represented by 15 genera with about 43 species, occur in Europe, Asia, northern Africa, and North America. The family includes a wide variety of rather generalized forms, most of which are Old World.

GENUS *NOTOPTHALMUS* Rafinesque

This genus contains 3 species, all found in eastern North America. One of these occurs in Alabama.

Notopthalmus viridescens (Rafinesque)

Four subspecies of this newt are recognized, 2 of which occur in Alabama.

Notopthalmus viridescens viridescens (Rafinesque)

Red-spotted Newt

Description (Fig. 161) A rather small, colorful salamander attaining a maximum total length of around 120 mm. Adults aquatic, but lacking gills except in neotenic individuals; dorsum yellowish olive to greenish brown with a scattering of black spots and a series of black-bordered red spots down each side; venter yellow with scattered small, black spots.

Tail of adult male more strongly compressed and deeper than that of female; hind legs of adult male enlarged, with horny excresences on lower surfaces, those of female not enlarged, lacking horny excresences.

Eft orange to red with 2 series of black-bordered red spots on dorsum; skin of eft spinose in contrast to smooth or slightly granular in adult.

Alabama distribution: (Fig. 162) Generally, the upland regions, intergrading with *N. v. louisianensis* along a broad front paralleling the Fall Line.

Habits: The optimal habitat for adult red-spotted newts is a quiet pool or pond, preferably one teeming with invertebrate life but lacking fish. They occur in quiet pools in some small streams, but are seldom abundant in stream habitats. Newts are neither fast nor elusive, and are easily captured with a seine or dipnet.

The red-spotted newt's life history deviates considerably from that of a "typical" salamander. A terrestrial immature stage, called the eft, is interposed between a gilled, aquatic larval form and an aquatic, non-gilled adult. Efts are usually found under rocks, logs, or other objects and in Alabama are less frequently encountered than adults.

FIG. 161. *Notopthalmus viridescens viridescens* x *louisianensis* (Lee County). The specimen shown here is an intergrade between the subspecies *N. v. viridescens*, the red-spotted newt, and *N. v. louisianensis*, the central newt. The ground color of dorsum is olive, and each side has a row of small red spots. (Photo by Robert Shealy.)

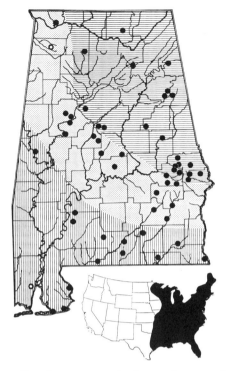

FIG. 162. Distribution of *Notopthalmus viridescens* and subspecific variation in Alabama. Horizontal hatching indicates the presumed range of *N. v. viridescens,* the red-spotted newt, and vertical hatching, the range of *N. v. louisianensis,* the central newt. The zone of intergradation is indicated by stippling. Solid symbols indicate localities from which the author examined specimens. Circles are literature records believed to be valid. The small map depicts approximately the known range of the species *N. viridescens* in the United States.

some parts of the species range the eft stage is omitted; neotenic individuals are not uncommon. Mecham (1967) reviewed the literature on this species.

Notopthalmus viridescens louisianensis (Walterstorff) Central Newt

Description: Generally similar to *N. v. viridescens* except as follows: red dorsal spots greatly reduced in size and intensity or, more frequently, absent; black spots reduced in size; body build more slender than in nominate form; and total length less (to approximately 100 mm as opposed to up to 120 mm maximum).

Alabama distribution: (Fig. 162) The Coastal Plain to within about 50 miles of the Fall Line, where intergradation with *N. v. viridescens* begins.

Habits: Generally similar to those of *N. v. viridescens.*

Breeding occurs in late winter and early spring. Fertilization is accomplished by means of a spermatophore. This is preceded by a period of courtship activity during which the male straddles the female, holding on with the hind limbs. The eggs are deposited singly and glued to stems and leaves of aquatic plants or other submerged objects. In

ORDER TRACHYSTOMATA—SIRENS

The sirens are included as a family within the salamanders by many workers. All are permanently aquatic and gilled throughout life. They have small, lidless eyes, well-developed front limbs, and an eel-like body. Hind limbs are lacking. Sirens occur in the Coastal Plain from Maryland to the Rio Grande Valley in Texas and Mexico, and in the Mississippi River system northward into Illinois and Indiana. Two genera with 3 species are included within a single family, Sirenidae. Two species are known from

Alabama, and the third has been collected in the Florida Panhandle within 20 miles of the Alabama boundary.

Siren intermedia Le Conte

Three subspecies of this species are recognized. One of these, *S. i. intermedia,* the easternmost, occurs in Alabama and another, *S. i. nettingi,* has been reported (Caldwell and Howell, 1966). For reasons indicated below, I consider the population on which that report was based to be intergradient between *S. i. nettingi* and the nominate form.

Siren intermedia intermedia Le Conte
Eastern Lesser Siren

Description: (Fig. 163) An elongate, aquatic amphibian attaining a maximum length of about 380 mm. Body eel-like; front limbs present, hind limbs lacking; permanently gilled, gills in 3 pairs, their rachises ranging in character from short and knobby to fairly long and plumose; tail compressed, with a fin. Dorsum brown, gray, or nearly black, sometimes dark-spotted; venter similarly colored but lighter. Juveniles usually with an orange or red spot near the tip of the snout, this connected to a facial stripe of the same color extending on each side to the gills; head markings becoming obscure with age; occipital markings characteristic of juvenile *S. i. nettingi* lacking.

Remarks: In this subspecies the number of costal grooves typically ranges from 31 to 34, the usual number 33. *Siren lacertina*, which is sympatric with *S. i. intermedia* in much of the Lower Coastal Plain, usually has 36 to 39 costal grooves.

Of those Alabama specimens of *S. i. intermedia* examined on which costal grooves could be counted accurately, two had 31, eight had 32, twenty had 33, and one had 34. The geographic distribution and size of the samples available were inadequate to determine whether geographic variation in this character occurs.

Most larvae examined conformed to previously published descriptions, but several lacked any trace of head markings. Some of the unmarked larvae were collected in Lake Jackson, Covington County, and the others in central Mobile County; both localities are in the Lower Coastal Plain.

FIG. 163. *Siren intermedia intermedia,* the eastern lesser siren (Macon County). This aquatic amphibian has external gills and 1 pair of limbs. It is smaller and has fewer costal grooves than the greater siren.

Alabama distribution: (Fig. 164) The Coastal Plain, except for the western portion of the Fall Line Hills, and possibly other areas of central western Alabama, where intergradation with *S. i. nettingi* occurs. (See account of that subspecies.)

Habits: The habits of the eastern and western lesser sirens are not known to differ significantly. Both forms are permanently aquatic and inhabit swamps and weedy ponds, pools, lakes, and sloughs. Streams with well-defined margins and large, open bodies of water with little aquatic vegetation seldom support populations of lesser sirens. Lesser sirens are mostly nocturnal, spending the day buried in the mud, in burrows, or concealed in vegetation.

Some suitable habitats dry up periodically. During such adverse periods, the sirens may burrow into the bottom and encapsulate in the mud, or seek refuge in crawfish burrows, a habit they share with *Amphiuma means* and possibly other amphiumas.

Lesser sirens are opportunistic feeders, but rely heavily on aquatic arthropods and worms for food. Algae and other vegetable matter are often present in the guts in considerable amounts. Little is known of the breeding habits. The few reports available indicate that nesting takes place in winter and early spring. A nest of *S. i. nettingi* has been found in a depression in the mud on the bottom of a pond. The mode of fertilization is unknown.

One curious aspect of the biology of lesser sirens is their tendency to emit clicking noises when disturbed or excited. The sounds have been recorded using an underwater microphone, and research continues in an effort to determine the significance of the phenomenon. The greater siren also produces sound, which is audible several feet away even when the animal is out of water. Martof (1973a) reviewed the literature on *S. intermedia*.

Siren intermedia nettingi Goin
Western Lesser Siren

Description: Differs chiefly from *S. i. intermedia* in the following respects: size somewhat larger, up to about 460 mm in total length; costal grooves more numerous, mostly between 34 and 36, the usual number 35; color lighter, typically slate gray or olive; spots or flecks on dorsum usually present and more conspicuous than on *S. i. intermedia;* venter usually light-spotted; juveniles of *S. i. nettingi* with a light band extending across the occiput which is lacking in those of nominate form.

Alabama distribution: (Fig. 164)

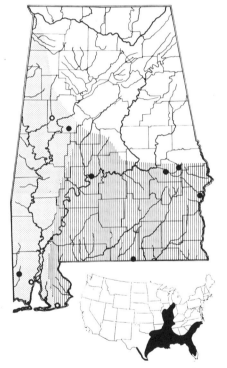

FIG. 164. Distribution of *Siren intermedia* and subspecific variation in Alabama. Vertical hatching indicates the presumed range of *S. i. intermedia*, the eastern lesser siren in Alabama. The stippled area is the zone of intergradation between *S. i. intermedia* and *S. i. nettingi*, the western lesser siren. Solid symbols indicate localities from which the author examined specimens. Circles are literature records believed to be valid. The small map depicts approximately the known range of the species *S. intermedia* in the United States.

Caldwell and Howell (op. cit.) identified a series of lesser sirens from Sipsey Swamp, near Shirley in Tuscaloosa County, as *S. i. nettingi.* They stated that "the top of the head, dorsum, and sides are slate gray, lacking the minute black spots typical of the Mississippi Valley *S. i. nettingi,*" but that "otherwise the coloration agrees with the original description given by Goin (1942)." Larvae were said to agree with the description of those of *S. i. nettingi.* In costal groove counts, nine specimens had 34 and nine had 33. On the basis of the information submitted by these investigators and on the geographic probability, I consider the Sipsey Swamp population to be intergradient between *S. i. nettingi* and *S. i. intermedia.* Another record of *S. intermedia* from Tuscaloosa County is based on a larva in the Auburn Museum collected from Big Sandy Creek. A Macon County specimen referred to by Caldwell and Howell (op. cit.) belongs to *S. i. intermedia.*

The Tuscaloosa County populations and one represented by a specimen from Dallas County are the only ones recorded for the species from western Alabama north of Mobile County. Lesser sirens undoubtedly occur locally throughout the intervening area, but their subspecific identity must await the acquisition of representative specimens.

Habits: See "Habits" under *S. i. intermedia.*

Siren lacertina Linnaeus
Greater Siren

Description: (Fig. 165) An elongate amphibian attaining a maximum total length of around 915 mm. Ultsch (1973), who studied the species, reported that the largest specimen he examined was 881 mm in length. Body eel-like, becoming stout with age; tail compressed, with a fin; permanently gilled, gills in 3 pairs; forelimbs present, hindlimbs lacking; costal grooves typically 36 to 39, the usual number 37 (specimens have been recorded from Florida with counts ranging from 33 to 40). Ground color variable, but usually some shade of gray or olive; back darker than sides; sides and belly with numerous small

FIG. 165. *Siren lacertina,* the greater siren (Henry County). This large aquatic species lacks hind limbs and is one of several eel-like amphibians called "Congo eel."

greenish spots and dashes, these less obvious on preserved specimens; dark spots visible on head, back, and sides of some individuals.

Remarks: Neill (1949b) described larvae of this species from Emanuel County, Georgia, as having a prominent light (yellowish) stripe on each side of the body, an indistinct light ventrolateral stripe, and a clear, yellowish white dorsal fin. The edge of the upper lip was said to be bordered by a light line. On the other hand, Duellman and Schwartz (1958) examined larvae from southern Florida and found no indications of lateral or ventrolateral light stripes. These larvae also lacked the clear dorsal fin. Instead, the dorsal fin was heavily pigmented with dark brown. A faint postocular stripe was present on most individuals. These workers suggested that larvae of greater sirens may vary geographically in details of color pattern. Larvae of S. i. intermedia apparently do, as is indicated by the specimens I have examined from Alabama. The larvae of S. lacertina have not, to my knowledge, been collected in Alabama.

Alabama distribution: (Fig. 166) Local in the Lower Coastal Plain westward, perhaps, to Mobile Bay. A population in a pond in Henry County, in southeastern Alabama, conforms closely to the general description of the species given above. A siren tentatively assigned to S. lacertina collected in the Fish River in Baldwin County does not conform. This specimen, which has 39 costal grooves and is 520 mm long, has a silvery gray ground color. The back, sides, and tail are profusely marked with conspicuous dark gray spots and vermiculations. The venter is unmarked. Additional specimens from that locality, as well as from some other localities to the east, will be needed to determine whether the specimen on hand is correctly assigned to species.

Habits: This large, eel-like amphibian is permanently aquatic and is found in ponds, lakes, sloughs, oxbows, and sluggish streams. In contrast to S. intermedia, it is often found in considerable numbers in large, open bodies of water. In Ala-

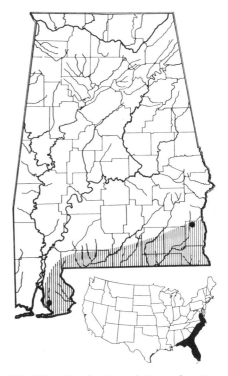

FIG. 166. Distribution of *Siren lacertina*, the greater siren. The presumed range in Alabama is indicated by hatching. Symbols indicate localities from which the author examined specimens. The circles are literature records believed to be valid. The small map depicts approximately the known range in the United States.

bama, specimens have been caught at night by fishing for them in a weedy pond in Henry County, and by "shocking" for fish in the Fish River in Baldwin County. Fish River is a sluggish, dark-water stream which empties into Mobile Bay.

Like lesser sirens and amphiumas, greater sirens burrow into the bottom when their habitats dry up. Carr (1940) found viable individuals in spherical chambers in the peat beneath the surface of a dry depression that formerly had held water. He further noted that some of the animals emitted "plaintive yelps," even after they had been excavated. The sounds reminded him of the call of *Hyla cinerea,* the green treefrog, heard from a distance.

Greater sirens feed on a variety of aquatic organisms, including crawfish, worms, insect adults and their larvae, and occasionally on fish. Large quantities of vegetable matter are often found in the stomachs of this species, as well as in those of *S. intermedia,* suggesting an omnivorous diet. Their reproductive hab-

its are poorly known. Ultsch (1973), who studied *S. lacertina* in Florida, summarized the available information. He concluded that the eggs are laid in shallow water, singly or in small groups, and that fertilization is probably external. He further concluded that, in Florida, breeding takes place mostly in February and March. Martof (1973b) reviewed the literature on *S. lacertina.*

ORDER CROCODILIA—CROCODILIANS

This order contains the only living reptilian remnants of the subclass Archosauria, which, mostly as dinosaurs, dominated the earth for 100 million years during the Mesozoic era. All crocodilians are aquatic, carnivorous, and oviparous. The male has a single penis, which is everted through the vent during copulation.

The order is represented on all continents except Europe and Antarctica, and

on many islands as well. Twenty-one species, several of which may be nearing extinction, are recognized and are usually categorized into 3 families. The American alligator, *Alligator mississippiensis,* is the only living crocodilian native to Alabama and is 1 of only 2 species native to the United States. The American alligator, along with 6 other crocodilian species, are placed in the family Alligatoridae. Four genera are included within

FIG. 167. *Alligator mississippiensis,* the American Alligator (Louisiana). The alligator persists in considerable numbers in the swampy country above Mobile Bay and is making a remarkable comeback in the Eufaula National Wildlife Refuge. (Photo by James Dobie.)

the family; the genus *Alligator* includes the only Old World representative, a form confined to the Yangtze River system in China.

Alligator mississippiensis (Daudin)
American Alligator

Description: (Fig. 167) A huge, aquatic reptile attaining a maximum total length of around 4,875 mm. Individuals over 12 feet long are now rare. The alligator is an unmistakable member of our native reptilian fauna and needs no de-

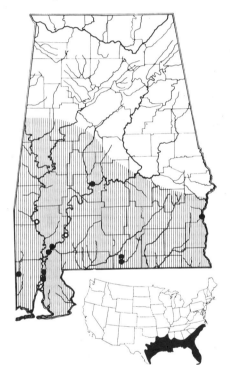

FIG. 168. Distribution of *Alligator mississippiensis*, the American alligator. The hatched area in Alabama has scattered individuals and populations of alligators and has habitat and climatic conditions thought to be capable of supporting breeding populations. Solid symbols are recent sightings by competent authorities of individuals thought to represent breeding populations. Circles are literature records of such individuals. Records which in the author's judgment represent recent releases are not shown. The small map depicts the presumed original range of the alligator in the United States.

tailed description here. In recent years caimans, close relatives of alligators, have been imported from South America for sale as pets and are sometimes mistaken for alligators. Caimans have a curved bony ridge in front of the eyes which is lacking in alligators, and are thus readily distinguishable from the latter. Caimans are not known to have established breeding populations anywhere in Alabama.

Alabama distribution: (Fig. 168) Apparently the alligator was at one time generally distributed throughout the Lower Coastal Plain in Alabama and occurred along the major streams and some of their larger tributaries northward nearly to the Fall Line. Today they persist in sizable numbers only in the anastomosing streams, lakes, and swamps which constitute the delta of the Mobile Bay drainage and in places where they are rigidly protected, such as Eufaula National Wildlife Refuge in Barbour County. Occasional individuals are sighted on the Tombigbee River as far north as Pickens County, on the Cahaba up to Marion in Perry County, and on the Alabama River up to Selma in Dallas County. Some private landowners in Alabama are in sympathy with the alligator and afford it protection on their property, accounting for some scattered reports of its occurrence.

Habits: Alligators make their homes in swamps, lakes, sloughs, and sluggish streams. Unless subjected to nearly constant exposure to people, they tend to be shy and wary and keep their distance. Normally, alligators do not attack people unless seriously provoked, and there is seldom cause for concern that an alligator is around. Most injuries by alligators have been inflicted on people who were teasing them while they were on land, attempting to catch them, or who have not heeded the advice to stay away from apparently "tame" alligators.

Alligators mate during the spring, usually at night. The male attracts the female, which he exceeds considerably in size, by bellowing loudly and giving off a musky secretion from glands under his chin. Sometime in May or June the female constructs a mound-shaped nest of leaves, mud, and rotting organic material about 7 feet in diameter and 3 feet high. Typically the nest is located fairly close to the water. The eggs are deposited in the center of the nest. Usually the clutch size is between 30 and 70, although up to 88 eggs have been recorded. The female then covers the eggs and spends much of her time in the vicinity of the nest until the time of hatching. During the incubation period she may contribute moisture to the nest by repeatedly crawling over it after she has entered and left the water. She also provides some protection against predators and will in some instances seek to drive away a human trespasser, claims to the contrary notwithstanding. I personally witnessed a display of aggression toward a human intruder by a female guarding a nest in the Okefenokee Swamp in Georgia.

The female reportedly rakes away the roof of the nest at the time of hatching, being stimulated to do so by yelping noises made by the hatching baby alligators. Some herpetologists question whether the female displays this behavior. In any event, the young are left to their own devices at an early age, certainly by the time they enter the water and begin to feed. Young alligators grow surprisingly fast, attaining a length of 5 to 6 feet in as many years, after which the growth rate begins to slow. During the first year predation may take a heavy toll. Alligators over 2 feet long have few natural enemies, except for larger alligators.

Alligators will eat almost any animal they can overpower. Insects, crustaceans, birds, fish, and mammals are all eaten, as well as turtles and snakes. Poisonous snakes are eaten without hesitation; cottonmouths are particularly susceptible to alligator predation and are seldom abundant in ponds where alligators are numerous. There are some indications that large alligators may suppress populations of beavers, which have become a nuisance in many parts of Alabama. Research is underway at Auburn University to investigate the efficacy of using alligators as beaver-control agents.

Should the alligator prove useful in controlling or suppressing beavers, it would gain many new allies among rural landowners, who are in a better position than anyone else to promote its survival. This would go far toward ensuring that the alligator would continue to "help keep up the fading color of our land" (quote from Archie Carr, 1967). Neill (1971) included a comprehensive account of the alligator in his book on crocodilians of the world.

ORDER SQUAMATA—LIZARDS AND SNAKES

Suborder Lacertilia—Lizards

The lizards comprise 19 families with about 3,000 species. They are generally found in greatest abundance in regions with warm, dry climates, such as the southwestern portion of the United States. Lizards exploit an amazing variety of habitats and modes of existence. Most are essentially ground-surface dwellers. Some, however, spend virtually their entire lives underground, others are almost completely arboreal, and a few are rather strongly aquatic.

The limbs of most lizards are well developed, although in many species they are either reduced in size or lacking altogether. Included among the latter are the 2 species of glass lizards found in Alabama that are legless and often mistaken for snakes.

The food habits of lizards vary extensively. Most are predatory, feeding on a variety of small animal life, especially insects and other arthropods. All the lizards of Alabama fall into this category. Many lizards, however, are vegetarians, and a few are scavengers.

Some lizards, including all that occur in our state, lay eggs, while others give birth to the young. Fertilization is internal, with copulation following a typically brief courtship. The male's copulatory organs are a pair of hemipenes, which when not in use are situated internally in the basal portion of the tail.

Only 2 lizards are known to be venomous, the Gila monster of the southwestern United States and Mexico and the beaded lizard of Mexico. Among the Alabama lizards only the broad-headed skink, *Eumeces laticeps*, is likely to bite hard enough even to break the skin, and it will not bite unless restrained.

Eleven species of lizards, distributed among 4 families, are native to Alabama. Two alien species apparently have established breeding populations in the state and are discussed in the section on introduced species (p. 25).

FAMILY ANGUIDAE – LATERAL-FOLD LIZARDS

This family, containing 10 genera and about 75 species, is widely distributed in both hemispheres, but is absent in Australia and in Africa south of the Sahara. Some of its members are legless. Two genera occur in the United States, 1 of which is represented in Alabama.

GENUS *OPHISAURUS* Daudin

Eleven species are included within this genus, which occurs in eastern North America, northern Africa, southern Europe, and southern Asia. Two species are found in Alabama.

Ophisaurus attenuatus Baird

Two subspecies of this lizard are recognized, 1 of which occurs in Alabama.

Ophisaurus attenuatus longicaudus McConkey
Eastern Slender Glass Lizard

Description: (Fig. 169, 170) An elongate, long-tailed, legless lizard attaining a maximum snout-vent length of around 330 mm and a total length of around 1,065 mm. (The former measurement is that of a specimen from Shelby County, Alabama, AM 3036, which is the largest of its species in terms of snout-vent length known to me.) Scales squarish to rhomboidal, hard and glossy, forming straight longitudinal and transverse series. Lower sides with deep grooves running along each side of the body. Dorsal ground color tan to brownish; dorsum of juveniles and some adults with a median dark stripe; dorsum of adults and some juveniles with irregular light, black-bordered crossbars which become more pronounced with increasing age; white markings on dorsum, when present, cen-

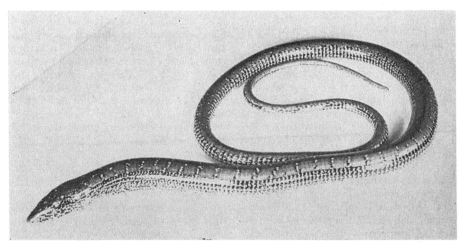

FIG. 169. *Ophisaurus attenuatus longicaudus*, the eastern slender glass lizard, adult (Macon County). This glass lizard has dark markings below the lateral groove. Glass lizards are sometimes erroneously referred to as "glass snakes" or "jointed snakes."

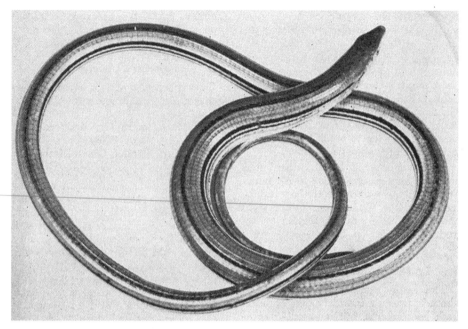

FIG. 170. *Ophisaurus attenuatus longicaudus,* the eastern slender glass lizard, subadult (Cleburne County). The adult of this species develops crossbars with age.

trally located on scales. Sides above lateral groove brown with 2 light stripes, these sometimes becoming obliterated in large adults. Venter light, usually with 2 rows of dark spots forming longitudinal stripes immediately below the lateral grooves.

In this subspecies, tail length in adults is greater than 2.4 times snout-vent length.

Remarks: Geographic variation among Alabama populations was not evident upon examination of the relatively small number of specimens available. Several specimens, however, deserve comment. In 2, AM 5175 and 11836, the characteristic dark striping under the lateral grooves is lacking except for faint indications of the uppermost stripe on the posterior region. Both are unusually light-colored and both are from northeastern Alabama (Etowah and Cleburne counties, respectively). AM 21007 and 18997 from the Lower Coastal Plain (Baldwin and Covington counties, respectively) are juveniles which show the

tendency to become crossbarred, as in adults.

Alabama distribution: (Fig. 171) Statewide, but more common in the upland provinces.

Habits: The slender glass lizard is most abundant in brushy, cut-over woodlands, around abandoned farms, and along stream courses. It is given to burrowing and is often unearthed by plowing. In southern Alabama where the species is sympatric with the eastern glass lizard, *O. ventralis,* it is not particularly common and is seldom found except in well-drained situations where the soil is loose and friable. (See "Habits" under *O. ventralis.*)

Many of the observations on glass lizards in the Southeast were made before McConkey (1954) showed that not 1 but 3 species were involved. Therefore, it is often impossible to determine the species to which the observation applies. Apparently, the females of all *Ophisaurus* lay eggs and attend the nest until the eggs hatch. Clutch size in *O. a. attenua-*

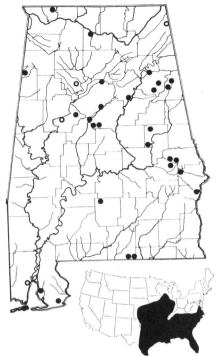

tus ranges from 6 to 17 (Fitch, 1970). Among the *O. a. longicaudus* from Alabama that I examined were 2 gravid females with 5 and 10 oviducal eggs. The captives I have had were nervous, but they fed readily on grasshoppers, roaches, and crickets. They made no attempt to bite. Holman (1971a) reviewed the literature on *O. attenuatus*.

A popular herpetological myth concerns a "snake" which shatters into pieces when struck. Later, it is said, the pieces miraculously reunite, and the "snake" crawls away. There is little doubt that the limbless glass lizards are at the root of this fallacy. Their long tails break readily, and it is likely that a blow across the tail region would cause breakage at several places. Although the animal will ultimately regenerate a new tail, there is, of course, no chance that the detached pieces will come back together. Glass lizards are easily distinguished from snakes in that they possess eyelids and ear openings.

FIG. 171. Distribution of *Ophisaurus attenuatus longicaudus,* the eastern slender glass lizard. This form is believed to occur statewide, or nearly so, in Alabama. Solid symbols indicate localities from which the author examined specimens. Circles are literature records believed to be valid. The small map depicts approximately the known range of the species *O. attenuatus* in the United States.

Ophisarus ventralis (Linnaeus)
Eastern Glass Lizard

Description: (Fig. 172) An elongate, long-tailed, legless lizard attaining a maximum snout-vent length of around 290 mm and a total length of around 1,080 mm. Scalation generally similar to that

FIG. 172. *Ophisaurus ventralis,* the eastern glass lizard (Lee County). This glass lizard usually lacks dark markings below the lateral groove and does not develop a barred dorsum with age.

of *O. a. longicaudus;* lateral groove present.

Dorsum tan in young, becoming brownish or greenish with age; dorsum lacking definite mid-dorsal stripe, but frequently with several longitudinal rows of small, dark spots; dorsum of many individuals becoming light-flecked; white markings, when present, peripherally located on scales. Sides above lateral groove with a longitudinal dark band containing rows of light flecks, band obscure or absent on dark individuals.

Venter white in young, becoming yellow with age; distinct dark striping below lateral groove, a characteristic of most *O. attenuatus,* usually lacking. (Three of the 52 specimens examined had one dark ventrolateral stripe.)

Alabama distribution: (Fig. 173) Generally distributed throughout most of the Coastal Plain, local in the Piedmont, Blue Ridge, and Ridge and Valley regions.

Habits: This is by far the most common "glass snake" of the Alabama Coastal Plain, except possibly in the northwestern portion. Eastern glass lizards occur in a variety of habitats but seem to prefer damp or mesic situations. They often turn up in overgrown vacant lots and under piles of debris in residential areas. Early morning and late afternoon are favored times of prowling. The numbers found dead on highways indicate that they move about rather extensively.

The diet consists mostly of insects and spiders; several reports state that other lizards and small snakes are also eaten. The female lays the eggs in protected places and broods them until they hatch. I found an attended nest with 7 eggs under a tire lying at the edge of an abandoned airstrip. James Keeler recorded in his field notes a nest of 8 eggs beneath a heavy paper bag near a pond in Montgomery County. The female was coiled over the eggs, which were in a slight depression. McConkey (1954) reported preserved gravid females with 8 and 10 oviducal eggs.

Captives are nervous and alert, but feed readily on insects, spiders, and bits of raw, lean meat. They must be handled

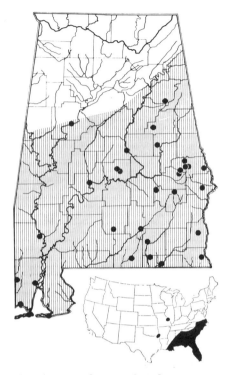

FIG. 173. Distribution of *Ophisaurus ventralis,* the eastern glass lizard. The presumed range in Alabama is indicated by hatching. Symbols indicate localities from which the author examined specimens. The small map depicts approximately the known range in the United States.

with care, however, to avoid breaking the tail. Holman (1971b) reviewed the literature on *O. ventralis.*

FAMILY IGUANIDAE – IGUANID LIZARDS

This family, with its more than 50 genera, is the largest in the New World. It is represented in the Old World by only 3 genera. Alabama has 2 native species, each belonging to a different genus.

GENUS *ANOLIS* Daudin

This genus is mostly tropical, occurring from southeastern United States southward into Bolivia and Paraguay. With about 200 species, it is the largest genus of the family. One species occurs in Alabama.

FIG. 174. *Anolis carolinensis carolinensis,* the green anole (Choctaw County). Color varies from green and gray-green to brown. This lizard is often called "chameleon" in Alabama.

Anolis carolinensis carolinensis Voigt
Green Anole

Description: (Fig. 174) A small or medium-sized lizard attaining a maximum snout-vent length of about 70 mm. Scales small, keeled, non-overlapping; ventral lamellae on next-to-last joint of toes expanded to form an elongate pad; males with an extensible reddish dewlap or throat fan; head long and pointed; color green, brown, or grayish, occasionally with an irregular, mid-dorsal light stripe.

Alabama distribution: (Fig. 175) Apparently statewide. Uncommon to rare in extreme northern Alabama, becoming increasingly common southward.

Habits: This lizard, called "chameleon" by many who recognize it, is best known for its ability to change color. It may be green, brown, or gray, depending on its "mood," the nature of the environment, and possibly other factors. Frightened or angered individuals, if not green initially, will usually turn green. At night, presumably when asleep, they are pale grayish in color. Mostly, however, chromatic fluctuations of anoles are unpredictable.

The green anole is largely arboreal and not too choosy about its habitat as long as vegetation and shade are abundant. In southern Alabama, anoles often abound in shady residential areas of cities and

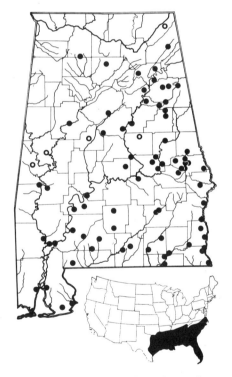

FIG. 175. Distribution of *Anolis carolinensis carolinensis,* the green anole. This form is believed to occur statewide, or nearly so, in Alabama. Solid symbols indicate localities from which the author examined specimens. Circles are literature records believed to be valid. The small map depicts approximately the known range of the species *A. carolinensis* in the United States.

FIG. 176. *Sceloporus undulatus undulatus* x *hyacinthinus,* fence lizard (Lee County). The spine-tipped scales on this common lizard will serve to distinguish it from other native Alabama lizards. The 2 subspecies found in Alabama are distinguishable chiefly on the basis of dorsal scale count.

towns. The hibernating instinct seems poorly developed in this species in comparison with other Alabama lizards. During the winter, individuals may be found under wood chips, pieces of bark, and in other relatively exposed situations where they are highly susceptible to temperatures below freezing. This factor doubtless contributes to their scarcity in extreme northern Alabama.

The breeding season in *A. carolinensis* extends throughout most of the summer. The eggs are laid one at a time in excavations about 1 to 2 inches deep in moist soil, sphagnum, leaf litter, or rotting wood. The male anole is strongly territorial. When approached by another male, or otherwise intimidated, he ex-

tends the conspicuous red dewlap, or throat fan. This behavior is accompanied by a few bobs of the head. If the other male continues his trespass, a heated battle is likely to ensue.

Captives should be provided with insects. Water should be supplied by sprinkling it over objects in the cage.

GENUS *SCELOPORUS* Wiegmann

This genus occurs from Canada to Mexico and contains about 95 species.

Sceloporus undulatus (Latreille)

Seven subspecies of this wide-ranging species are recognized. Two of these occur in Alabama.

TABLE 3. VARIATION IN NUMBER OF MID-DORSAL SCALES IN *Sceloporus undulatus* IN ALABAMA (COUNTED POSTERIORLY TO A POINT EVEN WITH BACK EDGE OF THIGH)

Section[1]	No. spec.	Number of mid-dorsal scales													Mean
		31	32	33	34	35	36	37	38	39	40	41	42	43	44	
NW	10							1	2		3	1	1	1	1	40.3
NE	11					1		1	2	1	3	2	1			39.2
WNC	36			1		2	6	8	6	7	4	1		1		37.8
ENC	32			2		1	4	4	5	6	5	5				37.3
WSC	18			1	2	1	3	6	1	2		1			1	37.1
ESC	69		1	5	9	10	17	15	5	4	2	1				36.0
SW	34	2	5	1	4	8	5	6	3							34.9
SE	21			1	5	5	3	3	1							34.8

[1] To show the geographic variation in this character, the state was divided into 8 roughly equal parts, 4 on each side of a north-to-south midline.

Sceloporus undulatus undulatus
(Latreille)
Southern Fence Lizard

Description: (Fig. 176) A medium-sized lizard attaining a maximum snout-vent length of around 85 mm. Body stout; scales keeled, overlapping, each with a spine. Color varies with age and sex. Females and young gray to brown or yellowish brown with dark wavy cross-bars, their venters light with small dark flecks and usually with traces of blue. Adult males dark gray to dark brown or bronze, the crossbars becoming obscure with increasing age; venter of adult males with conspicuous blue or blue-green patches, the intervening areas becoming black in some individuals.

In this subspecies dorsal scales are larger than in S. u. hyacinthinus, the other subspecies occurring in Alabama. Counting posteriorly from the back of the head to a point even with the posterior edge of the thighs, mid-dorsal scales usually number less than 38, as opposed to 38 or more in S. u. hyacinthinus (Table 3).

Habits: This abundant lizard prefers dry, open woodlands, abandoned farm buildings, rock outcrops, and piles of old lumber. Called rusty-backed lizard by most rural citizens of Alabama, it is usually conspicuous because of its size and its tendency to bask in exposed places and move readily when approached.

It usually tries to escape enemies by climbing the nearest tree or wall. However, by approaching the tree, peering around the trunk very carefully to determine the lizard's position, and then grabbing at a point level with or slightly above the lizard's head, the collector is often rewarded with success.

The male fence lizard is strongly territorial, advertising his presence to other members of the species with an elaborate ceremony involving head-bobbing and "push-ups." Another male may challenge the territory owner but more frequently will move away and avoid direct confrontation. If the other lizard is a female, mating may ensue. The female lays clutches of 6 to 15 eggs in a cavity she

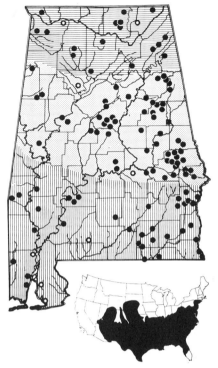

FIG. 177. Distribution of Sceloporus undulatus and subspecific variation in Alabama. Horizontal hatching indicates the presumed range of S. u. hyacinthinus, the northern fence lizard, and vertical hatching, the range of S. u. undulatus, the southern fence lizard. the zone of intergradation is indicated by stippling. Solid symbols indicate localities from which the author examined specimens. Circles are literature records believed to be valid. The small map depicts approximately the known range of the species S. undulatus in the United States.

digs in the soil. After covering the eggs, she pays no further attention to the nest. In Alabama, nesting activity usually begins in May. Apparently, 2 or more clutches of eggs may be laid each season. The life history of the southern fence lizard in Georgia was studied by Crenshaw (1955).

Sceloporus undulatus hyacinthinus
(Green)
Northern Fence Lizard

Description: Similar to S. u. undulatus except in having, usually, a mid-dorsal scale count of 38 or greater instead of 37 or less and, as adults, in being somewhat lighter in color.

Alabama distribution: (Fig. 177) Generally, the northern one-third of the state, intergrading with S. u. undulatus southward to the range of that subspecies.

Alabama distribution: (Fig. 177) Based on mid-dorsal scale count, the approximate range of the subspecies S. u. undulatus was determined to be the southern one-third of the state (Table 3). Intergradation with S. u. hyacinthinus occurs northward in a wide belt across central Alabama.

Habits: In Alabama, similar to those of S. u. undulatus.

FAMILY SCINCIDAE – SKINKS

This large cosmopolitan family contains about 49 genera with over 600 species, only a relatively few of which occur in the New World. Three genera are represented in the United States, 2 of which occur in Alabama.

GENUS *EUMECES* Wiegmann

This genus occurs in North and Central America, Africa, and Asia and contains about 40 species. Five species are found in Alabama. Three of these, *E. fasciatus, E. inexpectatus,* and *E. laticeps,* are closely related members of the five-lined skink group and in the juvenile stage are similar in general appearance.

Eumeces anthracinus (Baird)

Two subspecies of this lizard are currently recognized. One of these occurs in Alabama and the other exerts its influence in intergradient populations.

Eumeces anthracinus anthracinus (Baird)
Northern Coal Skink

Description: A fairly small lizard attaining a maximum snout-vent length of around 65 mm. Scales smooth, shiny, overlapping; postnasals lacking; postmental single (skinks of five-lined group have 2 postmentals); median subcaudals wider than those in adjacent rows. Each side of body with a dark lateral band bordered by a lateral and dorsolateral light stripe; an unbranched mid-dorsal light

FIG. 178. *Eumeces anthracinus pluvialis,* the southern coal skink (Blount County). The specimen shown laid eggs shortly after being photographed. In the coal skink, the postmental scale is undivided.

stripe often present, this always less conspicuous than dorsolaterals.

In this subspecies, head with a light stripe passing through posterior upper labials and continuing to ear; scale rows at mid-body usually 25 or fewer; juvenal pattern similar to adult; dorsum lacking dark markings between dorsolateral light stripes.

Alabama distribution: (Fig. 179) Genetic influence from this subspecies, as it is currently characterized, is detectable in coal skink populations in the northwesternmost portion of the species range in Alabama (Table 4). This area is essentially the northwestern portion of the Fall Line Hills and the adjacent portion of Sand Mountain in northwestern Alabama. In number of scale rows at mid-body, coal skinks from that area resemble *E. a. pluvialis*, but the labial striping is that of *E. a. anthracinus*. Coal skinks from other portions of the range in Alabama are fairly easily referable to *E. a. pluvialis*.

Habits: See "Habits" under *E. a. pluvialis*.

Eumeces anthracinus pluvialis Cope
Southern Coal Skink

Description: (Fig. 178) Differs from the nominate subspecies in having the following: posterior upper labials with light centers, sutures in between upper labials dark, producing a spotted appearance; scale rows at mid-body usually 26 or more; dorsum frequently with dark stripes or rows of spots between dorsolateral light stripes; juveniles dark, without evident markings.

Alabama distribution: (Fig. 179) *Eumeces a. pluvialis* has been collected in central Alabama in the lower portions of the Ridge and Valley region (in Shelby and Bibb counties); Blue Ridge (Chilton County); along the southern edge of Sand Mountain in St. Clair County; and in the Fall Line Hills in Tuscaloosa and Bibb counties. In western Alabama records are available from the Lower Coastal Plain in Mobile County, in the Red Hills in Monroe County, and from the Transitional Zone (between the Black Belt and Red Hills) in Choctaw County. The only records for eastern Alabama are for 2 localities in Russell County in the Fall Line Hills. It is not known whether the gaps indicated on the distributional map are real or only apparent.

Habits: The habits of the 2 subspecies are apparently similar. The 2 dozen or so specimens we have collected were all caught in hilly terrain in mixed pine-hardwood forests. Five were in sandy habitats, the others in relatively rocky situations. Most were found under logs or rocks, but at least 2 were foraging. Most were in close proximity to water. Dowling (1950a) reported collecting *E.*

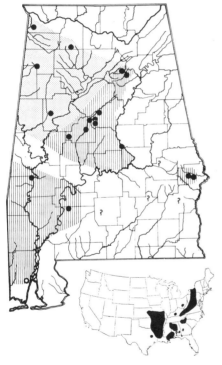

FIG. 179. Distribution of *Eumeces anthracinus* and subspecific variation in Alabama. The hatched area indicates the presumed range of *E. a. pluvialis*, the southern coal skink. The stippled area is the zone of intergradation between *E. a. pluvialis* and *E. a. anthracinus*, the northern coal skink. Solid symbols indicate localities from which the author examined specimens. The circle is a literature record believed to be valid. The small map depicts approximately the known range of the species *E. anthracinus* in the United States.

TABLE 4. SUMMARY OF CHARACTERISTICS OF INDIVIDUALS IN A SAMPLE OF ELEVEN *Eumeces anthracinus* FROM ALABAMA

AM Cat. No.	County	Mid-ventral scales	Scale rows mid-body	Number upper labials	Nature of light pigment on posterior upper labials	Nature of markings between dorsolateral light body stripes
4627	Choctaw	51	27	7-7	confined to center of scales, forming spots	each scale adjacent to dorso-lateral stripes with a dark spot
8730	Colbert	50	27	8-8	forming distinct light stripe, continuous to ear	dorsolaterals with narrow dark border, light mid-dorsal present
9356	Lawrence	52	28	7-7	forming distinct light stripe, continuous to ear	faint indication of mid-dorsal light stripe
4594	Marion	52	28	7-7	indistinct light stripe, continuous to ear	faint indication of submedian dark stripes
9363	Russell	49	27	7-7	specimen very pale, all labials light	none discernible
9780	Russell	52	27	7-7	confined to centers of scales, forming spots	faint indication of mid-dorsal light stripe
3254	Shelby	50	27	7-7	confined to centers of scales, forming spots	none discernible
3255	Shelby	50	27	7-7	confined to centers of scales, forming spots	none discernible
3256	Shelby	50	29	7-7	confined to centers of scales, forming spots	faint indication of median light stripe
3257	Shelby	55	27	7-7	confined to centers of scales, forming spots	one row of irregularly spaced small dark spots adjacent to each light stripe
3258	Shelby	51	26	7-7	confined to centers of scales, forming spots	none discernible

anthracinus from a lakeside in Tuscaloosa County.

The coal skink resembles at first glace an oversized *Scincella laterale*, but when alarmed it reacts quite differently. Whereas *Scincella* usually scurries underneath the ground litter, the coal skink usually runs or wriggles across the top.

Dowling (1950a) found a nest of 6 eggs, attended by the female, on June 10 under a piece of shale. Two of these hatched in the laboratory on July 4. A gravid female from St. Clair County contained 8 oviducal eggs when it was preserved. I witnessed copulation by a pair of captive coal skinks on March 10. The male seized the female by the neck, shifted his hold to a fold of skin just over the left leg, twisted his hindquarters under hers and effected coitus. The two remained in this position for about 1 minute without moving, following which the female terminated the act by crawling forward. This female laid 4 eggs on April 21. The young hatched on May 29 and measured approximately 24 mm in snout-vent length and 56 mm in total length.

Eumeces egregius (Baird)

Four subspecies of this southeastern skink are recognized, 1 of which occurs in Alabama.

Eumeces egregius similis McConkey
Northern Mole Skink

Description: (Fig. 180) A small, slender lizard attaining a maximum snout-vent length of about 55 mm. Scales smooth, overlapping; primary temporal lacking; limbs reduced; ear opening partially closed; body color gray or tan to brown with 2 long or short dorsolateral light stripes that begin on the head; mid-dorsal light stripe lacking.

In this subspecies, dorsolateral light stripes evident from hatching and neither widening nor diverging; tail red, reddish orange, orange, or reddish brown; scale rows at mid-body usually 18 to 21; upper labials 6 on each side. Adult males often with yellow or orange suffusion on lower sides and lips; average size of adult males somewhat less than that of females.

Alabama distribution: (Fig. 181) Local in the Piedmont, Ridge and Valley region, and Fall Line Hills westward to the Black Warrior River. Local in the Lower Coastal Plain westward at least to Baldwin County. Records for the Red Hills are confined to the eastern portion of that region. There are no records from the Black Belt.

Habits: This secretive lizard spends most of its time underground and is

FIG. 180. *Eumeces egregius similis,* the northern mole skink (Russell County). This burrowing skink has a reddish or pinkish tail. Ground color of the body ranges from gray to tan or brown.

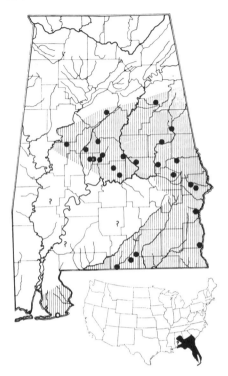

FIG. 181. Distribution of *Emeces egregius
similis*, the northern mole skink. The presumed range in Alabama is indicated by
hatching. Solid symbols indicate localities
from which the author examined specimens.
The circle is a literature record believed to
be valid. The small map depicts approximately the known range of the species *E.
egregius* in the United States.

rarely seen abroad. A frequent ecological
associate of the mole skink in the Coastal
Plain is the eastern pocket gopher, *Geomys pinetis*, a ratlike mammal mistakenly
called "salamander" by many residents
of southern Alabama. The pocket gopher
digs horizontal tunnels beneath the surface and at fairly regular intervals pushes
up the excess soil to form mounds on the
surface. The burrows apparently provide
ideal microhabitats for mole skinks, and
on warm, sunny days during late winter
and early spring, the skinks may "bask"
in the mounds. Raking through the
mounds at such times is one of the best
ways to locate these lizards. When a
mole skink is spotted, it must be secured
quickly or it will quickly wriggle out of

sight. Mole skinks are occasionally found
under logs, rocks, or other sheltering objects.

From 2 to 9 elliptical, whitish eggs
are laid in a cavity in the soil at a depth
of several inches to 6 feet. The nest is
attended by the female until the young
hatch and disperse. Mole skinks feed on
crickets, spiders, and other small arthropods. Mount (1968) reviewed the literature on *Eumeces egregius*.

Eumeces fasciatus (Linnaeus)
Five-lined Skink

Description: (Fig. 182, 183) A medium-sized lizard attaining a maximum
snout-vent length of about 85 mm. Scales
smooth, shiny, overlapping; chin with 2
postmentals; median subcaudals noticeably wider than scales in adjacent rows
(similar in this respect to 1 of its 2
close relatives in Alabama, *E. laticeps*,
but differing from the other, *E. inexpectatus*, in which median subcaudals are
about equal in width to those in adjacent
rows); upper labials usually 7; postlabials evident, usually 2 in number. Body
of juveniles and young adult females (except for venter) black or blue-black with
5 conspicuous yellowish stripes: a mid-
dorsal one, bifurcating anteriorly at back
of head and extending onto snout; 2 dorsolaterals beginning over the eyes; and
2 laterals beginning under the eyes; mid-
dorsal stripe usually somewhat wider
than that on *E. inexpectatus* or *E. laticeps*. Tail of juveniles bright blue above.
Juvenile colors and pattern becoming
faded with increasing age, especially in
adult males which may become virtually
uniform brownish; adults often with a
broad, dark, lateral stripe; heads of adult
males somewhat swollen and frequently
reddish in color.

Remarks: Occasionally a juvenile of
E. fasciatus is encountered that has one
or more features usually associated with
other Alabama members of the five-lined
skink group. Such individuals can be
identified with certainty only by experts
familiar with the total range of variation
within each form.

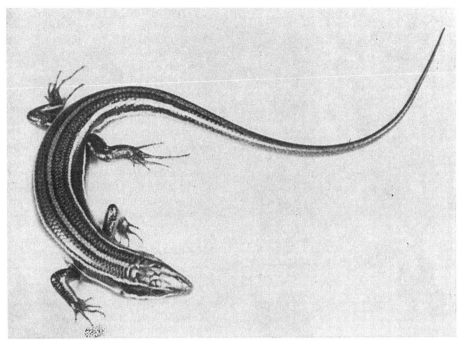

FIG. 182. *Eumeces fasciatus,* five-lined skink, adult female (Lee County). This common skink is 1 of 3 in Alabama to which the name "scorpion" is often applied erroneously.

FIG. 183. *Eumeces fasciatus,* the five-lined skink, adult male (Macon County). This is 1 of 3 species in Alabama in which the young are conspicuously striped and have bright blue tails. The males of all 3 develop reddish heads and tend to lose the dorsal striping as they increase in age.

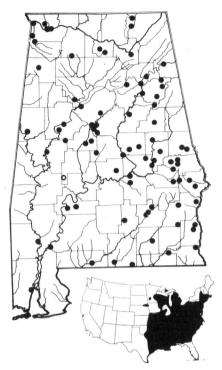

FIG. 184. Distribution of *Eumeces fasciatus,* the five-lined skink. This species is believed to occur statewide, or essentially so, in Alabama. Solid symbols indicate localities from which the author examined specimens. The circles are literature records believed to be valid. The small map depicts approximately the known range in the United States.

Alabama distribution: (Fig. 184) Statewide.

Habits: The five-lined skink, one of our most common lizards, is most often found in mesic forest habitats where it frequents rotting logs and stumps, rocky places, and trash piles. It is also common along the banks of streams in and around piles of woody debris deposited during periods of high water. Other favored habitats are abandoned farm houses and out-buildings. This species, along with *E. inexpectatus* and *E. laticeps,* is called "scorpion" throughout much of rural Alabama and erroneously believed to be venomous.

The tail of this species, as do those of other skinks, breaks off easily and when detached wiggles vigorously, becoming a source of distraction to a potential predator. When the tail is lost, a new, albeit shorter one is regenerated.

Eumeces fasciatus nests in spring and early summer in rotting logs or stumps, under rocks, and in cavities in sawdust piles. The female attends the 4 to 15 whitish eggs during incubation and assists the young in hatching. The diet of the five-lined skink consists almost entirely of arthropods. Fitch (1954) gave a comprehensive account of the life history and ecology of this species.

Eumeces inexpectatus Taylor
Southeastern Five-lined Skink

Description: (Fig. 185) A medium-sized lizard attaining a maximum snout-vent length of about 90 mm. Scales smooth, shiny, overlapping; chin with 2 postmentals; median subcaudals about the same width as those in adjacent rows (differing in this respect from each of its 2 close relatives in Alabama, *E. fasciatus* and *E. laticeps,* the median subcaudals in both of which are noticeably wider than those in adjacent rows); upper labials 7 or 8, usually followed by 2 enlarged postlabials. Body of juveniles and young adult females (except for venter) black or blue-black with 5 yellow or orange-yellow stripes: a mid-dorsal one, bifurcating anteriorly at back of head and extending onto snout; 2 dorsolaterals, beginning over the eyes; and 2 laterals, beginning under eyes. Mid-dorsal stripe relatively narrow when compared with that on *E. fasciatus.* Tail of juveniles and young adult females bright blue above. Adults, especially adult males, becoming tan or brownish in color with broad, dark lateral stripes; head of adult males becoming somewhat swollen and suffused with red.

Remarks: The range of variation in juvenile *E. fasciatus* overlaps that of juvenile *E. inexpectatus* in some characters, resulting in occasional individuals that are hard to identify with certainty.

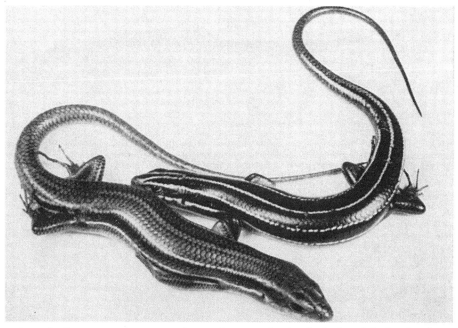

FIG. 185. *Eumeces inexpectatus,* the southeastern five-lined skink, adult female above, adult male below (Lee County). This species closely resembles *E. fasciatus* in general appearance. It is most abundant on the tops of ridges and other such dry habitats.

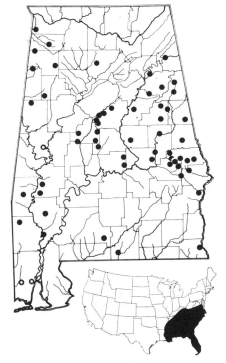

Alabama distribution: (Fig. 186) Apparently statewide, but uncommon or absent from much of the Tennessee Valley and Chert Belt.

Habits: The southeastern five-lined skink is most abundant in dry habitats, such as ridgetops, and well-drained, sandy places. It shuns heavily shaded, mesic ravines and coves, damp stream edges, and other such situations where habitat conditions are optimal for *E. fasciatus.* The ranges of ecological tolerance for the 2 species overlap somewhat, however, and they are frequently found together.

FIG. 186. Distribution of *Eumeces inexpectatus,* the southeastern five-lined skink. This species is believed to occur statewide, or essentially so, in Alabama. Solid symbols indicate localities from which the author examined specimens. The circles are literature records believed to be valid. The small map depicts approximately the known range in the United States.

FIG. 187. *Eumeces laticeps*, the broad-headed skink, adult male (Lee County). This skink attains an exceptionally large size in comparison with other Alabama skinks and spends much of its time in trees. The males develop conspicuously enlarged heads.

Rotting logs and stumps and rockpiles are favored microhabitats of *E. inexpectatus*, and in such places the female lays the eggs in a protected cavity. Data on nesting of this species are scarce. Two clutches of 11 eggs each have been reported, and I have observed clutches of 6 and 8 eggs. The southeastern five-lined skink feeds on a variety of arthropods and possibly on other forms of invertebrate life as well. It is almost wholly terrestrial, and in climbing ability is somewhat intermediate between *E. fasciatus* and *E. laticeps*.

Eumeces laticeps (Schneider)
Broad-headed Skink

Description: (Fig. 187, 188) A large lizard attaining a maximum snout-vent length of about 130 mm. Scales smooth, shiny, overlapping; chin with 2 postmentals; median subcaudals noticeably wider than scales in adjacent rows (similar in this respect to 1 of its 2 close relatives in Alabama, *E. fasciatus*, but differing from the other, *E. inexpectatus*, in which the median subcaudals are about equal in width to those in adjacent rows); upper

FIG. 188. *Eumeces laticeps*, broad-headed skink, adult female (Lee County). The juveniles of this large species have bright blue tails and narrow yellow or orange stripes. They are easily mistaken for *E. fasciatus* and *E. inexpectatus*.

labials usually 8; enlarged postlabials absent or, if present, usually 1 on each side. Body of juveniles (except for venter) black or blue-black with 5 yellowish to orange stripes: a mid-dorsal one, bifurcating anteriorly at back of head and extending onto snout, 2 dorsolaterals, beginning over the eyes, and 2 laterals, beginning under the eyes; mid-dorsal stripe relatively narrow when compared with that on *E. fasciatus*. Tail of juveniles and young adult females bright blue above. Juvenile pattern of light striping persisting in adult females except for fading, loss of sharp contrast, and obliteration of mid-dorsal stripe in some individuals; adult females with a broad, dark lateral stripe. Adult males virtually uniform brown or tan except for head, which becomes suffused with red; head of adult males considerably swollen.

Remarks: The range of variation in juvenile *E. laticeps* overlaps that of juvenile *E. fasciatus* in some characters, resulting in occasional individuals that are hard to identify with certainty.

Alabama distribution: (Fig. 189) Statewide.

Habits: In Alabama the broad-headed skink is considerably less abundant and apparently more habitat-specific than either of its 2 close relatives, *E. fasciatus* and *E. inexpectatus*. It frequents wooded areas having hollow trees or large rotting stumps or logs, living in the cavities that these provide. It climbs with much greater facility than other Alabama skinks and is elusive and often difficult to capture. When seized, the adults bite viciously; a large male will occasionally break the skin slightly. The bite is non-venomous, however, as are those of all other Alabama lizards, and the broad-headed skink is quite undeserving of the bad reputation it has among some people.

The eggs, usually laid in a cavity under the bark of a dead tree or stump, range in number from 6 to 16 per clutch and are attended by the female until hatching. The food of the broad-headed skink includes insects, spiders, and to a lesser extent, some other forms of small animal life.

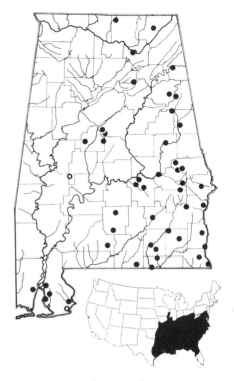

FIG. 189. Distribution of *Eumeces laticeps*, the broad-headed skink. This species is believed to occur statewide, or essentially so, in Alabama. Solid symbols indicate localities from which the author examined specimens. The circles are literature records believed to be valid. The small map depicts approximately the known range in the United States.

GENUS *SCINCELLA* Mittleman

The members of this genus are included by some authorities in *Leiolopisma* and by some others in *Lygosoma*. The genus contains 7 species and occurs in North and Central America. One species is found in Alabama.

Scincella laterale (Say)
Ground Skink

Description: (Fig. 190) A small, elusive lizard attaining a maximum snout-vent length of around 50 mm. Scales smooth, flat, overlapping; lower eyelid with a transparent "window;" color tan to dark brown, a dark dorsolateral stripe evident in relatively light-colored speci-

FIG. 190. *Scincella laterale*, the ground skink (Lee County). This small, brown skink is seen frequently in the forests of Alabama scurrying about among the leaves.

mens, obscure in dark-colored ones; venter yellowish to dull white.

Alabama distribution: (Fig. 191) Statewide.

Habits: The ground skink, one of our most abundant reptiles, is usually seen scurrying about among the leaves on the forest floor. It is surprisingly difficult to catch, and the would-be captor seldom gets more than one opportunity.

The ground skink exploits most forested, terrestrial habitat types and prefers mesic and dry sites over damp ones.

From 1 to 7, but usually 2 or 3, eggs are laid under a rock or in rotting wood or humus. Several clutches may be produced each season; unlike our other skinks, the ground skink does not protect its nest. Brooks (1963) reported on the food habits of the ground skink and in 1967 published on the population ecology of the species.

FAMILY TEIDAE – TEID LIZARDS

A New World group with 40 genera and about 200 species, this family contains mostly generalized, carnivorous lizards. The vast majority are found in South America. Only 1 genus, *Cnemidophorus*, occurs in the United States.

GENUS *CNEMIDOPHORUS* Wagler

This genus contains about 36 species and occurs from the United States southward to Argentina. It is well represented in some of our western states, and several of the forms that occur there are parthenogenetic. Only 1 species occurs in Alabama.

Cnemidophorus sexlineatus (Linnaeus)

Two subspecies of this lizard are recognized, 1 of which occurs in Alabama.

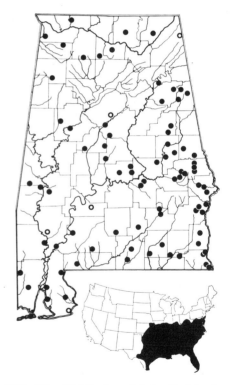

FIG. 191. Distribution of *Scincella laterale*, the ground skink. This species is believed to occur statewide, or essentially so, in Alabama. Solid symbols indicate localities from which the author examined specimens. The circles are literature records believed to be valid. The small map depicts approximately the known range in the United States.

FIG. 192. *Cnemidophorus sexlineatus sexlineatus,* the eastern six-lined racerunner, subadult (Elmore County). This speedy, elusive lizard is encountered in relatively open situations and is common in most parts of the state.

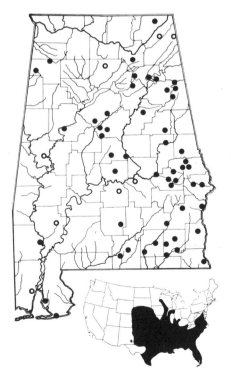

Cnemidophorus sexlineatus sexlineatus
(Linnaeus)
Eastern Six-lined Racerunner

Description: (Fig. 192) A medium sized, long-tailed lizard attaining a maximum snout-vent length of around 75 mm. Dorsal scales tiny, imparting a velvety texture to the skin; ventral scutes quadrangular, in 8 longitudinal rows. Color olive, brownish, or grayish with 6 well-defined yellow longitudinal stripes on the body (none of our skinks has more than 5 stripes).

Alabama distribution: (Fig. 193) Statewide.

FIG. 193. Distribution of *Cnemidophorus sexlineatus sexlineatus,* the eastern six-lined racerunner. This form is believed to occur statewide, or nearly so, in Alabama. Solid symbols indicate localities from which the author examined specimens. Circles are literature records believed to be valid. The small map depicts approximately the known range of the species *C. sexlineatus* in the United States.

Habits: This familiar lizard, often called sand-streak or sand-runner, inhabits dry, relatively open places, such as field roads, rights-of-way, and barren waste places. It relies chiefly on speed for protection, but if pressed will usually disappear into the burrow of a small rodent or mole, or into one it has dug for itself.

The racerunner is active and alert, on the move constantly when abroad, and operates most efficiently at high temperatures. It is one of the few terrestrial reptiles in Alabama that voluntarily exposes itself to full sunlight at midday during hot summer weather. In fact, it has been determined that the optimum body temperature for this species is around 40° C (104° F).

The female racerunner digs her shallow nest cavity in friable soil or in an old sawdust pile and deposits 1 to 5 softshelled, whitish eggs. She may lay 2 or possibly 3 clutches per season. After covering the eggs, she takes no further interest in the nest. Fitch (1958) provided a comprehensive account of the natural history of *C. sexlineatus* in Kansas.

Suborder Serpentes—Snakes

Snakes are distinctive in having an elongate, scaly body in combination with a lack of limbs, external ear openings, and eyelids. Snakes may be active year-round in warm tropical regions, but in temperate regions they overwinter in protected places, usually underground. In Alabama some species, such as the eastern diamondback rattlesnake, cottonmouth, and eastern garter snake, will emerge occasionally during warm spells in winter to bask or feed, while others, the coachwhip for example, are almost never seen abroad during the winter.

Snakes mate shortly after they emerge from overwintering, usually during March or April in Alabama. The male locates the female chiefly by scent, following which there is a brief, simple courtship culminating in copulation. Fertilization is accomplished by 1 of a pair of hemipenes, which is everted from the male's vent at the time of copulation.

When not in use, the hemipenes are located, 1 on each side, within the base of the tail.

Some species of snakes reproduce by laying eggs, others by giving birth. Maternal care of the eggs is practiced in a few snakes, including the pythons and, among Alabama species, the mud snake. None of the viviparous forms display maternal care.

External differences between males and females are not readily apparent in most snake species. In most forms the tails of males, on the average, are relatively longer than those of the females, and, correspondingly, the average number of subcaudal scutes is greater in the males of those forms. With experience one can often determine the sex of a snake by noting from the underside the relative width of the base of the tail — wider for males than for females.

Snakes are exclusively carnivorous and swallow their prey entire. A snake is capable of swallowing items considerably larger in diameter than its own head. Growth continues throughout life, although the rate declines following maturity. Periodically during the warm season, a snake sheds the outermost layer of its skin. Typically, it is shed all in one piece, beginning at the head. A week or so before shedding, the eyes develop a milky appearance, and the snake becomes inactive. The eyes become clear again 1 to 3 days prior to shedding. Snakes in Alabama usually shed 3 or 4 times each season. Rattlesnakes add 1 segment to the rattle each time they shed. Segments are lost from the end of the rattle from time to time, however, so it is seldom possible to determine the age of a large rattlesnake by counting the segments of its rattle.

Worldwide, there are about 2,700 species of snakes. The vast majority are harmless. Forty species of snakes are native to Alabama, all but 6 of which are harmless. Among our harmless species, however, are several that will bite viciously when cornered or handled, including the black racer, coachwhip, and water snakes of the genus *Natrix*. Others, such as the rough green snake, mud snake, rainbow snake, and hog-nosed snakes, can seldom be induced to bite under any circumstances. Kingsnakes (genus *Lampropeltis*) and rat snakes (genus *Elaphe*) are among those that are unpredictable. In any event, bites from our non-venomous snakes warrant no more concern than a scratch from a thorn or brier and are usually less painful. In fact, when catching a harmless snake, most herpetologists are inclined to treat the rear end with more respect than they do the head, because most snakes will smear the captor with an ill-smelling secretion of their anal glands, producing a sensation that is usually more unpleasant than being bitten.

The snakes of the United States and Canada are treated comprehensively in *Handbook of Snakes of the United States and Canada,* by Albert and Anna Wright, a 2-volume edition published by Comstock in 1957.

FAMILY COLUBRIDAE — COLUBRID SNAKES

This family, containing the great majority of living snakes, is essentially worldwide in distribution. Variation among its forms is extreme, and few obvious distinctive characteristics are shared by all. Some colubrids have grooved fangs in the rear of the mouth and are venomous. Only 2, however, both of them African, are dangerous to man. All of Alabama's harmless snakes belong to this family.

GENUS *CARPHOPHIS* Gervalis

This genus is composed of 1 polytypic species whose range is confined to the eastern United States.

Carphophis amoenus (Say)

The members of this species, called worm snakes, are divided into 3 subspecies, 2 of which occur in Alabama.

FIG. 194. *Carphophis amoenus helenae,* the midwest worm snake (Clay County). This secretive snake is usually found under rocks or logs in forested areas. It resembles the eastern worm snake, *C. a. amoenus,* except for a slight difference in head scalation. In both forms the dorsal and ventral colors meet abruptly, and the tail is short and spine-tipped.

Carphophis amoenus amoenus (Say)
Eastern Worm Snake

Description: (Fig. 38A and 194) A small snake, attaining a maximum total length of about 350 mm. Tail rather short, spine-tipped; head small, flattened, about the same width as neck; dorsal scales smooth, shiny, in 13 rows at midbody; anal divided. Dorsal color brown, gray-brown, or pinkish brown; ventral color pink, extending upward onto first or second scale row (counting from bottom), sharply delineated from darker dorsal color. In this subspecies internasals and prefrontals usually separate (approximately 95 percent frequency).

Ventral count in nineteen Alabama males: range 110 to 119, mean 114.1; in sixteen females: range 117 to 126, mean 122.1. Subcaudal count in the males: range 33 to 38, mean 34.9; in the females: range 22 to 30, mean 26.6

Alabama distribution: (Fig. 195) The range of this subspecies enters Alabama from the north through the Appalachian Plateaus region; broadens southward to include most of the remainder of the Appalachian Plateaus region except for the northeastern portion; extends westward into the Fall Line Hills in western Alabama; and extends southward to include the lower part of the Ridge and Valley region.

C. a. amoenus intergrades with C. a. helenae in the Chert Belt, in the extreme northwestern portion of the Fall Line Hills, and in several other areas around the periphery of its range.

Habits: The habits of the 2 subspecies of worm snakes in Alabama are not known to differ significantly. Optimum habitats for worm snakes in the state are mesic hardwood forests with abundant leaf litter and humus. These snakes are secretive and are usually found beneath rocks, logs, and debris. They will not bite.

Worm snakes are oviparous, laying 2 to 8 (usually 5) eggs in rotting logs, stumps, or sawdust piles. Earthworms constitute the bulk of the diet.

Carphophis amoenus helenae (Kennicot)
Midwest Worm Snake

Description: (Fig. 38B) Similar in most respects to C. a. amoenus except that in C. a. helenae the internasals and prefrontals are usually fused instead of separate (approximately 95 percent frequency) and, in Alabama, the average ventral count is somewhat higher.

Remarks: Mount (1972) reported an apparent difference in average ventral count between C. a. helenae from north of the Fall Line and C. a. helenae from the Coastal Plain. In a sample of eight-

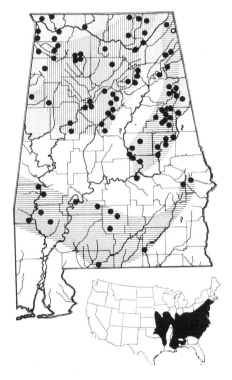

FIG. 195. Distribution of Carphophis amoenus and subspecific variation in Alabama. Horizontal hatching indicates the presumed range of C. a. helenae, the midwest worm snake, and vertical hatching, the range of C. a. amoenus, the eastern worm snake. The zone of intergradation is indicated by stippling. Solid symbols indicate localities from which the author examined specimens. Circles are literature records believed to be valid. The small map depicts approximately the known range of the species C. amoenus in the United States.

een males of the former, ventral count averaged 115.3 (range 109 to 120); in thirty-two females, the average was 124.3 (range 120 to 129). In seven males from the Coastal Plain, average ventral count was 118.9 (range 112 to 124); in three females the average was 126.3 (range 126 to 127). Geographic variation in subcaudal count was not detected within *C. a. helenae* or between *C. a. helenae* and *C. a. amoenus*.

Alabama distribution: (Fig. 195) In the Coastal Plain, *C. a. helenae* is known to occur in the central and eastern portions of the Fall Line Hills, Black Belt (1 locality), Transitional Zone, Red Hills, and Lower Coastal Plain (2 localities). Except in a few areas of the Red Hills and Fall Line Hills, *C. a. helenae* is infrequently encountered in the Coastal Plain. Above the Fall Line *C. a. helenae* is found throughout the Blue Ridge, in portions of the Piedmont and Ridge and Valley regions, and below the Tennessee River in the northeastern portion of the Appalachian Plateaus region.

Intergradation between *C. a. helenae* and *C. a. amoenus* occurs in most areas where the ranges of the 2 subspecies approach one another. The subspecific identity of worm snake populations in several areas of western Alabama has not been determined.

Habits: See "Habits" under *C. a. amoenus.*

GENUS *CEMOPHORA* Cope

This genus contains 1 polytypic species, which is found throughout much of the Southeast including Alabama.

Cemophora coccinea (Blumenbach)

Three subspecies of this snake are recognized, 1 of which occurs in Alabama.

FIG. 196. *Cemophora coccinea copei,* the northern scarlet snake (Russell County). In this secretive, nocturnal species the bands are red, black, and yellowish or white. The red bands are bordered on each side by black. The snout is red. In these respects it resembles the scarlet king snake. The venter of the scarlet snake is plain, however, while that of the scarlet king snake is banded.

Cemophora coccinea copei Jan
Northern Scarlet Snake

Description: (Fig. 196) A small to medium-sized snake, attaining a maximum total length of perhaps 800 mm, but averaging less than half that. Head small, not distinct from neck; scales smooth, usually in 19 rows at mid-body; anal single; rostral enlarged. Snout pointed, projecting well beyond lower jaw. Dorsal pattern of red saddles bordered by black on a ground color of white or light yellowish; snout red; venter unmarked.

Differs from other subspecies in having the following combination of characteristics: fewer than 185 ventrals, laterally closed body saddles, fewer than 6 upper labials, and first black body blotch usually touching parietals or joining with black head band.

Ventrals in twenty-five Alabama males: range 154 to 176, mean 165.2; in thirteen females: range 162 to 179, mean 169.5. Caudals in twenty-five males: range 34 to 46, mean 41.1; in thirteen females: range 32 to 40, mean 36.2.

Dorsal body blotches in twenty-five males: range 16 to 22, mean 18.6; in thirteen females: range 15 to 22, mean 18.5.

Alabama distribution: (Fig. 197) Statewide.

Habits: Relatively little is known of the habits of this secretive snake. It is seldom encountered during the day, although an occasional individual is found under a rock or under the bark of a rotting log. Scarlet snakes occur in a variety of forested and partially forested habitat types, but in general seem to be most abundant in well-drained areas with relatively loose soil. One of my students unearthed one in an abandoned fire ant mound. Most specimens are collected at night on black-topped roads.

The scarlet snake is oviparous and lays 3 to 8 elongate, whitish eggs. Natural nests are unknown. Eggs of other reptiles appear to be the preferred food. Other items have been reported in the diet, including small lizards, amphibians, insects, and small mammals. The scarlet snake does not bite, but usually fares poorly in captivity unless a supply of reptile eggs is available for food. Williams and Wilson (1967) provided an account of variation in the species along with some observations on its natural history. Palmer and Tregembo (1970) and Nelson and Gibbons (1972) supplemented this account with additional notes.

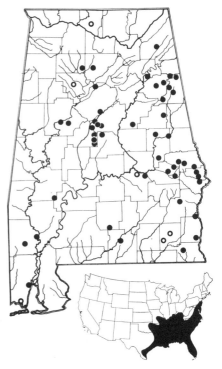

FIG. 197. Distribution of *Cemophora coccinea copei*, the northern scarlet snake. This form is believed to occur statewide, or nearly so, in Alabama. Solid symbols indicate localities from which the author examined specimens. Circles are literature records believed to be valid. The small map depicts approximately the known range of the species *C. coccinea* in the United States.

GENUS *COLUBER* Linnaeus

This genus, which also has representatives in Eurasia, is represented in the New World by 1 species.

Coluber constrictor Linnaeus

This species ranges from coast to coast and border to border and contains 8 currently recognized subspecies. Two of these occur in Alabama.

Coluber constrictor constrictor Linnaeus
Northern Black Racer

Description: (Fig. 198, 199) A long, fairly slender, black snake attaining a maximum length of about 1,955 mm. Head distinct from neck; eyes large; scales smooth, in 17 rows at mid-body; anal divided. Dorsum of adults uniformly dull black; venter black to dark gray except for the chin, which is often white or mottled. Juveniles up to 1 year of age distinctly patterned with 48 to 71 saddle-shaped, dark gray, brown, or reddish blotches, alternating with single or paired lateral dark blotches; belly with small semi-circular or crescent-like dark spots that become indistinct or absent posteriorly.

Differs from *C. c. priapus*, the other subspecies found in Alabama, in relative length of enlarged spine at the base of adult male's hemipenis (Fig. 39). In *C. c. constrictor*, spine usually less than 3 times as long as adjacent spine in same row; in *C. c. priapus*, basal hemipenial spine at least 3 times as long as adjacent spine.

Remarks: Some of the geographically variable characters in Alabama black racers do not vary concordantly with variation in hemipenial spine length. In pigmentation of upper labials, variation is somewhat chaotic, as it is in the color of the chin and neck. Populations in which the upper labials are mostly white occur in southern Baldwin County in southwestern Alabama and in Colbert, Franklin, and Lawrence counties in northwestern Alabama. Most other areas of the state yield some specimens whose upper labials are mostly white, but in a sizable series from central eastern Alabama (Lee, Macon, Bullock, Tallapoosa, and Russell counties) no such specimens were found. Individuals with the highest numbers of predominantly white chin

FIG. 198. *Coluber constrictor priapus*, southern black racer, adult (Lee County). Black racers are common throughout Alabama. The 2 subspecies found in our state differ chiefly in the length of the enlarged spine at the base of the hemipenis of the male.

FIG. 199. *Coluber constrictor priapus*, southern black racer, juvenile (Lee County). Juvenile black racers have conspicuous reddish blotches and bear little resemblance to the adults. The blotches are lost by the end of the second year.

TABLE 5. GEOGRAPHIC AND SEXUAL VARIATION IN THE NUMBER OF VENTRAL AND SUBCAUDAL SCUTES AMONG BLACK RACERS, *Coluber constrictor*, IN ALABAMA

Quadrant of state	Ventrals						Subcaudals					
	Males			Females			Males			Females		
	Range	Mean	No.	Range	Mean	No.	Range	Mean	No.	Range	Mean	No.
NW	171-180	177	(10)	176-184	179	(5)	94-103	98	(6)	89-96	93	(4)
NE	173-182	177	(13)	176-179	177	(4)	78-100	92	(11)	87-98	92	(3)
SW	164-178	171	(13)	169-178	173	(10)	80-102	92	(10)	75-99	86	(7)
SE	167-180	175	(20)	167-180	173	(9)	66-100	86	(15)	80-97	90	(4)

shields and anterior ventrals are found generally in southwestern Alabama in southern Baldwin County, in northwestern Alabama, and in the Blue Ridge and upper Piedmont of eastern Alabama.

Geographic variation in ventral and subcaudal counts is shown in Table 5. Populations in northern Alabama tend to have higher counts than those in southern Alabama.

Alabama distribution: (Fig. 200) Mountains, plateaus, and valleys of northeastern Alabama, in Jackson, De-Kalb, Cherokee, and Etowah counties and in portions of Cleburne, Calhoun, Marshall, and Madison counties. Intergrades with *C. c. priapus* to the west and south in a zone approximately 50 to 60 miles wide.

Habits: The habits of the northern black racer and those of the southern subspecies in Alabama are apparently similar. Black racers are active, diurnal snakes and are familiar to most Alabama citizens. They occur in nearly all of our terrestrial habitats but are most common in open woods, forest edges, and along brushy margins of streams, swamps, and lakes. Whether a racer will "chase" a person has been widely debated. Of the hundreds I have encountered, none has ever chased me, but if chased themselves and cornered, they have usually put up a vigorous defense. In any case, the black racer is absolutely harmless, its bite considerably less painful than a brier scratch.

The granular-surfaced, oblong eggs are laid in the soil, in a sawdust pile, in a rotting tree or stump, or under some sheltering object. The usual number per clutch is between 10 and 18. The conspicuously blotched hatchlings differ strikingly from the adults. Black racers eat snakes, small mammals, birds and bird eggs, frogs, toads, and lizards. The lack of dietary specialization in this species has probably contributed to its apparent success. Fitch (1963) presented an excellent account of the natural history of the racer, emphasizing the ecology and life history of the subspecies *flaviventris*. Auffenberg (1955) provided a taxonomic monograph of the species.

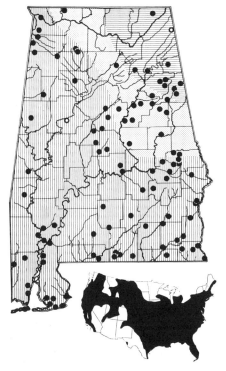

FIG. 200. Distribution of *Coluber constrictor* and subspecific variation in Alabama. Horizontal hatching indicates the presumed range of *C. c. constrictor*, the northern black racer, and vertical hatching, the range of *C. c. priapus*, the southern black racer. The zone of intergradation is indicated by stippling. Solid symbols indicate localities from which the author examined specimens. Circles are literature records believed to be valid. The small map depicts approximately the known range of the species *C. constrictor* in the United States.

Coluber constrictor priapus
Dunn and Wood
Southern Black Racer

Description: (Fig. 198, 199) The Alabama *C. c. constrictor* and *C. c. priapus* differ substantially from one another only in hemipenial spine length (Fig. 39). In *C. c. priapus*, enlarged basal spine on hemipenis longer, at least 3 times the length of adjacent spine in same series. (Other aspects of intraspecific variation among Alabama black racers are discussed in "Remarks" under *C. c. constrictor*.)

Alabama distribution: (Fig. 200) Generally the southern one-half and northwestern quadrant of the state. The range is delimited by the Fall Line in eastern Alabama. Intergrades with *C. c. constrictor* northward and eastward to the range of that subspecies.

Habits: In Alabama, the habits of *C. c. priapus* and *C. c. constrictor* are apparently similar (see above).

GENUS *DIADOPHIS* Baird and Girard

This genus is widely distributed in North America and is now thought to consist of 1 highly variable species.

Diadophis punctatus (Linnaeus)

Approximately 13 subspecies of the ringneck snake are recognized. The populations inhabiting most of Alabama represent intergradient combinations involving up to 3 of these.

Diadophis punctatus punctatus
(Linnaeus)
Southern Ringneck Snake

Description: (Fig. 201) A small, slender snake attaining a maximum total length of approximately 445 mm. Head small, somewhat flattened, scarcely distinct from neck; snout rounded; anal divided; scales smooth, in 15 rows at midbody; upper labials usually 8. Dorsum uniformly slate gray to blue-black (darkest in young) except for a narrow yellow or cream-colored neck ring, this some-

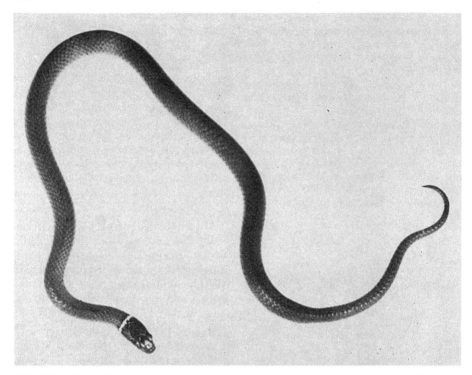

FIG. 201. *Diadophis punctatus punctatus* x *stictogenys,* ringneck snake (Lee County). The yellow neck ring in combination with the dark gray to blue-black dorsal color serves to identify *D. punctatus.* Most ringneck snake populations in Alabama are intergrades involving 2 or 3 subspecies.

times interrupted; venter yellow to orange, with a single row of fairly large, distinct, black "half-moons" down the midline; chin and labials with small black spots.

Alabama distribution: (Fig. 202) The species occurs statewide. Throughout the southern one-half of the state and in the northwestern quadrant, the populations are intergradient between *D. p. punctatus* and *D. p. stictogenys*. In the northeastern quadrant, except for northern portions of Jackson and DeKalb counties (the range of *D. p. edwardsi* in Alabama), the populations are influenced not only by *D. p. punctatus* and *D. p. stictogenys,* but by *D. p. edwardsi* as well.

Habits: The ringneck snakes are among the most commonly encountered snakes in Alabama. They occur in most terrestrial habitats but prefer those intermedi-

ate in moisture conditions. Rotting pine logs and stumps are favorable microhabitats, but ringnecks also live beneath rocks, in leaf litter, and in other protected places. Other small snakes frequently found in company with ringnecks include earth snakes (*Virginia* spp.) and worm snakes (*Carphophis amoenus*).

The elongate, whitish eggs are usually laid in rotting wood within a log or stump. Clutch size is most often 4 or 5. Food items include earthworms, insect larvae, amphibians, and small reptiles.

Ringneck snakes almost never bite when handled, but when freshly caught they will invariably attempt to smear the contents of the cloaca on the captor. Some individuals, when molested, will quickly curl the tail and turn it upside down, revealing the bright ventral color. This behavioral feature, shared with some other snake species, is thought to

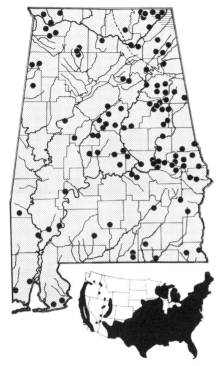

FIG. 202. Distribution of *Diadophis punctatus* and subspecific variation in Alabama. The horizontal hatching indicates the range of *D. p. edwardsi*, the northern ringneck snake. The stippled area included within the broken line is a zone of intergradation involving *D. p. edwardsi*, *D. p. punctatus* (the southern ringneck snake), and *D. p. stictogenys* (the Mississippi ringneck snake). The remainder of the state is a zone of intergradation between *D. p. punctatus* and *D. p. stictogenys*. The small map depicts approximately the range of the species *D. punctatus* in the United States.

tatus in having an unmarked venter (or one with a single row of very small markings), a relatively wide neck ring, unmarked chin and labials, and somewhat larger size (up to 570 mm). Also, ventral and subcaudal counts are higher than in *D. p. punctatus* (Table 6).

Alabama distribution: (Fig. 202) Extreme northeastern Alabama in portions of Jackson and DeKalb counties. Influence of *D. p. edwardsi* is evident in intergradient populations inhabiting much of the remainder of the northeastern quadrant of the state.

Habits: See "Habits" under *D. p. punctatus*.

Diadophis punctatus stictogenys Cope
Mississippi Ringneck Snake

Description: Differs from *D. p. punctatus* in the nature of the black ventral

startle some potential predators and in some instances enable the snake to escape unharmed.

Diadophis punctatus edwardsi (Merrem)
Northern Ringneck Snake

Description: Differs from *D. p. punc-*

TABLE 6. VARIATION IN NUMBER OF VENTRAL AND SUBCAUDAL SCUTES IN RINGNECK SNAKES, *Diadophis punctatus*, IN ALABAMA

Section of Alabama[1]	Males						Females					
	Ventrals			Subcaudals			Ventrals			Subcaudals		
	No.	Range	Mean	No.	Range	Mean	No.	Range	Mean	No.	Range	Mean
Northeast	7	145-155	151.6	7	49-59	52.9	5	151-163	157.8	5	43-57	51
Northwest	11	131-147	142.3	10	44-54	48.8	7	149-157	152.6	7	32-50	44
East north-central	8	137-147	142	7	48-56	51.9	11	140-152	148.1	10	41-46	43.2
Central	6	135-142	139	6	47-54	51	14	140-160	152.4	13	40-51	46.2
East south-central	27	131-146	137.3	26	42-56	48.7	30	133-154	144.1	29	34-54	44
Southwest	4	128-140	133.5	3	46-50	47.7	4	238-150	143.8	3	36-49	43.3
Southeast	3	132-143	137.3	3	41-47	43.7	4	130-147	140.8	4	36-46	42.3

[1] Counties making up the sections are: **Northeast**—Cherokee, Etowah, DeKalb, Jackson, Madison, Marshall; **northwest**—Colbert, Lauderdale, Lawrence, Marion, Morgan, Winston; **east north-central**—Calhoun, Clay, Cleburne, Randolph, Talladega; **central**—Autauga, Bibb, Chilton, Jefferson, Shelby; **east south-central**—Chambers, Elmore, Macon, Montgomery, Lee, Russell, Tallapoosa; **southwest**—Baldwin, Choctaw, Clarke, Conecuh, Mobile, Monroe, Wilcox; and **southeast**—Barbour, Butler, Covington, Geneva, Henry, Houston.

markings (irregular spotting or a row of paired black spots down the middle, as opposed to a single row of black half-moons); in frequency of occurrence of interrupted neck ring (high frequency, as opposed to low); and in usual number of upper labials (7 instead of 8). Chin and labials spotted as in *D. p. punctatus.*

Alabama distribution: (Fig. 202) Intergrades with *D. p. punctatus* in southern one-half and northwestern quadrant of the state. Intergrades with *D. p. punctatus* and *D. p. edwardsi* in northeastern quadrant, except for extreme northeastern corner.

Habits: Apparently similar to those of *D. p. punctatus.* (See account of that form.)

GENUS *DRYMARCHON* Fitzinger

This genus contains 1 polytypic species, which ranges from the southern United States to northern Argentina.

Drymarchon corais (Daudin)

Eight subspecies of this largely tropical snake are recognized, 1 of which is native to Alabama.

Drymarchon corais couperi (Holbrook)
Eastern Indigo Snake

Description: (Fig. 203) A large, fairly stout snake attaining a maximum total length of 2,630 mm. Head slightly, if at all, distinct from neck; anal undivided; scales large, smooth, shiny, in 17 rows at mid-body. Color uniform lustrous blue-black, except for some reddish or cream-colored suffusion about the chin, throat, and cheeks, this usually more prominent in females than in males.

Alabama distribution: (Fig. 204) Löding (1922) reported the indigo snake from Satsuma, Mobile County, and indicated having seen several individuals on the "palmetto-covered hills at Grand Bay

FIG. 203. *Drymarchon corais couperi,* the eastern indigo snake. This large, harmless snake is shiny blue-black. It is threatened virtually throughout its range and may have already been eliminated from Alabama.

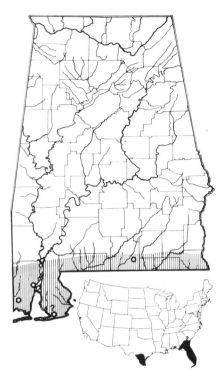

FIG. 204. Distribution of the *Drymarchon corais*. The Alabama map shows literature records and presumed range of *D. c. couperi*, the eastern indigo snake, until about 1940. The record for Baldwin County was listed by county only. The small map depicts approximately the present known range of the species *D. corais*.

made it an easy mark for people who kill snakes indiscriminately. In peninsular Florida the indigo snake persists in a few scattered areas that man has not completely overrun. In northern Florida, southern Georgia, and possibly southern Alabama, indigo snakes are found locally in a few desolate areas where gopher tortoise burrows occur in close proximity to stream or swamp-edge habitat. In these areas the snakes rely heavily, if not exclusively, on the tortoise burrows for overwintering sites. The practice of gassing gopher burrows in an attempt to drive out rattlesnakes may be contributing to the decimation of indigo snakes in much of the range (see Preface).

The indigo snake feeds on a wide variety of vertebrate animal life. Snakes, including poisonous ones, frogs, small mammals, birds, and even young turtles are all included. A freshly captured 7-foot indigo snake in my possession regurgitated its stomach contents, which consisted of the remains of a toad, a southern hognose snake, a pigmy rattlesnake, and a hatchling gopher tortoise.

Information on reproduction is based solely on data obtained on captives. Clutches of 5 to 11 eggs have been reported.

GENUS *ELAPHE* Fitzinger

This genus, considered here in the traditional sense, contains about 38 species and is widely distributed in both hemispheres. Four species occur in the United States, 2 of which are found in Alabama.

Elaphe guttata (Linnaeus)

Three subspecies are recognized, 1 of which occurs in Alabama.

Elaphe guttata guttata (Linnaeus)
Corn Snake

Description: (Fig. 205) A medium-sized to rather large snake attaining a maximum length of about 1,830 mm. Head distinct from neck: anal divided; scales smooth to weakly keeled, usually

in Mobile County," but was unable to catch one at that locality. Haltom (1931) listed the Mobile County records and also listed Baldwin County under Alabama distribution for this snake but gave no documentation for the latter. Neill (1954), in the most recent report of the indigo snake from Alabama, mentioned 2 specimens collected 12 miles north of Florala, Covington County. If the indigo snake still occurs in Alabama, it is exceedingly scarce.

Habits: Apparently, the eastern indigo snake has suffered more from the effects of civilization than any other southeastern snake. It is large, conspicuous, and relatively slow. These characteristics have

FIG. 205. *Elaphe guttata guttata*, the corn snake (Macon County). This docile species has red or reddish blotches on an orange background. It is one of our most attractive and most beneficial forms.

in 27 rows at mid-body; ventrals turning upward sharply near the ends. Patterned dorsally with black-bordered red or dark orange median blotches on a reddish orange or brownish orange ground color, these blotches alternating with a series of smaller lateral blotches that tend to become elongate and run together longitudinally; a third series of blotches involves the ends of the ventrals and adjacent 2 to 3 scale rows. Top of head usually with 2 convergent stripes that form a "spear-point," directed anteriorly. Venter white, conspicuously marked with quadrate black splotches; under surface of tail with 2 rows of black spots that tend either to coalesce and form convergent longitudinal stripes or to expand to involve the entire surface.

Ventrals in twenty-nine Alabama male corn snakes: range 206 to 222, mean 214.1; in fifteen females: range 206 to 223, mean 216.4. Subcaudals in twenty-four males: range 51 to 75, mean 66.7; in thirteen females: range 60 to 68, mean 63.8.

Remarks: Geographic variation in color is pronounced in Alabama corn snakes. Individuals from the Lower Coastal Plain are handsomely marked, the vivid orange and red markings on the juveniles persisting in undiminished intensity into adulthood. Those from the northernmost provinces are darker and less vividly marked. Variation in the intervening area appears to be clinal.

Alabama distribution: (Fig. 206) Statewide, relatively common throughout.

Habits: This attractive snake occurs in greatest abundance around abandoned farms and other places where small rodents are likely to thrive. Mice are the chief food of the adults; the juveniles will feed on lizards and small frogs. Corn snakes are rather strongly nocturnal and are often seen crossing the road at night.

Data on reproduction are scarce, and most reports deal with captives. Two Alabama captives in my possession laid

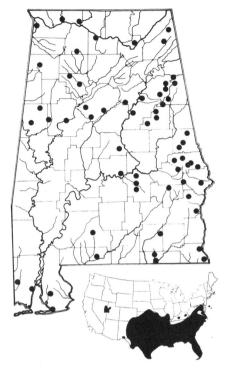

FIG. 206. Distribution of *Elaphe guttata guttata,* the corn snake. This form is believed to occur statewide, or nearly so, in Alabama. Symbols indicate localities from which the author examined specimens. The small map depicts approximately the known range of the species *E. guttata* in the United States.

11 and 16 eggs, respectively. Data on clutch size from captives from other areas indicate a range of from 3 to 21, with an average of about 10. Corn snakes are docile as captives and thrive when given proper care.

Elaphe obsoleta (Say)

Eight subspecies of this wide-ranging, highly variable species have been recognized. The validity of 3 of these, all confined to Florida, is problematical. At least 2 subspecies must be considered in the treatment of Alabama populations of this species.

FIG. 207. *Elaphe obsoleta obsoleta* x *spiloides,* rat snake (DeKalb County). The specimen shown is intergradient between the black rat snake and the gray rat snake. Rat snakes are among the more common large snakes in Alabama.

Elaphe obsoleta obsoleta (Say)
Black Rat Snake

Description: (Fig. 207) A large, moderately stout snake attaining a maximum length of about 2,565 mm. Head fairly distinct; tail relatively short; anal divided. Scales usually in 25 rows at midbody, keeled except for the lower 4 or 5 rows, which are smooth; ventrals turning sharply upward near the ends. Ground color of dorsum black to dark brown; blotches on body faintly if at all discernible; if discernible, blotches situated as in *E. o. spiloides* (see below) and usually outlined in white; interspaces between scales white; markings on venter black. Juveniles similar to those of *E. o. spiloides*.

Alabama distribution: (Fig. 208) The species occurs statewide. While individuals seemingly referable to *E. o. obsoleta* are encountered frequently in a portion of northeastern Alabama, the populations to which they belong are intergradient between that subspecies and *E. o. spiloides*. Such populations occur in Calhoun, Cherokee, Cleburne, DeKalb, Jackson, and Randolph counties.

Habits: Similar to those of *E. o. spiloides* as discussed below.

Elaphe obsoleta spiloides
(Duméril, Bibron and Duméril)
Gray Rat Snake

Description: (Fig. 209) Differs from *E. o. obsoleta* chiefly in characteristics of pigmentation and in maximum size attained (smaller, up to 2,135 mm in total length). Ground color gray to brown or yellowish brown. Dorsum with a series of median dark gray or dark brown blotches, the anteriormost usually having longitudinal extensions from their corners that may unite with extensions from neighboring blotches; sides with an alternating series of blotches, the anterior members of which tend to run together to form a longitudinal stripe; a third series of blotches present involving the lowermost 1 to 3 scale rows on each side and the ends of the ventrals.

Venter white with quadrate dark gray to brownish blotches and dark stippling, the latter becoming more intense posteriorly. Undersurfaces of tail with 2 convergent rows of dark spots that coalesce longitudinally to form stripes or expand to involve the entire surface. Juveniles similar to adults except for sharper contrast between ground color and markings.

Remarks: Variation in pigmentation among Alabama populations of this form is marked. In extreme southeastern Alabama most individuals are much lighter in color than are those from elsewhere in the state. The ground color is almost

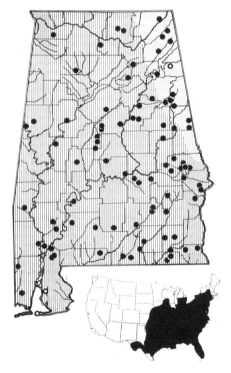

FIG. 208. Distribution of *Elaphe obsoleta* and subspecific variation in Alabama. The hatched area is the presumed range of *E. o. spiloides*, the gray rat snake, in Alabama. The stippled area is the zone of intergradation between *E. o. spiloides* and *E. o. obsoleta*, the black rat snake. Solid symbols indicate localities from which the author examined specimens. Circles are literature records believed to be valid. The small map depicts approximately the known range of the species *E. obsoleta* in the United States.

FIG. 209. *Elaphe obsoleta spiloides,* the gray rat snake. Rat snakes, often called chicken snakes or, in southeastern Alabama, oak snakes, feed predominantly on small mammals and are considered beneficial.

silvery gray in many, the blotches are only slightly darker, and brownish tones are usually lacking altogether. Northward the ground color tends to become darker and less uniform, with some individuals showing a distinctly brownish cast.

In the western half of the state, at least one-half of the individuals are decidedly brownish in overall appearance. In the westernmost tier of counties below Marion County, brownish orange contributes to the ground color of some. The blotches are often somewhat obscure. Many specimens from western Alabama more closely resemble *E. o. lindheimeri* than they do the light gray snakes from southeastern Alabama.

Substantial geographic variation in scale counts was lacking among Alabama specimens examined. Ventrals in five females from above the Fall Line: range 234 to 245, mean 240.8; in sixteen males from above the Fall Line: range 227 to 238, mean 233.2. Subcaudals in four of the females: range 70 to 81, mean 77.0;

in fifteen of the males: range 77 to 90, mean 83.8.

In nineteen females from below the Fall Line, the range in ventrals was 230 to 249, the mean 239.9; in eighteen males from below the Fall Line: range 229 to 242, mean 234.9. Subcaudals in fifteen of the females: range 66 to 89, mean 78.5; in sixteen of the males: range 77 to 96, mean 85.4.

Alabama distribution: (Fig. 208) Statewide except for a portion of northeastern Alabama where intergradation with *E. o. obsoleta* occurs.

Habits: *Elaphe obsoleta* is familiar to nearly all of our rural residents. In most parts of the state it is called "chicken snake," but is given the name "white-oak runner" or "oak snake" by many people in southeastern Alabama. It occurs in most kinds of terrestrial habitats but attains greatest densities in areas where forests and farmland are generally intermixed, and small rodents are relatively abundant. The gray rat snake is one of the few large snakes that frequently turns up in well-established residential areas around the edges of cities and towns in Alabama. It is an accomplished climber, and its presence in a tree is often revealed by a flock of screaming blue jays.

The whitish, oblong eggs are laid in rotting logs, stumps, sawdust piles, and other such places. Clutch size is usually between 12 and 18. The food of the young consists mainly of lizards and small frogs. Large individuals prefer warm blooded animals and eggs. Despite this snake's occasional depredations on the chicken house, it is usually considered beneficial because of its value in consuming rats and mice. Alabama farmers are becoming increasingly aware of this, and many now tolerate or even encourage its presence on their premises.

Gray rat snakes vary considerably in temperament. Many individuals, when threatened, defend themselves vigorously, striking repeatedly at the offender. Others allow themselves to be picked up by the body and handled without becoming overly alarmed. Gray rat snakes usually thrive in captivity and become quite docile, although many captives will bite if handled carelessly.

GENUS *FARANCIA* Gray

This genus, now considered to include *Abastor*, has 2 species; both are limited to the southeastern United States, and both occur in Alabama.

Farancia abacura (Holbrook)

Two subspecies are recognized both of which occur in Alabama.

Farancia abacura abacura (Holbrook)
Eastern Mud Snake

Description: (Fig. 210) A large snake attaining a maximum total length of about 2,055 mm. Body cylindrical, head and neck about the same width; eyes and tongue small; preoculars lacking; anal usually divided; tail short and stout, ending in a short, sharp spine. Dorsal scale rows smooth, in 19 rows at midbody (slight keels may be present pos-

terodorsally); dorsum shiny blue-black; ventral color mostly red (rarely white), extending upward on the sides to form a series of bars on the body and tail and occasionally meeting on the dorsum to form rings; dorsal color extending onto venter.

In this subspecies, light body bars usually 53 or more in number, their apices pointed instead of rounded; apices of corresponding bars on neck connecting or separated by no more than 3 dorsal scale rows; distal bars on tail uniting dorsally to form rings.

Remarks: I could detect no subspecific variation, or any other trenchant geographic variation, in ventral or subcaudal counts among Alabama populations of *F. abacura*. In a sample of nine Alabama males of mixed subspecific identity, ventral count ranged from 163 to 179 and averaged 166.3. In twelve females the range was 183 to 197 and the average 191.4. Subcaudal count in eight of the males ranged from 41 to 48 and averaged 45.0; in the twelve females, 35 to 41 with an average of 37.2.

Alabama distribution: (Fig. 211) Southern Baldwin County and Dauphin Island in Mobile County. Intergrades with *F. a. reinwardti* throughout most of the eastern one-half of the Coastal Plain.

Habits: The habits of the 2 subspecies *F. abacura* are apparently similar. Beaver swamps, ponds, and lakes with swampy margins and abundant aquatic vegetation, floodplains, and sluggish, mud-bottomed creeks are the habitats of the mud snake. The presence of *Amphiuma* spp. or *Siren* spp., the chief components of the diet, may be required to support mud snake populations. The mud snake spends most of its daylight hours in the water or in burrows in the mud. On rainy nights it prowls on the surface and may be found crossing roads in swampy areas.

The mud snake and its close relative the rainbow snake, *Farancia erytrogramma*, both have the habit of pressing the spinelike tip of the tail against the captor's skin, giving rise to the fallacy

FIG. 210. *Farancia abacura abacura* x *reinwardti,* mud snake (Butler County). The ground color is blue-black and the lighter color is usually red. The specimen shown here is an intergrade between the eastern and western subspecies. Called "hoop snakes" by some, mud snakes have a harmless spine at the tip of the tail.

that they are capable of delivering a venomous sting (see account of *F. erytrogramma*). Actually, both snakes are completely harmless, refusing even to bite.

The mud snake lays oblong or elliptical eggs in a flask-shaped cavity in the ground and remains with them, apparently, until they hatch. Wright and Wright (1957) indicate a range in clutch size of from 11 to 104 eggs for the species. These authors mention an egg sent to them from Auburn, Lee County, Alabama, on April 10. They noted that this egg hatched during shipment and reasoned, properly so, that it may have carried over from the previous year.

Food items mentioned in the literature other than sirens and amphiumas include tadpoles, frogs, small salamanders, and fish. I have induced juvenile mud snakes to eat tadpoles and small plethodontid salamanders, but the adults in my care would ordinarily feed only on amphiumas or sirens.

Farancia abacura reinwardti Schlegal
Western Mud Snake

Description: (Fig. 210) Differs from *F. a. abacura* as follows: lateral bars on body more sharply defined, rounded at tops, and usually numbering fewer than 53; tops of neck bars separated by 8 or more dorsal scale rows of dark dorsal color; distal light bars on tail, except sometimes the last, not uniting medially to form rings. Maximum total length less (about 1,830 mm).

Alabama distribution: (Fig. 211)

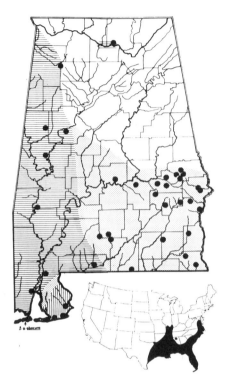

FIG. 211. Distribution of *Farancia abacura* and subspecific variation in Alabama. Horizontal hatching indicates the presumed range of *F. a. reinwardti*, the western mud snake, and vertical hatching, the range of *F. a. abacura*, the eastern mud snake. The zone of intergradation is indicated by stippling. Symbols indicate localities from which the author examined specimens. The small map depicts approximately the known range of the species *F. abacura* in the United States.

Roughly, the western one-third of the Coastal Plain except for Dauphin Island in Mobile County and lower Baldwin County. (See "Alabama distribution" under *F. a. abacura*.) The western mud snake also occurs in the Tennessee Valley. However, its presence in that region is documented by only 1 specimen (Madison County), and the extent of the range is not known.

Habits: See "Habits" under *F. a. abacura*.

Farancia erytrogramma (Palisot de Beauvois)

Two subspecies of this snake are recognized, 1 of which occurs in Alabama.

Farancia erytrogramma erytrogramma
(Palisot de Beauvois)
Rainbow Snake

Description: (Fig. 212) A large snake attaining a maximum total length of around 1,500 mm. Head and neck about the same width; eyes and tongue small; body cylindrical; tail short and stout, appended at the tip with a sharp spine; anal usually divided; preoculars lacking; dorsal scales smooth, in 19 rows at midbody (slight keels may be present posterodorsally). Dorsum shiny blue or blue-black with 3 narrow, longitudinal red stripes, venter red, each ventral scute with a black blotch at each end and usually with a smaller one in the middle; lower sides (between ventral scutes and dark dorsal ground color) yellow to red.

Ventrals in two Alabama males: 162 and 165, mean 163.5; in six females: range 175 to 178, mean 176.6. Subcaudals in two males: 48 each; in four females: range 39 to 41, mean 40.

Remarks: Neill (1964) and others have noted that in some rainbow snake populations, the mid-ventral spots of males are often more distinct than those of the females. This difference was not evident in the Alabama specimens.

Alabama distribution: (Fig. 213) Local in the Coastal Plain and possibly adjacent portions of upland provinces. Usually in or around rivers and medium- and large-sized creeks.

Habits: The rainbow snake, one of the most beautiful of Alabama's reptiles, is one of the least frequently encountered of our large snakes. Apparently it has a strong dietary preference for eels, perhaps explaining why rainbow snakes are usually found in or near streams. Other fish, tadpoles, and salamanders have been reported as occasional food items.

Rainbow snakes apparently are most active at night, but daytime feeding is

FIG. 212. *Farancia erytrogramma erytrogramma,* rainbow snake (Escambia County). This large, attractive snake has a red-striped, blue or blue-black dorsum. Found in or near water, it relies heavily on eels for food.

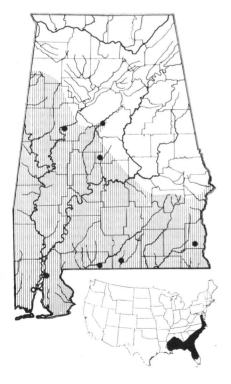

not uncommon. On two different occasions specimens were collected by Auburn students during the day in the Conecuh River. One seemed to be foraging underwater near the bank; the other was on the bank subduing an eel it had captured. Other rainbow snakes have been found in Alabama in piles of wet debris along the edges of streams and beneath a mat of vegetation along the edge of a land-locked pond. This last site was in southern Covington County. Eight specimens were found there at night along with 28 *Seminatrix pygaea* and one *Natrix fasciata.* All these snakes were within 100 feet of one another. The 8 rainbow snakes were all juveniles, but included individuals of at least 2 age groups, suggesting that the population was an established one.

FIG. 213. Distribution of *Farancia erytrogramma erytrogramma,* the rainbow snake. The presumed range in Alabama is indicated by hatching. Solid symbols indicate localities from which the author examined specimens. The small map depicts approximately the known range of the species *F. erytrogramma* in the United States.

Rainbow snakes have a sharp, spine-like scale at the end of the tail and when freshly captured will press the tip of this scale against the skin of the captor. The spine is devoid of venom, and I am not aware of any instances in which one has ever penetrated the skin. Nevertheless, this habit is probably responsible for the myth that this snake, along with *Farancia abacura* which shares the habit, will sieze the tail in the mouth, pursue an enemy by rolling like a hoop, and upon catching him will sting him to death. Stinging snake, hoop snake, and thunderbolt are among the names frequently applied to these snakes. Actually both are extremely docile. To my knowledge they never bite unless they mistake the handler for food. As a captive the rainbow snake often does well if provided with a diet of eels. Certain individuals may be induced to feed on salamanders and tadpoles.

The rainbow snake lays 22 to 52 eggs in a cavity in sandy soil 4 to 18 inches beneath the surface (Neill, 1964). Neill gives a laying record of July 8. A captive female in my possession laid 52 eggs on June 11.

GENUS *HETERODON* Latreille

Three species are included within this genus. The range includes much of the United States and portions of Mexico and Canada. Two species occur in Alabama.

Heterodon platyrhinos Latreille
Eastern Hognose Snake

Description: (Fig. 214, 215) A medium-sized, moderately stout snake attaining a maximum total length of about 1,155 mm. Tail short; scales keeled, usually in 23 or 25 rows at mid-body; anal divided; rostral keeled, projecting and pointed but not sharply upturned as in *H. simus;* prefrontals in contact. Color extremely variable, typically yellowish or tan with dark blotches but with individuals of other color phases, including black, reddish, gray, and brown regularly occurring. Ventral surface of tail usually conspicuously lighter than belly.

FIG. 214. *Heterodon platyrhinos*, the eastern hognose snake, blotched phase (Lee County). The name "spreading adder" is often applied to hog-nosed snakes in Alabama, and many people mistakenly believe them to be venomous.

Ventral count in thirty Alabama males: range 121 to 139, mean 129.4; in seven females: range 136 to 144, mean 138.9. Subcaudal count in twenty-seven males: range 40 to 55, mean 50.0; in five females: range 39 to 52, mean 45.2.

Alabama distribution: (Fig. 216) Statewide.

Habits: The eastern hognose snake, often called spreading adder, is one of our frequently encountered species. It is usually found in fields and areas of broken terrain. Hognose snakes are relatively sluggish in their movements, and they do not bite. A molested individual's first line of defense is a spectacular bluff. Hissing and jerking, it flattens its head and neck and inflates its body with air. The formidable aspect thus presented has led many to assume the hog-nosed snake to be dangerous. Should this behavior fail to intimidate the molester effectively, the snake begins to writhe as if in extreme agony. Mouth

FIG. 215. *Heterodon platyrhinos,* the eastern hognose snake, melanistic phase (Russell County). Melanistic individuals are common in most Alabama populations of this species.

agape and tongue lolling, it rolls over, belly up. During this ordeal it may disgorge a recent meal. Then it becomes still and limp, and takes on every aspect of death — except one; if turned right side up, the "dead" snake immediately rolls over again.

In captivity, hognose snakes usually lose the tendency to behave in this manner and become well adjusted. They will usually feed readily on toads, although an occasional individual will refuse to eat.

Platt (1969) studied the natural history of this species. Between 4 and 69 eggs are laid in sandy or gravelly soil usually at a depth of about 4 inches.

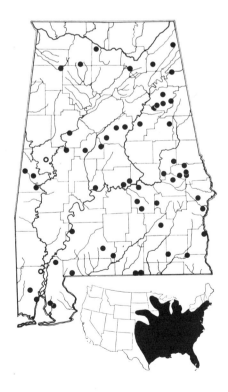

FIG. 216. Distribution of *Heterodon platyrhinos,* the eastern hognose snake. This species is believed to occur statewide, or essentially so, in Alabama. Solid symbols indicate localities from which the author examined specimens. The circles are literature records believed to be valid. The small map depicts approximately the known range in the United States.

FIG. 217. *Heterodon simus,* the southern hognose snake (Covington County). This species has a sharply turned-up snout and a short, stout body. It is often mistaken for the pigmy rattlesnake, *Sistrurus miliarius.*

The diet consists mostly of frogs, toads, insects, and lizards, many of which are apparently obtained by burrowing.

Heterodon simus (Linnaeus)
Southern Hognose Snake

Description: (Fig. 217) A short, stout snake attaining a maximum total length of around 300 mm. Generally similar to *H. platyrhinos* except as follows: rostral sharply upturned; prefrontals separated by small scales; undersides of the tail and belly about the same color. Color pattern more uniform than in *H. platyrhinos,* consisting of a series of mid-dor-

FIG. 218. Distribution of *Heterodon simus,* the southern hognose snake. The hatched area indicates the presumed range in Alabama. The area included within the broken line quite likely contains some scattered populations, but documentation is lacking. Solid symbols indicate localities from which the author examined specimens. Circles are literature records believed to be valid. The small map depicts approximately the known range in the United States.

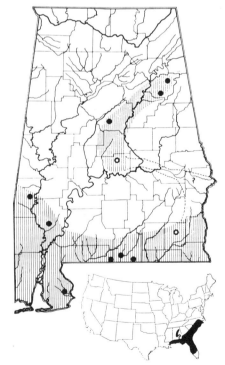

sal dark blotches alternating with smaller dorsolateral blotches on each side. Ground color grayish, yellowish, or light brown, often with tinges of red on dorsum. Melanistic individuals unknown.

Ventrals in eight Alabama males: range 113 to 118, mean 115; in five females: range 126 to 127, mean 126.8. Subcaudals in eight males: range 40 to 44, mean 42; in five females: range 32 to 34, mean 32.6.

Alabama distribution: (Fig. 218) Local in the Coastal Plain and Ridge and Valley region. Apparently absent from the Black Belt. Infrequently encountered.

Habits: The habits of this semi-fossorial snake are poorly known. Most of the specimens I have collected were in sandy, relatively open situations. Several were crossing roads. Apparently the behavior of H. simus does not differ greatly from that of H. platyrhinos. Natural nests are unknown. Price and Carr (1943) reported a clutch of 6 eggs laid in October by a captive female in Florida. Edgren (1955) found 10 eggs in a dead female from Georgia. The southern hognose snake apparently feeds almost exclusively on toads. It does not bite, and most individuals adjust readily to conditions of captivity.

GENUS LAMPROPELTIS Fitzinger

This widely distributed New World genus contains 7 species, 3 of which occur in Alabama.

Lampropeltis calligaster (Harlan)

Two subspecies of this species are recognized. One is found in Alabama, and influence from the other may occur in populations in the extreme northern portion of the state.

Lampropeltis calligaster rhombomaculata (Holbrook)
Mole Snake

Description: (Fig. 219, 220) A medium-sized snake attaining a maximum total length of around 1,145 mm. Head scarcely wider than neck; anal undivided; scales smooth, in 21 or 23 rows at mid-body. Color light brown or yellowish brown to pinkish brown with 33 to 60 black-edged dark brown to reddish spots down the back and alternating, less conspicuous spots on the sides. Pattern fading with age, the markings virtually disappearing in old individuals. Belly light, clouded, or spotted with brown. Juveniles with a conspicuous pattern of reddish spots.

Remarks: Variation in numbers of ventrals and subcaudals among the Alabama specimens examined is shown in Table 7. Although the samples are too small to permit accurate assessment, they suggest that average ventral count is higher in mole snakes in the southern portions of the range than in those in the northern portion. The number of dorsal body blotches ranged from 33 to 48. Most had between 36 and 45, and geographic trends were not indicated.

Alabama distribution: (Fig. 221) Apparently statewide, but records are lacking from some areas. The range of the subspecies L. c. calligaster approaches northwestern Alabama, but the presence of that form in our state has not been established. (See remark on L. c. cal-

TABLE 7. VARIATION IN NUMBER OF VENTRAL AND SUBCAUDAL SCUTES IN Lampropeltis calligaster rhombomaculata IN ALABAMA

Section of Alabama[1]	Males						Females			
	Ventrals			Subcaudals			Ventrals		Subcaudals	
	No.	Range	Mean	No.	Range	Mean	No.	Count	No.	Count
East north-central	5	199-204	201	4	44-51	47.5	1	207	1	43
Central	5	198-209	203.6	3	45-48	47	1	202	1	42
East south-central	6	190-203	198.2	4	43-51	47.3	1	205	1	40
Southwest	3	196-199	197	1		50	1	199	1	45

[1] Counties by section are: East north-central—Calhoun, Etowah; central—Bibb, Tuscaloosa, Shelby, Jefferson; east south-central—Lee, Russell; and Southwest—Mobile.

FIG. 219. *Lampropeltis calligaster rhombomaculata,* the mole snake, adult (Russell County). This secretive, burrowing snake is most often encountered on the road at night. The color is brown or yellowish brown.

FIG. 220. *Lampropeltis calligaster rhombomaculata,* the mole snake, juvenile (Russell County). The reddish blotches on the juvenile mole snake begin fading in intensity during the second year.

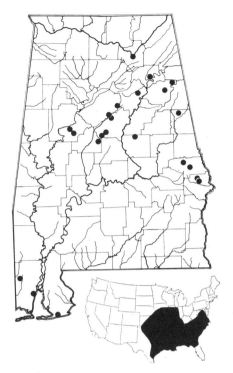

FIG. 221. Distribution of *Lampropeltis calligaster rhombomaculata,* the mole snake. This form is believed to occur statewide, or nearly so, in Alabama. Symbols indicate localities from which the author examined specimens. The small map depicts approximately the known range of the species *L. calligaster* in the United States.

ligaster under "Problematical Forms," p. 24.)

Most of the Alabama specimens have been collected in the Fall Line Hills and Ridge and Valley regions and from the vicinity of Mobile in the Lower Coastal Plain. I have seen none from the Black Belt, Tennessee Valley, or the Lower Coastal Plain east of Mobile County. Records are also lacking from the Red Hills, but that region has not been as intensively searched as some of the others.

Habits: The mole snake is mostly fossorial, and its appearances above ground are confined largely to night-time hours. Driving black-topped roads on warm

spring and summer nights has proven to be the most effective collecting method. Mole snakes collected in that fashion are most often males. Of 25 specimens from Alabama for which sex was recorded, 19 were males. At least 20 of the specimens were collected at night on the road.

Little is known of reproductive habits. Apparently no natural nests have been found. Food consists of lizards, small rodents, bird eggs, and snakes. Captives are unpredictable in their feeding habits, although most will eat mice or lizards if afforded maximum privacy.

Lampropeltis getulus (Linnaeus)

Seven subspecies of this wide-ranging species are currently recognized. Three subspecies occur in Alabama.

Lampropeltis getulus getulus (Linnaeus)
Eastern Kingsnake

Description: (Fig. 222) A large, relatively robust snake attaining a maximum total length of about 2,085 mm. Head not, or but slightly, distinct from neck; anal undivided; tail relatively short; scales smooth, polished, in 21 or 23 rows at mid-body. Body black with 23 to 52 narrow yellow or cream-colored transverse bands (these are occasionally broken) that typically divide on the sides and connect to a series of quadrate light spots. Belly checkered with yellow and black.

Remarks: Young are similar to adults. Variation in the number and width of light bands among Alabama *L. g. getulus* is considerable. Geographic variation in the latter is evident with band width tending to be greater in populations from the southeastern portion of the range (Barbour, Henry, Hale, Houston, Pike, Coffee, and Geneva counties) than in those from other portions. The narrowest bands tend to occur in populations inhabiting Lee, Macon, and Russell counties. Scale counts in randomly selected samples of ten males and ten females collected in Alabama: males, ventrals: range 209 to 224, mean 214.6; subcau-

FIG. 222. *Lampropeltis getulus getulus,* the eastern kingsnake (Macon County). This large, conspicuous snake feeds heavily on other species of snakes, including venomous ones.

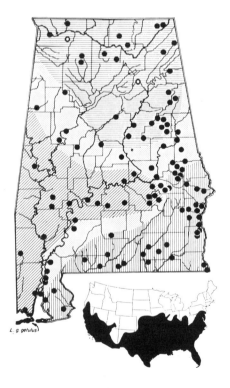

dals: range 39 to 54, mean 48.7. Females, ventrals: range 203 to 222, mean 212.8; subcaudals: range 36 to 51, mean 43.0.

Alabama distribution: (Fig. 223) Generally, eastern and extreme southern Alabama, northward in the former to Lee County and westward in the latter into Baldwin County and onto Dauphin Island in Mobile County. Intergrades fairly abruptly with the other Alabama subspecies along its range boundaries.

Habits: Within its range in Alabama, the eastern kingsnake occurs in nearly all of our terrestrial habitat types and is one

FIG. 223. Distribution of *Lampropeltis getulus* and subspecific variation in Alabama. Horizontal hatching indicates the presumed range of *L. g. niger,* the black kingsnake, vertical hatching, the range of *L. g. getulus,* the eastern kingsnake; and diagonal hatching, the range of *L. g. holbrooki,* the speckled kingsnake. Zones of intergradation are indicated by stippling. Solid symbols indicate localities from which the author examined specimens. Circles are literature records believed to be valid. The small map depicts the species *L. getulus* in the United States.

of the most frequently encountered large snakes. Optimal habitats include abandoned farms, rural garbage dumps, edges of floodplains, and brushy margins of streams and swamps. It is diurnal and almost exclusively ground-dwelling. A fairly conspicuous snake which moves rather slowly, it is easily killed or captured. Freshly captured individuals expel copious amounts of musk and may try to bite. If treated gently, however, they usually become calm and inoffensive.

Kingsnakes are constrictors, but may swallow small prey alive. Snakes are eaten, including poisonous ones, along with lizards, mice, and on occasion birds and amphibians. Many residents of rural Alabama recognize kingsnakes and refrain from killing them. Kingsnakes, when well cared for, usually thrive in captivity and show little resentment at being handled.

Most of the data on reproduction are based on observations of captives. Numbers of eggs laid, considered collectively for the 3 subspecies of *L. getulus* found in Alabama, range from 3 to 24 per clutch.

Lampropeltis getulus holbrooki Stejneger
Speckled Kingsnake

Description: (Fig. 224) Generally similar to *L. g. getulus* except in size and markings. Color black with an oval yellow or cream-colored spot in the center of each scale; contrasting colors intensifying with age; juveniles with 50 to 100 narrow light crossbands which persist into adulthood in some individuals but disappear in others. Maximum total length attained, about 1,675 mm.

Ventral counts in seven males from Alabama: range 207 to 216, mean 212.9; in seven females: range 209 to 225, mean, 218.6. Subcaudal counts in five males: range 44 to 49, mean, 46.8; in two females; 37 subcaudals each.

Alabama distribution: (Fig. 223) The range of this subspecies in Alabama is tongue-shaped. In extreme western Alabama it extends from the coast in Mobile County northward approximately to southern Lamar County. Eastward the range narrows rather abruptly, terminating in central Macon and Bullock coun-

FIG. 224. *Lampropeltis getulus holbrooki,* the speckled kingsnake (Autauga County). The markings on this snake provide excellent concealment in a grassy habitat.

ties, in central southeastern Alabama. Intergradation with *L. g. niger* and *L. g. getulus* occurs, respectively, along the northern and southern boundaries of the range.

Habits: Generally similar to those of *L. g. getulus*. Called "guinea snake" by many who know it, this kingsnake is well camouflaged in grassy situations and is one of the more common Black Belt forms. It attains greatest population densities along the edges of the floodplains of the large rivers which occur within its range.

Lampropeltis getulus niger (Yarrow)
Black Kingsnake

Description: (Fig. 225) Generally similar to *L. g. getulus* except in markings. Body with widely scattered yellow or cream-colored flecks, these more numerous and larger on the lower sides; dorsum in some individuals unpatterned, in others with faint crossbands; light markings on juveniles more numerous and relatively larger than on adults. Maximum total length, about 1,420 mm.

Ventral count in nine males: range 204 and 217, mean 211.6; in six females: range 207 to 218, mean 211.0. Subcaudal count in six males: range 48 to 58, mean 51.8; in two females: range 42 to 44, mean 43.0.

Alabama distribution: (Fig. 223) Most of northern Alabama, extending southward to near the Fall Line in central and eastern Alabama, and well into the Fall Line Hills region in western Alabama. Intergrades with the other subspecies along the southern margin of its range.

Habits: Generally similar to those of *L. g. getulus*.

FIG. 225. *Lampropeltis getulus niger,* the black kingsnake (Shelby County). Many rural people recognize kingsnakes and wisely permit them to live unmolested around their homes and outbuildings.

Lampropeltis triangulum (Lacépède)

The range of this species, which extends from Canada to northern South America, probably exceeds in area that of any other snake in the New World. In his monograph of the species, Williams (1970) recognized a total of 23 subspecies, including 6 new ones which he proposes to name.

The taxonomic history of the complex is lengthy and confusing and cannot be detailed here. Most of the confusion in recent years has stemmed from 2 sources. The first concerns the application of the trivial name *doliata*, which was used prior to *triangulum*. It is not clear whether Linnaeus, who first used the name, applied it to the scarlet snake or to the scarlet kingsnake. The current consensus favors the former interpretation. In 1967, the International Commission of Zoological Nomenclature acted favorably on a petition to suppress the name *doliata* and place it in the synonymy of *Cemophora coccinea* (the scarlet snake). The law of priority in this case was set aside because *doliata* had long been associated with the scarlet kingsnake.

The second element of confusion derives from the peculiar relationship between *L. t. elapsoides* (scarlet kingsnake) and populations of milk snakes in Alabama, Georgia, North Carolina, Tennessee, and Kentucky. Neill (1949a) noted that *L. t. elapsoides* and *L. t. triangulum* (eastern milk snake) occur in sympatry in northern Georgia without interbreeding. Williams (1970) stated that the 2 also occur together and behave as distinct species in the Tennessee Valley in eastern Tennessee, on the Cumberland Plateau of South Carolina and eastern Kentucky, and along the eastern edge of the Appalachian Mountains in parts of North Carolina and Georgia. He also noted that the 2 subspecies may be sympatric over the southwestern portion of the Piedmont in northwestern North Carolina and on the Coastal Plain in southern Virginia, and that they are "probably also sympatric in northern Alabama." He stated that the 2 forms intergrade in northern Virginia, Maryland, Delaware, and New Jersey.

Recent discoveries indicate that not 2, but 3, subspecies are involved in Alabama. I have examined 6 specimens of *L. triangulum* from northwestern Alabama, all from a relatively small area in Lawrence County in the Bankhead National Forest. Five of these were milk snakes referable to the red milk snake subspecies, *L. t. syspila*, and 1 was a scarlet kingsnake, *L. t. elapsoides*. Williams (1970) found some evidence that these forms intergrade in western Tennessee and northern Mississippi. I saw no evidence of intergradation in the series I examined, and I am convinced that they are reproductively isolated in the area where the series was collected.

The other specimens of milk snakes available from Alabama are 6 from the northeastern portion. One of these is referable to *L. t. triangulum*. It was collected 18 miles south-southwest of Mentone on Lookout Mountain, in DeKalb County, in the general vicinity of where Penn reported the subspecies in 1940. Four specimens are from Sand Mountain, which parallels Lookout Mountain to the northwest. These 4, and another from "Mud Creek Management Area" in Jackson County, are clearly intergrades between *L. t. triangulum* and *L. t. syspila*.

The presence of *L. t. elapsoides* in the same general area was established recently by James Adams, who collected a specimen from near the Georgia boundary on Sand Mountain. The specimen shows no indication of gene exchange between the population to which it belongs and the sympatric milk snake population.

Lampropeltis triangulum triangulum (Lacépède)
Eastern Milk Snake

Description: (Fig. 226) A medium-sized snake attaining a maximum total length of about 1,140 mm. Head slightly, or not at all, distinct from neck; anal undivided; scales smooth, usually in 21 rows at mid-body. Dorsum gray to tan with 24 to 54 (average 36) black-bordered dark gray or brownish blotches

FIG. 226. *Lampropeltis triangulum triangulum,* the eastern milk snake (DeKalb County). This subspecies occurs in Alabama only on Lookout Mountain and is rarely encountered. The blotches are reddish or reddish brown.

(red in juveniles), these usually terminating laterally on the third or fourth scale row (counting from bottom); a ventrolateral row (or 2 rows) of irregularly shaped dark blotches on each side alternating with the dorsal blotches. First body blotch usually connecting to dark markings on head, encircling a medial Y- or V-shaped light area on nape or back of head. Venter with rectangular black markings, these often arranged in checkerboard fashion.

Alabama distribution: (Fig. 227) Apparently confined to Lookout Mountain. The southwestern terminus of the range on the mountain is not known. Intergrades with *L. t. syspila* on Sand Mountain (see above).

Habits: Reportedly the eastern milk snake is rather secretive, spending much of its time under rocks, boards, logs, and in other protected places. In some parts of its range, forested areas appear to be the favored habitats, while in other parts, prairies are said to be frequently inhabited. The snake is said to be mostly nocturnal during hot weather and active during the day at other times. Some seasonal variation in habitat preference is indicated, the snake tending to frequent higher elevations during fall, winter, and spring months and to move into low, mesic areas during the summer.

The recently collected DeKalb County specimen of *L. t. triangulum* was found at night in June on a rocky ridge. The dominant vegetation at the site was Virginia pine (*Pinus virginiana*). The 5 *L. t. triangulum* x *syspila* mentioned above were all collected in May. Two were found under rocks along the edge of a mountain and 1 was dead in the road on a mountainside. The collection sites for the remaining 2 were not recorded.

The eastern milk snake may bite when captured but tends to become mild-mannered in captivity. Feeding response in captives is unpredictable, but most will feed on young mice. The idea that milk snakes suck milk from cows is, of course, a fallacy.

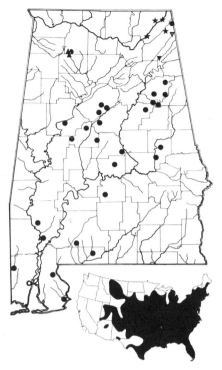

FIG. 227. Distribution of *Lampropeltis tri-angulum* and subspecific variation in Alabama. In Alabama the complex is found statewide, or essentially so. Solid symbols indicate localities from which the author examined specimens. Symbols with light centers are literature records believed to be valid. Circular symbols refer to *L. t. elap-soides*, the scarlet kingsnake; triangles in northwestern Alabama, to *L. t. syspila*, the red milk snake; inverted triangles (in north-eastern Alabama), to *L. t. triangulum*, the eastern milk snake; and stars, to intergrades between *L. t. triangulum* and *L. t. syspila*. The small map depicts approximately the range of the species *L. triangulum* in the United States.

FIG. 228. *Lampropeltis triangulum elapso-ides,* the scarlet kingsnake (Jefferson County). This fairly small, secretive snake has red, black, and yellow bands and a red nose. It is 1 of 2 Alabama snakes that is often mistaken for the venomous coral snake.

Lampropeltis triangulum elapsoides
(Holbrook)
Scarlet Kingsnake

Description: (Fig. 228) A fairly small, strikingly marked snake attaining a maximum total length of about 560 mm. Differs markedly from *L. t. triangulum* (described above) and *L. t. syspila* (see following). Scales usually in 17 or 19 rows at mid-body; body and tail ringed with red, black, and yellow (or white), the red and yellow rings always separated by black; red rings usually as wide or wider than intervening areas; pattern continuing onto head; snout red; ringed pattern often irregular on venter.

Alabama distribution: (Fig. 227) Probably statewide, but records are lacking from several large areas. Most abundant in Lower Coastal Plain and Fall Line Hills regions. Overlaps range of *L. t. syspila* in northwestern Alabama and those of *L. t. triangulum* and *L. t. triangulum* x *syspila* in northeastern Alabama.

Habits: This small kingsnake is extremely secretive and seldom ventures abroad during the day. Although an occasional individual is picked up on the road at night, most specimens are taken from rotting pine stumps, especially in the spring months.

Information on reproduction of scarlet kingsnakes in Alabama is lacking. Palmer

(1961) reported 6 eggs from inside a rotting pine stump in North Carolina, 3 of which hatched on August 23. I found a clutch of 2 eggs on September 10 in Hines County, Georgia, in a rotting pine stump. They were irregularly elliptic in shape and measured 38.5 x 11.5 mm and 30.0 x 11.0 mm, respectively. Hatching occurred on September 30.

Scarlet kingsnakes feed mostly on ground skinks and other small lizards. Other dietary items reported include small snakes, mice, fish, and earthworms. It seems unlikely that the last two are important. A captive will usually thrive on a diet of skinks. A piece of bark or other cover should be placed in the cage to provide a hiding place.

This snake and the one it superficially resembles, the scarlet snake, are both commonly mistaken for the venomous coral snake. Neither of the 2 mimics has the black nose of the coral snake, however, and on neither do the red and yellow (or white) rings come into contact with each other as is the case on the coral snake. The following rhyme may be kept in mind as an aid in remembering this:

"Red on yellow kill a fellow;
"Red on black, friend of Jack."

Lampropeltis triangulum syspila (Cope)
Red Milk Snake

Description: (Fig. 229) An attractive, medium-sized snake attaining a maximum total length of around 990 mm. Generally similar to *L. t. triangulum* in scalation but differing rather markedly in color characteristics. Body blotches, or saddles, typically red, wider and fewer in number (16 to 31, average 23), and extending downward on each side to about the first scale row (as opposed to the third or fourth in *L. t. triangulum*). General aspect, viewed dorsally, that of a banded or ringed snake as opposed to a more apparently blotched snake as in *L. t. triangulum*. Intervals between dorsal saddles white, cream, yellowish, or gray in color.

Head variously patterned, with red predominating on top; end of snout often predominantly light; first body blotch or saddle usually not connected to head pattern and separated from it by a light band or collar bordered posteriorly by black margin of first body blotch and anteriorly by a narrow black head band.

Ventrolateral surface often with a series of small blotches, similar in constitution to the dorsal ones and alternating with them. Venter light with large rectangular marks arranged irregularly or in checkerboard fashion.

Remarks: Considerable individual variation in pattern occurs in this subspecies. In old individuals, the saddles and blotches sometime become reddish brown or grayish brown.

I was able to examine in detail 3 red milk snakes from Lawrence County while

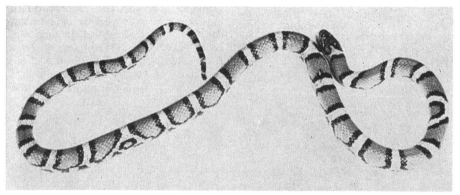

FIG. 229. *Lampropeltis triangulum syspila*, red milk snake (Lawrence County). This snake has black-bordered red saddles and, usually, a light collar. It is secretive and seldom encountered in Alabama.

they were alive. All were in reasonably close conformity to the definition given by Williams (1970). The color of the saddles in the 3 specimens ranged from bright red to brownish red. One had 25 saddles, the other two had 26. Each of the saddles, or the black margins thereof, reached the first scale row on each side. Each had a series of alternating ventro-lateral blotches on each side. One specimen, AM 21345, does not have the light collar. On this one the first body blotch communicates laterally with the head pattern, leaving a circular light spot on back of the head. This is the only feature I noted on any of Lawrence County milk snakes that conflicts with the definition of *L. t. syspila*.

Alabama distribution: (Fig. 227) Known only from the Bankhead National Forest in northwestern Alabama. Inter-grades between the red milk snake and eastern milk snake have been collected in DeKalb and Jackson counties, in north-eastern Alabama. There are several un-documented and unpublished reports of this form from Madison and Cullman counties.

Habits: Fitch and Fleet (1970) stud-ied the life history and ecology of the red milk snake in Kansas. The optimal habitat was said to be open woodland and woodland edge with an abundance of flat rocks and other types of cover, under which the snakes spend much of their time. Food items included lizards, snakes, and small mammals, with the reptilian component being most impor-tant. Alabama specimens in captivity fed readily on small mice but refused lizards and snakes.

The number of eggs laid by the red milk snake averages around 7 or 8. Aside from one report of a clutch of eggs in a manure pile, I know of no reference to natural nesting.

Information on this form in Alabama is limited to collection data and a few observations on captives. The Alabama specimens were all collected at relatively high elevations in the Bankhead National Forest. Except for 1, all were found by turning rocks and logs, and by breaking

open rotting logs, in relatively open, dry woodlands. Situations near rock outcrops seem to be favored. One specimen was found in the open on the forest floor. All were collected during April and May.

Several of the snakes collected had lost part of the tail, apparently due to tail rot, and one was acutely infected with fungus. This snake was collected in the spring of 1972, following a relatively warm, wet winter.

GENUS *MASTICOPHIS*
Baird and Girard

This New World genus contains 9 spe-cies and ranges from southeastern and western United States to northern South America. Alabama has 1 species.

Masticophis flagellum (Shaw)

Wilson (1970) recognized 7 subspe-cies of this wide-ranging species. One of these occurs in Alabama.

Masticophis flagellum flagellum (Shaw)
Eastern Coachwhip

Description: (Fig. 230) A long, slen-der snake attaining a maximum total length of about 2,590 mm. Head fairly distinct, but narrow; eyes large; tail long, whiplike in appearance; scales smooth, in 17 rows at mid-body (usually); anal divided. Head, neck, and anterior por-tion of body dark brown to nearly black, grading into tan posteriorly. Venter dark brown anteriorly, cream posteriorly.

Juveniles mostly lacking longitudinal transition in ground color; dorsum tan with dark bands, these more pronounced anteriorly. Venter of juveniles cream with a double row of spots in the neck region.

Remarks: The extent to which dark pigment covers the anterior portion of the body varies clinally from southeast to northwest within the subspecies range (Wilson, 1970). Individuals from the southeastern portion are usually predom-inantly pale, while those from the north-western portion are mostly dark. Pre-sumably this same trend will be found

FIG. 230. *Masticophis flagellum flagellum*, the eastern coachwhip (Lee County). The tail of this snake suggests the end of a braided whip. There is no truth to the widespread belief that the coachwhip will whip a person.

to occur within Alabama coachwhips, but the relatively small number of specimens currently available does not now permit accurate assessment of variation in this character. On the average, about one-third to one-half of the body is dark on the specimens I examined.

No significant geographic variation in scale counts was noted among the Alabama specimens examined. Ventrals in fourteen Alabama males: range 196 to 207, mean 202.8; in fifteen females: range 198 to 208, mean 202.0. Subcaudals in eleven males: range 94 to 111, mean 102.4; in twelve females: range 96 to 113, mean 104.0.

Alabama distribution: (Fig. 231) Statewide, apparently, except for some portions north of the Tennessee River. Specimens from north of the river are lacking altogether, but several reports I have received from competent observers lead me to conclude that the coachwhip does occur there, albeit very locally.

Habits: In Alabama the coachwhip is usually found in dry, relatively open places. The most favorable habitats are upland situations where open woods are interspersed with weedy fields. The coachwhip is lithe and graceful, and among North American snakes its speed and maneuverability are unmatched. It is an adept climber, and often ascends into bushes and small trees when pur-

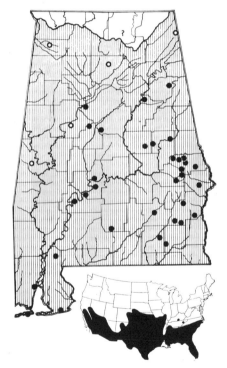

FIG. 231. Distribution of *Masticophis flagellum flagellum*, the eastern coachwhip. The presumed range in Alabama is indicated by hatching. Solid symbols indicate localities from which the author examined specimens. Circles are literature records believed to be valid. The small map depicts approximately the known range of the species *M. flagellum* in the United States.

sued. Its common name is based on the appearance of the tail, which is long and resembles the distal portion of a braided whip. The coachwhip puts up a vigorous defense when cornered, often aiming its strikes at the adversary's face. It will not, however, chase down a person and "flail him to death," as some people apparently believe.

The eggs are oblong with granular surfaces. Clutch size appears to average about 12. There are no observations from Alabama on its reproduction. Food reportedly consists of insects, lizards, small mammals, birds, and other snakes. Two I caught had recently eaten lizards. Coachwhips adjust rather poorly to captivity, and most I have had refused to eat. Wilson (1973) provided an updated review of the literature on this species.

GENUS *NATRIX* Laurenti

This genus, found in North America, Europe, Asia, and Africa, contains about 18 species.

Natrix cyclopion (Duméril and Bibron)

Natrix cyclopion was divided into 2 subspecies by Goff (1936). Specimens from Florida, South Carolina, and Georgia were placed in *N. c. floridana;* those from Mobile County, Alabama, westward were allocated to the nominate subspecies. Goff failed to find evidence of intergradation between the 2 forms, but postulated that intergrades would probably be found "where the ranges meet," somewhere "between Mobile, Alabama, and Leon County, Florida."

FIG. 232. *Natrix cyclopion cyclopion,* the green water snake. The ground color is dull, dark greenish. There is a row of subocular scales between the orbit and the upper labials.

Specimens of both *N. c. cyclopion* and *N. c. floridana* are available from Baldwin County, Alabama. Clear evidence of intergradation between the 2, however, is lacking. In a series of several specimens from a pond near Orange Beach, in extreme southeastern Baldwin County, the snakes' venters are slightly darker than those of most *floridana*, but otherwise they are clearly referable to that form. Specimens from other localities in Baldwin County have no indications of intermediacy and are easily referred to one or the other of the 2 forms. Moreover, Carr (1940) indicated that *N. c. cyclopion* occurred in Florida in Escambia and Leon counties and recalled having collected 2 specimens in the latter county. The green water snakes from Florida I have seen have all been apparently good *floridana*. Only 2, however, were from the Florida Panhandle (1 each from Walton and Escambia counties).

It is, thus, with some reservation that I list *floridana* as a subspecies of *N. cyclopion*. Further investigation of the problem is definitely warranted.

Natrix cyclopion cyclopion
(Duméril and Bibron)
Green Water Snake

Description: (Fig. 232, 233) A large, heavy-bodied aquatic snake attaining a maximum total length of about 1,270 mm. Tail fairly short; head distinct from neck; scales keeled (except for first row on each side), usually in 27 rows at midbody in males, 29 in females; anal divided; orbit separated from upper labials by a series of subocular scales.

Dorsal color dark olive to dark green, with a series of mid-dorsal dark blotches alternating with dark lateral bars, the markings becoming indistinct in old individuals.

Anterior one-third of the belly yellowish to white, the posterior two-thirds and undersurface of tail smoky gray to brown with light half-moons. Ventrals usually range in number from 136 to 146; subcaudals from 65 to 78 in males, 58 to 75 in females; lateral bars usually number between 38 and 48.

Ventral count in seven males from Ala-

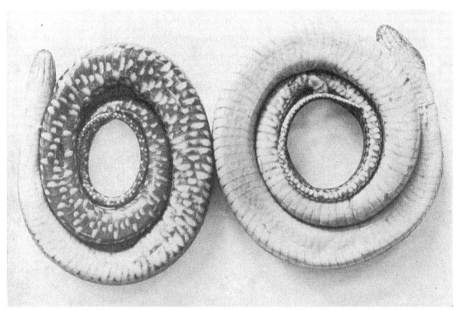

FIG. 233. Venters of the subspecies of *Natrix cyclopion*. On the left is *N. c. cyclopion* and on the right, *N. c. floridana*.

bama: range 139 to 144, mean 141.3; in seven females: range, 139 to 144, mean 141. Subcaudals in the males: range 65 to 77, mean 73.3; in the females: range 63 to 77, mean 70.0. Lateral bars in the males: range 39 to 45, mean 41.0; in the females: range 41 to 47, mean 44.2.

Alabama distribution: (Fig. 234) Specimens have been collected in swamps in lower Baldwin and Mobile counties and in the wooded swamps and tree-lined waterways between the Mobile and Tensaw rivers. The northern limit of the range in Alabama is unde-

FIG. 234. Distribution of *Natrix cyclopion* and subspecific variation in Alabama. The hatched area indicates the range of the species in Alabama. Solid circles indicate localities from which the author examined specimens referable to *N. c. cyclopion,* the green water snake. Triangles indicate locality records for specimens referable to *N. c. floridana,* the Florida green water snake. The starred symbol marks a locality from which specimens intermediate between *N. c. cyclopion* and *N. c. floridana* were examined. The small map depicts approximately the range of the species *N. cyclopion* in the United States.

termined but is probably the northern boundary of the Lower Coastal Plain. A Tuscaloosa County record, mentioned originally by Löding (1922), is doubtless invalid.

Habits: *Natrix c. cyclopion* prefers timbered swamps, oxbows, and sloughs associated with floodplains, and sluggish, tree-lined streams. In Alabama, it abounds in the tupelo gum-cypress swamps along the Tensaw and Mobile rivers and their associated waterways. It is fond of basking during late winter and spring, when numerous individuals may be seen, along with cottonmouths and other aquatic snakes, in bushes and on low tree branches that overhang the water. The snake is scarce or absent in much of the lower portion of the Mobile Bay delta area, where open expanses of marsh and grass flats are the prevalent habitats. Thus, the optimal habitat of this form may differ considerably from that of *N. c. floridana,* a snake frequently found in open situations, particularly those with an abundance of herbaceous vegetation.

Fish appear to be by far the most important food. Amphibians are eaten infrequently. The green water snake reproduces by giving birth, with litter size averaging about 15. Garton, *et al.* (1970) provided the most recent work on the habits of this form, concentrating their study on an Illinois population.

Natrix cyclopion floridana Goff
Florida Green Water Snake

Description: (Fig. 233, 235) Differs from *N. c. cyclopion* in having a predominantly light belly, usually yellow or white with only faint indications of markings; fewer ventrals on the average (usual range from 133 to 143); fewer caudals on the average (usual range from 73 to 83 in males, 65 to 75 in females); and a greater number of lateral bars (usual range from 46 to 58). Undersurface of tail similar in the 2 forms.

Alabama distribution: (Fig. 234) Local in the southern portion of Baldwin County.

FIG. 235. *Natrix cyclopion floridana,* the Florida green water snake (Baldwin County).

Habits: While optimum habitat for *N. c. cyclopion* is wooded swamp, that for *N. c. floridana* is weed-choked marsh or wet prairie. In peninsular Florida, the Florida green water snake is often the most commonly encountered aquatic snake in such habitats. My observations indicate that it is somewhat more nocturnal and less inclined to bask than *N. c. cyclopion.* Another possible dissimilarity between the two is inferred by a comparison of their geographic ranges. *Natrix c. cyclopion* in Alabama ranges inland at least 60 miles, perhaps to the upper edge of the Lower Coastal Plain, and in the Mississippi Valley the range extends northward to Illinois. *Natrix c. floridana,* on the other hand, is seldom found more than 30 miles from the coast, at least in the western part of its range (Alabama and the Florida Panhandle).

Collecting sites for the Florida green water snake in Alabama, all in lower Baldwin County, include a weedy roadside pond near the Perdido River; shallow, weedy ponds; and a freshwater inlet along the eastern shore of Mobile Bay. The food habits apparently differ from those of *N. c. cyclopion* in that frogs instead of fish constitute the most important component of the diet. The number of young in the Florida green water snake reportedly ranges from 10 to 67.

Natrix erythrogaster Forster

Four subspecies of this snake are recognized. One of these occurs in Alabama and another exerts strong genetic influence in intergradient populations.

Natrix erythrogaster erythrogaster (Forster)

Red-bellied Water Snake

Description: (Fig. 236, 237) A large, moderately heavy snake attaining a maximum total length of about 1,575 mm. Tail relatively short; head distinct from neck; scales strongly keeled, in 23 rows at mid-body; dorsum of adults unpatterned, dark brownish or grayish brown, becoming somewhat light on the sides; belly orange or reddish orange, unmarked except for a brownish gray suffusion on anterior edges of the ventrals. Young conspicuously patterned, often mistaken for those of *N. sipedon pleuralis;* anterior one-fourth to one-third of body with dark bands, these breaking up to form dark saddles and alternating vertical bars on remainder of body; light interspaces separating dorsal bands and saddles about 1 scale row wide; belly of juvenile yellowish or cream with dark pigment on anterior edges of ventrals.

Alabama distribution: (Fig. 238) The species occurs essentially statewide. Individuals of *N. erythrogaster* with reddish venters, indicative of influence of the subspecies *N. e. erythrogaster,* occur most frequently in southeastern Alabama but are not uncommon as far west as Butler County and as far north as Cleburne County. All populations in which

FIG. 236. *Natrix erythrogaster erythrogaster* x *flavigaster,* adult (Lee County). The specimen shown is an intergrade between the red-bellied water snake and the yellow-bellied water snake. The venter of this common water snake may be reddish orange, orange, or yellow.

such individuals occur, however, have a high incidence of yellow-bellied members and should, in my opinion, be considered intergradient. (See "Alabama distribution" under *N. e. flavigaster.*)

Habits: See "Habits" under *N. e. flavigaster.*

Natrix erythrogaster flavigaster Conant
Yellow-bellied Water Snake

Description: (Fig. 236, 237) Similar to *N. e. erythrogaster* except in characters of pigmentation. Dorsum of adults gray, greenish gray, or dark brown to almost black, usually unpatterned but occasionally showing traces of the juvenile pattern; venter yellowish or, rarely, cream-colored; juvenile similar to that of *N. e. erythrogaster.* Maximum total length in this subspecies to around 1,475 mm.

Remarks: Geographic variation in scale counts was not detectable among specimens of *N. erythrogaster* examined. Sexual dimorphism, however, was indicated. Following are data on scale counts taken from specimens selected randomly

from Alabama localities. Ventral count in thirty-nine males: range 138 to 150, mean 144.9; in forty-eight females: range 141 to 155, mean 146.6. Subcaudal count in twenty-six males: range 76 to 87, mean 80.6; in thirty-three females: range 63 to 75, mean 69.1.

Alabama distribution: (Fig. 238) The Tennessee River drainage in northern Alabama and southward in the western one-half of the state to the Gulf Coast. Intergrades with *N. e. erythrogaster* throughout the remainder of the state.

Habits: *Natrix e. erythrogaster* and *N. e. flavigaster* apparently have similar habits, and the following remarks apply to the species, as I know it in Alabama.

N. erythrogaster is one of the most abundant snakes in central Alabama and in parts of southern Alabama. It occurs in most kinds of permanently aquatic habitats, but seems best adapted to swamps, sluggish streams, floodplain pools, and lakes and ponds with swampy margins.

It is chiefly nocturnal, and on rainy nights is often seen crossing roads. At such times it tends to move into flooded

FIG. 237. *Natrix erythrogaster erythrogaster* x *flavigaster,* juvenile (Lee County). The dorsal pattern becomes obscure with age and in most individuals is lost altogether by the end of the second year. Patterned individuals are readily distinguishable from *N. sipedon pleuralis* by a difference in ventral markings.

ditches and other such places where frogs congregate to breed. Driving through low country on rainy nights and investigating these places is a good way to locate and collect *N. erythrogaster*, along with several other aquatic snakes.

Frogs and fish are the main food items of this species. It is viviparous, with the number of young usually ranging from 10 to 27. *N. erythrogaster* is rather disagreeable as a captive, but usually feeds well if properly cared for.

Natrix fasciata (Linnaeus)

The *Natrix fasciata* complex of 6 subspecies was separated taxonomically

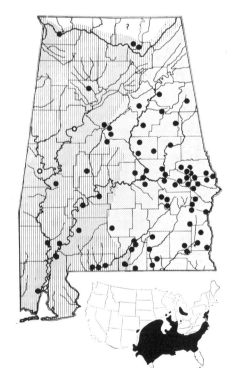

FIG. 238. Distribution of *Natrix erythrogaster* and subspecific variation in Alabama. The hatched area indicates the presumed range of *N. e. flavigaster,* the yellow-bellied water snake in Alabama. The stippled area is a zone of intergradation between *N. e. flavigaster* and *N. e. erythrogaster,* the red-bellied water snake. Solid symbols indicate localities from which the author examined specimens. Circles are literature records believed to be valid. The small map depicts approximately the range of the species *N. erythrogaster* in the United States.

from *N. sipedon* by Conant (1963) on the basis of a study of overlapping populations in the Carolinas and on reports that they occur in sympatry elsewhere in their ranges. Conant found evidence of interbreeding between the 2, but considered it to be a manifestation of introgression resulting from human disturbance of the habitats. Conant and Lazell (1973) reported additional evidence of interbreeding between *N. fasciata* and *N. sipedon* from the coastal area of North Carolina, and suggested that, in that case, hurricanes are causing the "apparent introgression."

Schwaner (1969) studied the relationship between *N. fasciata* ssp. and *N. sipedon pleuralis* in Alabama and found extensive interbreeding between them in 4 essentially unaltered streams in the Coastal Plain. However, a zone of intergradation between the two, in the traditional sense, appeared to be lacking.

It is apparent that considerable gene exchange is occurring between *N. fasciata* and *N. sipedon*. While a strong argument can be put forth for considering them conspecific, the complexity of the relationship and the inadequacy of our present knowledge favor retention of currently accepted nomenclature.

Subspecific variation in *N. fasciata* in Alabama involves 4 of the 6 recognized subspecies.

Natrix fasciata fasciata (Linnaeus)
Banded Water Snake

Description: (Fig. 239, 240) A relatively stout-bodied aquatic snake attaining a maximum length of around 1,525 mm. Tail fairly short; head distinct from neck; scales keeled; anal divided; labials swollen. Highly variable in coloration; dorsum tan, brown, or reddish brown, with darker crossbands, these often light-edged and sometimes irregular, but seldom broken; crossbands usually wider on dorsum than on sides; head with a dark postorbital stripe; venter yellowish with reddish to dark brown blotches that tend to be squarish or rectangular in shape and that seldom involve more than 1 ventral scute each.

FIG. 239. *Natrix fasciata fasciata*, banded water snake, light phase (Covington County). Freshwater forms of the species *N. fasciata* typically have unbroken dorsal bands. Populations intermediate between *N. fasciata* and *N. sipedon pleuralis* are found in many places in southern Alabama.

FIG. 240. *Natrix fasciata fasciata*, banded water snake, melanistic phase (Covington County). In Alabama melanistic individuals of *N. fasciata* are encountered most frequently in Houston and Geneva counties, where influence of the subspecies *N. f. pictiventris* is greatest.

Remarks: Ventral count in males of populations of this subspecies in Alabama, as well as in other populations of *N. fasciata* in the state, averages 1 or 2 less than in females. Subcaudal count in males averages 5 or 6 greater than in females. Overlap between sexes in both counts is extensive. The range in ventral count among Alabama specimens examined, sexes and subspecies combined, was 110 to 135. The range in subcaudals was 51 to 88.

Alabama distribution: (Fig. 241) The species *Natrix fasciata* occurs in suitable habitats throughout the Alabama Lower Coastal Plain and is confined to that region. Subspecific variation is complex. Records for *N. fasciata clarki* are limited to salt marshes in Baldwin and Mobile counties. I have not detected evidence of intergradation between *N. f. clarki* and the inland forms in Alabama, but I have seen obvious intergrades from the Florida Panhandle.

The pattern of subspecific variation among inland populations of *N. fasciata* is not clear. Boyles (1952) and Cliburn (1957) recognized the influence of *N. f.*

pictiventris in Houston County populations, in extreme southeastern Alabama. Schwaner (1969) found characteristics of that subspecies, in the form of worm-like ventral markings, in some specimens from as far west as Monroe and Escambia counties.

Schwaner detected strong influence of *N. f. confluens,* in the form of reduced number of crossbands and in ventral blotches that involve 2 to 4 scutes, in Mobile and Baldwin counties, nearly to the western limit of *N. f. pictiventris* influence.

The question thus arises as to whether unadulterated *N. f. fasciata* occurs in Alabama at all. Cliburn questioned the validity of the subspecies *fasciata* in 1957, noting that the holotype was collected within a zone of intergradation and that the topotypic material varied extensively. My own observations, however, indicate that our present concept of *N. f. fasciata* may appropriately be applied to populations inhabiting much of the Coastal Plain of the Carolinas and Georgia. In Alabama, individuals referable to *N. f. fasciata* appear to predominate in populations in that portion of the species range from Covington County to eastern Baldwin County, and, despite the complications, I shall tentatively accord them that designation.

In the Lower Coastal Plain stretches of the Pea, Choctawhatchee, Yellow, and Conecuh rivers, *N. fasciata* interbreeds extensively with *N. sipedon,* with characteristics of the latter predominating in those populations. Evidence of interbreeding can also be seen in specimens collected from ponds in Monroe and Washington counties (latter not indicated on map) near the northern edge of the Lower Coastal Plain.

Habits: The habits of the inland populations of *N. fasciata* are essentially similar. They occur in most kinds of permanently aquatic habitats. Banded water snakes are especially common in shallow sinkhole lakes and ponds, and in swamps with abundant vegetation. Stream habitats seldom support dense populations. The snakes are most active at night, particularly when heavy rains elicit an outburst of frog activity. At these times they tend to move out of their permanent-water habitats and into flooded ditches and other temporary accumulations of water where breeding frogs are abundant. *Natrix fasciata* shares this habit with *N. erythrogaster* and *Agkistrodon piscivorus.*

The young are usually born in July and August; litter size typically ranges from 10 to 35. The diet consists mostly of small fish and frogs, supplemented occasionally by salamanders and tadpoles.

Natrix fasciata is commonly mistaken for the venomous cottonmouth. It is extraordinarily disagreeable and is vigorous in defending itself if escape is prevented. Captives typically thrive but can seldom be trusted not to bite. The bites, however, like those of our other non-venomous species, are ordinarily no worse than brier scratches.

Natrix fasciata clarki (Baird and Girard)
Gulf Salt Marsh Water Snake

Description: (Fig. 242) A moderately stout, aquatic snake attaining a maxi-

mum total length of about 915 mm. Tail fairly short; head distinct from neck; scales keeled; anal divided; labials swollen. Color pattern conspicuously different from other *N. fasciata* found in Alabama. Dorsum dark gray to reddish brown, with mid-dorsal and dorsolateral yellowish stripes, the latter more conspicuous than the former. Venter black or black with tinges of yellow, having a sharply

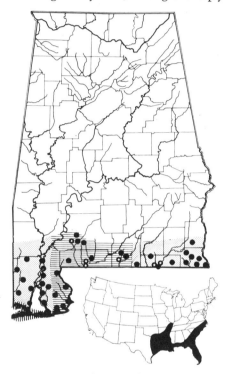

FIG. 241. Distribution of *Natrix fasciata* and subspecific variation in Alabama. Horizontal hatching indicates the presumed range of *N. f. fasciata,* the banded water snake, in Alabama; vertical hatching indicates that of *N. f. clarki,* the Gulf salt marsh water snake. The stippled area in southeastern Alabama is a zone of intergradation between *N. f. fasciata* and *N. f. pictiventris,* the Florida water snake. The stippled area in southwestern Alabama is a zone of intergradation between *N. f. fasciata* and *N. f. confluens,* the broad-banded water snake. Triangles are records of *N. f. clarki;* solid circular symbols are records for other specimens of *N. fasciata.* Starred symbols are records for specimens intermediate between *N. fasciata* ssp. and *N. sipedon pleuralis.* The small map depicts approximately the range of the species *N. fasciata* in the United States.

FIG. 242. *Natrix fasciata clarki,* the Gulf salt marsh water snake (Mobile County, Dauphin Island). This snake is confined to salt marshes in Mobile and Baldwin counties. It has longitudinal light stripes on the dorsum and a median yellow stripe on the venter.

contrasting median yellow stripe continuing well onto the tail, and a pair of ventrolateral yellow stripes, these involving the edges of the ventral scutes and the first row of dorsals. Lower labials, chin shields, and some upper labials typically light-centered.

Ventral count in two Alabama males: 130 and 131; in nine females: range 129 to 135, mean 131.9. Subcaudal count in two males: 79 and 82; in three females: range 68 to 71, mean 69.7.

Remarks: The color pattern is reported to be highly variable in this subspecies. All Alabama specimens I have examined, however, were in reasonable conformity with that in the above description.

Alabama distribution: (Fig. 241) Coastal salt marshes. (See "Alabama distribution" under *N. f. fasciata.*)

Habits: This snake is the only one in Alabama that habitually occupies the salt marsh habitat. It is active mostly at night, feeding on small fish and, occasionally, on crabs. Data on reproduction in Alabama are lacking. Reports from other areas indicate a range in litter size

of from 2 to 44. Available habitat for this snake in Alabama has rapidly diminished in recent years as a result of dredge-and-fill operations and encroaching real estate developments.

Natrix fasciata confluens Blanchard
Broad-banded Water Snake

Description: Generally similar to *N. f. fasciata* except as follows: dark bands much wider than the interspaces between them; venter more extensively dark-pigmented, the blotches usually occupying 3 or more scutes each and often merging extensively.

Alabama distribution: (Fig. 241) The Alabama populations of *N. fasciata* in freshwater habitats from the eastern boundary of the Mobile Bay drainage westward are considered intergradient between *N. f. confluens* and *N. f. fasciata.* (See "Alabama distribution" under *N. f. fasciata.*)

Habits: The habits of the freshwater populations of *N. fasciata* in Alabama are not known to differ subspecifically and are treated under *N. f. fasciata.*

Natrix fasciata pictiventris Cope
Florida Water Snake

Description: Differs from *N. f. fasciata* chiefly in having irregular, wormlike markings instead of rectangular blotches on the venter, and in having on the sides secondary dark spots between the bands.

Remarks: In some adults of this form and less frequently in some belonging to *N. f. fasciata*, the dorsal pattern is virtually obliterated by melanic suffusion in the interspaces between the bands. In such individuals indications of the bands may be indistinctly visible on the sides as bars of lighter color. This represents a curious reversal of the light-to-dark relationship that obtains in the young snakes and in the non-melanistic adults. Such individuals (Fig. 240) were found in Alabama in Houston, Geneva, and Covington counties, and in the Florida Panhandle farther westward, to Santa Rosa County.

Alabama distribution: (Fig. 241) Populations of *N. fasciata* in Alabama from Covington County eastward are considered to be intergradient between *N. f. fasciata* and *N. f. pictiventris*. (See "Alabama distribution" under *N. f. fasciata*.)

Habits: The habits of the freshwater populations of *N. fasciata* in Alabama are not known to differ subspecifically and are treated under *N. f. fasciata*.

Natrix rhombifera (Hallowell)

Natrix rhombifera was considered conspecific with *Natrix taxispilota*, another water snake species occurring in Alabama, by at least one worker as late as 1968 (Cagle, 1968). Mount and Schwaner (1970) presented evidence supporting the opposite view, which appears to be the consensus (Wright and Wright, 1957; Conant, 1958, 1969; Smith, 1961; and Anderson, 1965).

Three subspecies of *N. rhombifera* are recognized, 1 of which occurs in Alabama.

Natrix rhombifera rhombifera (Hallowell)
Diamond-backed Water Snake

Description: (Fig. 243) A large, thick-bodied snake attaining a maximum total length of around 1,600 mm. Tail short; head distinct from neck; scales keeled, in 25 to 31 rows; anal divided; suboculars absent; rear of parietals entire (as opposed to fragmented as in *N. taxispilota*); anterior temporals undivided; chin of large males bearing conspicuous papillae. Dorsum olive to brown with a median series of dark blotches, these usually connected by narrow, diagonal stripes at their corners to smaller, alternating dark blotches on each side; venter yellowish with dark semilunar spots, these more numerous posteriorly; chin shields immaculate (as opposed to dark-smudged in *N. taxispilota*).

Females exceed males in maximum size attained and in mean number of dorsal scale rows. Males exceed females in mean ventral count, mean subcaudal count and mean number of dorsal body blotches (Table 8).

Alabama distribution: (Fig. 244) The Coastal Plain, except for the extreme northwestern corner, eastward to the eastern periphery of the Mobile Bay drainage area.

Habits: This heavy-bodied snake is

TABLE 8. SEXUAL DIMORPHISM IN *Natrix rhombifera rhombifera* FROM ALABAMA

Specimens, No. and sex	Ventrals		Subcaudals		Scale rows at mid-body		Dorsal body blotches	
	Range	Mean	Range	Mean	Range	Mean	Range	Mean
Randomly collected specimens								
7 males	146-143	138.5	73-80	77.7	25-27	26.4	28-36	31.1
11 females	135-138	136.8	62-72	67.0	27-29	27.5	27-33	30.1
Composite of 3 litters								
39 males	133-145	140.9	74-84	77.4	25-29	26.8	26-36	30.9
31 females	132-143	138.1	63-74	65.4	27-29	27.6	27-35	30.5

FIG. 243. *Natrix rhombifera rhombifera,* the diamond-backed water snake (Baldwin County). This large, heavy-bodied water snake is olive brown with a dark, chainlike pattern on the dorsum. It occurs in a variety of aquatic habitats and is often mistaken for the venomous cottonmouth.

strongly aquatic and is found in greatest abundance in sloughs and lakes associated with rivers. Other habitats include streams of various sizes, swamps, and large farm ponds. It is active day and night, differing in this respect from *N. taxispilota,* which is rather strongly diurnal. Also, the diamond-backed water snake apparently basks somewhat less frequently than *N. taxispilota.* Fish and frogs are the dominant food items.

Three females captured in Alabama gave birth to litters of 23, 24, and 24 young. Much larger broods have been reported from some other areas.

The diamond-backed water snake will bite viciously when molested. In captivity it remains rather sullen and is untrustworthy. It is one of the water snakes

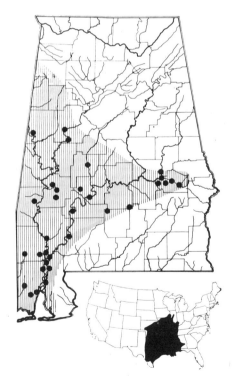

FIG. 244. Distribution of *Natrix rhombifera rhombifera.* The presumed range in Alabama is indicated by hatching. Symbols indicate localities from which the author examined specimens. The small map depicts approximately the known range of the species *N. rhombifera* in the United States.

most often mistaken for the venomous cottonmouth.

Natrix sipedon (Linnaeus)

A taxonomic problem concerning the relationship between *N. sipedon* and *N. fasciata* is discussed in the opening remarks under the latter.

Four subspecies of *N. sipedon* are currently recognized. Only 1, *N. s. pleuralis,* definitely occurs in Alabama. I could find no substantial evidence of influence from *N. s. sipedon* in populations in northern Alabama, although some previous workers have so indicated (Penn, 1940; Conant, 1958).

Natrix sipedon pleuralis Cope
Midland Water Snake

Description: (Fig. 245) An aquatic snake of relatively stocky proportions, attaining a maximum length of about 1,310 mm. Tail fairly short; head distinct from neck; scales keeled; anal divided; labials swollen. Ground color of dorsum gray, light brown, or reddish brown; dorsal pattern consisting of smooth-edged dark bands anteriorly and alternating dorsal and lateral blotches posteriorly; dark markings usually narrower than the spaces between them.

Venter typically yellow to cream colored, with a double row of cresent-shaped or half-moon-shaped red or reddish brown markings, these extending to near the tail tip.

Remarks: This form shows considerable individual and geographic variation in Alabama. On large individuals, the dorsal pattern is often obscure. The ventral markings on some individuals are indistinct, with indefinite boundaries. The juveniles of *N. erythrogaster* are easily mistaken for *N. s. pleuralis.* (See account of the former species.)

Variation in ventral and subcaudal scale counts was evident in some respects. Ventral count in eighty-one males from within the Alabama-Coosa-Tallapoosa river system averaged 132 (range 126 to 138), while that for one-hundred twenty-four females from the

FIG. 245. *Natrix sipedon pleuralis,* midland water snake. This is the most frequently encountered aquatic snake in most parts of Alabama. It is often referred to as "moccasin" even by those who recognize it as harmless.

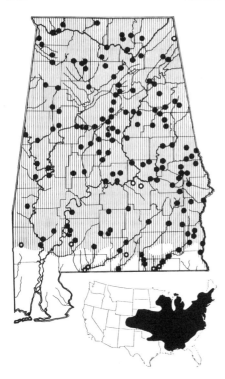

FIG. 246. Distribution of *Natrix sipedon pleuralis*, the midland water snake. The hatched area is the presumed range in Alabama. Solid symbols are localities from which the author examined specimens. Circles are literature records believed to be valid. Starred symbols are records for specimens intermediate between *N. s. pleuralis* and *N. fasciata* ssp. The small map depicts approximately the range of the species *N. sipedon* in the United States.

pleuralis, is present in about 20 percent of the latter in the Alabama Coastal Plain. Between 2 and 4 percent of *N. s. pleuralis* in Alabama are banded throughout their length, as in *N. fasciata.*

Alabama distribution: (Fig. 246) Statewide, but in the Lower Coastal Plain confined almost exclusively to streams that have at least some of their headwaters north of that province. Evidence of interbreeding between this form and *N. fasciata* has been found in the Choctawhatchee, Pea, Yellow, and Conecuh rivers and in some ponds in Washington and Monroe counties (see p. 215).

Habits: Throughout much of the state, the midland water snake is generally the most abundant aquatic snake. It inhabits farm ponds, lakes, streams, and most other permanently aquatic habitats.

However, in small, sluggish Coastal Plain streams, beaver swamps, and other such places in that province where the banks tend to be swampy or poorly defined, the midland water snake is often greatly outnumbered by *Natrix erythrogaster* or one of the other members of the genus. Cottonmouths are also likely to be more common in such places. The optimal habitat for *N. s. pleuralis* seems to be a moderate-sized stream with a rock, gravel, or sand bottom and an abundance of minnows and other small fish.

When threatened with harm or capture and escape is impossible, the midland water snake assumes a formidable appearance. Flattening its head and vibrating its tail, it strikes repeatedly at the offender. It is considered venomous and killed on sight by a large segment of the populace, who designate it "water moccasin." In spite of relentless persecution, the midland water snake persists in considerable abundance throughout nearly all of its range in our state.

Fish are the staple food of the midland water snake, many of which are caught at night. Other food items include frogs, tadpoles, and salamanders. Captives usually do well on a diet of

same system averaged 133 (range 123 to 142). These averages are somewhat lower than those in snakes from the Tennessee and Tombigbee-Warrior river systems and slightly higher than those in populations inhabiting the Chattahoochee River system and the systems contained entirely within the Coastal Plain.

Subcaudal count in sixty-three males from the Alabama-Coosa-Tallapoosa averaged 75 (range 65 to 84) and in one-hundred and four females, 65 (range 42 to 77). Geographic variation in subcaudal counts was not detected.

A dark postocular stripe, present in *N. fasciata* but reportedly absent in *N. s.*

FIG. 247. *Natrix taxispilota*, the brown water snake (Russell County). This large, aquatic snake has alternating dorsal and lateral body blotches. It frequently basks in trees overhanging the water or on protruding snags. "Water rattler" is a misnomer often applied to this species.

whole, small fish and can usually be induced to eat fillets of large ones. Live fish may be placed in water in a shallow container in the cage.

The midland water snake is viviparous, as are other *Natrix*, with the newborn appearing from July to early September. The usual number per litter is between 12 and 30.

Natrix taxispilota (Holbrook)
Brown Water Snake

This species has been considered by some workers to include *Natrix rhom-bifera*. Recent work has shown rather conclusively that the latter is a separate species. (See account of *N. rhombifera*.)

Description: (Fig. 247) A large, thick-bodied, aquatic snake attaining a maximum total length of around 1,750 mm. Tail short; head distinct from neck; scales keeled, in 25 to 33 rows; anal divided; suboculars usually absent; parietals fragmented behind; anterior temporals usually divided (80 percent). Dorsum brownish with a series of 22 to 29 median dark blotches alternating with a series of lateral blotches on each side;

TABLE 9. NUMBER OF VENTRAL AND SUBCAUDAL SCUTES IN ALABAMA *Natrix taxispilota*, BY SEX AND RIVER DRAINAGE SYSTEM

Drainage system	Number of ventrals						Number of subcaudals					
	Males			Females			Males			Females		
	No.	Range	Mean	No.	Range	Mean	No.	Range	Mean	No.	Range	Mean
Chattahoochee	10	135-142	137.9	4	132-136	133.5	10	70-82	77.6	4	67-74	69.5
Choctawhat-chee-Pea	5	136-142	138.2	11	131-137	135.5	4	75-83	78.7	7	67-73	69.1
Yellow	2	137-138	137.5				2	74-79	76.5			
Escambia-Conecuh	5	132-140	136.4	3	130-131	130.7	3	73-83	78.3	3	63-70	66.0
Perdido-Styx	1		136	3	129-136	131.0	1		75	2	70-71	70.5

venter yellowish, heavily patterned with blackish spots; chin shields smudged with dark pigment.

Remarks: Females exceed males in maximum size attained and slightly in mean number of scale rows at mid-body (thirty-eight females: range 26 to 33, mean 29.0; thirty seven males: range 25 to 31, mean 28.4). Males exceed females in mean ventral and subcaudal counts. There is an indication that the population inhabiting the Choctawhatchee-Pea river drainage has a greater mean ventral count than other populations in Alabama (Table 9).

Alabama distribution: (Fig. 248) The Coastal Plain east of the Mobile Bay drainage and that portion of the Pied-mont drained by the Chattahoochee River.

Habits: In Alabama the brown water snake is most frequently encountered in streams and stream impoundments. It is formidable in appearance and greatly feared by many who live within its range. The name "water rattler" is often applied to this snake in southern Alabama, based on the erroneous assumption that it is a timber or "canebrake" rattlesnake that has adopted aquatic habits and lost its rattle. The brown water snake is rather strongly diurnal and spends much of its time basking over the water in trees and bushes. Large numbers of basking individuals are seen each spring at Lake Eufaula on the Chattahoochee River in southeastern Alabama. *N. taxispilota* puts up a vigorous defense and is capable of delivering a painful though non-venomous bite.

Fish and frogs constitute the bulk of the diet. The young, ranging in number from 14 to 58 per litter, are born in late summer and early fall.

GENUS *OPHEODRYS* Fitzinger

This genus occurs in Asia and North America, and is represented in Alabama by 1 of its 8 species.

Opheodrys aestivus (Linnaeus) Rough Green Snake

Description: (Fig. 249) An extremely slender snake attaining a maximum total length of around 1,160 mm. Head distinct from neck; tail long, slender; scales keeled, in 17 rows at mid-body; anal divided. Color above light green, becoming bluish in preservative; belly white or yellowish.

Ventrals in twenty-four Alabama males: range 152 to 165, mean 156.4; in twenty-three females, range 147 to 168, mean 159.1. Subcaudals in twenty males: range 123 to 161, mean 137.3; in twenty females: range 118 to 144, mean 132.1.

Alabama distribution: (Fig. 250) Statewide; fairly common in every region.

Habits: This docile snake is perhaps

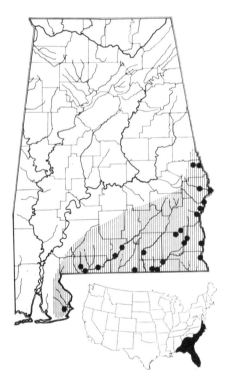

FIG. 248. Distribution of *Natrix taxispilota*, the brown water snake. The presumed range in Alabama is indicated by hatching. Symbols indicate localities from which the author examined specimens. The small map depicts approximately the known range in the United States.

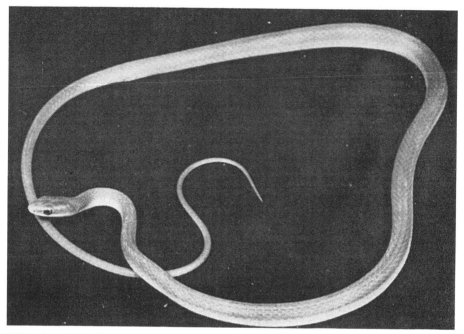

FIG. 249. *Opheodrys aestivus,* the rough green snake (Lauderdale County). The dorsal color is bright green. This familiar snake is often found in vegetation along stream banks.

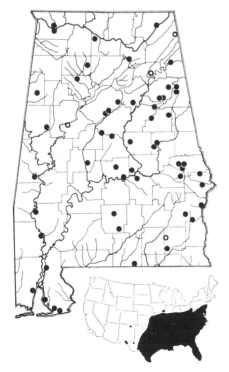

the most familiar of all our species. It is unmistakable, and its life is frequently spared, even by those who are inclined to kill all snakes on sight. The green snake is often found among shrubbery and overhanging vegetation around lakes and streams. Although an agile climber, it moves rather slowly and relies chiefly on concealment for protection. It feeds mainly on soft-bodied arthropods, particularly spiders.

The green snake lays 2 to 12 elongate eggs. A clutch of 2 eggs was discovered under a rock in Jackson County by J. R. Jordan, Jr., on July 15. One of these eggs hatched. The color of the hatchling was dull greenish gray. Other nests of this species have been found under rot-

FIG. 250. Distribution of *Opheodrys aestivus,* the rough green snake. This species is believed to occur statewide in Alabama. Solid symbols indicate localities from which the author examined specimens. The circles are literature records believed to be valid. The small map depicts approximately the known range in the United States.

ting cardboard boxes in Texas (Sabath and Worthington, 1959) and under a rock in Illinois (Smith, 1961). The green snake is noted for its docile nature and does not bite.

GENUS *PITUOPHIS* Holbrook

This genus occurs from Canada southward to Guatemala. While workers continue to disagree on the number of species represented by the various described forms, the concensus seems to be 3. Alabama has 1 species.

Pituophis melanoleucus (Daudin)

The pine snake-bull snake complex is now thought to consist of 1 polytypic species. Three of the 10 recognized subspecies occur in Alabama.

Pituophis melanoleucus melanoleucus (Daudin)
Northern Pine Snake

Description: (Fig. 251) A large snake attaining a maximum total length of about 2,110 mm. Body moderately stout; tail fairly short; head small, only slightly wider than neck; anal undivided; scales keeled except for some of lowermost row; rostral scale enlarged, curving backward between internasals and ending in a point. Dorsal ground color gray, cream, or yellowish; dorsum with 25 to 31 dark blotches or saddles (excluding tail blotches), blotches somewhat poorly defined and blackish anteriorly, becoming sharply defined and dark reddish brown toward the tail; side with a series of dark blotches, these more distinct posteriorly. Venter glistening white with a row of distinct, black spots down each side, each spot involving the ends of 1 to 3 ventrals anteriorly and 3 to 5 ventrals posteriorly; tail with reddish saddles or rings.

Remarks: No significant geographic variation in scale counts was noted among the relatively small number of Alabama pine snakes I examined. Ventrals in thirteen males, subspecies combined: range 203 to 220, mean 214.0; ventrals in four females: range 213 to 223, mean 218. Subcaudals in the thirteen males: range 44 to 63, mean 52.5; subcaudals in the four females: range 29 to 31, mean 30.0.

FIG. 251. *Pituophis melanoleucus melanoleucus,* the northern pine snake (DeKalb County). An infrequently encountered form of dry habitats above the Black Belt, this snake is believed to spend much of its time underground.

Alabama distribution: (Fig. 252) Local in the mountains, ridges, and plateaus above the Fall Line, exclusive of the Piedmont, and in sandy areas of the Fall Line Hills region eastward to the Coosa River. Intergrades with *P. m. mugitus* in scattered areas of suitable habitat within the Fall Line Hills of eastern Alabama between the Coosa River and the range of that subspecies. (See "Alabama distribution" under *P. m. mugitus*.)

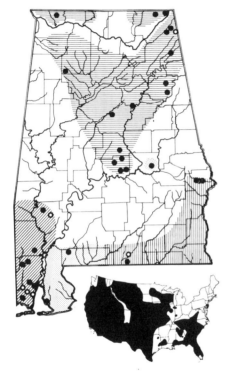

FIG. 252. Distribution of *Pituophis melanoleucus* and subspecific variation in Alabama. Horizontal hatching indicates the presumed range of *P. m. melanoleucus*, the northern pine snake, in Alabama; the vertical hatching, that of *P. m. mugitus*, the Florida pine snake; and the diagonal hatching, that of *P. m. lodingi*, the black pine snake. The stippled areas show zones of intergradation. Solid symbols indicate localities from which the author examined specimens. Circles are literature records believed to be valid. The small map depicts approximately the range of the species *P. melanoleucus* in the United States.

Habits: The ecology of the pine snakes, which comprise the 4 subspecies of the *Pituophis melanoleucus* complex found in the Southeast, is poorly understood. Nowhere, apparently, are pine snakes common; Conant (1956), in his review of the subspecies *lodingi* and *ruthveni*, suggested as an explanation of this apparent scarcity the "inherent tendency for the pine snake to hide, to take refuge in burrows and cavities or beneath vegetation, or to burrow into the arenaceous substratum."

In Alabama, pine snakes are encountered most frequently in xeric habitats. Most of the specimens from below the Fall Line have come from longleaf pine-turkey oak or sandhill associations or from dry pine flatwoods areas. Above the Fall Line, pine snakes have been collected on several occasions in the vicinity of Ider, DeKalb County. The soil there is sandy, and forested areas nearby are often dominated by *Pinus virginiana*. Other pine snake localities in northern Alabama with which I am familiar are gravelly, upland sites that support mixed pine-hardwood forests.

Pine snakes are oviparous; in *P. m. melanoleucus*, clutches of 7 to 24 eggs have been reported. The eggs are large, ranging in length from 50 to 64 mm. Nests have been found in cavities or burrows in sandy soil several inches below the surface.

Pine snakes are known to feed on small mammals, birds, and bird eggs. Young individuals may eat lizards. Temperament varies considerably from snake to snake. Many will hiss loudly and strike at the molester, but will usually keep the mouth closed. Others are even-tempered and docile. Most specimens will do well in captivity if afforded maximum privacy.

Pituophis melanoleucus lodingi Blanchard
Black Pine Snake

Description: (Fig. 253) Differs from *P. m. melanoleucus* chiefly in color. Adults

FIG. 253. *Pituophis melanoleucus lodingi,* the black pine snake, juvenile (Mobile County). This form has a restricted range and is one of the least frequently encountered of Alabama snakes.

typically almost uniformly dark brown to black; a trace of pattern visible on some individuals, with blotches most evident posteriorly; a few white scales present on some individuals; venter dark brown to black, occasionally with a few light markings mainly near the tail. Young similar to adults except lighter, having more light scales. Maximum total length attained, about 1,875 mm.

Alabama distribution: (Fig. 252) Southwestern Alabama in the Lower Coastal Plain and Red Hills regions west of the Alabama River. Specimens are known only from Mobile, Clarke, and Washington counties, but it is probable that the range includes southern Choctaw County as well. Intergrades between *P. m. lodingi* and *P. m. mugitus* have been collected in Baldwin County (Conant, 1956) and in Escambia County (AM-6351). A specimen collected by W. T. Neill from 12 miles south of Andalusia, and reported by Conant (op. cit.), was tentatively assigned intergradient status. This snake, a photograph of which appears in Conant's work, was almost uniformly tan dorsally and had

a white belly, except for encroachments of the dorsal color onto the posterolateral corners of the ventrals. I have examined several pine snakes from southern Covington County, all of which were referable to *P. m. mugitus.* None showed detectable influence from *P. m. lodingi.* I strongly suspect that the questionable snake is an aberrant *P. m. mugitus,* and in the absence of further evidence to the contrary shall so regard it.

The Black Belt in Alabama apparently is uninhabited by pine snakes. If so, the ranges of *P. m. lodingi* and *P. m. melanoleucus* are widely separated, and it is doubtful that the forms intergrade.

Habits: The habits of this subspecies are poorly known, but there is no evidence that they differ substantially from those of *P. m. melanoleucus.* (See Conant, 1956, and Cliburn, 1962).

Pituophis melanoleucus mugitus Barbour
Florida Pine Snake

Description: (Fig. 254) Differs from *P. m. melanoleucus* chiefly in coloration. Ground color gray anteriorly to rusty

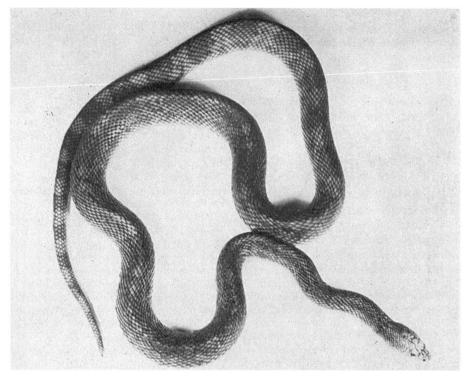

FIG. 254. *Piuophis melanoleucus mugitus,* the Florida pine snake (Russell County). This snake has become scarce in Alabama in recent years. The practice of "gassing" the burrows of gopher tortoises may be contributing to this scarcity. (See Preface.)

brown posteriorly; anterior dorsal blotches indistinct; venter white, but not glistening; ventrals with brownish spots appearing at irregular intervals on their ends. Maximum total length attained about 2,285 mm.

Alabama distribution: (Fig. 252) Local in the southeastern quadrant of the state, except for the Black Belt, where pine snakes apparently are absent. Actual records are available only from Covington and Russell counties. *P. m. mugitus* intergrades with *P. m. lodingi* in Escambia and Baldwin counties.

A specimen from near Tallassee in Elmore County appears to be intergradient between *P. m. mugitus* and *P. m. melanoleucus.* The specimen, which is currently a captive in the Auburn Museum, is the only pine snake I have seen from the area in Alabama between the known ranges of those subspecies. Other pine snakes may ultimately be found in Macon County, which contains several areas of seemingly suitable habitat, and which lies between Elmore County and Russell County.

Habits: The habits of the Florida pine snake are not known to differ significantly from those of *P. m. melanoleucus.* An inhabitant of areas with sandy soil, it is often found in close proximity to gopher tortoise burrows, which it uses as retreats.

Neill (1951) reported on clutches of 4, 5, and 8 eggs from captive female *P. m. mugitus.* The eggs varied from cream to white in color and from 71 to 109 mm in length.

GENUS *REGINA* Baird and Girard

Five species are usually included within this genus. Four of these are placed in the genus *Natrix* by some herpetologists. The genus is confined to the eastern United States. Two species occur in Alabama.

Regina rigida (Say)

Three subspecies of this species are recognized, 1 of which occurs in Alabama.

Regina rigida sinicola (Huheey)
Gulf Glossy Water Snake

Description: (Fig. 255) A relatively small aquatic snake attaining a maximum total length of about 780 mm. Body fairly stout; head small, scarcely or not at all distinct from neck; eyes small; scales somewhat shiny, keeled (except for the first row on each side), in 19 rows at mid-body; anal divided; upper labials not swollen. Dorsal ground color olive brown, becoming paler on the sides; 2 faint longitudinal dark stripes on back and 2 more on the sides often detectable; belly yellowish to cream with 2 rows of conspicuous dark spots which usually coalesce to form stripes; stripes convergent anteriorly and uniting on the throat; underside of tail usually with a median dark line. In this subspecies, chin and gular region virtually immaculate; usually 2 preoculars on each side.

Ventral count in eight males from Alabama: range 131 to 134, mean 132.5; in nine females: range 132 to 139, mean 134.7. Subcaudal count in seven males: range 58 to 69, mean 62.7; in eight females: range 50 to 56, mean 53.5.

Remarks: The subcaudal counts for the Alabama sample are considerably lower than those reported by Huheey (1959) for the subspecies *R. r. sinicola* (males: 61 to 71, mean 67.6; females: 55 to 64, mean 58.8), and are in fact very close to those he reported for *R. r. rigida* (males 57 to 67, mean 62.7; females: 50 to 59, mean 54.6). Most of the *R. r. sinicola* examined by Huheey, however, were from Texas, Louisiana, and Mississippi, in the western portion of the subspecies range. He examined only 3 representatives from the Georgia-Florida-Alabama portion of the range.

Alabama distribution: (Fig. 256) The

FIG. 255. *Regina rigida sinicola*, the Gulf glossy water snake (Russell County). This secretive, nocturnal snake is brown above and has 2 conspicuous longitudinal stripes on the venter.

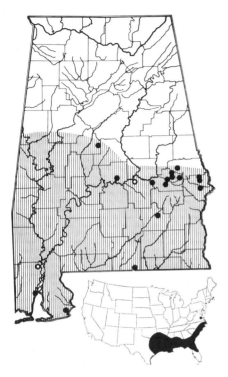

FIG. 256. Distribution of *Regina rigida sinicola*, the Gulf glossy water snake. The presumed range in Alabama is indicated by hatching. Solid symbols indicate localities from which the author examined specimens. Circles are literature records believed to be valid. The small map depicts approximately the known range of the species *R. rigida* in the United States.

Coastal Plain except possibly for the northwestern portion.

Habits: Highly secretive, the glossy water snake is seldom seen in Alabama except at night during rainy weather. Most specimens have been collected on roads traversing floodplains and other low, damp places and around the edges of ponds and swamps. At Lake Jackson in Covington County, specimens have been found in mats of aquatic vegetation that occur around the water's edge. An individual was collected in Lee County while basking on a limb overhanging a small stream.

The glossy water snake reportedly feeds on a variety of aquatic animals, in-cluding fish, frogs, sirens, and crawfish. Huheey (1959) and Rossman (1963a) suggested that crawfish are perhaps more important in the diet than most earlier investigators realized. There is a strong possibility that glossy water snakes rely heavily on crawfish burrows for retreats.

Information on reproduction is scarce. Huheey (1959) reported examining a newborn litter of 11 young and found 9 and 14 ova in 2 gravid females. A gravid female in the Auburn collection contained 8 ova.

Regina septemvittata (Say)
Queen Snake

In 1963, Neill proposed subspecific recognition (as *R. s. mabila*) for a population of queen snakes inhabiting D'Olive Creek in Baldwin County, Alabama. Spangler and Mount (1969) studied variation in Alabama queen snakes and concluded that the available evidence did not justify continued recognition of *mabila*, an opinion to which I still adhere.

Description: (Fig. 257) A small to medium-sized aquatic snake attaining a maximum total length of around 920 mm. Body slender to moderately stout; head small, scarcely or not at all distinct from neck; scales keeled, in 19 rows at mid-body; anal divided; upper labials not swollen. Dorsal ground color olive brown to almost black; 3 obscure dark stripes occasionally visible on dorsum; a ventrolateral light stripe on each side; venter of juveniles, adult males, and young females off-white with 2 dark stripes that converge anteriorly; venter of old females predominantly dark.

Remarks: Ventral count shows a north-to-south cline in Alabama with populations in the northern part of the state having higher average counts than those to the south (Spangler and Mount, 1969). The total range in ventrals in thirty-six Alabama males: 127 to 148. Mean ventral count for four males from the Tennessee River drainage: 142.5; for six males from localities well below the Fall Line in southern Alabama: 126.5.

FIG. 257. *Regina septemvittata,* the queen snake (Lee County). This docile snake is seen most frequently around creeks as it drops into the water from overhanging limbs.

In subcaudal count the lowest values are found in snakes from the Tennessee River drainage: four males, range 67 to 77, mean 72; three females, range 63 to 74, mean 71.5. There are no significant geographic trends in subcaudal count among specimens from south of the Tennessee drainage: eighteen males, range 78 to 90, mean 85; thirty-six females, range 64 to 87, mean 79.5.

Alabama distribution: (Fig. 258) Common to abundant above the Fall Line; local in the Coastal Plain. The limits of the range in western Alabama are not known.

Habits: Queen snakes are almost always found along streams or impoundments of streams. Above the Fall Line

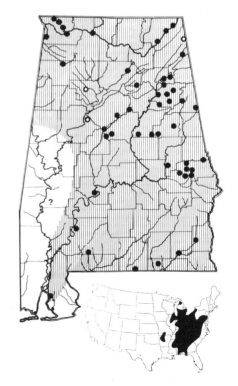

FIG. 258. Distribution of *Regina septemvittata,* the queen snake. The range in Alabama is indicated by hatching. Solid symbols indicate localities from which the author examined specimens. The circles are literature records believed to be valid. The small map depicts approximately the known range in the United States.

FIG. 259. *Rhadinaea flavilata*, the pine woods snake or yellow-lipped snake (Washington County). This small, yellowish brown snake has been collected in Alabama on relatively few occasions. It is usually encountered under or within a log in damp pine flatwoods.

they are common along many of the rivers as well as along the smaller streams. In the Coastal Plain they frequent small, clear creeks with sandy or rocky bottoms.

Queen snakes spend much of their time basking on limbs of bushes and trees that overhang the water. They feed almost exclusively on crawfish and are active day and night. The young are born during the summer, with litter size averaging about 12. Aside from the habit of discharging the cloacal contents at the time of capture, the queen snake is inoffensive and seldom bites. Branson and Baker (1974) conducted a rather detailed study of the ecology and life history of this species in Kentucky.

GENUS *RHADINAEA* Cope

This New World genus contains about 24 species, whose collective ranges extend from the southern United States to central South America. One species occurs in Alabama.

Rhadinaea flavilata (Cope)
Pine Woods Snake
(Yellow-lipped Snake)

Description: (Fig. 259) A small snake attaining a maximum total length of around 390 mm. Head slightly distinct from neck; tail relatively long; scales smooth, in 17 rows at mid-body; anal divided. Dorsum golden brown; diffused mid-dorsal and lateral stripes sometimes visible; top of head darker than body, often marked with pale vermiculations; a dark band extends from the snout through the eye to the corner of the mouth; upper labials yellowish, some with dark spots; venter yellowish white to yellow.

Alabama distribution: (Fig. 260) Local in the Lower Coastal Plain; known only from Baldwin, Mobile, and Washington counties.

Habits: This poorly known, secretive species inhabits damp pine flatwoods where rotting logs and stumps are abundant. It is usually encountered within or under a log, stump, or some other sheltering object during March, April, or early May, especially when the water table is high.

The food of the pine woods snake consists mostly of small amphibians and reptiles, which are swallowed alive or are killed or inactivated with a mildly venomous saliva before being eaten. Enlarged maxillary teeth in the rear of the mouth assist in envenomating the prey. The snake is completely harmless to man and makes no attempt to bite. Captives feed on small lizards and frogs. Cricket frogs

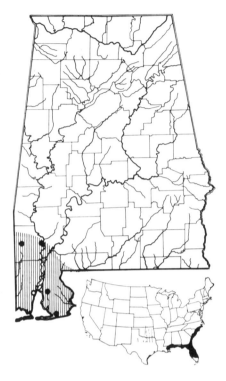

FIG. 260. Distribution of *Rhadinaea fla-vilata*, the pine woods snake or yellow-lipped snake. The presumed range in Alabama is indicated by hatching. Solid symbols indicate localities from which the author examined specimens. The circle is a literature record believed to be valid. The small map depicts approximately the known range in the United States. (Note: A recent record of this species for Dauphin Island, Mobile County, is not indicated on the Alabama map.)

(*Acris spp.*) were readily consumed by captives in my possession.

Natural nests are unknown. Myers (1967) in his account of this species concluded that between 2 and 4 eggs are laid and that the laying season lasts from May to August.

GENUS *SEMINATRIX* Cope

This genus contains a single polytypic species, which is confined to the southeastern United States.

Seminatrix pygaea (Cope)
Black Swamp Snake

Three subspecies of this small, secretive snake are recognized; the range of

FIG. 261. *Seminatrix pygaea pygaea*, North Florida black swamp snake (Covington County). This small snake is rather shiny black above and has a predominantly red venter. The scales are smooth, but faint longitudinal light lines, especially near the tail, give the impression that they are keeled.

1 of these barely extends into southern Alabama.

Seminatrix pygaea pygaea (Cope)
North Florida Black Swamp Snake

Description: (Fig. 261) A small snake attaining a maximum total length of about 425 mm. Head slightly distinct from neck; tail short; anal usually undivided; scales smooth, in 17 rows at mid-body; dorsum shiny black; first 3 to 4 scale rows with obscure light longitudinal lines; venter red. In this subspecies, ventrals, usually more than 117; venter immaculate or patterned with long, narrow, curved black bars on leading edges of scutes.

FIG. 262. Distribution of Seminatrix pygaea pygaea, the North Florida black swamp snake. The presumed range in Alabama is indicated by hatching. Symbols indicate localities from which the author examined specimens. The small map depicts approximately the known range of the species S. pygaea in the United States.

Ventral counts for six Alabama males: 122, 124, 124, 124, 126, and 128 (mean 124.6); for three females: 122, 122, and 125 (mean 123.0). Subcaudals in the six males: range 40 to 52, mean 48.2; in the three females: range 36 to 39, mean 37.7.

Alabama distribution: (Fig. 262) Known from only 3 localities, all in extreme southern Covington County. A shed skin which appeared to be of this form was found in a weedy pond in southern Houston County.

Habits: Most of our information about this secretive snake comes from the work of Dowling (1950b). Rossman (1956) provided observations on the behavior of a captive specimen. The preferred habitats are swamps, ponds, and lakes with abundant emergent vegetation. In Florida floating mats of water hyacinths (Eichornia crassipes) provide ideal habitats. In Alabama we have collected specimens from under mats of water pennywort (Hydrocotyle umbellata) around the edges of ponds and lakes.

The food of S. pygaea, eaten mostly at night, includes oligochaete worms, leeches, tadpoles, small frogs, and small fish. The species is viviparous, with litter size ranging from 2 to 11. A female collected at Lake Jackson, Covington County, on June 28 gave birth to a litter of 7 on August 1. The female was 384 mm in total length and the young averaged 135 mm in length. The black swamp snake does not bite.

GENUS STORERIA Baird and Girard

Found from the eastern United States to Guatemala and Honduras, this genus contains 2 polytypic species, both of which are represented in Alabama.

Storeria dekayi (Holbrook)

Seven subspecies of this wide-ranging species are recognized. Treatment of Alabama populations requires consideration of 3 of these.

FIG. 263. *Storeria dekayi wrightorum*, the midland brown snake (Lee County). *Storeria dekayi* is often encountered in and around towns and cities in the northern one-half of the state. It is one of several small, harmless snakes that are called "ground rattlers" by a surprisingly large number of people.

Storeria dekayi dekayi (Holbrook)
Northern Brown Snake

Description: A small snake attaining a maximum total length of about 440 mm. Head more or less distinct; tail short; anal divided; dorsal scales keeled, in 17 rows at mid-body; ground color gray to brown; dorsum with a median light stripe about 4 scale rows wide, outlined by a row of dark spots on each side; side of head with a vertical or diagonal dark bar involving the anterior temporal and generally the sixth and seventh upper and lower labials. Venter light with 1 or 2 rows of small black dots along the edges. Juveniles with a yellowish collar across neck.

Remarks: The combined count of ventrals and subcaudals is used by some to separate *S. d. dekayi* from *S. d. wrightorum*. For reasons discussed below, I feel that the dorsal pattern provides a more appropriate basis for defining these subspecies.

Alabama distribution: (Fig. 264) The lack of dorsal crossbars on some specimens of *S. dekayi* from extreme northeastern Alabama can be interpreted as influence from *S. d. dekayi*. The populations thus represented are herein designated *S. d. dekayi* x *wrightorum;* they are found in DeKalb and Jackson counties.

Habits: Similar to those of *S. d. wrightorum,* which are discussed below.

Storeria dekayi limnetes Anderson
Marsh Brown Snake

Description: Generally similar to *S. d. wrightorum* (described below) except as follows: dorsum usually not crossbarred; dark bar on anterior temporals horizontal

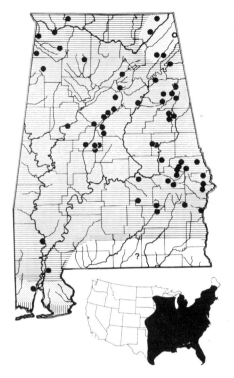

FIG. 264. Distribution of *Storeria dekayi* and subspecific variation in Alabama. Horizontal hatching indicates the presumed range of *S. d. wrightorum*, the midland brown snake, in Alabama; that of *S. d. limnetes*, the marsh brown snake, by vertical hatching. The stippled area in southwestern Alabama is a zone of intergradation between *S. d. wrightorum* and *S. d. limnetes*. The stippled area in northeastern Alabama is a zone of intergradation between *S. d wrightorum* and *S. d. dekayi*, the northern brown snake. Solid symbols indicate localities from which the author examined specimens. The circle is a presumably valid literature record. The small map depicts the range of the species *S. dekayi* in the United States.

(instead of vertical or diagonal) (Fig. 37B); sixth and seventh labials usually unpigmented.

Alabama distribution: (Fig. 264) Sabath and Sabath (1969) found specimens referable to *S. d. limnetes* along the Gulf Coast as far east as Pensacola, Florida. They did not examine specimens from the Alabama coastal region, but by inference they included it within the range of that subspecies. I have examined 4 specimens of *S. dekayi* from Mobile, Mobile County. Three of these have the characteristics of *S. d. wrightorum*, the form occurring throughout most of the species range in Alabama. The fourth, USA 1175, has crossbars as in *S. d. wrightorum*, but the anterior temporals are marked as in Figure 1H in Sabath and Sabath (1969), a condition considered intermediate between *S. d. wrightorum* and *S. d. limnetes*. I have not examined specimens of *S. dekayi* from the coastal marshes of Alabama, but it is not unreasonable to assume that *S. d. limnetes* will be the subspecies found to occur there. The Mobile population is tentatively regarded as *S. d. wrightorum* x *limnetes*.

Habits: Inhabits coastal marshlands. Other aspects are little known but are presumably similar to those of *S. d. wrightorum*.

Storeria dekayi wrightorum Trapido
Midland Brown Snake

Description: (Fig. 263) Generally similar to *S. d. dekayi* except that the dorsal spots in most cases are fused to form crossbars. Differs from *S. d. limnetes* in having a diagonal or vertical dark temporal bar (rather than a horizontal one) (Fig. 37A) and in having dark pigment on the sixth and seventh labials. Maximum total length about 425 mm. A Lee County specimen, the largest examined during the study, had a total length of 423 mm.

Remarks: The barred dorsum characterizes about 90 percent of the individuals in brown snake populations sampled in Alabama except those in the extreme northeastern portion. The specimens from that area indicate that the barred condition is less than 50 percent in frequency of occurrence, and they are considered intergrades.

A relatively low ventral-plus-subcaudal count, presumably indicative of influence from the subspecies *S. d. dekayi*, occurs not only in populations in northern Alabama, where such influence might be

TABLE 10. NUMBER OF VENTRAL AND SUBCAUDAL SCUTES IN ALABAMA *Storeria dekayi*

Section of Alabama	Sex	No.	Ventrals		Subcaudals		Total of ventrals and subcaudals	
			Range	Mean	Range	Mean	Range	Mean
Northeast[1]	Males	4	122-125	123	50-57	53.2	173-179	176
	Females	13	124-135	128	43-50	46.5	170-177	174
Northwest[2]	Males	2	118-118	118	52-53	52.5	170-171	170.5
	Females	3	127-131	129	43-48	45.6	170-179	174
Central[3]	Males	3	121-124	123	52-58	55	173-182	178
	Females	10	127-135	131	39-52	46.1	168-185	177
East-central[4]	Males	7	122-127	124	46-59	53.5	171-185	177
	Females	17	124-135	130	44-55	47.7	172-187	178
Southwest[5]	Males	2	124-126	125	48-58	53	174-182	178
	Females	2	124-128	126	42-48	46	170-172	171

[1] Blount, Calhoun, Cherokee, Cleburne, Etowah, and Jackson counties.
[2] Colbert, Franklin, and Lauderdale counties.
[3] Bibb, Jefferson, St. Clair, and Shelby counties.
[4] Clay, Lee, Macon, Russell, and Tallapoosa counties.
[5] Mobile County.

anticipated, but in populations in extreme southwestern Alabama as well (Table 10). Moreover, in samples from central and eastern-central Alabama, the ranges of variation in this character, from 168 to 185 and from 171 to 187, respectively, virtually span the spectrum from one extreme to the other. For these reasons, it seems most appropriate to rely on dorsal pattern to differentiate between *S. d. wrightorum* and *S. d dekayi*.

Alabama distribution: (Fig. 264) Populations of brown snakes from DeKalb and Jackson counties and the one in the immediate vicinity of the city of Mobile are considered intergradient and have been discussed previously. Specimens are unavailable from the immediate coastal area, but it is postulated that *S. d. limnetes* occurs there. The remainder of the state where brown snakes occur is inhabited by *S. d. wrightorum*. Brown snakes are common to abundant throughout most of the northern three-fourths of the state. In parts of the Red Hills region and in the Lower Coastal Plain from Escambia County eastward they are unaccountably rare or absent.

Habits: *Storeria dekayi* is one of the most common snake species north of the Red Hills. It thrives in urban communities as well as in rural environs. A vacant lot or golf course rough often satisfies its ecological requirements. It tends to hide under logs, pieces of tin, and other debris, but is often seen abroad. The scarcity or absence of this species in much of the Lower Coastal Plain is perplexing, particularly in view of the fact that it is abundant around Mobile. I can as yet offer no explanation.

Storeria dekayi is docile in temperament; I have never known one to bite. The diet includes earthworms, slugs, spiders, and, on rare occasions, small amphibians. The young are born, with litter sizes varying from 3 to 31. The latter number, apparently a record for the species, was recorded by George W. Folkerts for a litter from a female *S. d. wrightorum* from Lee County, Alabama.

Storeria occipitomaculata (Storer)

Three subspecies of the red-bellied snake are recognized, 2 of which must be considered in interpreting intraspecific variation among Alabama populations of the species.

Storeria occipitomaculata occipitomaculata (Storer)
Northern Red-bellied Snake

Description: (Fig. 265) A small snake attaining a maximum total length of about 405 mm. Head blunt, more or less distinct from neck; tail short; anal divided; scales keeled, in 15 rows at

FIG. 265. *Storeria occipitomaculata occipitomaculata*, the northern red-bellied snake. The dorsum often has a median longitudinal light band. The belly varies from yellow to red.

mid-body. Extremely variable in ground color and pattern. Dorsum gray, brown, or black, patternless or with a median light stripe; belly pink to orange or reddish (rarely black), usually with a longitudinal row of black spots on each side. Head black to light brown, seldom uniform; nape with 3 pale spots, the central one largest; fifth upper labial with a light spot, bordered below by black.

Alabama distribution: (Fig. 266) Apparently, the red-bellied snake, in one form or another, occurs throughout Alabama. It is rather common in the northern half of the state, but becomes decreasingly so southward. Influence of *S. o. occipitomaculata* predominates in nearly all of the populations sampled, but their subspecific status is far from clear. This matter is considered in greater detail under the description of *S. o. obscura*.

Habits: Red-bellied snakes occur most abundantly in mesic, forested habitats where the soil is moderately heavy and the topography is hilly or mountainous. They are often found in close association with *Virginia valeriae* and, like individuals of that species, spend most of their time under logs, rocks, and other sheltering objects.

Storeria occipitomaculata gives birth to the young. Litter sizes of 1 to 21 have been reported. Nelson (1969) reported an average of 15.5 young for six Minnesota females, a larger number than is indicated by previous records for the species. A specimen from Auburn, Lee County, Alabama, gave birth to a litter of 8 on July 31.

The food of the red-bellied snake consists of insects, snails, isopods, and other small invertebrates. The snake has a peculiar habit of curling the upper lip upward on one or both sides when freshly captured. The snake is, however, completely harmless and does not bite. Jordan (1970) reported death-feigning

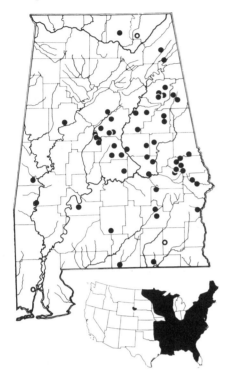

FIG. 266. Distribution of *Storeria occipit-omaculata occipitomaculata,* the northern red-bellied snake. This form is believed to occur statewide, or nearly so, in Alabama. Solid symbols indicate localities from which the author examined specimens. Circles are literature records believed to be valid. The small map depicts approximately the known range of the species *S. occipitomaculata* in the United States.

in a female of this species from Alabama.

The 2 subspecies are not known to differ markedly in habits.

Storeria occipitomaculata obscura
Trapido
Florida Red-bellied Snake

Description: The following are said to characterize this subspecies: top of head black; light spots on back of head fused to form a collar; fifth upper labial with light spot extending to lower margin of scale; ventrals average somewhat less and subcaudals somewhat more than in *S. o. occipitomaculata.*

Remarks: A total of 22 of the 52 red-bellied snakes examined from Alabama had 1 or more of the first 3 character-istics listed. Five had black heads, 8 had the light collar, and on 14 the light labial spots extended to the lower margin of the scale. A vast majority of the avail-able material came from the northern two-thirds of the state. Oddly, most of the specimens that closely resembled *S. o. obscura* were from an area near the center of the state, centered around Shelby County, and not from the east-ern portion where strong *obscura* influ-ence might be expected.

Other specimens having *obscura* char-acteristics came from such widely sep-arated areas as Calhoun County, Russell County, and Wilcox County. A specimen from Geneva County, the only one exam-ined from extreme southeastern Ala-bama, showed no features suggesting *obscura* influence.

Because of the complexity of variation in the diagnostic characters and because of a lack of specimens from many areas of the state, designation of my Alabama populations as *S. o. obscura* seems un-warranted at present. I recommend that such designation be deferred until suf-ficient material is available to make an objective determination or until the status of *S. o. obscura* is reassessed.

Significant geographic trends in scale counts were not evident among the red-bellied snakes examined from Alabama. Ventrals in twenty-one males: range 111 to 121, mean 115; in thirty-one females: range 111 to 126, mean 118.2. Sub-caudals in twenty males: range 44 to 63, mean 53; in twenty-seven females: range 35 to 51, mean 44.2.

Habits: See "Habits" under *S. o. oc-cipitomaculata.*

GENUS *TANTILLA* Baird and Girard

This genus, found from the United States to Argentina, includes almost 47 species, 1 of which is found in Alabama.

Tantilla coronata Baird and Girard
Southeastern Crowned Snake

In his revision of the southeastern *Tantilla*, Telford (1966) placed *T. coronata wagneri* and T. *coronata mitrifer* in the synonymy of *T. coronata*. The populations inhabiting peninsular Florida were considered to represent 2 new species, which he described. Following Telford, I shall recognize *T. coronata* as a monotypic species.

Description: (Fig. 267) A small, delicate snake attaining a maximum total length of about 215 mm. Head slightly or not at all distinct from neck; scales smooth, in 15 rows at mid-body; anal divided; upper labials 6 or 7; hemipenis with 2 basal hooks. Color of dorsum tan to pinkish brown; venter white, cream, or pinkish; head black, bordered behind by a light parietal band which is followed by a black collar on the neck.

Ventrals in thirty-four Alabama males: range 128 to 144, mean 135.1; in sixteen females: range 136 to 147, mean 142.0. Subcaudals in thirty-three males: range 31 to 52, mean 43.5; in fourteen females: range 31 to 45, mean 41.3.

Alabama distribution: (Fig. 268) Locally common statewide.

Habits: This small, harmless snake is an inhabitant of dry hillsides, ridgetops, and other xeric habitats, where it hides under rocks, logs, piles of debris, and in rotting stumps. Frequently associated with it in the same microhabitats is the rough earth snake. Although it is relatively common, there is little information on the crowned snake's habits. Neill (1951) reported finding copulating individuals in Georgia in April and early May. He found a nest of this species containing 3 small, oval eggs in a cup-shaped cavity in a pile of woody debris. The food of the crowned snake consists of small invertebrates. Captives apparently will feed on termites.

FIG. 267. *Tantilla coronata*, the southeastern crowned snake (Macon County). A small, secretive species, the snake is usually found under logs or rocks in dry situations.

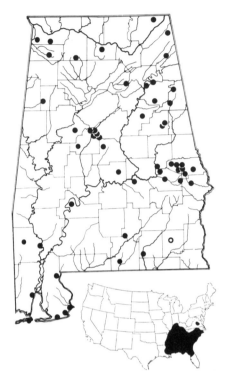

FIG. 268. Distribution of *Tantilla coronata*, the southeastern crowned snake. This species is believed to occur statewide, or essentially so, in Alabama. Solid symbols indicate localities from which the author examined specimens. The circle is a literature record believed to be valid. The small map depicts approximately the known range in the United States.

GENUS *THAMNOPHIS* Fitzinger

This genus, found from Canada to Costa Rica, contains about 22 species, 2 of which occur in Alabama.

Thamnophis sauritus (Linnaeus)

Four subspecies of this snake are recognized, 1 of which occurs in Alabama.

Thamnophis sauritus sauritus (Linnaeus)
Eastern Ribbon Snake

Description: (Fig. 269) A small or medium-sized snake attaining a maximum total length of about 955 mm. Body slender; tail slender and long, up to 39 percent of total length; anal undivided; scales prominently keeled, in 19 rows at mid-body. Belly yellowish, unmarked; dorsum brown or reddish brown; 3 conspicuous yellow stripes present, a median one and a lateral one on each side involving the third and fourth scale row above the ventrals.

Remarks: Females attain larger sizes than males. There seems to be little difference between Alabama males and females in scale counts. Ventrals in twenty-one females: range 143 to 163, mean 153.0; in five males: range 147 to 160, mean 154.6. Subcaudals in nine females; range 95 to 129, mean 119.9; in three males: range 97 to 132, mean 120.0.

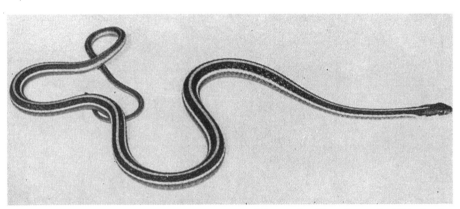

FIG. 269. *Thamnophis sauritus sauritus*, eastern ribbon snake (Lee County). This slender, docile snake is found most frequently in the vicinity of water. The venter of the ribbon snake is unmarked.

Alabama distribution: (Fig. 270) Statewide, but somewhat local.

Habits: The ribbon snake is semi-aquatic in habits, preferring more or less open, damp situations. Such places include marshes, beaver swamps, weedy lake shores, stream margins, and low wet meadows. Fish hatcheries often provide optimal habitat conditions. The ribbon snake is alert, agile, and a good climber. It is nervous in temperament but does not bite. It usually does well in captivity.

The ribbon snake is viviparous and usually gives birth in July or August. A female from Montgomery County produced a litter of 23 on July 26. Data from other sources, summarized by Ross-

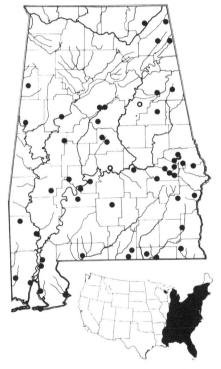

FIG. 270. Distribution of *Thamnophis sauritus sauritus*, the eastern ribbon snake. This form is believed to occur statewide, or nearly so, in Alabama. Solid symbols indicate localities from which the author examined specimens. The circle is a literature record believed to be valid. The small map depicts approximately the known range of the species *T. sauritus* in the United States.

man (1963b), indicate a range in litter size of from 3 to 26. Fish and amphibians constitute the bulk of the diet. A recent summary of the literature on *T. sauritus* was provided by Rossman in 1970.

Thamnophis sirtalis (Linnaeus)

Twelve subspecies of this snake, which ranges from coast to coast, are recognized. Only 1 of these occurs in Alabama.

Thamnophis sirtalis sirtalis (Linnaeus)
Eastern Garter Snake

Description: (Fig. 271) A medium-sized snake attaining a maximum total length of about 1,220 mm. Head distinct from neck; anal undivided; scales strongly keeled, in 19 rows at mid-body. Color and pattern variable; dorsum dull greenish, brown, or bluish with a yellow, tan, or red stripe occupying the mid-dorsal scale row and one-half of each adjacent row and, usually, with a light ventrolateral stripe on each side occupying scale rows 2 and 3 (counting up from ventrals); 2 rows of alternating dark spots or squarish blotches often present between the stripes on each side; belly yellowish, greenish, or bluish with 1 or 2 rows of dark spots down each side.

Remarks: The only obvious geographic variation in this species in Alabama involves the color of the mid-dorsal stripe. In a majority of the live specimens I have seen from the lower two-thirds of Baldwin and Mobile counties, the stripe is decidedly red. This condition was not encountered elsewhere in the state.

Ventrals in twenty-one Alabama males: range 133 to 152, mean 145.8; in eighteen females: range 134 to 156, mean 143.3. Subcaudals in twelve males: range 62 to 82, mean 74.0; in twelve females: range 56 to 79, mean 68.9.

Alabama distribution: (Fig. 272) Statewide.

Habits: From the standpoint of its ecological requirements, the eastern gar-

FIG. 271. *Thamnophis sirtalis sirtalis*, the eastern garter snake (Lee County). The ventral scutes of this common snake have a black spot at each end.

ter snake is a generalized form, and though not overly abundant, it can be found in almost all terrestrial habitat types. Its food consists mostly of frogs, toads, and earthworms; but fish, salamanders, small mammals, and even snakes are eaten occasionally (Fitch, 1965). The garter snake gives birth to the young, usually 7 to 20 per litter, although litters of up to 80 have been recorded.

Garter snakes tend to be somewhat ill-tempered and will not hesitate to bite when captured. In their inclination to bite and smear the captor with musk, they resemble some of the species of *Natrix*. Ordinarily they adjust reasonably well to captivity, however, feeding readily and becoming fairly docile.

FIG. 272. Distribution of *Thamnophis sirtalis*, the eastern garter snake. This form is believed to occur statewide in Alabama. Solid symbols indicate localities from which the author examined specimens. Circles are literature records believed to be valid. The small map depicts approximately the known range of the species *T. sirtalis* in the United States.

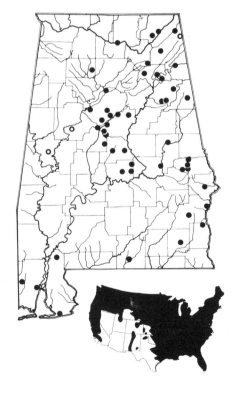

GENUS *VIRGINIA* Baird and Girard

The ranges of the 2 species which comprise this genus are both confined to the eastern United States. Both are found in Alabama.

Virginia striatula (Linnaeus)
Rough Earth Snake

Description: (Fig. 273) A small, moderately slender snake attaining a maximum total length of around 320 mm. Head small; snout pointed; tail short; anal divided; scales small, keeled, in 17 rows at mid-body; upper labials usually 5; prefrontal and loreal entering eye. Color above brownish to gray; back of head of most juveniles and some adults with a light band; venter cream to yellowish.

Ventrals in thirty-nine Alabama males: range 112 to 130, mean 121.2; in four-teen females: range 120 to 129, mean 124.8. Subcaudals in thirty-three males: range 26 to 48, mean 39.5; in twelve females: range 29 to 44, mean 34.2.

Alabama distribution: (Fig. 274) Most of the Coastal Plain and lower portions of the Piedmont, Blue Ridge, and Ridge and Valley regions. Possibly occurs in other upland regions, but records are lacking.

Habits: This small, secretive snake is most abundant in relatively dry Coastal Plain woodlands. It is usually encountered when rocks or logs are overturned or when rotting pine logs and stumps are pulled apart. The eastern crowned snake, *Tantilla coronata*, is one of its frequent associates. *V. striatula* is more tolerant of xeric conditions than the smooth earth snake, *V. valeriae*.

Reported food items include a variety of small invertebrates, in addition to

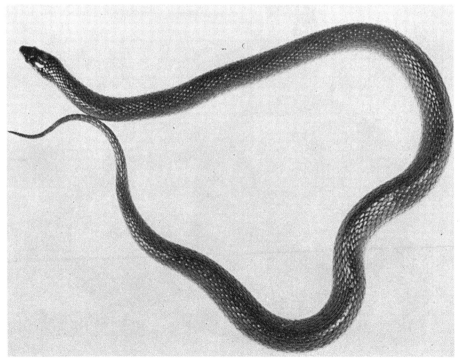

FIG. 273. *Virginia striatula*, the rough earth snake (Russell County). A small secretive snake, this species is usually found under rocks and logs in dry habitats. It has a small, pointed head and keeled scales.

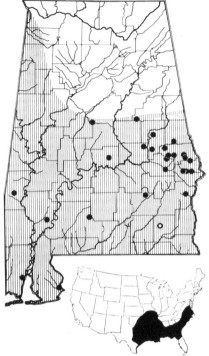

FIG. 274. Distribution of *Virginia striatula*, the rough earth snake. The presumed range in Alabama is indicated by hatching. Solid symbols indicate localities from which the author examined specimens. The circle is a literature record believed to be valid. The small map depicts approximately the known range in the United States.

small frogs and lizards. The rough earth snake is viviparous, with 2 to 13 young being born in mid- or late summer.

Virginia valeriae Baird and Girard

Three subspecies of this small snake are recognized; one subspecies occurs in Alabama and influence from another is evident in intergradient populations.

Virginia valeriae valeriae Baird and Girard
Eastern Smooth Earth Snake

Description: (Fig. 275) A small snake attaining a maximum total length of

FIG. 275. *Virginia valeriae valeriae*, the eastern smooth earth snake (Macon County). This small, short-tailed snake is found most frequently under logs and rocks. It has smooth scales and a gray to brown or yellowish brown ground color. The snout is pointed.

about 325 mm. Head small, pointed; anal divided; tail short; scales smooth or, rarely, very slightly keeled, in 15 rows at mid-body; dorsum gray to brown or yellowish brown with widely scattered small, dark flecks; color of venter light gray to white, not sharply delineated from dorsal color as in *Carphophis amoenus,* a species with which the smooth earth snake is often confused.

Ventrals in fifteen Alabama males: range 109 to 115, mean 111.7; in thirty-six females: range 112 to 128, mean 118.5. Subcaudals in fourteen males: range 30 to 42, mean 34.6; in thirty-three females: range 22 to 31, mean 26.2.

Alabama distribution and remarks: (Fig. 276) The species *V. valeriae* apparently occurs statewide, although documentation of its presence in some areas is lacking. Both *V. v. valeriae* and *V. v. elegans,* the western smooth earth snake, have been presumed to occur in Alabama, the latter in the extreme western portion. The only samples I have examined from that area were from Mobile and Sumter counties, and both were intermediate in phenotype. (The Sumter County record is not indicated on the distribution map.) It seems appropriate, therefore, to consider extreme western Alabama to be within a zone of intergradation between the two subspecies.

Habits: This small, secretive snake occurs most abundantly in mesic forests, where it hides beneath rocks and logs and in piles of organic debris. It is frequently encountered in wooded residential areas of cities and towns and is one of several species of small snakes mistakenly called "ground rattlers." (See account of *Sistrurus miliarius.*) With the approach of cold weather, smooth earth snakes often congregate in small numbers, sometimes in company with individuals of *Virginia striatula,* and overwinter under large rocks.

Smooth earth snakes feed predominantly on earthworms. The young are born alive and number from 4 to 14, the latter number reported by Groves (1961) for a female from Maryland.

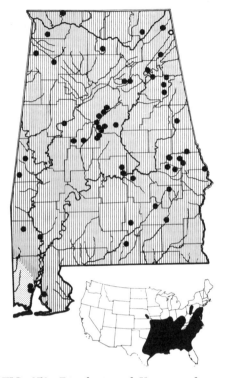

FIG. 276. Distribution of *Virginia valeriae* and subspecific variation in Alabama. Vertical hatching indicates the presumed range of *V. v. valeriae,* the eastern smooth earth snake, in Alabama. The stippled area is a zone of intergradation between *V. v. valeriae* and *V. v. elegans,* the western smooth earth snake. Solid symbols indicate areas from which the author examined specimens. The circle is a literature record believed to be valid. The small map depicts approximately the range of the species *V. valeriae* in the United States. (Note: A Sumter County record of *V. v. valeriae* x *elegans* was inadvertently omitted from the Alabama map.)

Virginia valeriae elegans Kennicott
Western Smooth Earth Snake

Description: Generally similar to *V. v. valeriae* except in having 17 rows (at mid-body) of *faintly keeled scales,* as opposed to 15 rows of *smooth scales.*

Alabama distribution: See "Alabama distribution and remarks" under *V. v. valeriae.*

Habits: Apparently similar in most respects to those of *V. v. valeriae.*

FAMILY ELAPIDAE – ELAPID SNAKES

This large family of around 215 species contains the cobras, kraits, coral snakes, and their allies. The ranges of most are tropical or subtropical; the family is particularly well represented in Australia. All elapids are venomous, although some are so small and mild-mannered that they are considered harmless. All the New World species are considered dangerous to man. The venom is conducted by a pair of erect, grooved fangs, which are situated near the front on the upper jaws.

GENUS *MICRURUS* Wagler

This genus contains about 46 species and is distributed from the southern United States to Peru and Argentina. One species, the only one found in the United States, occurs in Alabama.

Micrurus fulvius (Linnaeus)

Two subspecies of this snake are recognized, 1 of which occurs in Alabama.

Micrurus fulvius fulvius (Linnaeus)
Eastern Coral Snake

Description: (Fig. 277) A medium-sized, fairly slender snake, attaining a maximum total length of about 1,090 mm. Head short, blunt, only slightly distinct from neck; upper jaw with a pair of immovable, erect fangs near the front; scales smooth, in 15 rows at midbody; anal divided. Top of head and nose black, occiput with a broad yellow band; pattern on body typically of alternating, complete red and black bands separated by narrow yellow rings; red bands in this subspecies containing black pigment which tends to coalesce dorsally into a pair of spots and ventrally into a single spot. Aberrant color patterns occur regularly.

Ventral count in four Alabama males: range 199 to 205, mean 202; in one female: 218. Subcaudal count in the males: range 37 to 41, mean 40.3; in the female: 30.

Alabama distribution: (Fig. 278) Generally distributed and relatively common

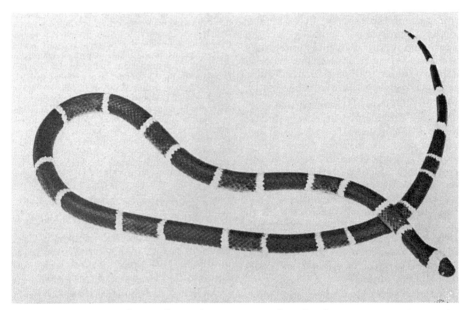

FIG. 277. *Micrurus fulvius fulvius*, the eastern coral snake (Geneva County). In this dangerously venomous snake, the snout is black and the sequence of bands is red-yellow-black-yellow-red-yellow . . . The coral snake has short fangs, and most bites have occurred when the snakes were being handled.

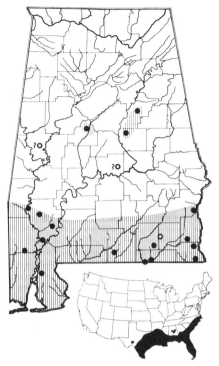

FIG. 278. Distribution of *Micrurus fulvius fulvius*, the eastern coral snake. Vertical hatching indicates the presumed range of the coral snake in Alabama. Solid symbols indicate localities from which the author examined specimens. The circle in southeastern Alabama is a relatively recent literature record believed to be valid. The circle in Greene County (western Alabama) is an old literature record (Yarrow, 1882) as is that in Autauga County (central Alabama) (Holt, 1924).

in the Lower Coastal Plain, infrequent in the Red Hills, and rare elsewhere within the range. Northern limit of range undetermined. Specimens have been collected above the Fall Line as far north as the vicinity of Blockton in Bibb County, in central Alabama, and Shocco Springs, Talladega County, in eastern Alabama. At least 1 specimen has been collected in Coosa County.

Habits: The eastern coral snake apparently spends much of its time underground. Activity on the surface is confined mostly to early morning and late afternoon hours, and most Alabama speci-

mens have been collected at those times. Habitat types exploited range from hardwood forests to pine flatwoods. Friable soil seems to be a requisite.

The reproductive habits are poorly known. The eggs apparently are laid in loose soil or in rotting organic matter. Clutch size reportedly varies from 3 to 12. Small snakes and lizards constitute the coral snake's diet.

The eastern coral snake is dangerous and its venom is fully capable of causing death. There are many reports, most of them old, to the effect that coral snakes are docile and inoffensive, and that they may be handled with impunity. Many people who have been bitten were probably of this school of thought. Most of the coral snakes I have caught readily turned and bit the objects with which they were being restrained. Often when restrained, a coral snake will ball the tail and wave it about in a bit of deception that can easily cause an inexperienced collector to mistake the tail for the head, adding danger to attempts to capture it. The best practice is to leave coral snakes alone and under no circumstances handle them.

FAMILY VIPERIDAE — VIPERS

This large family, circumglobal in distribution, contains about 190 species, all of which are dangerously poisonous. The venom is conducted by recurved, retractable, hollow fangs situated near the front of the upper jaws. Members of the family have undivided subcaudal scutes (except for those near the tail-tip), and the vast majority have elliptical eye pupils. The family is divisible into 3 subfamilies, the largest of which, Crotalinae, with about 138 species, contains all the New World members. The crotalines, commonly called pit vipers, are also represented in Asia and are distinctive in having a heat-sensitive depression, the "pit," on each side of the head between the eye and the nostril. Five of Alabama's 6 venomous species of snakes are pit vipers.

GENUS *AGKISTRODON* Beauvois

This genus has representatives in Europe, Asia, and North America. It is represented in Alabama by 2 polytypic species.

Agkistrodon contortrix (Linnaeus)

Five subspecies of this species are recognized, 2 of which are found in Alabama.

Agkistrodon contortrix contortrix
(Linnaeus)

Southern Copperhead

Description: (Fig. 279) A moderately large, fairly stout snake attaining a maximum total length of about 1,320 mm. Scales keeled, usually in 25 rows at midbody; anal undivided, subcaudals typically undivided except near end of tail. Head distinct from neck, with a facial pit or depression on each side between eye and nostril; front of upper jaw with recurved, movable fangs; pupils of eye vertically elliptical; loreal present. Body light brown, tan, or pinkish with 16 to 21 hourglass-shaped transverse dark bands, these constricted in width to 2 or 3 scale-lengths at mid-dorsum, or the 2 halves failing to meet altogether. Ven-

trolateral spots present but not of equal intensity, those opposite the body bands pale and diffuse, the alternating ones dark and well defined.

Remarks: No significant geographic variation in scale counts was detected in this subspecies or, for that matter, among any of the populations of Alabama copperheads sampled. Sexual dimorphism is detectable in means of both ventral and subcaudal counts, with counts for males averaging more than those for females. Ventral count for thirty-four Alabama male copperheads, subspecific allocation disregarded: range, 140 to 152, mean 146.4. Ventrals in twenty-four females: range 141 to 151, mean 144.5. Subcaudals in the males: range, 39 to 51; mean, 45.0. Subcaudals in twenty-two of the females: range, 38 to 49; mean, 43.3.

Color pattern shows considerable individual variation in all populations, particularly in the nature of the dark crossbands. Occasionally, an individual is encountered with a deviation so exceptional that it would not be recognized on the basis of its pattern. Such an individual is AM 19709, a copperhead (*A. c. contortrix X mokeson*) obtained from Calhoun County by Thomas Yarbrough, in which the dark pigment forms longitudinal dorsolateral

FIG. 279. *Agkistrodon contortrix contortrix* x *mokeson*, copperhead (Barbour County). Copperheads are common in most parts of the state. The individual shown here is an intergrade between 2 subspecies, *A. c. contortrix*, the southern copperhead, and *A. c. mokeson*, the northern copperhead. Although rarely resulting in fatality, a copperhead bite should be regarded as serious.

stripes instead of transverse bands. Occurrences such as this emphasize the danger of attempting to identify a snake without seeing it. For example, there are no *species* or *subspecies* of poisonous snakes in Alabama that typically have a longitudinally striped pattern, but in this case we have an example of an *exceptional individual* so marked.

Alabama distribution: (Fig. 280) The Lower Coastal Plain, intergrading with *A. c. mokeson* northward to the range of that subspecies in extreme northern Alabama. Within the broad zone of intergradation are many individuals whose features conform precisely to those given for *A. c. contortrix*. These represent one end of a spectrum of individual variation that characterizes the populations to which they belong.

Habits: Aside from those implied by a consideration of their ranges, there seem to be no important differences between the habits of *A. c. contortrix* and *A. c. mokeson* in Alabama. Above the Fall Line, copperheads occur in greatest abundance in forested areas with rocky bluffs and ravines. Preferred habitats in the Coastal Plain provinces seem to be floodplains, the edges of swamps, and hilly terrain dominated by hardwood trees. Copperheads are common in the Black Belt, where they are usually found along streams, hedge rows, and in places overgrown with kudzu (*Pueraria lobata*). Throughout the range, abandoned farms often provide ideal habitat conditions. Only in some of the excessively sandy, dry areas of extreme southern Alabama do copperheads appear to be scarce or absent.

In the spring and fall, copperheads are active during the day. During hot weather, they are mainly nocturnal. The food habits are generalized. Included in the diet are small mammals, frogs, lizards, and insects. Hatchling turtles have been reported in at least 2 instances. The tails of newborn copperheads are yellow and are possibly used for luring prey in a manner similar to that employed by young cottonmouths. (See account of *A. piscivorus*.)

Mating in copperheads occurs shortly after emergence from hibernation. I found a pair copulating in Shelby County on April 8. The air temperature was about 75°F. The young are born during August and September, and average 5 or 6 per litter.

Although the copperhead is relatively docile, it is dangerous and capable of causing death. Fatalities from copperhead bites are rare, however, and serious problems seldom arise when reasonable therapy is preformed. Copperheads usually thrive in captivity when properly cared for. The life history and ecology

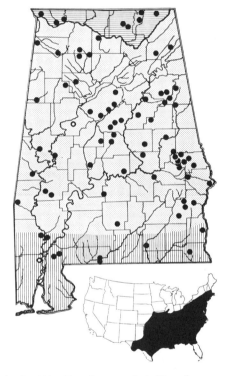

FIG. 280. Distribution of *Agkistrodon contortrix* and subspecific variation in Alabama. Horizontal hatching indicates the presumed range of *A. c. mokeson*, the northern copperhead, and vertical hatching, the range of *A. c. contortrix*, the southern copperhead. The zone of intergradation is indicated by stippling. Solid symbols indicate localities from which the author examined specimens. Circles are literature records believed to be valid. The small map depicts approximately the known range of the species *A. contortrix* in the United States.

of the copperhead were treated in detail by Fitch (1960).

Agkistrodon contortrix mokeson
(Daudin)
Northern Copperhead

Description: (Fig. 279) Generally similar to A. c. contortrix except as follows: ground color usually darker and more reddish or brownish than in A. c. contortrix; transverse bands, when complete, only moderately constricted at mid-dorsum, to 3 to 5 scale-lengths in width; ventrolateral spots of nearly equal intensity.

Alabama distribution: (Fig. 280) From the Alabama-Tennessee boundary southward approximately to the Tennessee River and possibly in extreme northeastern Alabama below the Tennessee River. Intergrades with A. c. contortrix southward to the range of that subspecies. To determine precisely the boundary between the range of A. c. mokeson and the intergrade zone will require considerably more specimens from northern Alabama than are currently available.

Habits: See "Habits" under A. c. contortrix.

Agkistrodon piscivorus (Lacépède)

Three subspecies of this species are currently recognized, all 3 of which occur in Alabama.

Scale counts for the 3 subspecies are presumably diagnostic, but they overlap considerably, and other diagnostic characters are subject to marked indi-

FIG. 281. Agkistrodon piscivorus piscivorus, eastern cottonmouth, adult (Lee County). The venomous cottonmouth is but one of the several snakes that occur in aquatic habitats in Alabama. Variation in coloration among adult cottonmouths, even among individuals of the same population, is extensive. Many adults are dark and almost patternless, such as the one shown here, while others are as vividly marked as the juvenile shown in Fig. 282.

vidual variation. For these reasons, as well as for others mentioned below, subspecific allocation of populations in Alabama has been difficult and must be regarded as tentative.

Agkistrodon piscivorus piscivorus
(Lacépède)
Eastern Cottonmouth

Description: (Fig. 281, 282) A large, heavy-bodied aquatic snake attaining a maximum total length of about 1,520 mm. Scales keeled, in 25 rows at midbody; anal undivided; subcaudals typically undivided except near end of tail. Head distinct from neck, with a facial pit or depression on each side between eye and nostril; front of upper jaw with recurved, movable fangs; pupil of eye vertically elliptical; loreal absent. Ground color light brown to nearly black; pattern, when visible, of transverse dark bands with serrated edges, with bands narrowest at mid-dorsum. Juveniles much more conspicuously marked than adults.

In this subspecies, end of snout typically brownish without conspicuous markings; top of head brownish, often with light patches in mature individuals; crossbands on body often contrasting rather strongly with ground color; markings on face and lower jaws typically less conspicuous than on A. p. conanti, but more so than on A. p. leucostoma; overall color lighter than that of A. p. leucostoma.

Mean subcaudal count (46 for males, 44 for females) somewhat higher than for A. p. leucostoma, but lower than for A. p. conanti.

Alabama distribution: (Fig. 283) Statewide except for southeastern and southwestern portions. (See "Alabama distribution" under other subspecies.) Cottonmouths are common and generally

FIG. 282. *Agkistrodon piscivorus piscivorus*, eastern cottonmouth, juvenile (Monroe County). Juvenile cottonmouths are vividly marked and often mistaken for copperheads. As in copperheads, the end of the tail of the newborn is bright yellow.

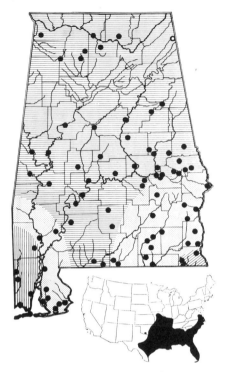

FIG. 283. Distribution of *Agkistrodon piscivorus* and subspecific variation in Alabama. Horizontal hatching indicates the presumed range of *A. p. piscivorus,* the eastern cottonmouth, in Alabama; vertical hatching, that of *A. p. leucostoma,* the western cottonmouth; and diagonal hatching, that of *A. p. conanti,* the Florida cottonmouth. Stippled areas are zones of intergradation. Solid symbols are localities from which the author examined specimens. The circle is a literature record believed to be valid. The small map denotes approximately the range of the species *A. piscivorus* in the United States.

Plain, cottonmouths are found on occasion in such seemingly unlikely places as small, clear brooks in mountainous areas of the state.

The food habits are generalized. Food items, as reported from variou.s portions of the range, include insects, snails, fish, frogs, baby alligators, lizards, turtles, snakes, birds, bird eggs, small mammals, and carrion.

Cottonmouths, when aroused, tend to be pugnacious in disposition when approached on land or prevented from escaping. Often the first reaction is to expel from the anal glands a quantity of musk, which has an odor remarkably like that of a male goat. Cottonmouths have the habit of gaping repeatedly at an intruder, jerking the head with each gape. This behavior reveals the light mouth linings and has given rise to the colloquial name. Several other water-inhabiting snakes in Alabama are collectively termed "water moccasins" by novices and are mistaken for cottonmouths, but they seldom display this gaping habit. Another habit of cottonmouths that may aid in recognition is the tendency to swim with the head well out of the water, in contrast to other aquatic snakes. Also, they frequently appear more buoyant when swimming and less inclined to dive when threatened than the others.

Cottonmouths give birth to the young, usually during August and September. Burkett (1966), in his work on the natural history of the species, stated that an average litter is 6 or 7. The tail of the young cottonmouth is sulfur yellow. When in motion it resembles a worm and is thought to serve as a luring device which aids in the capture of food (Whatron, 1960). Most cottonmouths do well and tend to become sluggish in captivity. The bite of a cottonmouth is serious, however, and the snakes must be handled with extreme caution.

Agkistrodon piscivorus conanti Gloyd
Florida Cottonmouth

Description: (Fig. 284) Generally similar to *A. p. piscivorus* except as

distributed in the Coastal Plain and adjacent portions of other provinces. Elsewhere they tend to be rather uncommon and local in occurrence.

Habits: The habits of the 3 subspecies of cottonmouths are similar in most respects and are considered here collectively. The species shows wide ecological tolerance in Alabama, occurring in almost every type of permanently aquatic habitat. Although the greatest population densities are attained in the swamps, sloughs, and bayheads of the Coastal

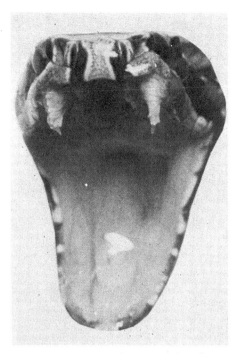

FIG. 284. Front of the snout of *Agkistrodon piscivorus conanti*, the Florida cottonmouth (Houston County). The vertical dark markings on the snout are characteristic of *A. p. conanti* and occur only rarely in populations outside the range of influence of that subspecies.

follows: Size larger, up to about 1,880 mm; sides of the rostral and adjacent prenasals and upper labials with a conspicuous dark stripe; upper labials with 1 or 2 dark spots; markings on head and undersurfaces of jaws more distinct than in *A. p. piscivorus*, especially when old individuals are compared. Mean subcaudal count (males, 50; females, 45) higher than in either *A. p. piscivorus* or *A. p. leucostoma*.

Alabama distribution: (Fig. 283) Southern Houston County in extreme southeastern Alabama. Influence of this subspecies can be seen in populations intergradient with *A. p. piscivorus* as far north as Lee County and as far west as Butler and Covington counties. Two specimens from Wilcox County (AM 18566-67) and one from Limestone County (AM 2914) have rostral stripes suggestive of *A. p. conanti*, but other considerations are against assigning them intergradient status.

Habits: See "Habits" under *A. p. piscivorus*.

Agkistrodon piscivorus leucostoma
(Troost)

Western Cottonmouth

Description: Generally similar to *A. p. piscivorus* except as follows: top of head uniform dark brown to black; dark markings on sides of head obscure; transverse bands on body not readily apparent in mature individuals; overall appearance darker than in either of the other 2 forms. Mean subcaudal count (males, 44; females, 42) lower than for either *A. p. piscivorus* or *A. p. conanti*.

Alabama distribution: (Fig. 283) Extreme southwestern Alabama, in Mobile County and southern Washington County. The northernmost extent of the zone of intergradation between this and the nominate subspecies in Alabama has not been accurately determined.

Habits: See "Habits" under *A. p. piscivorus*.

GENUS *CROTALUS* Linnaeus

Thirty-six of the 39 species of rattlesnakes are contained within this genus, which ranges from Canada to Argentina. The genus is represented in Alabama by 2 species.

Crotalus adamanteus Beauvois

Eastern Diamondback Rattlesnake

Description: (Fig. 285) An extremely large, heavy-bodied snake attaining a maximum total length of about 2,440 mm. Tail short, stout, with a rattle or "button" at the end; scales keeled, in 27 to 29 rows at mid-body; anal undivided. Head large, sharply distinct from neck, with a pit on each side between eye and nostril; front of upper jaws with movable, recurved fangs; top of head in back of eyes with small scales. Ground color

FIG. 285. *Crotalus adamanteus,* the eastern diamondback rattlesnake (Covington County). The most dangerous of the venomous snakes found in Alabama, the eastern diamondback is capable of attaining lengths well in excess of 7 feet.

of dorsum brownish; dorsal pattern consisting of dark diamonds with light centers and yellow borders; head with dark band extending obliquely from eye to labials, band bordered on each side by a light streak; snout with rostral outlined by yellow and with a vertical yellow stripe on each side in front of nostril. Belly yellowish to white, lightly suffused with brownish at sides.

Ventrals in four Alabama males: range 165 to 170, mean 167.8; in five females: range 162 to 176, mean 171.2. Subcaudals in the males: range 26 to 31, mean 28.3; in the females: range 21 to 27, mean 23.4.

Alabama distribution: (Fig. 286) Generally distributed and locally common in the Lower Coastal Plain. Local in areas of suitable habitat in the Red Hills.

Habits: Relatively dry pine flatwoods and longleaf pine-turkey oak hills are the favored habitats of this extremely dangerous snake. Abandoned farm land and other such places where rabbits and small rodents abound are also likely to support sizable diamondback populations. The burrow of the gopher tortoise often serves as a refuge, particularly during cold

weather (see account of *Gopherus polyphemus,* p. 307). Where gopher burrows are scarce or absent, a stump hole may be used. During the winter the diamondback is not a "heavy sleeper," and on warm, sunny days it may emerge to bask or to prowl on the surface.

During an encounter with man the diamondback conducts itself with poise and dignity. When not in the open, it is loath to move or rattle and will often remain perfectly still until actually touched. When touched, or when a direct confrontation is imminent, the snake assumes the defensive attitude, body coiled, rattle errect and buzzing, with the head near the center and the neck flexed laterally 2 or more times. From this position a strike of up to two-thirds of the snake's length is possible. Once in this stance, the rattler, particularly if it is large and away from shelter, tends to hold its ground until the threat of danger has passed.

During late summer and early fall the females seek sheltered places and give birth. The litters range in size from about 8 to 15; the average length of the newborn is about 355 mm. Mice and rats are the chief foods of small diamond-

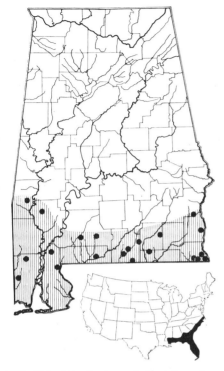

FIG. 286. Distribution of *Crotalus adamanteus*, the eastern diamondback rattlesnake. The presumed range in Alabama is indicated by hatching. Symbols indicate localities from which the author examined specimens. The small map depicts approximately the known range in the United States.

backs, while rabbits seem to be the principal diet of large ones. Occasional food items include squirrels and ground-dwelling birds.

A diamondback destined for captivity should be treated gently during capture and transport. The residence cage should contain a box big enough for the snake to hide in and should be kept in a place that affords a maximum of privacy. Under such conditions a diamondback will often thrive for years. Young individuals adjust more readily to captivity than do old ones.

Crotalus horridus Linnaeus
Timber Rattlesnake
(Canebrake Rattlesnake)

Until recently the southern populations of *C. horridus*, incuding those inhabiting most of Alabama, were recognized collectively as the subspecies *C. h. atricaudatus*. In 1972, Pisani, *et al.* put forth a convincing argument against continued recognition of *atricaudatus*, showing that geographic variation in the most significant diagnostic characters tends to be clinal. Thus, *C. horridus* is considered here to be monotypic.

Description: (Fig. 287) A large,

FIG. 287. *Crotalus horridus*, the timber rattlesnake or canebrake rattlesnake. This large rattlesnake is found statewide and is erroneously called "diamondback rattlesnake" by many residents of northern Alabama. It is fully capable of causing death but is considerably less dangerous than the diamondback.

heavy-bodied snake attaining a maximum total length of about 1,880 mm. Tail short, stout, with a rattle or "button" at the end; scales keeled, in 23 or 25 rows at mid-body; anal undivided. Head moderately large, sharply distinct from neck, with a pit on each side between eye and nostril; front of upper jaws with movable, recurved fangs; top of head behind the eyes with small scales. Ground color yellowish, brownish, pink, gray, or occasionally nearly black; dorsal pattern a series of dark, chevron-shaped transverse bands, some of which may be broken. Tail usually black. Belly dull white to yellowish with patches of dark stippling.

Remarks: Most populations of timber rattlesnakes in Alabama have been allocated to the former subspecies *C. h. atricaudatus* and have characteristics traditionally associated with that phenotype. These include a tan or reddish brown mid-dorsal stripe, a dark postocular stripe, a vivid pattern, and 25 scale rows at mid-body. The only significant geographic variation detected among Alabama specimens I examined was a tendency toward reduction in intensity of the mid-dorsal stripe and postocular stripe in populations inhabiting DeKalb and Jackson counties, in the extreme northeastern portion of the state.

Slight differences between males and females in mean numbers of ventrals and subcaudals is indicated by the Alabama specimens. Ventral count in twenty-three males: range 159 to 170, mean 165.0; subcaudal count in this sample: range 22 to 26, mean 24.2. Ventral count in eighteen females: 164 to 170, mean 167.4; subcaudal count: range 19 to 26, mean 22.0.

Alabama distribution: (Fig. 288) Statewide.

Habits: The timber rattlesnake, also called canebrake rattlesnake in much of the South, is most abundant in sparsely settled, forested areas. In the Lower Coastal Plain, where it is sympatric with the eastern diamondback rattlesnake, the timber rattler is seldom found in the same habitats with its larger relative. In that region the diamondback is usually found in relatively dry, sandy situations, whereas the timber rattler is restricted mostly to swampy areas and floodplains. Northward the timber rattler is much less habitat-specific, occurring in both uplands and lowlands.

The timber rattler usually gives birth in August or September. It feeds on a variety of small mammals and, infrequently, on ground-dwelling birds. It is rather "mild-mannered" in disposition and in general less dangerous than the diamondback. Its bite, however, is capable of causing death. The timber rattler adjusts rather well to captivity if treated

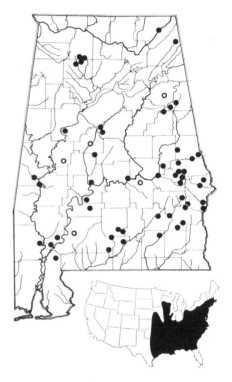

FIG. 288. Distribution of *Crotalus horridus*, the timber or canebrake rattlesnake. The presumed range in Alabama is indicated by hatching. Solid symbols indicate localities from which the author examined specimens. The circle is a literature record believed to be valid. The small map depicts approximately the known range in the United States.

gently during capture and afforded maximum privacy in its quarters.

GENUS *SISTRURUS* Garman

This genus of rattlesnakes is represented in the United States and Mexico. Three species are recognized, 1 of which occurs in Alabama.

Sistrurus miliarius (Linnaeus)

Three subspecies of *S. miliarius* are recognized, all of which are represented in Alabama. The zones of intergradation are extensive, and their limits poorly defined.

Sistrurus miliarius miliarius (Linnaeus)
Carolina Pigmy Rattlesnake

Description: (Fig. 289, 291) A short, stout-bodied snake attaining a maximum total length of about 535 mm. Tail attenuated at the tip, with a small rattle or button. Scales keeled, usually in 23 rows at mid-body; anal undivided. Head distinct from neck, with a pit on each side between eye and nostril; movable

FIG. 289. *Sistrurus miliarius miliarius* x *streckeri,* pigmy rattlesnake (Fayette County). The pigmy rattlesnake, called "ground rattler" by many in Alabama, is capable of delivering a painful bite from which serious complications can arise if judicious treatment is not applied. The individual shown here is an integrade between *S. m. miliarius,* the Carolina pigmy rattlesnake, and *S. m. streckeri,* the western pigmy rattlesnake.

recurved fangs near front of upper jaws; top of head with 9 large symmetrical plates; loreal large, completely separating preoculars from postnasal. Dorsum light brown or gray, often with a pinkish cast, with a median series of 25 to 36 dark brown or black blotches (males average 30, females 33); median blotches usually oval shaped with regular edges, about equal in longitudinal dimension to light interspaces; lateral spots present in 2 series, the mid-lateral ones opposite mid-dorsal blotches, relatively round, with indistinct edges.

Venter white to cream, blotched with grayish brown, the blotches elliptical and occupying the width of 2 ventral scutes.

Ventral count in three Alabama males: range 127 to 129, mean 128.3; in one female: 135. Subcaudal count in the males: range 31 to 32, mean 31.7; in the female: 30.

Alabama distribution: (Fig. 290) This subspecies occurs across the northern one-third of Alabama and in the eastern portion of the state southward to Lee County. Populations in adjoining areas are intergradient.

Habits: The habits of the 3 subspecies of pigmy rattlesnakes in Alabama appear to be similar in most respects. In the Lower Coastal Plain pigmy rattlesnakes occur in most of the terrestrial habitat types represented except for extensive, hardwood-dominated floodplains. In central and northern Alabama, mixed pine-hardwood forests seem to be favored.

The pigmy rattlesnake is seldom encountered except during late summer. Most specimens are found as they cross roads in late afternoon or at night. This small snake is pugnacious in its attitude toward a molester. Most Alabamians who know it call it "ground rattler." This leads to considerable confusion, because many people apply that name loosely to any small snake they do not recognize. This tendency has doubtless contributed to the widespread belief that the pigmy rattler has no rattle. A rattle is, of course, present, even though it is small and can scarcely be heard more than 3 feet away.

Pigmy rattlesnakes have been reported to feed on mice, lizards, frogs, insects, and spiders. The young are born between July and September. The usual number is between 4 and 10, but Carpenter (1960) reported an unusually large litter of 32 from a pigmy rattler (*S. m. streckeri*) from Oklahoma. Data on reproduction in Alabama are scarce. A female pigmy rattler from Chilton County in my possession gave birth to 6 young on August 15. A paper by Palmer and Williamson (1971) dealt with the natural history of *S. m. miliarius*.

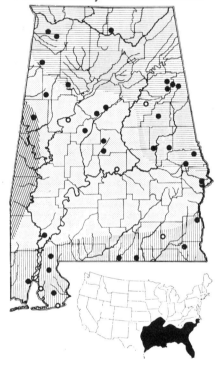

FIG. 290. Distribution of *Sistrurus miliarius* and subspecific variation in Alabama. Horizontal hatching indicates the presumed range of *S. m. miliarius,* the Carolina pigmy rattlesnake in Alabama; vertical hatching, that of *S. m. barbouri,* the dusky pigmy rattlesnake; and diagonal hatching, that of *S. m. streckeri,* the western pigmy rattlesnake. The stippled area is a zone of intergradation. Solid symbols indicate localities from which the author examined specimens. Circles are literature records believed to be valid. The small map depicts approximately the range of the species *S. miliarius* in the United States.

The bite of the pigmy rattlesnake is not likely to be serious in an adult because of the small amount of venom injected, but it can produce several days of considerable discomfort.

Sistrurus miliarius barbouri Gloyd
Dusky Pigmy Rattlesnake

Description: (Fig. 291) Similar to *S. m. miliarius* but having the following distinctive combination of features: dorsal ground color dark gray, heavily stippled with black; dorsum with a median reddish or reddish brown stripe; dark lateral blotches in 3 series; scale rows at midbody usually 23 or 25, more often the latter; venter white with sharply contrasting dark brown to black blotches which tend to coalesce posteriorly. Maxi-

mum size larger than *S. m. miliarius,* up to about 760 mm.

Alabama distribution: (Fig. 290) Restricted to the Lower Coastal Plain where it is fairly common in sandy pinelands and scrubby areas. Influence from this subspecies can be seen in intergradient populations throughout most of the remainder of the southern one-half of the state.

Habits: See "Habits" under *S. m. miliarius.*

Sistrurus miliarius streckeri Gloyd
Western Pigmy Rattlesnake

Description: (Fig. 289) Similar to *S. m. miliarius* except in having the following combination of characteristics:

FIG. 291. *Sistrurus miliarius miliarius,* the Carolina pigmy rattlesnake (Lee County). The ground color of the specimen shown here is somewhat darker than is usual for the nominate subspecies, approaching that of *S. m. barbouri.*

dorsal ground color light gray or brownish, usually with a pinkish cast; a reddish median dorsal stripe occasionally present; mid-dorsal blotches 23 to 42, wider than long, often irregular in shape but narrower longitudinally than interspaces; lateral spots in 1 or 2 series, those opposite the mid-dorsals usually higher than wide; mid-body scale rows usually 21; venter pale with indistinct

blotches, these usually confined to a single scute. Maximum total length about 635 mm.

Alabama distribution: (Fig. 290) Extreme western portion of central Alabama. Limits not precisely known. Intergrades over an extensive area with *S. m. miliarius* and *S. m. barbouri.*

Habits: See "Habits" under *S. m miliarius.*

ORDER TESTUDINATA—TURTLES

Turtles, as a group, are our oldest living reptiles, having been on the earth for nearly 200 million years. Not only do they constitute a valuable food resource, but they also provide a source of enjoyment for a large and growing number of people who like to keep them as pets or merely observe them in their natural habitats.

While varying considerably in size, shape, and color, all turtles are easily recognizable as such. Each species has a shell, consisting of an upper portion, the carapace, which joins laterally with a lower portion, the plastron. A close inspection of the shell of most turtles will reveal an inner layer of bony plates and an outer layer of horny epidermal scutes. In the soft-shelled turtles, the bony elements are greatly reduced, and the outer layer of the shell is composed of leathery skin.

The life histories of turtles vary in details but are similar in basic aspects. All species are oviparous. Fertilization is internal, accomplished by means of a penis which is extruded from the vent of the male at the time of copulation. Courtship activities prior to copulation vary, and the details of this behavior are known for relatively few species. In the Alabama species of *Pseudemys* and in *Chrysemys,* the male strokes and titillates the head of the female with the long front toenails. In the gopher tortoise, *Gopherus polyphemus,* courtship is accompanied by head-bobbing on the part of the male. Occasionally, the male

gopher may pound the side of the female's shell with the front end of his plastron. The male box turtle (*Terrapene* spp.) bites and nips at the front of the female's carapace during courtship. Males of some *Graptemys* vibrate the head against the top and sides of those of the females; in other male *Graptemys* the claws are used in a manner similar to males of *Pseudemys.*

The male turtle typically mounts the female from the rear, twisting his tail beneath hers. In several species of turtles, the male's plastron has a concavity which facilitates assumption of the copulatory position. This plastral concavity is especially pronounced in the male box turtle. Male turtles may hold to the female's shell with all four feet, with just the hind feet, or with the feet and tail. The tails of male mud turtles and musk turtles are adapted to hook under the female's carapace during copulation. In back of the "knee" of the hind leg of males of these genera are opposable patches of horny skin in which the tail of the female is grasped and pulled to one side.

The nest cavity is excavated by the female using the hind feet. In some cases the female expels fluid from the bladder during the process; this softens the soil and makes digging easier. Following oviposition the female covers the eggs, again using only the hind feet. The eggs of some turtles, such as those of the tortoises, soft-shelled turtles, and musk and mud turtles, have hard shells, but those of most, including the remainder of the Alabama species, are somewhat leathery in texture.

Sexual dimorphism is evident in most species of turtles. The tail of the male is longer and thicker than that of the female. The vent of the male is usually well behind the edge of the carapace when the tail is extended, whereas in the female the vent is under the carapace. In most turtle species, the female attains a greater size than the male. Size difference is especially pronounced in some species of *Graptemys*. In these species the females not only exceed the males in size, but in most they develop greatly enlarged heads as well, a change that does not occur in the males.

Sexual dimorphism in color is pronounced in some turtles. In the females of our soft-shelled turtles, the juvenile carapace patterns become obscured and ultimately replaced by considerably different ones, while those of the males remain essentially unchanged. In the red-eared pond slider, the reddish bar on the side of the head is retained well into adulthood in most females, but becomes obscured by melanism in most adult males.

The two most recent comprehensive works devoted chiefly to the turtles of the United States are *Handbook of Turtles* (Carr, 1952) and *Turtles of the United States* (Ernst and Barbour, 1972). The latter is a superbly illustrated, up-to-date treatment of the life history, ecology, and behavior of U.S. turtles. Unlike the former, however, it does not deal with details of distribution or geographic variation, and is thus of limited value to the taxonomist or zoogeographer.

The world's turtle fauna consists of about 336 species and is divisible into 2 suborders, Pleurodira and Cryptodira. The pleurodires, or "side-necked turtles," comprise 2 families with 13 genera; they occur in South America, Africa, Madagascar, New Guinea, and Australia. Cryptodira, with 9 families and 54 genera, is by far the larger suborder and is represented on every continent except Antarctica. All living North American turtles are cryptodires. Alabama's turtle fauna is exceptionally rich and diverse relative to those of most other areas of comparable size in the world. Exclusive of sea turtles, it consists of 22 species, with 5 families and 12 genera represented. Two additional species are known to occur within a few miles of Alabama's western boundary and may ultimately be found within the state.

FAMILY CHELONIIDAE – SEA TURTLES (EXCEPT LEATHERBACK)

The family Cheloniidae is represented in warm seas throughout the world. It includes 4 genera, *Caretta, Chelonia, Eretmochelys,* and *Lepidochelys,* any of which might be encountered along the Alabama coast. Only *Caretta,* however, habitually nests on our beaches.

GENUS *CARETTA* Rafinesque

This genus, containing only 1 species, is widely distributed in warm seas in both hemispheres.

Caretta caretta (Linnaeus)

Two subspecies of this marine turtle are recognized, 1 of which is found along the Alabama coast.

Caretta caretta caretta (Linnaeus)
Atlantic Loggerhead Turtle

Description: A huge salt-water turtle attaining a maximum carapace length of about 2,130 mm. Feet modified into paddle-like flippers; head large, with 2 pairs of prefrontals; front of carapace often with a concavity; carapace with a keel which is less evident in old individuals; scutes of carapace not overlapping, pleurals in 5 or more pairs; bridge with 3 enlarged scutes. Carapace reddish brown, shaded, or mottled with olive; soft parts brown and yellowish. Juveniles light brown above, whitish beneath; carapace with 3 keels, plastron with 2.

Alabama distribution: Coastal waters of Mobile and Baldwin counties.

Habits: Apparently, the loggerhead is the sea turtle encountered most frequently along the Alabama coast, and the only one that habitually nests on our beaches. Jackson and Jackson (1970) state that the loggerhead regularly nests on the southern, seaward beaches of Dauphin Island in Mobile County. However, Alabama beaches are rapidly becoming unsuitable for nesting due to the increasing presence of humans and their activities.

Loggerheads are almost wholly carnivorous, feeding on a variety of crustaceans, molluscs, echinoderms, and other available marine animal life, including fish on occasion. There are several reports of their feeding on Portuguese men-of-war, keeping their eyes closed to protect them from repeated stings. The flesh of the loggerhead is not highly regarded as food.

Nesting occurs from May through August, with a peak about mid-June. The gravid female intent on nesting crawls from the water, usually shortly after dark, and ascends to a point somewhere between the high-tide mark and the dune front. Using all 4 flippers, she scoops out a shallow depression and then, using the hind flippers only, digs the nest chamber, a cavity ranging in depth from 18 to 26 inches. The eggs, which are roughly spherical in shape, are deposited in groups of 2 or 3 until a clutch of 60 to 200 is laid. The nest is then covered with sand and packed. Before leaving the water, the female makes sweeping movements with her front and hind limbs, scattering the sand and obscuring the precise location of the nest. Anywhere from 1 to as many as 4 or 5 clutches of eggs may be laid in a single season.

Predation on the incubating eggs is heavy. In most cases, raccoons, feral dogs, and sand crabs are the most serious predators. In some places, hogs destroy many of the nests. To this list of predators man must be added; despite legal constraints, thoughtless people rob many nests each year. Incubation to hatching takes an average of 65 days, and, as-suming a clutch hatches successfully, the baby turtles wiggle and thrash about in the cavity until they break through to the surface. Emergence usually occurs at night, and those few that break through during the day are often killed by the heat of the sun or are consumed by predators. The hatchlings from a given nest usually appear at the surface in groups, and several days may elapse before the entire brood has left the nest. Caldwell, et al. (1959) provided an account of the natural history of the Atlantic loggerhead.

GENUS *CHELONIA* Latreille

Chelonia contains a number of forms of undetermined relationship and is widely distributed in warm seas in both hemispheres.

Chelonia mydas (Linnaeus)
Green Turtle

According to Carr (1967) there may be as many as 8 statistically separable populations of *C. mydas*. He states, however, that recognition of subspecies in this case is not particularly appropriate.

Description: A large salt-water turtle attaining a maximum carapace length of at least 1,525 mm. Feet modified into paddle-like flippers, prefrontals on head 2; shell broad, low, flattened, keelless in adults; pleural scutes 4 on each side, the first not touching the nuchal; scutes of carapace not overlapping. Carapace light to dark brown, often shaded or mottled with blotches or radiating lines of darker color; soft parts brownish dorsally. Juveniles with 2 keels on plastron and 1 on carapace; ends of their flippers black, edged with white.

Alabama distribution: Although the usual range of this turtle in the Gulf of Mexico is well south of Alabama, an occasional straggler might be expected along our coast.

Habits: The Atlantic green turtle is principally an inhabitant of shallow waters of tropical seas. It is a herbivore, and within its range is most common where vegetation, especially eelgrass, is abundant. Prized for its flesh and eggs, the green turtle's numbers have declined steadily through the years, prompting Archie Carr of the University of Florida to conduct an intensive, long-term study of the animal's ecology and habits and to develop a program to insure its survival. It now appears that this ambitious undertaking will be successful. Dr. Carr's book, *So Excellent A Fishe* (Natural History Press, 1967) is primarily an account of the natural history of the green turtle, with notes on other sea turtles.

GENUS *ERETMOCHELYS* Fitzinger

Eretmochelys is a monotypic genus which is widely distributed in warm marine waters of both eastern and western hemispheres.

Eretmochelys imbricata (Linnaeus)

Two subspecies of this marine turtle are recognized, 1 of which occurs in the Gulf of Mexico and might be expected along our coast.

Eretmochelys imbricata imbricata (Linnaeus)
Atlantic Hawksbill

Description: A salt-water turtle attaining a maximum carapace length of around 915 mm. Feet modified into paddle-like flippers; head with 2 pairs of prefrontals; carapace keeled, heart-shaped or shield-shaped, with scutes overlapping (except in very old individuals); pleurals in 4 pairs, the first not touching the nuchal. Carapace color reddish brown, with small markings of lighter colors; plastron yellow; soft parts predominantly brown above, yellow below. Juveniles with 1 keel on the carapace and 2 on the plastron.

Alabama distribution: Occasional visitor to the coast.

Habits and remarks: The Atlantic hawksbill, an omnivore, frequents coast-al waters of the American tropics and occurs along the northern Gulf Coast only as an occasional migrant. It is perhaps the most persecuted of all the sea turtles. The quality of its meat is said to compare favorably with that of the green turtle. Its eggs are used extensively for food. But it is exploited principally for its carapace, which is, along with that of its subspecific counterpart the Pacific hawksbill, the source of tortoise-shell.

GENUS *LEPIDOCHELYS* Fitzinger

This genus contains 2 species and has a wide distribution in the warm marine waters of both eastern and western hemispheres.

Lepidochelys kempi (Garman)
Atlantic Ridley

Description: The smallest of the Atlantic sea turtles, attaining a maximum carapace length of around 700 mm. Feet modified into flippers, head large with 2 pairs of prefrontals; carapace short, wide, nearly circular with 5 pairs of pleural scutes, the first touching the nuchal; carapace keeled; 4 enlarged scutes on bridge (3 on that of *Caretta caretta*); scutes on carapace not overlapping. Carapace color gray, plastron white or cream. Young darker, with 4 tuberculate ridges on carapace, 3 on plastron.

Alabama distribution: Found in the Gulf of Mexico and probably an occasional visitor to our coastal waters.

Habits and remarks: The Atlantic ridley was at one time called by some the "bastard turtle" because of the erroneous assumption that it was a hybrid between a loggerhead and a green turtle. Until little more than a decade ago, concrete proof to the contrary was lacking because it had never been found nesting. The discovery that ridleys nest along the beaches in Tamaulipas, Mexico, first reported to the scientific community by Dr. Henry Hildebrand at a meeting in 1961, finally solved the "riddle of the ridley." The ridley is mostly carnivorous, and its flesh is considered inferior to that of the green turtle.

FAMILY CHELYDRIDAE – SNAPPING TURTLES

This family of large freshwater turtles is found throughout the eastern United States and the adjacent portion of Canada southward to Ecuador. It consists of 2 genera, both of which are represented in Alabama.

GENUS *CHELYDRA* Schweigger

This genus consists of 4 recognized taxa, all of which are considered by most authorities to belong to the same species, *C. serpentina.*

Chelydra serpentina (Linnaeus)

Chelydra serpentina occurs throughout the United States east of the Rocky Mountains and southward to northern South America. It is represented in Alabama by the nominate subspecies.

Chelydra serpentina serpentina (Linnaeus)
Common Snapping Turtle

Description: (Fig. 292) A large aquatic turtle attaining a carapace length of up to 470 mm. Carapace with 3 keels (not as well developed as in *Macroclemys* and often lacking in old individuals); eyes evident when viewed from above; snout in front of eyes elongate, with a moderately hooked beak; plastron small; soft parts warty; chin with 3 barbels; tail long with 3 dorsal rows of tubercles, the median row conspicuous and platelike.

Alabama distribution: (Fig. 293) Statewide.

Habits: In Alabama the common snapper inhabits a wide variety of permanently aquatic habitats, ranging from small farm ponds and creeks to the largest lakes and rivers. Only in some of the sandy-bottomed, clear creeks of the Lower Coastal Plain does it appear to be scarce or absent. This turtle is rather thoroughly aquatic and seldom leaves the water except for egg-laying. In the water it is inoffensive and not disposed to bite; when removed from the water, it is vicious and aggressive, lunging and striking repeatedly at the offender. The long tail makes a convenient handle for carrying, but large specimens may be injured when carried in this manner, and care must be taken to avoid being bitten on the leg.

The eggs are round with soft shells and are laid in a flask-shaped cavity dug by the female, often well away from water. The usual number per clutch is between 20 and 30. White and Murphy

FIG. 292. *Chelydra serpentina serpentina,* the common snapping turtle (Cleburne County). A familiar form throughout Alabama, the common snapper will bite viciously when out of water.

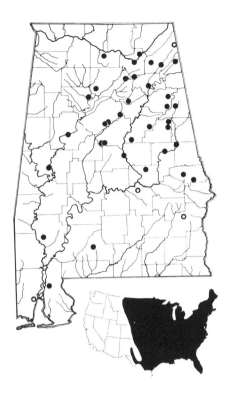

FIG. 293. Distribution of *Chelydra serpentina serpentina,* the common snapping turtle. This form is believed to occur statewide in Alabama. Solid symbols indicate localities from which the author examined specimens. Circles are literature records believed to be valid. The small map depicts approximately the known range of the species *C. serpentina* in the United States.

(1973) reported on the reproductive cycle of the snapping turtle in Tennessee.

Snappers are omnivorous. Fish, carrion, and some vegetable matter constitute the bulk of the diet. They usually thrive in captivity. Snappers are good to eat, but they are not eagerly sought by most Alabamians.

GENUS *MACROCLEMYS* Troost

This genus contains 1 extant species, which occurs in streams of Gulf drainage systems from northern Florida to Texas, northward to Illinois and Iowa.

Macroclemys temmincki (Troost)
Alligator Snapping Turtle

Description: (Fig. 294) An extremely large aquatic turtle attaining a maximum carapace length of over 660 mm. Cara-

FIG. 294. *Macroclemys temmincki,* the alligator snapping turtle (Monroe County). The world's largest freshwater turtle, the alligator snapper has a sharply hooked beak and a row of scutes, the supramarginals, between the marginals and pleurals.

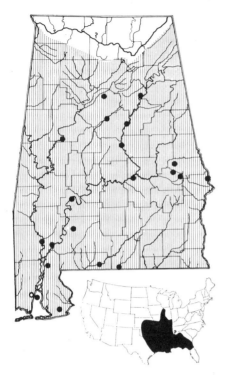

FIG. 295. Distribution of *Macroclemys temmincki*, the alligator snapping turtle. The presumed range in Alabama is indicated by hatching. Symbols indicate localities from which the author examined specimens. The small map depicts approximately the known range in the United States.

pace brown, rough, with 3 conspicuous longitudinal ridges, which may be worn down in old individuals; carapace generally with a row of supramarginal laminae above marginals on each side. Snout in front of eyes elongate, terminating in a strongly hooked break; eyes on sides of head and, in contrast with those of *Chelydra*, not evident when viewed directly from above. Tail long; plastron relatively small; chin and neck with numerous dermal projections.

Alabama distribution: (Fig. 295) Apparently statewide, or nearly so. Reports of its occurrence in the Tennessee River system in Alabama are not, however, documented by specimens. The alligator snapper has been collected from Bear Creek, a tributary of the Tennessee River, in Mississippi.

Habits: This spectacular animal, capable of attaining weights in excess of 200 pounds, is the world's largest freshwater turtle. The alligator snapper usually inhabits rivers, oxbows, and sloughs, but is found occasionally in medium-sized creeks. Unlike the common snapper, it is almost never found in isolated ponds and lakes and leaves the water only to nest.

The alligator snapper is sluggish and spends nearly all of its time lying on the bottom. Along the coast it may inhabit brackish water for considerable periods. Jackson and Ross (1971) reported barnacles on the shell of a specimen from near the mouth of Dog River, Mobile County, Alabama, and a similarly infested specimen, from Baldwin County, is in the Auburn Museum (AMP 195).

One unique feature of this turtle is a wormlike luring device attached to the tongue. Lying on the bottom, mouth agape, the snapper wiggles this appendage and feeds on fish that are attracted to it. Fish are by no means, however, its sole food. Virtually anything of animal origin, including carrion, is eaten, and James Dobie (personal communication) found an individual whose stomach was filled with palmetto fruits and another which had engorged itself with acorns.

Data on nesting are limited to observations of captives by Allen and Neill (1950) and to Fred Cagle's discovery of a natural nest, as reported by Dobie (1971). The nest had been dug in a mounded area about 8 feet from the edge of a Louisiana bayou. The site was concealed by thick underbrush. The nest, approximately 8 inches beneath the surface, had been disturbed by a predator, and top layer of eggs had been removed. The eggs of *M. temmincki* are round with leathery shells. Based on a study of corpora lutea, Dobie concluded that 16 to 52 eggs are produced per female per season.

Lacking the agility and viciousness of the common snapper, the alligator snapper when removed from water, gapes at the captor. It will bite objects placed in or near the mouth, but the widely accepted ideas that it can bite through a broomhandle is a gross exaggeration. The alligator snapper thrives in captivity and will live for many years if cared for properly.

FAMILY DERMOCHELIDAE – LEATHERBACK SEA TURTLE

This family contains a single monotypic genus, *Dermochelys* Blainville. Its range includes tropical seas in both hemispheres, but visits to the temperate zone are recorded regularly.

Dermochelys coriacea (Linnaeus)

Two races of this cosmopolitan marine turtle are usually recognized. One of these is occasionally seen in the Gulf of Mexico and might be found in Alabama coastal waters.

Dermochelys coriacea coriacea (Linnaeus)
Atlantic Leatherback

Description: An enormous salt-water turtle attaining a maximum carapace length of 2,438 mm, making it the world's largest chelonian. Unmistakable on the basis of the flipper-like feet and smooth skin of the carapace and plastron, which have no laminae. Carapace with 7 longitudinal ridges; plastron with 5 ridges. Color black or dark brown with patches of white. Young covered with numerous small scales and more vividly marked than adults.

Alabama distribution: Records are lacking, but the leatherback may visit our coast on rare occasions. Robert M. Shealy recently showed me the remains of a leatherback that had washed ashore near Pensacola, Florida.

Habits: Leatherback turtles nest mostly in the tropics, but there are 2 reliable records of their nesting in the United States, both on the Atlantic coast of Florida. The flesh of this species is considered inedible, but the eggs are eaten regularly in some parts of the world. Leatherbacks are apparently carnivorous and rely heavily on jellyfish as a dietary staple when migrating in the open sea.

FAMILY EMYDIDAE – EMYDID TURTLES

With 26 genera and approximately 80 species, Emydidae is the world's largest turtle family. Its range is circumglobal, but excludes Australia and most of Africa. The family is especially well represented in southeastern Asia and in the southeastern United States. Six genera and 13 species are known to occur in Alabama.

GENUS *CHRYSEMYS* Gray

This genus contains a single species whose extensive range includes most of the United States. Several recent authorities have concurred in a proposal that the genus be expanded to include *Pseudemys;* the 2 are herein considered separately.

Chrysemys picta (Schneider)

Four subspecies of this species are recognized. Three of these occur in Alabama.

Chrysemys picta picta (Schneider)
Eastern Painted Turtle

Description: (Fig. 296) A medium-sized aquatic turtle attaining a maximum carapace length of about 180 mm. Carapace smooth, dark, and somewhat depressed; seams of second and third vertebral scutes in nearly the same transverse line as those of adjacent pleurals; plastron yellowish, usually unmarked; marginals conspicuously marked with red. Head with a pair of yellow spots behind the eyes and another pair above and behind these; lighter markings on legs and other soft parts red.

Alabama distribution: (Fig. 297) Sev-

FIG. 296. *Chrysemys picta picta,* the eastern painted turtle (Lee County). Painted turtles have a smooth carapace and red suffusion on the marginals.

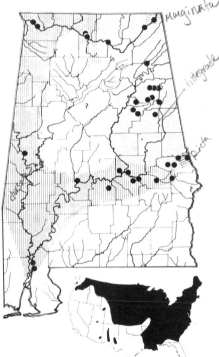

eral painted turtles from the Chattahoochee River drainage area in eastern Alabama are referable to *C. p. picta.* All are from above the Fall Line in Lee County. Painted turtles are not available from the Chattahoochee drainage below the Fall Line. Influence from *C. p. picta* is detectable in intergradient populations in the remainder of the species' range in eastern Alabama northward to the southern limit of the Tennessee River drainage area. (See "Alabama distribution" under *C. p. dorsalis* and *C. p. marginata.*)

FIG. 297. Distribution of *Chrysemys picta* and subspecific variation in Alabama. Horizontal hatching (extreme northeastern Alabama) indicates the presumed range of *C. p. marginata,* the midland painted turtle in Alabama; vertical hatching, that of *C. p. dorsalis,* the southern painted turtle; and diagonal hatching, that of *C. p. picta,* the eastern painted turtle. The stippled area is a zone of intergradation. Symbols indicate localities from which the author examined specimens. The small map depicts approximately the range of the painted turtle in the United States.

Habits: The habits of painted turtles in Alabama do not, to my knowledge, show substantial subspecific variation and will here be considered collectively.

Painted turtles are locally abundant in Alabama in many lakes, ponds, sloughs, and oxbows having mud or silt bottoms and abundant aquatic vegetation. They also occur in the main channels of some of our large sluggish streams, but they are seldom abundant in these habitats.

The basking habit is strongly developed in painted turtles, and they are often found wandering on land. Food habits are generalized, with arthropods and molluscs predominating. Some vegetation and carrion are consumed.

The females usually dig their nest cavities sometime between mid-May and the end of June. Data on clutch size from Alabama are lacking; reports from other areas indicate a range of from 4 to 11 eggs.

Chrysemys picta has probably been studied more intensively than any other American emydid turtle. Recent works include those by Gibbons (1967, 1968a, 1968b) and Ernst (1967, 1970, 1971a). Ernst (1971b) provided a review of the literature on the species.

Chrysemys picta dorsalis Agassiz
Southern Painted Turtle

Description: (Fig. 298) Differs chiefly from *Chrysemys p. picta* as follows: Carapace with a conspicuous red, orange, or yellow median stripe; vertebral and pleural scutes of carapace alternating; major yellow markings on head forming longitudinal stripes. Maximum carapace length attained, about 150 mm.

Alabama distribution: (Fig. 297) The eastern one-half of the area drained by the Tennessee River system and that portion of the Mobile Bay drainage below the Fall Line. Intergrades with *C. p. marginata* and *C. p. picta* above the Fall Line in the Coosa and Tallapoosa river systems of the Mobile Bay drainage. (See "Alabama distribution" under *C. p. picta* and under *C. p. marginata.*)

FIG. 298. *Chrysemys picta dorsalis,* the southern painted turtle (Montgomery County). The presence of a conspicuous mid-dorsal red or orange stripe characterizes this subspecies.

Habits: See "Habits" under *C. p. picta.*

Chrysemys picta marginata Agassiz
Midland Painted Turtle

Description: Differs chiefly from *C. p. picta* as follows: vertebral and pleural scutes of carapace alternating; plastron with a centrally located dark blotch, this varying in size and often barely discernible in adults. Maximum carapace length about 190 mm.

Alabama distribution: (Fig. 297) Two specimens from the Tennessee River at Bridgeport, Jackson County, are referable to *C. p. marginata.* On this basis I am tentatively including the extreme northeastern corner of the state within the range of that subspecies. From Bridgeport downstream in the river approximately to Decatur, Morgan County, *C. p. marginata* intergrades with *C. p. dorsalis.* Farther westward, the population is referable to the latter subspecies.

Below the Tennessee River drainage in eastern Alabama, *C. p. marginata* intergrades with *C. p. picta.* Intergradation among all 3 subspecies involved is evident in some populations in Lee County, in extreme east-central Alabama. Specimens of painted turtles were unavailable from a large portion of central Alabama.

Habits: See "Habits" under *C. p. picta.*

GENUS *DEIROCHELYS* Agassiz

The single species belonging to this genus is limited almost entirely to the southeastern Coastal Plain.

Deirochelys reticularia (Latreille)

Three subspecies of this southeastern turtle are recognized, 1 of which occurs in Alabama.

Deirochelys reticularia reticularia (Latreille)
Eastern Chicken Turtle

Description (Fig. 299) A medium-sized turtle attaining a maximum carapace

FIG. 299. *Deirochelys reticularia reticularia,* the eastern chicken turtle (Macon County). Borrow pits formed by removing fill-dirt and gravel, when filled with water, have created optimum habitats for chicken turtles. The exceedingly long neck of the chicken turtle is distinctive when compared with other turtles of Alabama.

length of about 255 mm. Neck noticeably long when extended, its length
sometimes approaching that of the
carapace; carapace dark, oval in outline,
not expanded, marked with a typically
inconspicuous reticulum of greenish or
yellowish lines, and often rimmed with
yellow. Plastron rigid, yellow, typically
unmarked or, when marked, having a
dendritic pattern following the seams;
bridge usually with an elongate black
blotch or series of spots; marginals near
the bridge often having dark spots on
their undersurfaces. Ground color of
soft parts dark brown or black; forelimbs
with a broad yellow stripe on anterior
surface at lower edge; rump with vertical yellow stripes.

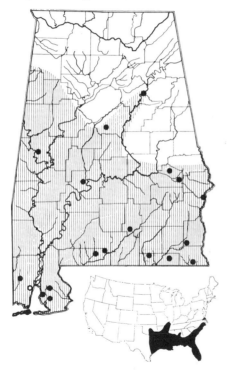

FIG. 300. Distribution of *Deirochelys reticularia reticularia*, the eastern chicken turtle. The presumed range in Alabama is indicated by hatching. Solid symbols indicate
localities from which the author examined
specimens. The circle is a literature record
believed to be valid. The small map depicts
approximately the known range of the species *D. reticularia* in the United States.

Alabama distribution: (Fig. 300) The
Coastal Plain and Ridge and Valley region. Infrequent in the latter. Most
abundant in the Lower Coastal Plain.

Habits: Shallow, weedy ponds, swamps
and borrow pits with standing water are
the usual habitats of the chicken turtle.
It is not strongly aquatic and often moves
about on land, especially during the
spring. Data on breeding in Alabama
are lacking. Carr (1952) states that in
Florida, laying in *Deirochelys r. chrysea*
apparently may occur at any time of the
year. He found nests in plowed lakeside fields and reported clutch sizes ranging between 7 and 15 eggs. Gibbons
(1969) reported on some aspects of the
ecology and population dynamics of the
chicken turtle, and Zug and Schwartz
(1971) reviewed the literature on the
species.

Chicken turtles apparently feed on a
wide variety of animal life. The long
neck and wide gape seem to enhance
their predatory capacity. They usually
do well in captivity, but tend to be aggressive and may kill smaller turtles
kept with them.

GENUS *GRAPTEMYS* Agassiz

Members of this genus occur in the
eastern one-half of the United States
and in a small, adjacent portion of Canada. The genus is divisible into 4 groups.
The *pseudogeographica* group, containing
G. pseudogeographica, G. kohni, G. versa,
and *G. caglei*, has the least specialized
members but is taxonomically the most
confusing. Members of a single monotypic species, *G. geographica*, comprise
the second group. The adult females
of this relatively early offshoot are highly
specialized for feeding on molluscs. Similar, though independently derived, dietary specializations are found in the
pulchra group, a somewhat later deriva-
tive composed of 2 allopatric species, *G.
pulchra* and *G. barbouri*. The most recent divergence gave rise to the *oculifera* group, with 3 allopatric species of
the mid-Gulf Coastal Plain region having rather generalized (though wholly
carnivorous) feeding habits. They are

G. oculifera, G. flavimaculata, and *G. nigrinoda.* All four of these groups are represented by the *Graptemys* occurring in Alabama, three with 1 species each and one with 2 species.

Graptemys barbouri Carr and Marchand
Barbour's Map Turtle

Description: (Fig. 301) A large, aquatic turtle attaining a maximum carapace length of about 270 mm in females and 130 mm in males. Carapace with a median keel accentuated by spines or prominent knobs on some of the vertebrals, these most pronounced on the second and third vertebrals and becoming inconspicuous on large females; carapace serrate behind; plastron large, rigid. Carapace ground color olive or greenish, tips of spines or knobs black; pleurals typically with yellowish circular or C-shaped markings; upper surfaces of marginals with narrow yellowish markings; lower surfaces of marginals and bridge with dark markings; carapace of adult females becoming dark with age, the markings becoming obscure. Plastron

unmarked except for narrow dark lines following seams.

Head with a large greenish or yellow-green blotch behind each eye; top of head predominantly light; chin with an isolated light bar paralleling the lower jaw, followed by a light inverted U-shaped mark. Limbs and tail striped.

Remarks: Sexual dimorphism is pronounced. In addition to attaining a much larger overall size than the male, the female develops a greatly enlarged head, while that of the male remains relatively small.

This species closely resembles its near relative, *G. pulchra.* The ranges of the two forms are mutually exclusive, however, and if collection data are available, there is no problem mistaking one for the other.

Alabama distribution: (Fig. 302) The Chattahoochee River northward at least to Russell County. It is remotely possible that populations also occur in some tributaries of the Chattahoochee River and in Big Creek and Cowart's Creek in southern Houston County. The latter

FIG. 301. *Graptemys barbouri,* Barbour's map turtle, adult male (Baker County, Georgia). Barbour's map turtle resembles *G. pulchra,* the Alabama map turtle, but has a yellow stripe on the chin following the curvature of the jaw that is not connected to other yellow markings.

streams are headwaters of the Chipola River, in which *G. barbouri* occurs.

Graptemys barbouri is not known to occur anywhere outside the Apalachicola River drainage. The record often indicated for the Escambia River is erroneous (Dobie, 1972).

Habits: Barbour's map turtle is found exclusively in streams that contain substantial numbers of molluscs, the dietary requisite of the adult females. It is fond of basking, utilizing for this purpose logs, snags, stumps, and the slanting bases of living trees that protrude from the water. When basking, the adult females are exceedingly wary and difficult to approach. They are easily caught underwater in clear streams by competent swimmers, however, and under some

FIG. 302. Distribution of *Graptemys barbouri,* Barbour's map turtle. The presumed range in Alabama is indicated by hatching. Symbols indicate localities from which the author examined specimens. The small map depicts approximately the known range in the United States.

conditions may be taken at night while they sleep near the surface. The population in Florida's Chipola River has been reduced substantially within recent years by overzealous collectors who take advantage of the turtles' vulnerability in that stream's clear water.

Barbour's map turtle is wholly carnivorous. Adult males and juveniles of both sexes are mostly insectivorous, while adult females, with their enlarged heads and expanded oral crushing surface, feed almost entirely on mussels and snails. The imported Oriental mussel, *Corbicula manilensis,* now abounds in most of the streams within the turtle's range, constituting an important food source. Captive *G. barbouri* will feed on liver, fish, and other kinds of fresh, lean meat.

The most significant contribution on reproduction in this species was by Walquist and Folkerts (1973). They found nests and recently hatched young along the Flint River in southwestern Georgia in late August. The nests were at depths of about 3 to 6 inches in moist sand on a small, steep-sloping sandbar along the river bank. Distances from the water's edge ranged from about 12 to 24 inches. One nest contained 8 hatchlings, and the other two had clutches of 8 and 9 dull white, ellipsoidal eggs. The eggs were brought to the laboratory, where one clutch began hatching on September 10 and the other on September 25. It was postulated that the same female was responsible for all 3 nests. The hatchlings averaged about 35 mm in length.

Graptemys geographica (Le Sueur)
Map Turtle

Description: (Fig. 303, 304) A large aquatic turtle attaining a maximum carapace length of about 150 mm in males and 270 mm in females. Carapace relatively low with a weak mid-dorsal keel; low spines or tubercles on rear of some vertebrals in juveniles; carapace somewhat serrate behind; plastron large, rigid. Carapace color greenish to olive brown, plain or with a pattern of circular, semicircular, and reticulate yellow or orange

FIG. 303. *Graptemys geographica,* the map turtle, adult female (Lawrence County). The map turtle has an isolated yellow spot on each side of the head and a reticulum of yellowish lines on the carapace.

FIG. 304. *Graptemys geographica,* the map turtle, juvenile (Shelby County). Map turtles are often found in smaller, shallower creeks than are suitable for most other emydid turtles.

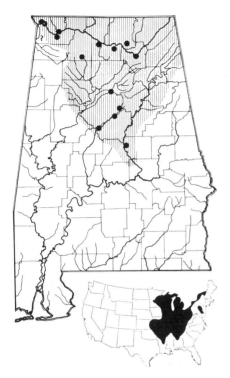

FIG. 305. Distribution of *Graptemys geographica,* the map turtle. The presumed range in Alabama is indicated by hatching. Symbols indicate localities from which the author examined specimens. The small map depicts approximately the known range in the United States.

markings; plastron yellowish, with dark lines along the seams and occasionally with other dark markings; undersides of marginals with concentric circular or semi-circular dark markings at the seams; bridge with dark, longitudinal lines. Head greenish to olive with yellow stripes and a detached yellow spot behind the eye; head considerably enlarged in old females.

Alabama distribution: (Fig. 305) Streams of the Tennessee River system and in the Black Warrior, Cahaba, and Coosa river systems above the Fall Line.

Habits: This shy turtle is seen most frequently basking on logs and rocks in creeks and rivers. Unlike other Alabama species of *Graptemys,* it will on occasion move well up into small brooks.

The juveniles and adult males feed on a wide variety of small animal life. The mature females feed mostly on mussels and snails.

Graptemys geographica is not particularly common anywhere in Alabama, and data on its reproduction in the state are lacking. Cahn (1937) reported that in Illinois, it laid 10 to 16 elliptical, leathery-shelled eggs during the morning hours in May and June.

Graptemys nigrinoda Cagle

Two subspecies are currently recognized, both of which occur in Alabama.

Graptemys nigrinoda nigrinoda Cagle
Northern Black-knobbed Sawback

Description: (Fig. 306) A medium-sized aquatic turtle attaining a maximum carapace length in females of at least 155 mm (males to about 115 mm). Carapace with medial knob-like projections on the second and third vertebrals, and a smaller one on the first vertebral; medial projections reduced to small, pointed swellings in old females; carapace serrate behind; plastron large, rigid. Carapace ground color greenish olive to brown; medial projections black; pleurals with yellow or white circles; sides of vertebrals with light reticular markings; plastron yellowish with dark lines bordering the sutures or with a dark figure occupying not more than 30 percent of the plastral area; undersides of marginals with concentric dark rings at the seams. Head small, olive to brown with yellowish stripes and a pair of crescent-shaped, strongly recurved postocular yellowish marks, these usually connected posteriorly to longitudinal stripes on head; lower surfaces of soft parts predominantly light-colored.

Alabama distribution: (Fig. 307) The Coosa, Tallapoosa, and Cahaba rivers from the Fall Line southward, and the Alabama River downstream to approximately the level of the Wilcox-Monroe County line, where integradation with *G. n. delticola* begins. Folkerts and Mount (1969) considered the northern-

FIG. 306. *Graptemys nigrinoda nigrinoda,* the northern black-knobbed sawback, juvenile (Wilcox County). Found exclusively in rivers, black-knobbed sawbacks are commonly seen basking on logs and snags. In this subspecies, the soft parts are predominantly yellow and the dark plastral figure, if present, is less extensive than that of *G. n. delticola.*

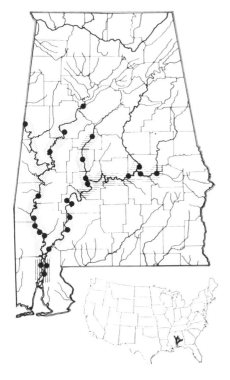

most populations of *G. nigrinoda* in the Warrior River to be of the nominate subspecies, but we are now inclined to consider them intergradient. Populations farther south in the Warrior River are also intergradient, as are those in the Tombigbee River southward at least to Jackson, Clarke County.

Habits: The habits of the 2 subspecies of *G. nigrinoda* are not known to differ and may be considered collectively. In the Coastal Plain stretches of the large rivers that drain into Mobile Bay, *G. nigrinoda* is present in relative abun-

FIG. 307. Distribution of *Graptemys nigrinoda* and subspecific variation in Alabama. Horizontal hatching indicates the presumed range of *G. n. nigrinoda,* the northern black-knobbed sawback, and vertical hatching, the range of *G. n. delticola,* the southern black-knobbed sawback. The zone of intergradation is indicated by stippling. Symbols indicate localities from which the author examined specimens. The small map depicts approximately the known range of the species *G. nigrinoda* in the United States. (Note: Map in error. Wilcox County has *G. n. nigrinoda.*)

THE REPTILES AND AMPHIBIANS OF ALABAMA

dance and appears to be the dominant turtle species. Despite its abundance, it was not described until 1954.

The turtle is confirmedly fluviatile and seems never to leave the water except to lay eggs or to bask, the latter a habit to which it is strongly addicted. Waters (1973) studied basking behavior in the black-knobbed sawback in Alabama. *G. nigrinoda* is mostly, if not entirely, carnivorous, but details of its food habits are not known. In the feces of freshly captured individuals kept at Auburn, insect remains were the only identifiable materials. Captives will feed readily on raw liver, chopped fish, and canned dog food.

Data on reproduction are scarce. A female collected in the Tombigbee River in Marengo County on July 1 contained 2 oblong oviducal eggs, each about 37 mm x 22 mm. Also present were 4 large ovarian eggs. On August 4 a nest of 6 eggs was uncovered about 4 inches beneath the surface on a sandy bank of the Tensaw River in Baldwin County. The nest was about 30 feet from the edge of the water and the eggs averaged 34.3 mm x 25.2 mm. Hatching began on August 30. The hatchlings were patterned essentially like older individuals. James Dobie found nests of *G. nigrinoda* on the sandy beach on Gravine Island, in the Tensaw River, Baldwin County.

Graptemys nigrinoda delticola Folkerts and Mount
Southern Black-knobbed Sawback

Description: (Fig. 308) A medium-sized aquatic turtle attaining a maximum carapace length of 195 mm in females and about 115 mm in males. Similar to *G. n. nigrinoda* except as indicated: plastral pattern complex, expanded along plastral sutures and occupying more than 60 percent of the plastral area; postorbital marks neither crescent-shaped nor strongly recurved laterally, often disconnected from longitudinal stripes on head; soft parts predominantly dark, usually black, the light stripes narrower than dark interspaces; average relative shell height greater than in nominate subspecies.

Alabama distribution: (Fig. 307) Confined to Alabama where it occurs in the Mobile, Tensaw, and other anastomosing freshwater streams and lakes which con-

FIG. 308. *Graptemys nigrinoda delticola,* the southern black-knobbed sawback, adult female (Baldwin County). In this subspecies the plastron has an extensive dark figure, and the soft parts are predominantly black.

stitute the upper portion of the delta of the Mobile Bay drainage, in Baldwin and Mobile counties.

Habits: See "Habits" under *G. n. nigrinoda.*

Graptemys pseudogeographica (Gray)

Three subspecies of this turtle are usually recognized, 1 of which occurs in Alabama.

Graptemys pseudogeographica ouachitensis Cagle
Ouchita Map Turtle
(False Map Turtle)

Description: (Fig. 309) A fairly large aquatic turtle attaining a maximum carapace length of around 255 mm in females, 115 mm in males. Carapace with a median keel accentuated by prominent knobs or blunt spines on at least the second and third vertebrals; carapace serrate behind; plastron large, rigid. Carapace color brown or greenish olive with an often-interrupted black mid-dorsal stripe and a network of yellowish lines, these usually forming circles or semicircles on the pleurals. Plastron yellowish with a dark complex figure that becomes obscure with age; undersides of marginals with concentric dark rings at the seams; bridge with dark lines; head brownish or olive with yellow lines; a rectangular-to-oval yellow spot behind each eye; 1 to 3 yellow lines below this spot entering orbit; an oval spot below each eye, one on each side of the lower jaw, and one on the chin.

Alabama distribution: (Fig. 310) Confined in Alabama to the Tennessee River and its associated backwaters.

Habits: This turtle is essentially an inhabitant of large impoundments and low-gradient streams. The map turtle, *Graptemys geographica,* with which it shares much of its range, is often found in small, shallow creeks well upstream

FIG. 309. *Graptemys pseudogeographica ouachitensis,* the Ouachita map turtle or false map turtle, adult male (Jackson County). This turtle usually has a rather elaborate plastral figure and 3 conspicuous light spots under the lower jaw. It is found in Alabama only in the Tennessee River system.

FIG. 310. Distribution of *Graptemys pseudogeographica ouachitensis*, the Ouachita map turtle. The presumed range in Alabama is indicated by hatching. Symbols indicate localities from which the author examined specimens. The small map depicts approximately the known range of the species *G. pseudogeographica* in the United States.

from their mouths, but *G. p. ouachitensis* seldom ascends the small tributaries.

This turtle, like the other *Graptemys*, is fond of basking and is frequently seen in considerable numbers on logs, snags, and stumps, especially during the spring months. Courtship involves face-to-face confrontation in which the male vibrates the front toenails against the snout and face of the female. The nesting habits are not well known. The egg complement reportedly varies from 7 to 13 and is laid in a flask-shaped excavation in the soil. Nesting has not been observed in Alabama.

The food habits are not well known. The few reports available seem to indicate that the young are entirely carnivorous, while the adults supplement a predominantly carnivorous diet with some plant material.

FIG. 311. *Graptemys pulchra*, the Alabama map turtle, adult female (Escambia County). The turtle shown here has the markedly humped carapace that characterizes old adult females of this species in the Escambia-Conecuh and Yellow river drainages.

FIG. 312. *Graptemys pulchra*, Alabama map turtle, adult male (Escambia County). The male of this species fails to develop the conspicuously enlarged head that characterizes the mature female.

Graptemys pulchra Baur
Alabama Map Turtle

Our knowledge of the life history, ecology, and habits of this turtle in Alabama results chiefly from the work of Robert M. Shealy, who studied the species in conjunction with his doctoral research at Auburn University. Dr. Shealy has kindly permitted me to use some of his data in preparing this account.

Description: (Fig. 311, 312) A large, aquatic turtle attaining a maximum carapace length of about 285 mm in females and 120 mm in males. These sizes apparently exceed previously published maxima and were attained by AM 21970 and AM 21971, respectively. Carapace with a median keel accentuated by spines or prominent knobs on some of the vertebrals, these most pronounced on the second and third vertebrals, becoming less conspicuous with age, and virtually unnoticeable on large females; carapace serrate behind; plastron large, rigid. Carapace ground color olive to dull green, with a median, longitudinal black stripe, stripe broken on occasional individuals; pleurals unmarked or with light reticular markings of varying intensity;

upper marginals with light bars, lines, or C-shaped markings of varying width; lower surfaces of marginals and bridge with dark markings; pleurals usually not noticeably convex; plastral pattern of scattered dark markings and dark lines

FIG. 313. Variation in plastral markings in *Graptemys pulchra*, the Alabama map turtle. Upper left, Conecuh River, Escambia County; upper right, Opintlocco Creek, Tallapoosa River system, Macon County; lower left, Uphapee Creek, Tallapoosa River system, Macon County; lower right, Pintlalla Creek, tributary of Alabama River, Montgomery County.

which follow the seams, or reduced to the latter (Fig. 313).

Head with large yellow or greenish yellow blotches behind the eyes and a patch of the same color on the top of the head and snout, with which the lateral head blotches may or may not be connected; chin pattern variable, but usually involving a combination of connecting longitudinal and laterally oriented light stripes or bars. Tail and limbs striped.

Sexual dimorphism pronounced, with females attaining much greater sizes than males and developing greatly enlarged heads, as in *Graptemys barbouri*, the closest living relative.

Remarks: *Graptemys pulchra* shows considerable geographic variation, only the essentials of which can be presented here. In Alabama, populations inhabiting the Escambia-Conecuh and Yellow river drainages are rather well differentiated

from those in the Mobile Bay drainage. In the former the shell is relatively high, at least in individuals exceeding 80 mm carapace length. The anterior portion of the carapace of large females becomes markedly humped. Yellow markings on the upper marginals are conspicuous. Plastral markings on these turtles are usually limited to narrow dark lines following the seams (Fig. 313). On the back of the head of most individuals is a pair of oval light spots, homologous to the anterior-most portions of the paramedial stripes (those adjacent to the median stripe) on individuals lacking the spots (Fig. 314).

In *G. pulchra* inhabiting the Mobile Bay drainage, the shell is relatively low. The anterior portion of the carapace of large females is less markedly humped. Yellow markings on the upper marginals are relatively narrow and inconspicuous. The plastron not only has the dark seam outlines, but usually other figures as well,

FIG. 314. Variation in head markings of *Graptemys pulchra*, the Alabama map turtle. Left, Tombigbee River, Marengo County; center, Conecuh River, Escambia County; right, Warrior River, Jefferson County.

especially on the posterior portion (Fig. 313). Head and neck markings are variable, but rarely include the 2 oval spots on the back of the head that characterize most individuals of the Escambia-Conecuh and Yellow river drainages (Fig. 314).

In shell dimensions and shell pigmentation, the *G. pulchra* of the Escambia-Conecuh and Yellow river drainages resemble those from the Pascagoula and Pearl river drainages in Mississippi and Louisiana more than they do those of the intervening Mobile Bay drainage. A noticeable constriction of the carapace at the level of the fifth and sixth marginals in males of the western populations is lacking in both the Alabama groups, however, and in neither of the latter are the yellow bars on the upper marginals as wide as they are on the turtles of the Pascagoula and Pearl drainages.

Alabama distribution: (Fig. 315) *Graptemys pulchra* occurs in suitable habitats throughout the Yellow River drainage, Escambia-Conecuh river drainage, and Mobile Bay drainage, except possibly for the Tallapoosa River system above the Fall Line. It has not been found in the Blackwater River or Perdido River drainages. Neither has it been recorded from Big Creek or the Escatawpa River, Alabama's 2 tributaries to the Pascagoula River, a Mississippi stream within which *G. pulchra* occurs in relative abundance.

Habits: The Alabama map turtle inhabits streams ranging in size from medium-sized creeks to large rivers. The primary requisite of a candidate stream of sufficient size appears to be an abundance of molluscs, especially mussels, on which the adult females depend almost solely for food. The scarcity of molluscs in some of the streams that arise within the Lower Coastal Plain, such as the Perdido River and Escatawpa River, may account for the turtle's scarcity or absence from those streams. Males and juvenile females feed mostly on insects and other arthropods.

Other factors that contribute to a stream's capacity to support a sizable population of Alabama map turtles include the presence of nesting sites in the form of expansive sandbars and sandy banks, pools of water deep enough to provide shelter, and an abundance of snags, logs, and appropriately suited tree trunks to serve as basking sites, hiding places, and substrates for the attachment and development of food organisms. The practice of removing snags and logs from streams doubtless effects *G. pulchra* adversely, as it does most other stream-dwelling animals.

Nesting activity in *G. pulchra* begins in late April or early May, reaches a peak in June, and continues through July and August. Up to 6 to 7 clutches, aver-

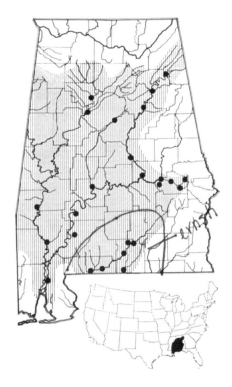

FIG. 315. Distribution of *Graptemys pulchra*, the Alabama map turtle. The presumed range in Alabama is indicated by hatching. Symbols indicate localities from which the author examined specimens. The small map depicts approximately the known range in the United States.

aging 4 to 6 eggs each, are laid by the females. Nest destruction by predators is heavy. Shealy (1973) estimated that each year more than 90 percent of the nests were destroyed in a study area on the lower reaches of the Conecuh River. Raccoons and fish crows were determined to be the most important predators.

The Alabama map turtle does reasonably well in captivity if properly nourished and cared for. Beef liver is an acceptable staple food for small and medium-sized individuals; large females will frequently eat crawfish and molluscs.

GENUS *MALACLEMYS* Gray

This genus consists of a single polytypic species whose range extends along the coast from New England to Mexico.

Malaclemys terrapin (Schoepff)

This species occurs in suitable habitats along the Atlantic and Gulf coasts. Seven subspecies, some of which may be invalid, are currently recognized. One of these occurs along the Alabama coast.

Malaclemys terrapin pileata (Wied)
Mississippi Diamondback Terrapin

Description: (Fig. 316) A medium-sized turtle of the salt marshes attaining a maximum carapace length of about 200 mm. Shell broadly oval, its sides nearly parallel; carapace variable but usually dark gray to black and unmarked in adults; large laminae with deep, conspicuous growth rings; all vertebrals except the last (fifth) with medial swellings, those on the third and fourth prominent, rounded, and knoblike. Plastron large, rigid, and yellowish with a profusion of dark spots and blotches; ground color of head and neck gray or greenish gray; upper lips and dorsal surface of head often dark; cheeks, neck, and chin light with rounded dark spots; limbs almost uniformly dark.

Carapace of young predominantly light-colored. Adult females larger in overall size than males; head of adult females conspicuously enlarged.

Alabama distribution: (Fig. 317) Salt

FIG. 316. *Malaclemys terrapin pileata*, the Mississippi diamondback terrapin (Mobile County, Dauphin Island). This turtle is becoming scarce in many places where it was formerly abundant as man continues to encroach on its salt marsh habitat.

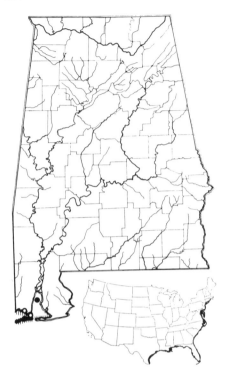

FIG. 317. Distribution of *Malaclemys terrapin pileata*, the Mississippi diamondback terrapin. In Alabama, this turtle is confined to salt and brackish-water marshes along the coast. Solid symbols indicate localities from which the author examined specimens. The small map depicts approximately the known range of the species *M. terrapin* in the United States.

marshes and adjacent shallow waters along the Gulf Coast and Mobile Bay.

Habits: This turtle is restricted to salt marsh and estuarine habitats. The adult females feed almost exclusively on molluscs, which are crushed between the expanded alveolar surfaces of the jaws. The reproductive habits are probably similar to those of other races of diamondback terrapins. If so, the eggs, between 4 and 12 per clutch, are laid in flask-shaped nests dug on high ground. Between 2 and 5 nestings per season have been reported in other subspecies.

Diamondback terrapins were common on Dauphin Island until as recently as 1964. Apparently, the population

there has been declining since that time. Jackson and Jackson (1970) noted that Hurricane Camille, a powerful storm which struck the mainland west of Dauphin Island in August 1969, washed away part of the western tip of the island. The western end of the island had provided most of the remaining suitable habitat for diamondbacks, and the effects of the storm no doubt hurt the dwindling population.

GENUS *PSEUDEMYS* Gray

About 14 species (or as few as 8 according to some authorities) are contained within this genus of freshwater turtles. The genus range extends from the United States to Argentina. Four species occur in Alabama.

Pseudemys alabamensis Baur
Alabama Red-bellied Turtle

Description: (Fig. 318) A large, robust turtle, attaining a maximum carapace length of about 335 mm in females (AUMP 1906) and 295 mm in males. Shell deep; carapace oval, slightly serrate behind; becoming wrinkled longitudinally with age. Plastron large, rigid; bridge deep. Carapace olive to dark brown, with variable light markings that usually include a light vertical bar on the second pleural scute. Plastron reddish, occasionally plain but more often with an elaborate figure of dark bars and variably shaped, light-centered dark figures which may be separate or connected (Fig. 319); plastron and, less frequently, the carapace freckled or marked with brownish vermiculations in some large individuals. Bridge plain or with diagonally oriented dark markings; undersides of marginals with light-centered single or double dark rings.

Soft parts and head olive to black with yellow striping; eye with a transverse dark bar. Front of upper jaw with a terminal notch flanked on each side by a distinct cusp, a feature found in no other aquatic emydid turtle in Alabama.

Hatchlings with a greenish, conspicu-

FIG. 318. *Pseudemys alabamensis,* the Alabama red-bellied turtle, adult male (Baldwin County). This turtle is confined to the lower portion of the Mobile Bay drainage. The plastron is reddish, and the carapace has vertical light markings.

FIG. 319. Variation in plastral pigmentation among juvenile *Pseudemys alabamensis,* Alabama red-bellied turtles. These turtles were all collected on the same date by Lee Barclay from near the mouth of Chickasaw Creek, Mobile County.

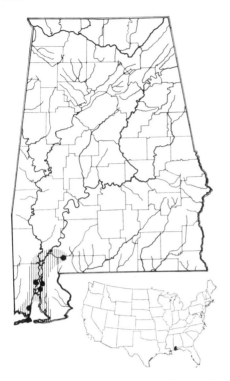

FIG. 320. Distribution of *Pseudemys ala-bamensis*, the Alabama red-bellied turtle. The presumed range in Alabama is indicated by hatching. Symbols indicate localities from which the author examined specimens. The small map depicts approximately the known range in the United States.

ously marked carapace, resembling most closely, among Alabama turtle species, those of *P. f. floridana*, but invariably distinguishable from the latter by the presence of the maxillary cusps.

Alabama distribution: (Fig. 320) Waterways associated with the lower portion of the Mobile Bay drainage. In Mobile Bay itself the turtle is found chiefly in the uppermost portion. The northern limit of the range is not known. There was, and may still be, a population in Little River State Park Lake, in southern Monroe County. This lake is a headwater of Little River, which forms the boundary between Monroe and Baldwin counties.

Remarks: This poorly known form has confused herpetologists for a good many

years, and its taxonomic status still is not clear. Carr (1952) treated it as a variant of *"Pseudemys floridana mobilensis,"* but in 1957, with Crenshaw, placed it in the *"rubriventris group,"* along with *P. rubriventris* and *P. nelsoni*. Although they returned it nomenclaturally to species status, they did so reservedly, pointing out the possibility that it may be subspecifically related to *P. nelsoni*.

Carr and Crenshaw mentioned having seen both *P. alabamensis* and *P. nelsoni* from the Florida Panhandle, cited a record of *P. alabamensis* from Texas, and reported the occurrence of a turtle with the *"alabamensis* phenotype" from Shelby County, Tennessee. I have not seen *P. alabamensis* from outside Alabama. James Dobie informs me that he has seen one of the *"alabamensis"* from Florida referred to by Carr and Crenshaw, and that he considers it to be *P. nelsoni*. *Pseudemys nelsoni* occurs westward in Florida to Jackson County. The Texas record is almost surely based on a misidentified *P. concinna texana*, and the Tennessee specimen is probably a variant of either *P. concinna* or *P. floridana*.

Based on information currently available, I concur in Carr and Crenshaw's treatment of *alabamensis* as a species within the *rubriventris* group, but consider its occurrence outside Alabama problematical.

Habits: Although the Alabama red-bellied turtle occurs sparingly in and around Mobile Bay and is captured occasionally, perhaps as a waif, on Dauphin Island (Jackson and Ross, 1972; James D. Williams, personal communication), it is by no means a salt marsh form, as was stated by Ernst and Barbour (1972). It is most abundant in fresh to moderately brackish water which supports an abundance of submergent aquatic vegetation, the turtle's principal food. Optimum habitat conditions obtain in the stretch of the Tensaw River between Hurricane and Spanish Fort in Baldwin County.

The "red-belly" is fond of basking, and is trapped for food at its basking sites by some who live within its range. The most frequent turtle associates of *P. alabamensis* are *P. c. concinna* (see following account) and *Graptemys nigrinoda delticola.* There are no observations on courtship and mating or on nesting habits of the species, and virtually nothing is known of its population dynamics.

Pseudemys concinna (Le Conte)

This species ranges from the Pecos River in New Mexico and Texas to the Atlantic coast. Five subspecies, 3 of which have been reported in Alabama, are currently recognized. In the discussion below, I have recommended that 3 of the subspecies be placed in the synonomy of the nominate form.

Pseudemys concinna concinna (Le Conte)
River Cooter

Description: (Fig. 321, 322) A large aquatic turtle attaining a maximum carapace length of about 415 mm in females and 300 mm in males. Carapace oblong to oval, somewhat serrate and flaring be-

hind (especially in males); carapace color olive-brown to nearly black, with concentric light markings on pleural scutes and usually with a C-shaped light figure on the second pleural. Plastron large, rigid, yellow to orange in ground color, occasionally plain but more often with dark pigmentation along at least some of the seams, the pattern becoming obscure or disappearing entirely with age (especially in females). Undersides of marginals, including the hindmost, with light-centered dark spots or rings; bridge with dark spots or longitudinal markings.

Head, limbs, and tail olive-brown to black with greenish yellow to reddish orange stripes; cutting edge of upper jaw smooth or serrate, but the Alabama populations lacking the 2 anterior subterminal cusps characteristic of *P. alabamensis;* eye with or without a transverse dark bar.

Carapace of first-year young lighter, olive to greenish, with light markings more conspicuous; plastral markings, if present, conspicuous and well defined.

FIG. 321. *Pseudemys concinna concinna,* the river cooter, adult female (Coffee County, Pea River).

FIG. 322. *Pseudemys concinna concinna,* the river cooter, juvenile in third year (Tallapoosa River, Tallapoosa County). In the river cooter, the plastral markings tend to follow the seams.

Remarks: According to most recent workers, 3 subspecies of *P. concinna* are represented in Alabama (See Conant, 1958). *Pseudemys c. concinna* reportedly occurs in the eastern portion; *P. c. mobilensis* (Holbrook) in the southwestern portion; and *P. c. hieroglyphica* (Holbrook) in the remainder of the state. A fourth form, *P. c. suwanniensis* Carr, is presumably a Floridian subspecies whose range closely approaches Alabama from the southeast. The fifth recognized subspecies of *P. concinna, P. c. texana* Baur, does not occur east of Texas and warrants no special consideration here.

The scheme presently used for dividing *P. concinna* into subspecies is based on Carr's interpretation (1952) as amended by Crenshaw (1955). Crenshaw established that *P. concinna* and *P. floridana* are separate species, but showed that the two hybridize. Crenshaw did not elaborate on distributional and morphological relationships among the *P. concinna* subspecies.

The 4 eastern subspecies (*texana* considered here the "western subspecies") have been defined on the basis of various combinations of characteristics that involve shape and pigmentation of the shell, color of the soft parts, and nature of the alveolar surfaces of the lower jaw, as follows:

P. c. concinna

1. Shell relatively low, long, and narrow.

2. Ground color of soft parts light brown to dark brown.

3. Ground color of carapace brown, with light markings conspicuous.

4. Stripes on head and limbs yellow to orange.

5. Fore- and hindfeet dark, unstriped.

6. Tail not striped above.

7. Alveolar surfaces of lower jaws relatively narrow, without high, iso-

lated conical teeth on the median ridge.

P. c. hieroglyphica

1. Shell relatively long, low, and narrow, and often constricted at the region of the sixth marginals.

2. Ground color of soft parts light brown to dark brown.

3. Ground color of carapace brown, its light markings conspicuous.

4. Stripes on head and limbs yellow to orange.

5. Fore- and hindfeet marked with continuations of leg stripes.

6. Tail striped above.

7. Alveolar surfaces of lower jaw relatively broad with a few high, isolated conical teeth on the median ridge.

P. c. mobilensis

1. Shell relatively high and broad.

2. Ground color of head, legs, and carapace light to dark brown.

3. Stripes on head and limbs yellow, orange yellow, or reddish.

4. Outer surface of forelimbs with 4 lines.

5. Usually 7 or more lines between the eyes.

P. c. suwanniensis

1. Shell relatively high and broad.

2. Ground color of carapace, legs, and head lustrous, sooty black.

3. Stripes on head and limbs light greenish yellow.

4. Outer surface of foreleg with 2 or 3 lines or narrow stripes, that of the hindleg not striped.

5. Usually 5 lines between the eyes.

In an attempt to determine the pattern of subspecific variation in Alabama P. concinna, specimens were examined not only from Alabama, but from adjacent portions of Georgia, Florida, and Mississippi. A series from Florida from the Santa Fe River, which is within the range of P. c. suwanniensis, was also examined. Geographic variation was found to be inconsistent with previous reports and assumptions. Although most characters that have been used at the subspecific level vary geographically within the area studied, predictability is low, and concordance among the varying characters is generally lacking.

In ground color of carapace and soft parts, the darkest specimens were generally from the southeastern portion of the state and the lightest from the northern portion; the overall effect is irregularly clinal. Geographic variation in mean shell width and mean shell height is detectable in adults. Mean shell width was greatest in the samples from the Tennessee River and Black Warrior River systems and least in the sample from the lower portion of the Mobile Bay drainage. Overlap in range between these samples, however, was extensive. Mean shell height was greatest in the Chattahoochee River system sample and least in that from the Warrior River system. The latter difference was pronounced in specimens over 215 mm in carapace length, and the sample ranges did not overlap when comparison was limited to such specimens. Large specimens from the Tennessee River system were unavailable for comparison with the others.

A constriction in the shell at the region of the sixth marginals occurred in greatest frequency among specimens from the Tennessee River system and upper portion of the Mobile Bay drainage. However, the condition also characterized several specimens from the lower portion of the latter, an area which is near the center of the supposed range of P. c. mobilensis.

Color of the light head and limb stripes is of questionable value in making subspecific assignments. The orange or reddish color was observed most frequently in adults and subadults from southern central Alabama, but appeared in populations from other areas as well. Moreover, it was noted that stripe color may change in direct response to changes in the animal's environment. This came to my attention when the stripes on a large adult female from the Chattahoochee River changed from orange to lemon yellow after 3 hours' exposure to laboratory conditions. The factors responsible for this change were not determined.

In every specimen examined from Alabama, the upper surface of the tail was striped. Stripes were also present on the outer surfaces of the hind limbs and feet of every specimen. Except for a few specimens from the Tallapoosa River system, all adult P. concinna examined from Alabama had relatively well-developed cusps on the alveolar surfaces of the lower jaw.

The only characters that showed reasonably predictable patterns of variation among the Alabama P. concinna examined involved eye pigmentation and plastral pattern. The former, assessable only in live animals, has not been mentioned previously, to my knowledge, in connection with variation in P. concinna. In nearly all members of the populations inhabiting the Coosa, Tallapoosa, Cahaba, and Tennessee River systems, and in occasional individuals from elsewhere in the state, the iris of the eye is virtually free of dark pigment. In others, dark pigment invades the iris from the anterior and posterior. Occasionally these invasions extend to the pupil, producing the "barred eye" characteristic of the other species of Pseudemys found in Alabama.

In individuals from the Chattahoochee River system the dark plastral figure consistently occupies a greater area than in those from elsewhere in the state, except in some from the Tennessee River system. Variation in this character is extensive among P. concinna in the Mobile Bay drainage, but relatively few individuals from that drainage have an elaborate pattern and, on some, the plastron is unmarked.

In view of the overall inconsistency of geographic variation in P. concinna in Alabama and the discordance among characters assumed to be of taxonomic value at the intraspecific level, subspecific allocation of the Alabama populations is, in my opinion, largely arbitrary. Moreover, continuing to make such allocations perpetuates the notion that the eastern P. concinna are appropriately divisible into subspecies when, in fact, they may not be.

Two reasonable alternatives remain: (1) consider all the Alabama populations intergradient, with various combinations of up to 4 subspecies represented, or (2) as I have chosen to do, allocate them all to P. c. concinna. As a corollary to the latter, P. c. hieroglyphica, P. c. mobilensis, and P. c. suwanniensis are relegated to the synonomy of P. c. concinna.

Hybridization between P. concinna and P. floridana occurs in Alabama, most frequently in the extreme southwestern portion. The populations inhabiting most of the small streams entering Mobile Bay are apparently hybrid. One juvenile turtle examined from the Tennessee River in Lauderdale County was an apparent hybrid between P. concinna and P. scripta, the only such specimen I have seen.

Alabama distribution: (Fig. 323) Statewide.

Habits: The river cooter is chiefly a resident of streams and relatively large lakes. It is often seen basking on logs or rocks, and under such circumstances is exceedingly wary, plunging into the water at the slightest indication of human presence. The mature females are particularly difficult to approach. The river cooter is strongly aquatic and, unlike P. scripta, a species with which it often occurs, seldom ventures onto land except to nest.

In courtship the male approaches the female from above and vibrates the long fingernails against her head. Nesting occurs in sandy, friable soil on elevated sites near the water. As many as 19 eggs in one clutch have been reported. Most of our information on the life history of P. concinna is from a study of the species in northern Florida by Jackson (1964). The hatchlings appear in August and September, although some overwinter in the nest and emerge the

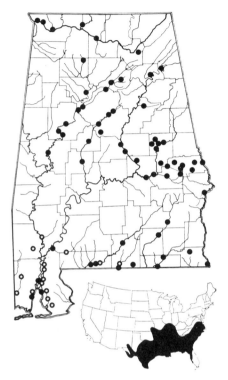

FIG. 323. Distribution of *Pseudemys con-cinna concinna*, the river cooter. The form apparently occurs statewide in Alabama. Solid symbols indicate localities from which the author examined specimens of *P. c. concinna*. Starred symbols are localities from which apparent hybrids between *P. c. concinna* and *P. f. floridana* were examined. The small map depicts approximately the known range of the species *P. concinna* in the United States.

following spring. River cooters hibernate during the coldest months of the year in most parts of Alabama, but in some streams in the Lower Coastal Plain they are active virtually year-round.

Adult river cooters are almost entirely herbivorous, feeding on a wide variety of plant material. The baby turtles are omnivorous. River cooters are eaten by some Alabamians, especially in the south-western portion of the state. There they are often included with *P. floridana* under the name "mobilians."

Pseudemys floridana (Le Conte)

Three subspecies of *P. floridana* are currently recognized. Two of these, *P. f. floridana* and *P. f. hoyi,* have been reported to occur in Alabama. I have seen no substantial evidence of the latter's presence and consider its occurrence problematical (p. 24.)

Pseudemys floridana floridana (Le Conte)
Florida Cooter

Description: (Fig. 324) A large, robust aquatic turtle attaining a maximum carapace length of about 400 mm (females). Males are smaller. Carapace oval, relatively high-domed in females, somewhat serrate and often flaring behind; carapace color dark brown to nearly black with yellowish markings, the most conspicuous one a vertical bar forked at either or both ends, on the second pleural scute (*P. concinna* usually has a C-shaped light mark on the second pleural).

Plastron large, rigid, immaculate yellow; bridge plain or with 1 or more dark spots; undersides of some or all of the anterior marginals with dark spots, which may or may not have light centers; undersurfaces of posterior marginals unmarked (in contrast to other species of *Pseudemys* in Alabama).

Head, limbs, and tail black, or nearly so, with yellow stripes; stripes on top of head not hairpin-shaped (in contrast to *P. f. peninsularis*); head stripes not numerous, broken, and twisted (in contrast to *P. f. hoyi*). Eye with a complete, transverse dark bar.

Hatchlings greenish above with numerous yellow markings, vertical mark on second pleural scute present but not particularly outstanding.

Remarks: *Pseudemys floridana* often hybridizes with *P. concinna* in Alabama, especially in the western portion of its range.

Alabama distribution: (Fig. 325) The Lower Coastal Plain. Reports of this species from elsewhere in Alabama are

FIG. 324. *Pseudemys floridana floridana,* the Florida cooter, adult male (Holmes County, Florida). This form hybridizes extensively with *P. c. concinna* in Alabama, but maintains its integrity in several lakes in the Lower Coastal Plain.

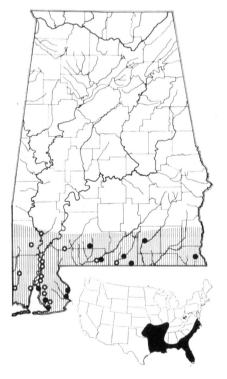

quite possibly based on misidentified variants of *P. concinna.*

Habits: In Alabama *P. f. floridana* occurs in greatest numbers in large ponds and lakes with abundant aquatic vegetation. Lake Jackson, a large sinkhole lake in Covington County, provides particularly favorable habitat. This turtle also occurs in oxbows and sloughs associated with rivers and in some of the small, sluggish rivers, such as the Perdido, that have aquatic vegetation along their edges. It is seldom seen in the main channel area of relatively deep, swift Coastal Plain streams, such as the Conecuh and Choctawhatchee rivers, a

FIG. 325. Distribution of *Pseudemys floridana floridana,* the Florida cooter. The hatched area is the presumed range of *P. f. floridana* in Alabama. Solid symbols indicate localities from which the author examined specimens of *P. f. floridana.* Starred symbols indicate localities from which apparent hybrids between *P. f. floridana* and *P. c. concinna* were examined. The small map depicts approximately the range of the species *P. floridana* in the United States.

habitat type well suited to *P. concinna.* Nesting occurs from late May until August. Clutch size ranges from 4 to 22, with most females laying 2 or more times each season. Sandy areas are chosen as nesting sites.

Hatchlings are seen in greatest abundance in the spring, suggesting that they overwinter in the nest. During the first year, the young turtles feed on both plant and animal life. After that they become almost totally herbivorous, feeding on a wide variety of plants.

Thomas (1972) reported on certain aspects of the life history and ecology of *P. f. floridana* in southern central Alabama and in the Florida Panhandle.

Pseudemys scripta (Schoepff)

This species, whose range extends from coast to coast and from the Great Lakes southward to Argentina, includes at least 12 and possibly as many as 18 or more subspecies. Two subspecies occur in Alabama.

Pseudemys scripta scripta (Schoepff)
Yellow-bellied Pond Slider

Description: (Fig. 326, 327) A moderately large, robust, aquatic turtle attaining a maximum carapace length of about 275 mm. Carapace rounded to slightly oval, relatively high-domed, longitudinally wrinkled in old individuals, olive green to black with a broad, vertical yellow stripe on each pleural scute. Head with a large yellow blotch behind the eye; chin and neck stripes relatively broad and few in number. Eye with a transverse dark bar; upper jaw with a terminal notch, but this not flanked by projecting cusps.

Plastron large and rigid; typically with 2 spots, one on each gular scute; spots on bridge small or lacking; lower surface of each marginal with a dark spot, smaller in area than the yellow ground color; rump typically with longitudinal yellow stripes.

Pattern on shell and soft parts obscure on many adults, especially males,

FIG. 326. *Pseudemys scripta scripta* x *elegans*, pond slider, subadult male (Monroe County). Pond sliders are the most frequently encountered aquatic turtles in most parts of Alabama.

as melanism increases with age. Ground color of hatchlings greenish.

Alabama distribution: (Fig. 328) The species occurs statewide. Populations referable to *P. s. scripta* occur in isolated lake, pond, and swamp habitats in the Lower Coastal Plain and in the shallow streams which have their headwaters mostly within that province. In the remainder of the state, except for portions of northwestern Alabama, and in major streams within the Lower Coastal Plain, *P. s. scripta* exerts its influence in intergradient populations.

Habits: This turtle seems best adapted to aquatic environments with abundant vegetation. Within its range, such habitats include lakes, ponds, swamps, sloughs, and low-gradient, shallow streams. Overland migrations are common in *P. s. scripta,* accounting for its frequent occurrence in semi-permanent bodies of water.

In the first year of growth, the young yellow-bellied pond sliders are rather strongly carnivorous, relying heavily on aquatic insects and other invertebrate life for food (Clark and Gibbons, 1969). The older ones are mostly herbivorous, including in their diet a wide variety of aquatic plants. Many farm pond owners assume that pond sliders are harmful to fish populations and destroy them regularly. Moss (1955) showed this assumption to be incorrect.

The eggs, usually between 10 and 15 per clutch, are laid in a flask-shaped excavation, usually within 300 feet of the water. The largest numbers of hatchlings appear in the spring, indicating that many overwinter in the nest.

The adults of this form are rather ill-tempered and are more inclined to bite than our other *Pseudemys,* but they do rather well in captivity.

Pseudemys scripta elegans (Weid)
Red-eared Pond Slider

Description: (Fig. 326) Differs from *P. s. scripta* as follows: shell of adults smoother and more depressed; carapace

FIG. 327. *Pseudemys scripta scripta,* the yellow-bellied pond slider, adult female, Geneva County. In this subspecies, the head has a yellowish blotch behind the eye (except in old, melanistic individuals), and the plastron typically has only 2 dark spots, these on the gulars.

more elongated, with a tendency to flare; stripes on carapace narrow.

Side of head with an orange to red longitudinal bar behind the eye, as opposed to a large yellow blotch; each plastral scute with a large dark spot or smudge (this sharply defined and frequently ocellate in young); undersides of marginals and bridge with more black than yellow.

Alabama distribution: (Fig. 328) The western half of the Tennessee River drainage area and the Tombigbee River drainage area above the mouth of the Warrior River.

Influence of *P. s. elegans* is evident in

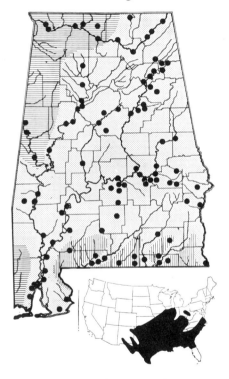

FIG. 328. Distribution of *Pseudemys scripta* and subspecific variation in Alabama. Horizontal hatching indicates the presumed range of *P. s. elegans*, the red-eared pond slider, and vertical hatching, the range of *P. s. scripta*, yellow-bellied pond slider. The zone of intergradation is indicated by stippling. Symbols indicate localities from which the author examined specimens. The small map depicts approximately the known range of the species *P. scripta* in the United States.

intergradient populations in most of the remainder of the state except for those in the Lower Coastal Plain in isolated pond, lake, and swamp habitats and small streams.

Within the zone of intergradation, the influence of *P. s. elegans* is strongest in the large streams. On a directional basis this influence declines from west to east and from north to south.

Remarks: Chermock (1952), Conant (1958), and others have indicated that a third subspecies of *P. scripta*, *P. s. troosti* (Holbrook), occurs in extreme northeastern Alabama, and Holman (1961) reported *troosti* influence from as far south in Alabama as Jefferson County.

The currently held concept of *P. s. troosti* is that of a pond slider inhabiting the Cumberland River and upper Tennessee River system that is (1) similar to *P. s. elegans* in shell shape; (2) similar to *P. s. scripta* in chin and neck striping and in carapace markings; (3) intermediate between the two in the amount of black on the bridge and undersurfaces of the marginals; and (4) unique in having a narrow, yellow (never red or orange) temporal bar that is not more than twice as wide as the stripe continuing posteriorly from it.

Davidson (1971) studied variation in populations of pond sliders in Alabama and in some adjacent areas and could find no *P. s. troosti* influence in the state. He concluded that earlier reports so indicating were based on populations having influence from *P. s. scripta*. He detected the latter, in the form of expanded temporal markings, in populations throughout the northeastern quadrant of the state, and from as far north in the Tennessee River system as Kingston, Roane County, in eastern Tennessee. The chin and neck stripes on the Roane County specimens were narrow and numerous as in *P. s. elegans*. Davidson proposed that these populations be designated *P. s. scripta* x *elegans*.

Habits: *Pseudemys s. elegans* inhabits a wide variety of permanently aquatic habits, but is generally most abundant in lakes and sluggish rivers. Apparently, it is better adapted to life in large streams than *P. s. scripta,* which could account in part for its strong influence in and around the rivers that flow through the Red Hills and Lower Coastal Plain regions otherwise inhabited by populations whose characteristics are predominantly or exclusively those of *P. s. scripta.*

The eggs of this form, varying in number from 4 to 20 per clutch, are laid in cavities dug by the females, often at considerable distances from the water. Up to 3 clutches may be laid in one season. Most of the baby turtles overwinter in the nest. The food of *P. s. elegans* consists chiefly of aquatic animal life, supplemented with vegetation. The hatchlings are produced and collected commercially in some states and provide the basis for most of the baby turtle trade in this country.

GENUS *TERRAPENE* Merrem

Four species of this genus are currently recognized, 2 of which occur in the United States and the other 2 in Mexico. One species occurs in Alabama.

Terrapene carolina (Linnaeus)

Seven subspecies of this wide-ranging terrestrial turtle are currently recognized (Milstead, 1969). Known as box turtles, the members of the species are easily distinguished from all other Alabama turtles by the nature of the plastron, which is large, hinged, bilobed, and capable of completely sealing the shell.

Box turtles in Alabama occur in a bewildering array of shapes and color patterns. Three of the 7 subspecies, *T. c. carolina, T. c. major,* and *T. c. triunquis,* are involved.

FIG. 329. *Terrapene carolina carolina* x *triunguis,* box turtle (Lee County). Most box turtle populations in Alabama are intergradient combinations involving 2 or 3 subspecies. The turtle shown here is an intergrade between *T. c. carolina,* the eastern box turtle, and *T. c. triunguis,* the three-toed box turtle, with characteristics of the former predominating.

Terrapene carolina carolina (Linnaeus)
Eastern Box Turtle

Description: (Fig. 329) A medium-sized, terrestrial turtle, attaining a maximum carapace length of around 165 mm. Shell without a bridge; carapace high-domed, rounded; third vertebral scute not elevated to form a hump; fifth vertebral scute not convex; posterior marginals flaring only slightly or not at all.

Plastron large, hinged, capable of completely sealing the shell; hind lobe of plastron in adult males with a deep concavity; hind feet with 4 toes; carapace, head, and forelimbs brownish to black with variable yellow or orange markings (carapace of occasional individuals olive-brown without noticeable markings). Iris of eye of male usually red, that of female usually brown.

Plastron of young dark-centered; plastral pigmentation becoming highly variable with age; carapace of young dark with a small yellow spot on each vertebral and pleural.

Remarks: Milstead (1969) noted distinct subspecific differences at the population level in certain plastral ratios. Milstead's data are shown in Table 11, along with those I obtained for Alabama box turtles. Most Alabama populations are intergradient. In some ratios Alabama populations seem to conform to the expected trends. In others, they apparently do not. Larger samples are needed to evaluate accurately the pattern of variation in plastral ratios among Alabama box turtles.

Alabama distribution: (Fig. 330) The species occurs statewide. The subspecies *T. c. carolina* occurs in the extreme northern portion; its influence in intergradient populations extends throughout most of the remainder of the state.

Habits: Box turtles are well known to Alabamians, who usually refer to them as "tarrapins." They show little habitat specificity, but are generally most abundant in moist, forested areas. During hot, dry weather they tend to move to floodplains, stream banks, and spring-heads and become somewhat sedentary.

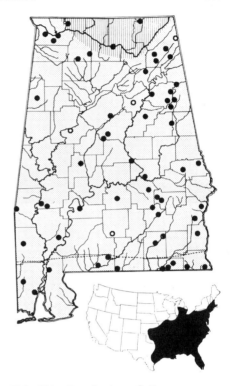

FIG. 330. Distribution of *Terrapene carolina* and subspecific variation in Alabama. The hatched area is the presumed range of *T. c. carolina,* the eastern box turtle, in Alabama. The stippled area southward to the broken line is a zone of intergradation between *T. c. carolina* and *T. c. triungius,* the three-toed box turtle. South of the broken line, influence from a third subspecies, *T. c. major,* the Gulf Coast box turtle, is evident. Solid symbols indicate localities from which the author examined specimens. Circles are literature records believed to be valid. The small map depicts the range of the species *T. carolina* in the United States.

A light rain during a droughty period will often bring about a burst of box turtle activity, and at such times the turtles are likely to be seen in abundance on the highways.

The food requirements of box turtles, like their other ecological requirements, are seldom restrictive. Berries, fungi, earthworms, insects, and even carrion are included. Captives will eat grasshoppers and crickets, and some will fare nicely

TABLE 11. VARIATION IN SELECTED PLASTRAL RATIOS AMONG SUBSPECIES AND AMONG ALABAMA POPULATIONS OF *Terrapene carolina* (RATIOS ARE EXPRESSED AS PERCENTAGES; MEANS ARE IN PARENTHESES)

Subspecies or sample area of Alabama[1]	No. samples	No. specimens	Intergular seam/ ant. lobe	Interhumeral seam/ ant. lobe	Interpectoral seam/ ant. lobe	Interabdominal seam/ post. lobe	Interfemoral seam/ post. lobe	Interanal seam post. lobe
T. c. carolina[2]	11		47-52	18-23	29-31	34-35	9-12	53-56
T. c. major[2]	1		45	29	26	35	12	53
T. c. triunguis[2]	12		47-52	18-22	29-34	32-36	12-16	52-55
Northeast		2	44-52	21-25	27-36	32-35	12-16	52
			(48)	(23)	(31.5)	(33.5)	(14)	(52)
East north-central		5	37-52	12-26	32-37	34-37	11-12	51-55
			(45.2)	(19.4)	(34.2)	(35.2)	(11.2)	(53.6)
Northwest		7	41-47	14-31	28-42	30-41	9-16	48-58
			(45)	(22.3)	(32.6)	(34.6)	(12.3)	(53.3)
East south-central		10	40-56	16-32	24-38	28-39	6-18	45-58
			(46.2)	(23.8)	(30)	(34.9)	(11.7)	(53.6)
West south-central		11	37-50	15-29	24-36	30-41	9-20	44-56
			(45)	(21.5)	(34)	(36)	(12.7)	(51.6)
Southeast		8	46-52	12-26	25-38	31-42	7-15	51-60
			(48.5)	(20.6)	(31.1)	(34.4)	(11.3)	(54.4)
Southwest		8	44-50	20-30	25-35	32-38	8-14	52-57
			(45.3)	(24)	(31)	(35)	(10.6)	(54.8)

[1] Counties included in the sample areas are: *Northeast*—Jackson, DeKalb; *east north-central*—Calhoun, Etowah, Cherokee, Coosa; *northwest*—Jefferson, Winston, Walker, Morgan, Lawrence, Colbert; *west south-central*—Perry, Marengo, Clarke, Wilcox, Monroe, Lowndes; *southeast*—Henry, Houston, Geneva, Coffee, Covington; and *southwest*—Mobile, Baldwin, Escambia.

[2] Numbers given for these are sample means and are from Milstead (1969).

on a diet of canned dog food and table scraps.

During mating, the male mounts the female from the rear and holds on with the hind feet. The concavity in the male's plastron facilitates assumption of the mating position. The female later deposits 2 to 7 elongate white eggs in a cavity she constructs in the soil. Apparently 2 or 3 clutches are laid per season. Curiously, baby box turtles are not often encountered. Most of those I have found have been under logs in moist habitats. I have seen no evidence that they are aquatic, as some workers have suggested.

Terrapene carolina major (Agassiz)
Gulf Coast Box Turtle

Description: A rather large terrestrial turtle, attaining a maximum carapace length of over 210 mm. Differs from *T. c. carolina* and *T. c. triunguis* in the following: size larger; fifth vertebral scute convex, forming a hump; posterior marginals with strong tendency to flare and turn upward to form a gutter (not a characteristic unique to this subspecies, however). Differs from *T. c. triunguis*, but not from *T. c. carolina*, in having 4 instead of 3 claws on hind foot; in having a relatively deep plastral concavity in the male; and in lacking the elevation of the third vertebral scute. Plastral ratios reportedly differ among subspecies. (See description of *T. c. carolina* and also Table 11.)

Alabama distribution: (Fig. 330) Until the work of Auffenberg (1958) and Milstead (1969), the range of *T. c. major* was thought to include the coastal areas of Alabama. In fact, 3 of the 6 specimens constituting the original type series are from Mobile. The currently held concept of *T. c. major*, however, limits the range to the coastal area of the eastern portion of the Florida Panhandle. Accordingly, box turtles along the coast of Alabama should be considered intergradient between *T. c. major* and *T. c. triunguis*. Northward in Alabama, influence from *T. c major* is evident in intergradient box turtle populations in the Lower Coastal Plain to approximately the level of the Escambia-Conecuh county line.

Habits: Not known to differ significantly from those of *T. c. carolina*, except in the types of habitats exploited, as dictated by the subspecies' range.

Terrapene carolina triunguis (Agassiz)
Three-toed Box Turtle

Description: A medium-sized terrestrial turtle attaining a maximum carapace length of around 165 mm. Differs from *T. c. carolina* and *T. c. major* in the following: hind feet usually with 3 instead of 4 claws; third vertebral scute of carapace elevated, forming a hump; hind lobe of plastron of male flat or only slightly concave; ground color of carapace, head, and forelimbs frequently olive or horn-color; carapace frequently unmarked. Differs from *T. c. major*, but not from *T. c. carolina*, in lacking the strong convexity of the fifth vertebral scute. Degree of flaring of the posterior marginals intermediate between *T. c. major* and *T. c. carolina*.

Remarks: Subspecific differences in plastral ratios, as indicated by Milstead (1969), are shown in Table 11. (Also see description of *T. c. carolina*.)

Alabama distribution: (Fig. 330) Apparent influence from *T. c. triunguis* can be seen in box turtle populations throughout Alabama except in the extreme northern portion. A determination of whether "good" *T. c. triunguis* occurs in the state must await the accumulation of additional specimens from extreme western Alabama.

Habits: Not known to differ significantly from those of *T. c. carolina*.

FAMILY KINOSTERNIDAE – MUD AND MUSK TURTLES

This family includes 4 genera and ranges throughout most of the eastern and southern United States southward to northern South America. Two genera are represented in Alabama.

GENUS *KINOSTERNON* Spix

This genus is the most widely distributed one of its family and also the most confusing taxonomically. As many as 15 species are recognized by some authorities. Four species occur within the United States, 1 of which is found in Alabama.

Kinosternon subrubrum (Lacépède)

Three subspecies are recognized. One of these occurs in Alabama, and strong influence from another is evident in intergradient populations.

Kinosternon subrubrum subrubrum
(Lacépède)
Eastern Mud Turtle

Description: (Fig. 331) A small turtle attaining a maximum carapace length of around 120 mm. Carapace plain brown to black, smooth, dome-shaped; pectoral laminae of plastron triangular in shape; forelobe of plastron slightly movable. Ground color of soft parts dark brownish, head and neck typically mottled with dull yellow or yellowish brown.

Adult male with a well-developed, blunt spine or nail at end of tail and with rough patches on insides of hind legs; plastron of male usually smaller; width of hind lobe of plastron, as a percentage of carapace length, in a sample of eight Lee County adult males: range 38.7 to 43.6, mean 41.0; in eight females: range 39.0 to 46.5, mean 43.6. Length of plastron as a percentage of carapace length in the eight males; range 80.5 to

FIG. 331. *Kinosternon subrubrum subrubrum*, the eastern mud turtle (Lee County). This rather plain turtle is abundant in Alabama and may be encountered on land as well as in the water.

90.0, mean 85.1; in the eight females: range 86.5 to 96.7, mean 90.5. Plastron of hatchling reddish orange to yellowish with dark central figure.

Remarks: Average plastron length appears to be greater in the turtles belonging to populations above the Fall Line than to those below it. This is exemplified by a comparison of 2 samples of females. In four females from well above the Fall Line, plastron length as a percentage of carapace length ranged from 92.0 to 99.5, and averaged 95.3. In eight females from well below the Fall Line, the range was 88.5 to 95.6, with an average of 91.2.

Alabama distribution: (Fig. 332) Statewide, except for the Mobile-Baldwin County area where it intergrades with *K. s. hippocrepis*.

Habits: The eastern mud turtle is abundant in Alabama and may be found in ponds, lakes, swamps, marshes, and flooded roadside ditches. About the only aquatic habitats likely to be shunned are free-flowing creeks and rivers.

The eastern mud turtle frequently wanders about on land, is more active at night than during the day, and seldom basks. In its aquatic habitats, it is usually seen crawling about on the bottom. Mud turtles are active year-round, and I have on several occasions seen them on winter nights foraging on the bottom of rain-filled depressions. On 2 such occasions, they were feeding on the entrails of gravid frogs, (*Pseudacris ornata* and *Rana pipiens*), which they had presumably captured.

The nest of this species is dug in the ground or in piles of organic matter. I found one nest in an abandoned beaver dam and one in Georgia in an old alligator nest. Most nests contain 2 to 5 eggs. The eggs are hard-shelled and quite resistant to desiccation.

Captive *K. subrubrum* vary considerably in temperament. As a rule freshly captured individuals tend to be shy and disinclined to bite, while other, "better adjusted" ones tend to be aggressive and snappy. Some individuals emit a rather malodorous musk when handled. Captives usually feed well and, as in their

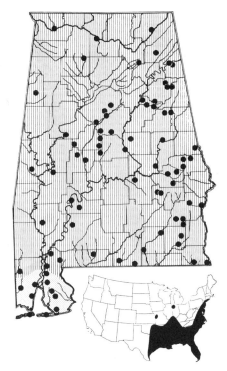

FIG. 332. Distribution of *Kinosternon sub-rubrum* and subspecific variation in Alabama. The hatched area is the presumed range of *K. s. subrubrum*, the eastern mud turtle, in Alabama. The stippled area is a zone of intergradation between *K. s. subrubrum* and *K. s. hippocrepis*, the Mississippi mud turtle. Symbols indicate localities from which the author examined specimens. The small map depicts approximately the known range of the species *K. subrubrum* in the United States.

natural habitats, will eat a wide variety of animal foods.

Kinosternon subrubrum hippocrepis Gray
Mississippi Mud Turtle

Description: Similar to *K. s. subrubrum* except in its possession of 2 yellowish stripes which begin at the eye and extend backward onto the neck.

Alabama distribution: (Fig. 332) Mud turtle populations inhabiting the Mobile-Baldwin County area are intergradient between this subspecies and *K. s. subrubrum*.

Habits: Similar to those of *K. s. subrubrum*.

GENUS *STERNOTHERUS* Gray

Three species are recognized within this genus, all of which occur within the United States. Two of these species are known to occur within Alabama, and another, whose range extends to within a few miles of the state's western boundary, may eventually be encountered.

Sternotherus minor (Agassiz)

Three subspecies of this turtle are recognized. All 3 occur in Alabama and 1, which is endemic to the state, is considered by some to be a full species.

Sternotherus minor minor (Agassiz)
Loggerhead Musk Turtle

Description: (Fig. 333) A moderately small, aquatic turtle attaining a maximum carapace length of about 130 mm. Carapace with scutes overlapping; plastron relatively small, its anterior lobe slightly movable; pectoral scute rectangular or quadrangular in shape; 1 gular scute present; barbels present on chin only. Carapace with 3 distinct keels, these most pronounced in juveniles and often absent in old adults; carapace brown, with dark spots or streaks, these becoming obscure in old adults. Top of head and snout light brown to gray, with numerous, mostly rounded spots and blotches; top and sides of neck with similar but somewhat less regular markings; tail spotted (useful for identification only in males). Plastron pink in young, becoming yellow with age. Head usually greatly enlarged in old adults.

Remarks: In this form, sexual dimorphism obtains in the following relative measurements: pre-anal tail length, which is greater in males; and in plastron length, inter-anal seam length, and bridge length, all of which are greater in females (Tinkle, 1958).

Alabama distribution: (Fig. 334) Southeastern Alabama, in the Apalachi-

FIG. 333. *Sternotherus minor minor* x *peltifer* (Lee County). The turtle shown here is an intergrade between *S. m. minor*, the loggerhead musk turtle, and *S. m. peltifer*, the stripe-necked musk turtle. In the former subspecies, the head and neck are usually spotted, while in the latter, the neck is striped and the head markings are variable. All musk turtles belonging to the species *S. minor* show a strong preference for streams as habitats.

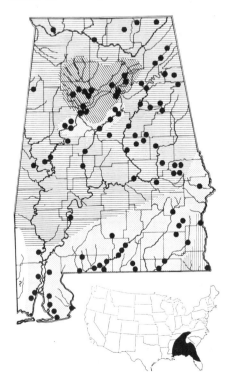

cola River drainage in Houston, Henry, and Barbour counties. Intergrades with *S. m. peltifer* in the remainder of the Apalachicola drainage to the north, and in other drainages across southern Alabama to the area of the Tensaw and Mobile rivers. Influence from *S. m. minor* is not evident in the Mobile Bay drainage north of the Lower Coastal Plain. The subspecific status of *S. minor* populations in the Pascagoula River drainage in Alabama, if any occur there, is not known.

Habits: Although this musk turtle turns up occasionally in farm ponds and other

FIG. 334. Distribution of *Sternotherus minor* and subspecific variation in Alabama. Horizontal hatching indicates the presumed range of *S. m. peltifer*, the stripe-necked musk turtle, in Alabama; vertical hatching, that of *S. m. minor*, the loggerhead musk turtle; and diagonal hatching, that of *S. m. depressus*, the flattened musk turtle. Stippled areas are zones of intergradation. Symbols are localities from which the author examined specimens. The small map depicts approximately the known range of the species *S. minor* in the United States.

isolated lentic habitats, it is primarily an inhabitant of creeks and rivers and their associated aquatic environments. It is frequently encountered early in the morning, crawling on the bottom around logs, rocks, and masses of vegetation. Insects and molluscs are the principal food items; the large heads and expanded crushing surfaces of the jaws in adults are presumably adaptations to feeding on the latter.

Sternotherus minor is seldom seen basking in the open in the manner of aquatic emydid turtles but will often climb onto the leafy branch of a tree protruding from the water. Otherwise, it seldom leaves the water except to nest. The hard-shelled eggs are laid singly, or in pairs, in the soil.

Sternotherus minor depressus Tinkle and Webb
Flattened Musk Turtle

Description: (Fig. 335) Characterized as follows: carapace extremely flattened; top of head greenish with a reticulum of dark markings, this often breaking up to form spots and blotches on top of snout. Plastron color pinkish in young, yellowish in adults. Heads of old adults not greatly enlarged.

Alabama distribution: (Fig. 334) Confined to Alabama, where it occurs in permanent streams of the Black Warrior River system above the Fall Line. Intergrades with *S. m. peltifer* in the upper Cahaba River system and in a small portion of the Warrior River system along the Fall Line.

Remarks: This form was described as a full species and is still so regarded by some workers. Estridge (1970) found evidence of intergradation between it and *S. m. peltifer* in the Warrior River system in the form of a few intermediate specimens. He noted considerable intermediacy between *depressus* and *peltifer* in the population inhabiting the upper Cahaba River system. Estridge stated, however, that his evidence was inconclusive and recommended that *depressus* be retained as a full species.

FIG. 335. *Sternotherus minor depressus*, the flattened musk turtle (Walker County). The reticulum on the head is greenish yellow. This fairly small, flat turtle, an Alabama endemic, is confined to streams of the Warrior River system above the Fall Line.

Since that work was completed, additional specimens intermediate between *depressus* and *peltifer* have been collected from the Warrior River system. Also, repeated efforts to find concrete evidence of sympatry have failed. It thus appears that *depressus* is more appropriately accorded subspecific rank.

Habits: The habits of this exceedingly shy turtle remain poorly known. Most specimens have been collected on the bottom of relatively clear, rock-bottomed streams at depths of 1 to 5 feet, which apparently provide good habitat. Deep impoundments with little shallow water are less suitable and may not be capable of supporting breeding populations. Ponds and temporary watercourses are not inhabited.

The food of *S. m. depressus* consists largely of molluscs, although other invertebrates may be eaten. Early morning appears to be the time of greatest activity. Basking has not been reported.

Data on reproduction are scarce. Tinkle (1958), by counting ovarian follicles, estimated a reproductive potential of around 6. Estridge (1970) reported on an egg laid by a captive female on June 16. The oblong, brittle egg, which hatched on October 16, measured 32 mm by 16.4 mm. Emergence of the hatchling took 12 hours, and its carapace, after expansion, was 25 mm long and 20 mm wide. The depth of its shell was 7.8 mm. Carapace markings were present, but somewhat obscure.

Sternotherus minor peltifer Smith and Glass

Stripe-necked Musk Turtle

Description: (Fig. 333) Similar to *S. m. minor* except as follows: Carapace lacking lateral keels; top of head with irregular dark markings anteriorly, these coalescing to form longitudinal stripes posteriorly on back of head and on back and sides of neck; tail with longitudinal stripes (useful for identification only in males). Maximum carapace length 120 mm, this measurement from AM 9323, a specimen collected from the Cahaba River in Perry County.

Alabama distribution: (Fig. 334) The Tennessee River system and the Mobile Bay drainage area southward to the Lower Coastal Plain, except for the Black Warrior and Cahaba river systems above the Fall Line. Intergrades with *S. m. minor* in the Lower Coastal Plain portion of the Mobile Bay drainage and eastward across southern Alabama to the range of that subspecies. Intergrades with *S. m. depressus* in the Cahaba River system above the Fall Line and in the Warrior River system along the Fall Line.

To my knowledge, *S. minor* has not been collected from within the Pascagoula River drainage in Alabama. The Escatawpa River and Big Creek, in extreme southwestern Alabama, are streams of that drainage in which the species may eventually be found and, if so, the resident populations will probably be referable to *S. m. peltifer*.

Habits: Generally similar to those of *S. m. minor*. Folkerts (1968) reported on the food habits of *S. m. peltifer* in Alabama.

Sternotherus odoratus (Latreille)

Common Musk Turtle (Stinkpot)

Description: (Fig. 336) A moderately small, aquatic turtle attaining a maximum carapace length of about 135 mm. Scutes of carapace not apparently overlapping except in young; plastron relatively small, its anterior lobe slightly movable; pectoral scute rectangular or quadrangular in shape; 1 gular scute present; barbels present on chin and neck. Carapace light olive brown to dark brown, often with radiating dark streaks; carapace of juveniles with a median keel. Head with 2 light stripes, except in an occasional adult in which stripes are lacking or are reduced to a series of longitudinal light markings. Plastron brownish to yellowish.

Small young with mottled or marbled plastron; marginals with light markings; head with conspicuous stripes. Adult males with a blunt spine or nail at end of tail and rough patches on insides of

FIG. 336. *Sternotherus odoratus,* the common musk turtle or stinkpot (Lee County). This turtle has 2 yellow stripes on the head and barbels on the chin and neck. It frequents a wide variety of aquatic habitats but is most frequently found in ponds and lakes.

hind legs, as in *S. minor* ssp. and *Kinosternon subrubrum* ssp.

Remarks: No appreciable geographic variation was detected among Alabama populations of this species. Differences between adult males and females, other than those already noted, include a difference in relative plastron length, which tends to be greatest in the latter. Plastron length as a percentage of carapace length in 32 males over 75 mm ranged from 63.0 to 77.3, and averaged 69.1. In 24 females over 75 mm, the range was 68.0 to 78.1, and the average was 73.3.

Alabama distribution: (Fig. 337) Statewide.

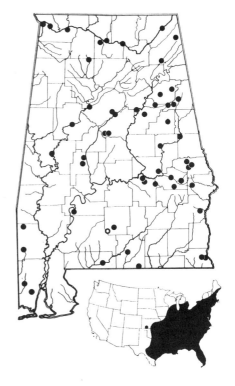

FIG. 337. Distribution of *Sternotherus odoratus,* the common musk turtle or stinkpot. This species is believed to occur statewide, or essentially so, in Alabama. Solid symbols indicate localities from which the author examined specimens. The circle is a literature record believed to be valid. The small map depicts approximately the known range in the United States.

FIG. 338. *Gopherus polyphemus,* the gopher tortoise (Geneva County). This large, harmless turtle lives in dry, sandy areas of the Coastal Plain.

Habits: In Alabama the common musk turtle inhabits ponds, lakes, sloughs, and other still- or sluggish-water habitats. In streams, I have found it in abundance only in the Tennessee River. Extremely aquatic, it spends most of its time crawling about on the bottom and seldom basks.

A small complement of elongate, hardshelled eggs, usually 3 to 5, is laid in a shallow excavation in a mound of loose soil or in a pile of rotting organic debris. The nest may be dug in a decaying log or stump.

The food of *S. odoratus* includes carrion, a wide variety of small animal life, and small amounts of vegetation. Freshly captured individuals often secrete an illsmelling musk and will bite if given the opportunity. This species usually does well in captivity.

FAMILY TESTUDINIDAE — TORTOISES

Tortoises occur in North and South America, Africa, Europe, and Asia. Approximately 40 species are recognized. Authorities disagree on the number of genera, with opinions ranging from 7 to 10. One genus occurs in the United States.

GENUS *GOPHERUS* Rafinesque

This genus is found only in the United States and Mexico. Four species are currently recognized, 1 of which occurs in Alabama.

FIG. 339. Distribution of *Gopherus poly-phemus,* the gopher tortoise. The presumed range in Alabama is indicated by hatching. Solid symbols indicate localities from which the author examined specimens. The circle is a literature record believed to be valid. The small map depicts approximately the known range in the United States.

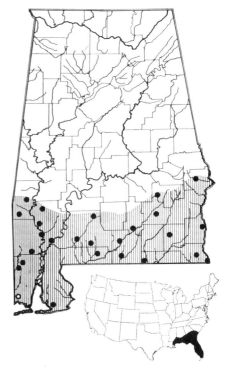

Gopherus polyphemus (Daudin)
Gopher Tortoise

Description: (Fig. 338) A large ter-restrial turtle attaining a maximum cara-pace length of about 355 mm. Top of head conspicuously scaled; front toenails large and flattened; hind feet elephan-tine; gulars of plastron protruding well forward. Carapace brown, the scutes yellow-centered in young; soft parts yel-lowish brown in young, darkening to brown or almost black in adults. Plastron of adult males somewhat concave.

Alabama distribution: (Fig. 339) Re-stricted to the Coastal Plain. Fairly com-mon in the Lower Coastal Plain, local elsewhere in the range. Absent from the Black Belt. Only 1 native population, this a small one in Russell County, is known to occur in the Fall Line Hills, a region with several areas of seemingly suitable habitat. Harper (1943) reported seeing abandoned tortoise burrows in the Fall Line Hills in an area north of Selma, Dallas County, and Dan W. Speake in-formed me that he has seen abandoned burrows in that region in southern Lee County. These reports suggest that the gopher was widely distributed in the Fall

FIG. 340. The mouth of a burrow of *Gopherus polyphemus,* the gopher tortoise (Mobile County). The burrows of this tortoise provide valuable retreats not only for the gopher but for numerous other animals, including some of our threatened and endangered species.

Line Hills in relatively recent times. At least 1 population occurs in the transitional zone between the Black Belt and Red Hills, a small one occupying portions of Pike and Bullock counties.

Habits: Gopher tortoises live in dry, sandy places, where they construct sloping burrows up to 30 feet or more in length (Fig. 340). Habitats in Alabama capable of supporting gopher populations are usually dominated by turkey oak (*Quercus laevis*) and longleaf pine (*Pinus palustris*) and are referred to as high pine-turkey oak or sandhill habitats (see Fig. 4).

The gopher burrows, described in detail by Hansen (1963), provide shelter not only for the gophers but for an assortment of other animals as well. These include invertebrates as well as vertebrates. Among the latter are mammals of several species, gopher frogs, pine snakes, indigo snakes, coachwhips, and eastern diamondback rattlesnakes. (See Preface.)

The gopher tortoise is herbivorous, feeding on a variety of herbs and berries. A staple food at many localities is wiregrass (*Aristida stricta* and *Sporobolus junceus*). The gopher is inoffensive and cannot be induced to bite.

Courtship in the gopher tortoise involves nipping and head-bobbing (Auffenberg, 1966). Nesting occurs from May to July. Between 4 and 7 round, hard-shelled eggs are laid in a cavity approximately 6 inches beneath the surface (Carr, 1952; Arata, 1958). The nest-hole is usually dug within a few feet of the burrow entrance.

FAMILY TRIONYCHIDAE – SOFT-SHELLED TURTLES

This family occurs in North America, Africa, southern Asia, and the Indonesian area. It contains about 23 species included within 7 genera. The 4 North American species all belong to the genus *Trionyx*. Webb (1962) provided a comprehensive account of North American trionychid turtles.

GENUS *TRIONYX* Geoffroy St. Hilaire

This genus occurs in North America, northern Africa, southern Asia, and Indonesia and contains about 15 species. Three of these are found in Alabama.

Trionyx ferox (Schneider)
Florida Softshell

Description: (Fig. 341) A large, aquatic turtle attaining a maximum carapace length of about 460 mm in females and 285 mm in males. Body flattened; shell lacking horny epidermal scutes, covered instead with soft, leathery skin; snout prolonged into a tubular proboscis. Leading edge of carapace with low, rounded prominences; anterolateral edge of carapace folded over forming a ridge having a distinct inner margin. Carapace of juveniles with a light margin and with conspicuous dark blotches, these sometimes light-centered. Carapace pattern becoming obscure with age. Large females with enlarged, flattened knobs in nuchal region of carapace and posteriorly in its center.

Alabama distribution: (Fig. 342) Restricted to the Lower Coastal Plain, where it occurs locally in the extreme southern portion westward to Mobile Bay.

Habits: The Florida softshell, an inhabitant of sluggish streams, lakes, and ponds, spends much of its time buried on the bottom with only the head protruding. It feeds on a wide variety of animal life, including crawfish, insects, molluscs, frogs, and fish. As in the case with other softshells, this species is rather thoroughly aquatic and leaves the water only to bask or to lay eggs. Out of the water it is extremely pugnacious and, because of the long neck, is difficult to handle without being bitten. Two or possibly 3 clutches of 7 to 22 eggs each are laid in a flask-shaped cavity constructed in sand or sandy soil.

Trionyx muticus Le Sueur
Smooth Softshell

Two subspecies are currently recognized, both of which occur in Alabama.

FIG. 341. *Trionyx ferox*, the Florida softshell, juvenile (Covington County). This species is recorded from only 3 localities in Alabama. The fold along the anterolateral edge of the carapace is distinctive.

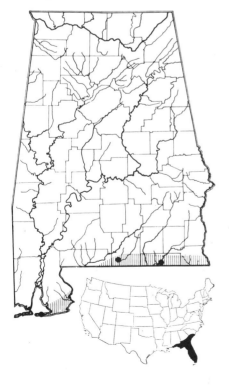

Trionyx muticus muticus Le Sueur
Midland Smooth Softshell

Description: (Fig. 343) A moderately large aquatic turtle attaining a maximum carapace length of about 355 mm in females and about 175 mm in males. Body flattened, carapace and plastron lacking horny epidermal shields, covered instead with soft skin; snout ending in a tubular proboscis; septal ridges in nostrils lacking; top of snout with light stripes except in large females. Leading edge of carapace smooth; carapace grayish to light brownish, light-bordered; carapace pattern in juveniles of dusky spots and short lines or dashes, becoming obscure or absent in some adult males, and being replaced by a pattern of mottling

FIG. 342. Distribution of *Trionyx ferox*, the Florida softshell. The presumed range in Alabama is indicated by hatching. Symbols indicate localities from which the author examined specimens. The small map depicts approximately the known range in the United States.

FIG. 343. *Trionyx muticus muticus*, the midland smooth softshell, adult female (Limestone County). This form is restricted to streams and lakes within the Tennessee River system. The leading edge of the carapace is smooth, and the juvenile's carapace lacks the large, round dark spots characteristic of *T. m. calvatus*.

or irregular blotches in adult females. Head with a dark-bordered postorbital light stripe. Top of snout with inconspicuous light stripes in front of eyes.

Alabama distribution: (Fig. 344) Confined to the Tennessee River drainage, where it occurs in the river itself, its backwaters, and possibly in some of its larger tributaries.

Habits: The 2 subspecies of *T. muticus* are not known to differ in habits. Smooth softshells are confirmed stream-dwellers and are strongly aquatic, forsaking the water only to nest or to bask along the edge. Rapid swimmers, they would be difficult to collect were it not for the habit of burying themselves in mud or sand in shallow water. A slightly mounded, disturbed area often reveals a turtle's presence to the collector.

As with other *Trionyx*, *T. muticus* is almost wholly carnivorous, feeding on such items as crawfish, insects, molluscs, fish, frogs, and tadpoles. In contrast to the other 2 species of softshells in Alabama, *T. muticus* is not particularly aggressive when handled.

Nesting takes place during May, June, and July. The flask-shaped nest cavity is usually dug on an exposed sandy bank or sand bar. (See Webb, 1962; and Mount and Folkerts, 1968.) The eggs, which reportedly number from 4 to 33 per clutch, are spherical and hardshelled.

Trionyx muticus calvatus Webb
Gulf Coast Smooth Softshell

Description: (Fig. 345, 346) Differs from nominate subspecies as follows: light stripes on top of head or snout lacking; carapace of juveniles and most males with a pattern of large, circular spots;

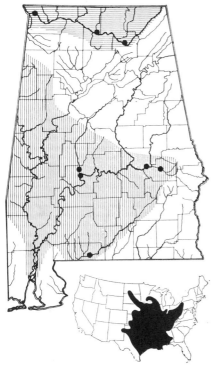

FIG. 344. Distribution of *Trionyx muticus* and subspecific variation in Alabama. Horizontal hatching indicates the presumed range of *T. m. muticus*, the midland smooth softshell, in Alabama, and vertical hatching, that of *T. m. calvatus*, the Gulf Coast smooth softshell. Symbols indicate localities from which the author examined specimens. The small map depicts approximately the known range of the species *T. muticus* in the United States.

dark borders of postorbital light stripes wider than in *T. m. muticus*.

Remarks: The taxonomic characters used to separate the 2 subspecies are of little or no value in the case of large females. A specimen of *T. m. calvatus* (AM 14286), a female from Dallas County, Alabama, has a carapace 287 mm in length, and apparently is the record-sized specimen for the subspecies. This is the specimen shown in Fig. 345.

Alabama distribution: (Fig. 344) In Alabama known only from the Coastal Plain in the Cahaba, Conecuh, Talla-poosa, and Alabama rivers and from Up-happee Creek, a tributary of the Talla-poosa River. A Mississippi record from the Tombigbee River establishes the presence of *T. m. calvatus* in that river system.

Habits: See "Habits" under *T. m. muticus*.

Trionyx spiniferus Lesueur

Six subspecies are recognized, 2 of which occur in Alabama.

Trionyx spiniferus spiniferus Le Sueur
Eastern Spiny Softshell

Description: (Fig. 347) A large aquatic turtle attaining a maximum carapace length of about 430 mm in females, and about one-half that size in males. Body flattened, carapace and plastron lacking horny epidermal shields, covered instead with soft skin; snout ending in a tubular proboscis. Leading edge of carapace with tubercles or spiny projections; cara-pace with a single encircling dark line inside the margin; carapace of juveniles and males with well-defined ocelli and spots; carapace of adult females irregu-larly mottled with dark and light mark-ings, these contrasting more sharply than in *T. s. asper*, the other subspecies occur-ring in Alabama; undersurfaces of legs and edges of plastron conspicuously mot-tled.

Carapace of large females with en-larged flattened knobs in the nuchal re-gion and posteriorly in the center; cara-pace of adult males "sandpapery" in texture.

Alabama distribution: (Fig. 348) Streams of the Tennessee River system and possibly some ponds and lakes in the area drained by those streams.

Habits: The optimal habitat of this form in Alabama is a free-flowing creek or river with a sand-gravel subtrate. The midland smooth softshell, *T. m. muticus*, a turtle with which it is sympatric in Alabama, seems best adapted to streams or backwaters of streams having deposits of silt, or sand and silt, on the bottom and along the margins. The impound-ment of the Tennessee River throughout

FIG. 345. *Trionyx muticus calvatus,* the Gulf Coast smooth softshell, juvenile (Macon County). The large, dark carapacial spots occur on the juveniles and adult males of this form.

FIG. 346. *Trionyx muticus calvatus,* the Gulf Coast smooth softshell, adult female (Dallas County). This softshell is found exclusively in streams.

FIG. 347. *Trionyx spiniferus spiniferus,* the eastern spiny softshell, adult male (Wayne County, Tennessee). Confined mainly to streams within the Tennessee River system, this form is uncommon in Alabama. The damming of the Tennessee River was probably detrimental to the eastern spiny softshell.

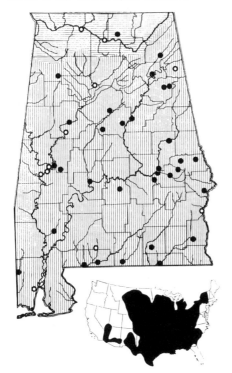

its length in Alabama has apparently favored the midland smooth softshell and has been detrimental to the eastern spiny softshell.

The habits of the eastern spiny softshell in Alabama are not well known. Presumably they are generally similar to those of *T. s. asper,* which is considerably more abundant.

Trionyx spiniferus asper (Agassiz)
Gulf Coast Spiny Softshell

Description: (Fig. 349, 350) Generally similar to *T. s. spiniferus* except as

FIG. 348. Distribution of *Trionyx spiniferus* and subspecific variation in Alabama. Horizontal hatching indicates the presumed range of *T. s. spiniferus,* the eastern spiny softshell, in Alabama, and vertical hatching that of *T. s. asper,* the Gulf Coast spiny softshell. Solid symbols indicate localities from which the author examined specimens. Circles are literature records believed to be valid. The small map depicts approximately the known range of the species *T. spiniferus* in the United States.

FIG. 349. *Trionyx spiniferus asper,* the Gulf Coast spiny softshell, adult male (Russell County). The pattern on the adult male and juvenile are similar. The most common soft-shell throughout most of Alabama, this form may be recognized by the spines or tubercles on its carapace and the presence of 2 or more dark lines around the edge of the carapace.

FIG. 350. *Trionyx spiniferus asper,* Gulf Coast spiny softshell, adult female (Macon County). The juvenile pattern is replaced in the female by one of irregular splotches and mottling, beginning in the second year.

follows: 2 or more dark lines around edge of carapace instead of 1; plastron relatively shorter than in *T. s. spiniferus;* dark and light mottling on undersurfaces of legs absent or, if present, contrasting less sharply than on *T. s. spiniferus.* Maximum carapace length in this subspecies about 455 mm.

Alabama distribution: (Fig. 348) Rivers, creeks, lakes, and permanent ponds throughout Alabama except for that portion drained by the Tennessee River and its tributaries, where it is replaced by *T. s. spiniferus*

Habits: Outside the Tennessee River drainage, *T. s. asper* is by far the most common softshell in Alabama. The Gulf Coast spiny softshell exploits most kinds of permanently aquatic habitats, ranging from small creeks and farm ponds to the largest rivers and lakes.

This softshell, when out of water, is ill-tempered and a large individual can deliver a painful bite. In handling a large specimen, it is advisable to grasp it with both hands by the rear of the carapace. *T. s. asper* is carnivorous and seems to eat almost anything available in the way of animal life. The dominant food items are invertebrates, and there is nothing to indicate that this turtle harms fish populations.

The nesting season begins in May and ends in July. From 3 to 25 eggs are laid in flask-shaped nests constructed in sandy places. Exposed sand bars and beaches are especially favored as nesting sites. The females probably lay up to 3 clutches each per season.

COLLECTING AND PRESERVING SPECIMENS

Collecting

Methods the collector must use to locate and capture reptiles and amphibians will vary according to the habits of the species he wishes to procure. Some species are located most effectively by turning over rocks, logs, and other sheltering objects, some by "road riding," and others require a different approach. The reader should refer to the specific accounts for precise information on habits and habitats.

Some turtles, especially map turtles and sawbacks, are collected most effectively by swimming downstream in the streams they inhabit and capturing them while they bask. Scuba diving may be employed to good advantage to collect aquatic turtles in certain habitats. Water snakes basking within a few feet of the water are often easily approached and captured by a stealthy swimmer. Techniques involving swimming are hazardous, however, and are not recommended for the inexperienced.

Funnel traps, hoop nets, and other such contrivances are occasionally used with success in capturing some aquatic turtles. Live fish or crawfish in a small wire box may be used as bait, although some turtles are more readily attracted to the flesh of dead animals. Submerged traps should be checked every few hours to prevent the captives from drowning.

Hellbenders, sirens, waterdogs, and amphiumas can often be taken at night on hook and line. Minnows, worms, or crawfish may be used for bait. These forms can also be collected on occasion by seining or, if the water is clear, by dipnetting, especially at night.

Novices usually capture snakes by pinning their heads to the ground with a stick or some other implement, then grasping them behind the head. Often the snake experiences considerable trauma when this method is used and, as a result, may refuse to feed and otherwise fare poorly in captivity. The experienced collector uses gentler methods, designed to minimize trauma and excitement, particularly if he intends to hold the snake in captivity for an extended period. If the specimen is of a nonvenomous species and has not been overly aroused, the collector attempts to pick it up slowly and deliberately by the body and transfer it to a cloth bag. This can usually be accomplished without the collector being bitten. If the snake is one which often bites, and has been aroused or is attempting to escape, it is grasped by the rear of the body, or by the tail if necessary, and quickly swung headfirst between the legs, which are closed at once. The snake may then bite only the collector's pants. He then pulls the snake slowly forward, keeping the legs together, until he can gently but securely grasp it behind the head.

A wise collector avoids handling venomous snakes with the hands whenever possible. Often a venomous snake can be lifted gently into an open receptacle, using a stout stick or some other appropriate implement, without causing it to become overly alarmed. If the snake is on the move, it can often be induced to crawl into a receptacle of its own accord. Many venomous snakes when placed in captivity refuse food and ultimately die of starvation. Such adverse reactions often result from physical and psychological trauma experienced during capture.

Escape-proof wooden boxes or close-mesh cloth bags are best for transporting captured snakes, except for tiny ones. Small snakes, lizards, and frogs, as well as most salamanders, are transported best in ventilated cans or jars containing damp moss or leaf litter In all cases care must be taken to prevent overheating; many species will die if subjected for any length of time to temperatures exceeding those to which they are accustomed. An insulated ice-chest or cooler containing a leak-proof plastic bag of ice is handy for transporting heat-sensitive animals during the summer. Under no conditions should any captive be subjected to prolonged exposure to sunlight or left in a car with the windows up during warm weather.

Killing

Reptiles can be killed by etherization or by injecting a small amount of sodium pentobarbital (0.1 to 2.0 cc, depending on size) into the abdominal cavity. If neither of these methods is available, the specimen may be drowned by complete submersion in water. Amphibians can be killed by placing them in a solution of chloretone (1 part saturated solution to 4 parts water) for 5 to 15 minutes. They may also be killed by placing them in warm water.

Fixing and Preserving

The tails and abdominal cavities of reptiles should be injected with 10 percent formalin (1 part stock solution to 9 parts water) and the specimen placed in formalin solution to harden; the hardening or fixing process requires 4 to 14 days, depending on specimen size. If a syringe is not available, incisions should be made through the body wall and along the undersurface of the tail to permit formalin to come into contact with the viscera and other tissues. The legs, feet, and head musculature of large lizards and turtles should also be injected.

Amphibians, except for large ones, do not require injection and should be placed directly into formalin. The mouths of salamanders may be propped open for convenience in examining the teeth. The mouths of turtles should also be propped open before fixing.

Proper positioning of the animal in the fixing receptacle varies. Ordinarily, snakes are coiled, with the head inside or, if the specimen is positioned in a vertical coil, with the head on top. Other forms are placed in a more or less natural position, with the toes extended. The tails of lizards should be curved forward and extended alongside the body; the limbs, heads, and tails of turtles should be extended.

Following fixation the specimen should be rinsed briefly and placed in preservative. For most purposes, a solution of 70 percent ethyl alcohol or one of 33 percent isopropyl alcohol is an appropriate preservative. Formalin at a strength of 4 or 5 percent may be used if alcohol is unavailable. Eggs of amphibians should be fixed and preserved in 5 percent formalin. Care must be taken in all cases to keep the preserving fluids clean and up to strength.

REPTILES AND AMPHIBIANS AS CAPTIVES

Many species of reptiles and amphibians fare well in captivity if given proper care. Few people, however, are willing or able to provide the necessary requirements of captives for any length of time, and in most cases the creatures die or are released in a weakened condition in a foreign environment. For those devotees who would like to keep these animals in captivity, the following recommendations, along with those provided in some of the species accounts, may be helpful. Additional information can be obtained from a number of sources, including Robert Snedigar's book *Our Small Native Animals — Their Habits and Care*, (1963, Dover Pub., Inc.) and Carl Kauffeld's *Snakes: The Keeper and the Kept* (1969, Doubleday and Co., Inc.).

Snakes and Lizards

Snakes and lizards should be provided with a clean, well-ventilated cage, preferably one with a screen top and glass front. For most forms, temperatures between 75° and 85° F are preferred. Clean drinking water should be provided in a suitable receptacle (one that will not overturn easily) for snakes, skinks, and glass lizards, and in the form of sprinkled droplets for anoles and fence lizards. Otherwise the quarters should be kept dry. Newspaper may be used on the floor of the cage. Do not use wood chips and sawdust as they may be inadvertently ingested and cause strangulation or intestinal blockage. A box with an entrance hole should be placed within the cage for needed privacy. A tree limb may be added for climbing species.

Most lizards should be fed insects or spiders, preferably on a daily basis. Snakes may be fed less often, at intervals of 3 to 12 days, depending on the size of the snake and the meal. Refer to the species accounts to determine the food preference of the snake being held captive.

Some snakes are exceedingly difficult to maintain in captivity, either because of their specialized food habits or general inadaptability. These include coral snakes, rainbow snakes, mud snakes, green snakes, glossy water snakes, coachwhips, and scarlet snakes. The snakes that tend to adjust most readily to captivity include rat snakes and corn snakes (*Elaphe* sp.), hog-nosed snakes, water snakes of the genus *Natrix*, garter snakes, ribbon snakes, and kingsnakes. It must be remembered, however, that adaptability to conditions of captivity varies not only among species but among individuals of the same species and that generalizations do not apply in every case.

Rattlesnakes, cottonmouths, and copperheads frequently thrive in captivity if they have not been mishandled (see section on collecting and preserving, p. 315), and if they are provided with optimum conditions during captivity. *Venomous snakes should be kept only by mature, experienced people.*

Turtles

Aquatic turtles should be kept in clean water in an aquarium and, except for snappers, provided with a way to get out of the water to bask. They should be fed daily, according to the species' requirements (see accounts). Some of the newer kinds of pelleted turtle food apparently provide a staple diet for many small aquatic turtles, but this should be supplemented with fresh foods. Most turtles need periodic exposure to sunlight or some other source of ultraviolet radiation to remain healthy. Water temperature should be kept around 80°F. A piece of hardened plaster of paris in the water will help supply calcium, which is necessary for the development of bones and shell.

Box turtles should be kept in an outside pen, provided with shelter and water, and fed fresh lean meat or canned dog food, with an occasional supplement of fruits and vegetables. Box turtles will also eat crickets, grasshoppers, and a variety of other insects. The captives should be brought inside or buried under a thick layer of pine straw or similar insulating material during cold weather.

Frogs, Toads, and Salamanders

Terrestrial amphibians can be kept in terraria containing a few inches of moist soil. Plants may be included for the benefit of treefrogs and to enhance the terrarium's appearance. Ranid frogs quite often eat smaller amphibians, and large salamanders may eat smaller ones, so one must take care to maintain species compatibility. Food should be provided in the form of earthworms, adult insects, and insect larvae; a shallow, sunken bowl of water is beneficial. Sick or diseased individuals should be removed, and the container should not be overcrowded. A screen top must be provided to prevent escape.

Aquatic Amphibians and Larvae

Tadpoles, salamander larvae, newts, sirens, and amphiumas should be kept in aquaria. The water should be reasonably clean and fairly well oxygenated. Tadpoles of most frogs will eat algae, but washed, cooked spinach should be added as a supplement.

Salamander larvae, newts, sirens, and amphiumas are all carnivorous and must be supplied with animal life of suitable size (see accounts). It is often possible to induce these forms to eat small chunks of liver or other raw, lean meat. Small individuals may be fed brine shrimp or mosquito larvae. Sirens, amphiumas, and newts will feed on pelleted turtle food.

Waterdogs and hellbenders are difficult to maintain in captivity. These forms require well-oxygenated, cool water and hiding places. A pump to provide continuous recirculation should be installed for best results.

POISONOUS SNAKES AND SNAKEBITE TREATMENT

Only 6 of the 40 species of snakes that occur in Alabama are dangerous to humans. Five of these, the cottonmouth, copperhead, and the 3 rattlesnakes, are pit vipers, and are recognizably distinct from all our other snakes in having an elliptical eye pupil, a pit or depression on each side of the face between the eye and nostril, and undivided scutes under the tail (except for those near the end of the tail). The sixth is the eastern coral snake, which has a black nose and a red-yellow-black-yellow-red . . . banded color pattern.

The venom of pit vipers, while producing some neurological symptoms, is largely histolytic in action — that is, it destroys tissue. Severe pain and local swelling rapidly follow envenomation. The coral snake's venom is largely neurotoxic, producing, in most cases, less pain and swelling but causing major malfunctions within the central nervous system. Particularly susceptible are some of the

vital autonomic reflex centers such as those associated with breathing and rate of heartbeat. Vomiting is a frequent symptom of snakebite, indicating direct involvement of the nervous system and, quite possibly, anxiety.

In our region, the eastern diamondback rattlesnake is the most dangerous snake species, chiefly because of its large size, long fangs, and large reservoir of venom. This species is restricted to the southern portion of Alabama. The copperhead is the most common poisonous snake in most parts of Alabama and undoubtedly is responsible for more snakebite cases than any other. Fortunately, fatalities from copperhead bites are extremely rare. Coral snake bites are serious, but they occur rarely and have produced few fatalities.

In some instances of persons being bitten by pit vipers, little or no venom is injected. When this happens, local symptoms are absent or are extremely mild, and there is little or no systemic involvement. In such cases, antivenin therapy should not be employed.

On the average, snakebite accounts for no more than about 14 fatalities each year in the entire country. In Alabama, the annual average is probably less than one. It is clear, then, that much of the apprehension over the snakebite problem is unwarranted. There are, however, certain reasonable precautions that should be taken by any person engaging in outdoor activities in areas inhabited by poisonous snakes. Some of these are:

1. Watch your step. Most poisonous snakes, including most rattlesnakes, rely on camouflage as their first line of protection, and if stepped on are likely to bite. Wearing leather boots or leggings when hiking or working where poisonous snakes occur is a wise practice.

2. Keep your hands out of holes, crevices, and other places into which you cannot see.

3. Leave all snakes alone unless you are positive of their identity. Do not handle poisonous snakes. Probably one-half or more of snakebite victims have been people who were either handling the snakes or keeping them in captivity.

4. Usually, it is best not to try to kill snakes. Many snakebite incidents have resulted from such attempts.

5. Do not handle "dead" poisonous snakes. Some people have been bitten by snakes they felt certain were dead.

6. Be particularly wary if you are alone in the woods. In the unlikely event that snakebite does occur, the victim should be urged to relax and remain calm. The snake should be secured, if possible, for identification. The bite of a pit viper typically produces two deep puncture wounds and considerable pain and swelling. A coral snake's fangs are fairly short and its bite is less painful. The tooth punctures made by harmless snakes are usually very shallow, often little more than scratches, and except for those of very large individuals, there is little pain.

The victim of a poisonous snake bite should be seen by a physician or transported to the nearest medical facility as soon as possible. Exertion on the part of the victim, which hastens the spread of the venom, should be minimized. If a medical facility is more than an hour away, a tourniquet should be applied, but care must be taken to keep it loose enough to permit the flow of arterial blood. Otherwise, the tourniquet can produce effects worse than those caused by the snake bite.

If, at a medical facility, it is determined that the bite is serious, antivenin will probably be administered. Antivenin injections may have beneficial effects for up to 24 hours or more after the patient has been bitten. Antivenin should be administered only by a trained person because of the danger of infection and anaphalyxis.

The "cut and suck" method of treating snakebite should be used only in exceptional circumstances (e.g., the bite of coral snake on a digit), or if no other treatment is available. It should be kept in mind that many a snakebite victim has suffered greater injury from improper treatment than from the effects of the bite itself.

To summarize the important points:

1. Try to keep the victim calm and relaxed.

2. Get medical help as soon as possible.

3. Keep in mind that snakebite seldom results in fatality.

GLOSSARY

This section gives the meanings of technical terms used in the text that are not illustrated in figures or defined at the time they are used.

ADPRESSED LIMBS. The hind limb pressed forward alongside the body and the forelimb on the same side pressed backward.

ANAL. When used as a noun in descriptions of snakes, the scute immediately anterior to the anus or vent.

ALLOPATRIC. A term applied to two or more species occupying mutually exclusive geographic ranges.

ATTENUATE. Tapering gradually and pointed at the tip.

BAND. (1) A completely encircling broad area of color differing from the ground color. (2) A broad area of color on the dorsum extending downward on each side to the edge of the ventral surface. (3) A broad area of such color oriented lengthwise on the dorsum or side of the body or tail.

BARBEL. A fleshy protuberance, usually on the head or neck.

BARRED. (1) Possessing vertical marks of contrasting color on the body or tail. (2) Possessing regularly spaced, transversely oriented markings of contrasting color across the top of the back, as in *Storeria dekayi wrightorum* (syn. crossbarred).

BLOTCH. A relatively large area of color contrasting from the ground color, usually squarish or rounded.

BORROW PIT. A relatively shallow depression created by the removal of soil or gravel for fill or for construction purposes.

CAUDAL. Pertaining to the tail. (Also see "subcaudal.")

CHEVRONATE. V- or chevron-shaped.

CIRRUS. One of a pair of fleshy downward projections from the upper lip of some salamanders.

CHAOTIC. Irregular; patternless.

CLINAL. Changing gradually, especially with respect to geographic variation.

CLOACA. The chamber receiving the contents of the intestinal and genito-urinary ducts.

COLLAR. A band of color across the neck.

COMMISSURE. The line or seam along which the jaws meet when the mouth is closed.

COMPRESSED. Flattened from side to side.

CONCORDANT. In conformity or agreement with.

CROSSBARRED. Having a barred dorsum.

CUSP. A pointed, toothlike projection.

DEPAUPERATE. Lacking in richness or diversity.

DEPRESSED. Flattened from top to bottom.

DISCORDANT. Not in conformity or agreement with.

DORSAL. (1) Pertaining to the back. (2) Any one of the scales on a snake's body above the enlarged ventral scutes.

DORSOLATERAL. Along the side of the back.

DORSUM. The upper surface of the body.

DOT. A small area of color contrasting from the ground color.

ECOTYPE. A phenotype or recognizable form of a species which owes its peculiar characteristics to the selective effects of the local environment. Ecotypes, as opposed to subspecies, are usually discontinuously distributed within the range of the species to which they belong and are often restricted to specific microhabitat types.

EMARGINATE. Having the margin interrupted or with an irregularity.

ENDEMIC. Confined to or indigenous to.

ENTIRE. (1) Complete. (2) Uninterrupted.

EXTANT. Still in existence (antonym of extinct).

FIMBRIAE. The ultimate branches of the external gills of salamanders.

GULAR. As an adjective, meaning located under the throat.

HABITUS. General aspect or build.

HAMMOCK. A forest community dominated by evergreen hardwood trees.

HERPETOFAUNA. The reptiles and amphibians of an area, considered collectively.

HIATUS. A gap.

HUMIC. Rich in organic soil or humus.

HYDRIC. Wet.

INTERRUPTED. Discontinuous or having a gap; not entire.

INTERSPACE. The area of ground color between spots, blotches, bands, etc.

INTROMITTENT ORGAN. The structure on or within a male animal used for internal fertilization.

JUVENAL. Pertaining to juvenile.

JUVENILE. Young; immature; not adult.

KEEL. An elongate, longitudinally oriented structure or development which may or may not be strongly compressed.

LABIAL. (1) Of or pertaining to the lips. (2) One of the scales on the lips of a snake or lizard.

LARVA. An immature but postembryonic stage that differs markedly in morphology from the adult.

LATERAL. Located on or pertaining to the side.

MEDIAL. Toward the midline.

MEDIAN. In the middle.

MELANIC or MELANISTIC. Unusually darkened with dark brown or black pigment.

MESIC. Intermediate in moisture conditions; not hydric or xeric.

MONOTYPIC. Having but one immediately subordinate taxon, as referring to a genus having but one species, or, in the case of a monotypic species, a species not divided into subspecies. (antonym of polytypic)

MORPHOTYPE. See "Phenotype."

MOTTLED. Marked with spots and blotches or differing color.

NASOLABIAL GROOVE. A groove running from the nostril to the edge of the upper lip in salamanders of the family Plethodontidae.

NEONATE. Newly hatched or newborn.

NEOTENY. In salamanders, the attainment of sexual maturity by an individual that retains the appearance of a larvae.

OCCIPUT. The back of the head.

OCELLATE. Possessing one or more eye-like spots.

ONTOGENETIC. Having to do with age or stage of development.

ORBITAL. Of or pertaining to the eye-socket.

PAPILLA. A small, nipple-like or pimple-like projection.

PAPILLATE. Possessing papillae.

PAROTOID. The large, swollen, glandular area lying behind the eye or on the shoulder region of some toads.

PEDICEL. A slender stalk or stem.

PERIPHERY. The edge or outer border.

PHENOTYPE. As used herein, a distinctive morphological type to which certain male and female individuals of a species conform.

PHYSIOGRAPHY. Natural or physical geography.

PLICATE. Having folds or parallel ridges and deep grooves.

POLYMORPHISM. Condition in which two or more distinct types of individuals, other than males and females, occur within the same population of the same species. (See also "sexual dimorphism.")

POLYTYPIC. Having two or more immediately subordinate taxa, as referring to a genus having two or more species, or a species with two or more subspecies. (antonym of monotypic)

POSTLABIAL. Any one of several large scales lying posterior to and in line with the labials.

PUSTULE. A small wart.

RETICULUM. A network of linear markings resembling the mesh of a net; adjective reticulate.

RUGOSITY. A wrinkle or fold; adjective rugose.

SADDLE. A blotch extending down the sides.

SCUTE. A large scale.

SEXUAL DIMORPHISM. Condition in which males and females differ in characters other than those associated with the anatomy of the reproductive system.

SINUATE. Wavy, as opposed to straight.

SPATULATE. Broadened and depressed.

SPOT. A relatively small, round area of color differing from the ground color; smaller than a "blotch" but larger than a "dot."

SUBCAUDAL. A scale or scute on the ventral surface of the tail of a reptile.

SYMPATRIC. A term applied to two or more species (or forms) occupying the same geographic area or having broadly overlapping ranges.

SYMPATRY. Condition in which two or more closely related forms occur in the same area without interbreeding.

TAXON. A taxonomic category.

TAXONOMY. The science dealing with classification of organisms.

TUBERCLE. A small, rounded bump or knob on the skin; adjective tuberculate.

TYPE LOCALITY. The place where the type specimen or holotype of a species or subspecies was collected.

TYPE SPECIMEN (HOLOTYPE). The specimen designated by the describer of a species or subspecies to insure the taxonomic fixity of the group.

VENTER. The undersurface of the body.

VENTRAL. (1) Pertaining to the venter. (2) Any one of the scutes on the venter of a snake, beginning with the first scute that makes full contact with the first row of dorsals and ending with the one that contacts the anal or anal plate.

WART. A prominence on the skin, usually more or less hardened, but not necessarily so. A small wart may be referred to as a pustule.

XERIC. Dry.

LITERATURE CITED

AGASSIZ, L. 1857. Contributions to the Natural History of the United States of America. Little, Brown, and Co., Boston, Vol. 1-2, 452 pp.

ALLEN, E. R. 1938. Notes on Wright's Bullfrog (*Rana heckscheri*). Copeia, 1938:50.

———————— and W. T. NEILL. 1950. The Alligator Snapping Turtle *Macrochelys temminckii*, in Florida. Sp. Pub. Ross Allen's Rept. Inst. 4:1-15.

ALTIG, R. 1970. A Key to the Tadpoles of the Continental United States and Canada. Herpetologica, 26:180-207.

ANDERSON, J. D. 1967a. *Ambystoma texanum*. Cat. Amer. Amphib. Rept: 37.1-37.2.

————————. 1967b. *Ambystoma opacum*. Cat. Amer. Amphib. Rept: 46.1-46.2.

————————. 1967c. *Ambystoma maculatum*. Cat. Amer. Amphib. Rept: 51.1-51.4.

———————— AND R. E. GRAHAM. 1967. Vertical Migration and Stratification of Larval *Ambystoma*. Copeia, 1967: 371-74.

ANDERSON, P. 1965. The Reptiles of Missouri. Univ. of Mo. Press, Columbia. 330 pp.

ANDERSON, P. K. 1954. Studies on the Ecology of the Narrow-mouthed Toad, *Microhyla carolinensis carolinensis*. Tulane Stud. Zool., 2:15-46.

————————. 1961. Variation in Populations of Brown Snakes, genus *Storeria*, bordering the Gulf of Mexico. Amer. Midl. Nat. 66:235-249.

ARATA, A. A. 1958. Notes on the Eggs and Young of *Gopherus polyphemus* (Daudin). Quart. J. Fla. Acad. Sci., 21:274-280.

AUFFENBERG, W. 1955. A Reconsideration of the Racer *Coluber constrictor* in Eastern United States. Tulane Stud. Zool., 2:89-155.

————————. 1958. Fossil Turtles of the Genus *Terrapene* in Florida. Bull. Fla. St. Mus., 3:53-92.

————————. 1966. On the Courtship of *Gopherus polyphemus*. Herpetologica, 22:113-117.

BAILEY, J. R. 1937. Notes on Plethodont Salamanders of the Southeastern United States. Occas. Pap. Mus. Zool. Univ. Mich., 364:1-10.

BAUR, G. 1893. Two New Species of North American Testudinata. Amer. Nat., 27:675-76.

BAYLESS, L. E. 1969. Ecological Divergence and Distribution of Sympatric *Acris* Populations (Anura: Hylidae). Herpetologica, 25:181-187.

BISHOP, S. C. 1943. Handbook of Salamanders: the Salamanders of the United States, of Canada, and of Lower California. Comstock Publ. Co., Ithaca, N.Y., XIV + 555 pp.

BLAIR, ALBERT P. 1967. Tail Prehensile in *Phaeognathus hubrichti*. Herpetologica, 23:67.

BLANCHARD, F. N. 1920. A Black *Pituophis*. Copeia, old ser., 81:31-33.

————————. 1921. A Revision of the King Snakes: Genus *Lampropeltis*. Bull. U.S. Nat. Mus., 114:1-260.

————————. 1923. The Snakes of the Genus *Virginia*. Pap. Mich. Acad. Sci., 3:343-365.

————————. 1924. A Name for the Black *Pituophis* from Alabama. Pap. Mich. Acad. Sci., Arts and Lett., 4:531-32.

————————. 1925. The Forms of *Carphophis*. Pap. Mich. Acad. Sci., Arts and Lett., 4, pt. 1:527-530.

————————. 1938. Snakes of the Genus *Tantilla* in the United States. Field Mus. Nat. Hist., Zool. Ser. 10:369-76.

————————. 1942. The Ring-necked Snakes of the Genus *Diadophis*. Bull. Chicago Acad. Sci., 7:1-144.

BLANEY, R. M. AND K. RELYEA. 1967. The Zig-zag Salamander, *Plethodon dorsalis* Cope, in Southern Alabama. Herpetologica, 23:246-247.

BOYD, C. E. 1964. The Distribution of Cricket Frogs in Mississippi. Herpetologica, 20:201-202.

BOYLES, J. M. 1952. Variation and Distribution of Water Snakes of the Genus *Natrix* in the State of Alabama. M.S. thesis, Univ. of Ala., Tuscaloosa. 70 pp.

BRANDON, R. A. 1965. Morphological Variation and Ecology of the Salamander *Phaeognathus hubrichti*. Copeia, 1965:67-71.

——————. 1966a. Additional Locality Records for *Ambystoma texanum* in Alabama, with Comments on Site of Oviposition. J. Ohio Herp. Soc., 5:104-105.

——————. 1966b. Amphibians and Reptiles Associated with *Phaeognathus hubrichti* Habitats. Herpetologica, 22:308-310.

——————. 1966c. *Phaeognathus* and *P. hubrichti*. Cat. Amer. Amphib. Rept: 26.1-26.2.

——————. 1966d. Systematics of the Salamander Genus *Gyrinophilus*. Ill. Biol. Monogr., 35:1-86.

BRANSON, B. A. AND E. C. BAKER. 1974. An Ecological Study of the Queen Snake, *Regina septemvittata* (Say) in Kentucky. Tulane Stud. in Zool. and Bot., 18:153-171.

BRIMLEY, C. S. 1904. The Box Tortoise of Southeastern North America. J. Elisha Mitchell Soc., 20:1-8.

——————. 1907. Notes on Some Turtles of the Genus *Pseudemys*. J. Elisha Mitchell Soc., June, pp. 76-84.

——————. 1910. Records of Some Reptiles and Batrachians from the Southeastern United States. Proc. Biol. Soc. Washington, 23:9-18.

——————. 1920. Notes on *Amphiuma* and *Necturus*. Copeia, old ser., 77:5-7.

——————. 1928. Two New Terrapins of the Genus *Pseudemys* from the Southern States. J. Elisha Mitchell Soc., 44:66-69.

BRODE, W. E. 1969. A Systematic Study of the Genus *Necturus* Rafinesque. Ph.D. diss., Univ. of Sou. Miss., Hattiesburg. 137 pp.

BROOKS, G. R. 1963. Food Habits of the Ground Skink. Quart. J. Fla. Acad. Sci., 26:361-367.

——————. 1967. Population Ecology of the Ground Skink, *Lygosoma laterale* (Say). Ecol. Monogr., 37:71-87.

BROWN. J. S. 1956. The Frogs and Toads of Alabama. Ph.D. diss., Univ. of Ala., Tuscaloosa. 323 pp.

——————, AND H. T. BOSCHUNG. 1954. *Rana palustris* in Alabama. Copeia, 1954:226.

BROWN, L. E. 1969. (1970). Natural Hybrids between Two Toad Species in Alabama. Quart. J. Fla. Acad. Sci., 32:285-290.

BRUCE, R. C. 1970. The Larval Life of the Three-lined Salamander, *Eurycea longicauda guttolineata*. Copeia, 1970:776-779.

——————. 1972. The Larval Life of the Red Salamander, *Pseudotriton ruber*. J. Herpetol., 6:43-51.

BURKETT, R. D. 1966. Natural History of the Cottonmouth Moccasin, *Agkistrodon piscivorus* (Reptilia). Univ. Kans. Pub. Mus. Natur. Hist., 17:435-491.

BURT, C. 1939. The Lizards of the Southeastern United States. Trans. Kans. Acad. Sci., 40:349-366.

CAGLE, F. R. 1952. The Status of the Turtles *Graptemys pulchra* Baur and *Graptemys barbouri* Carr and Marchand, with Notes on Their Natural History. Copeia, 1952:223-234.

——————. 1954. Two New Species of the Genus *Graptemys*. Tulane Stud. Zool., 1:167-186.

——————. 1968. Reptiles, p. 213-268. In W. Frank Blair, *et al.* Vertebrates of the United States. 2nd ed., McGraw-Hill, Inc. New York.

CAHN, A. R. 1937. The Turtles of Illinois. Ill. Biol. Monogr. 35:1-218.

——————. 1939. The Barking Frog, *Hyla gratiosa*, in Northern Alabama. Copeia, 1939:52-53.

CALDWELL, D. K., A. F. CARR, JR., AND L. H. OGREN. 1959. Nesting and Migration of the Atlantic Loggerhead Turtle. Bull. Fla. St. Mus., 4:295-308.

CALDWELL, R. D. AND W. M. HOWELL. 1966. *Siren intermedia nettingi* from Alabama. Herpetologica, 22:310-311.

CARPENTER, C. C. 1960. A Large Brood of Western Pigmy Rattlesnakes. Herpetologica, 16:142-143.

CARR, A. F., JR. 1937. A New Turtle from Florida, with Notes on *Pseudemys floridana mobiliensis* (Holbrook). Occ. Pap. Mus. Zool. Univ. Mich., 348:1-7.

————————. 1938. A New Subspecies of *Pseudemys floridana*, with Notes on the *floridana* Complex. Copeia, 1938:105-109.

————————. 1940. A Contribution to the Herpetology of Florida. Univ. Fla. Pub., Biol. Sci. Ser., 3:1-118.

————————. 1952. Handbook of Turtles. The Turtles of the United States, Canada, and Baja California. Comstock Publ. Assoc., Ithaca, N.Y. XVIII + 542 pp.

————————. 1967a. Alligators. Dragons in Distress. Nat. Geographic, 131:133-148.

————————. 1967b. So Excellent a Fishe. Natural History Press, Garden City, N.Y. xii + 248 pp.

CARR, A. F., JR. AND J. W. CRENSHAW, JR. 1957. A Taxonomic Reappraisal of the Turtle *Pseudemys alabamensis* Baur. Bull. Fla. St. Mus., 2:25-42.

———————— AND L. J. MARCHAND. 1942. A New Turtle from the Chipola River, Florida. Proc. New England Zool. Club, 20:95-100.

CHERMOCK, R. L. 1952a. A Key to the Amphibians and Reptiles of Alabama. Geol. Surv. Ala., Mus. Pap. 33:1-88.

————————. 1952b. Additional Records of Salamanders from Alabama. J. Ala. Acad. Sci., 21:48.

————————. 1955. A Record of the Northern Pine Snake, *Pituophis melanoleucus* Copeia, 1955:141.

CHRISTMAN, S. P. 1970. *Hyla andersoni* in Florida. Quart. J. Fla. Acad. Sci., 33:80.

CLARK, D. B. AND J. W. GIBBONS. 1969. Dietary Shift in the Turtle *Pseudemys scripta* (Shoepff) from Youth to Maturity. Copeia, 1969:704-706.

CLIBURN, J. W. 1957. Some Southern Races of the Common Water Snake, *Natrix sipedon*. Herpetologica, 13:193-202.

————————. 1960. The Phylogeny and Zoogeography of North American *Natrix*. Ph.D. diss., Univ. of Ala., Tuscaloosa. 319 pp.

————————. 1961. The Ribbon Snake of Southern Mississippi. Herpetologica, 17:211-212.

————————. 1962. Further Notes on the Behavior of a Captive Black Pine Snake (*Pituophis melanoleucus lodingi* Blanchard). Herpetologica, 18:34-37.

CONANT, R. 1949. Two New Races of *Natrix erythrogaster*. Copeia, 1949:1-15.

————————. 1956. A Review of Two Rare Pine Snakes from the Gulf Coastal Plain. Amer. Mus. Novitates, No. 1781:1-31.

————————. 1958. A Field Guide to Reptiles and Amphibians of the United States and Canada East of the 100th Meridian. Houghton-Mifflin Co., Boston. xviii + 366 pp.

————————. 1963. Evidence for the Specific Status of the Water Snake *Natrix fasciata*. Amer. Mus. Novitates, No. 2122:1-38.

————————. 1969. A Review of the Water Snakes of the Genus *Natrix* in Mexico. Bull. Amer. Mus. Nat. Hist. 142 (Art. 1):1-140.

CONANT, R. AND J. D. LAZELL, JR. 1973. The Carolina Salt Marsh Snake: A Distinct Form of *Natrix sipedon*. Breviora, No. 400:1-13.

CONWAY, C. H. AND D. E. METTER. 1967. Skin Glands Associated with Breeding in *Microhyla carolinensis*. Copeia, 1967: 672-673.

COOPER, J. E. 1968. The Salamander *Gyrinophilus palleucus* in Georgia with Notes on Alabama and Tennessee Populations. J. Ala. Acad. Sci., 39:182-185.

———————— AND M. R. COOPER. 1968. Cave-associated Herpetozoa II: Salamanders of the Genus *Gyrinophilus* in Alabama Caves. Natl. Speleol. Soc. Bull., 30:19-24.

COPE, E. D. 1880. On the Zoological Position of Texas. Bull. U.S. Nat. Mus., No. 17:1-51.

————————. 1889. The Batrachia of North America. Bull. U.S. Nat. Mus., No. 34:1-525.

————————. 1900. The Crocodilians, Lizards and Snakes of North America. U.S. Natl. Mus. Rept. for 1898:153-1270.

CRENSHAW, J. W., JR. 1955a. The Ecological Geography of the *Pseudemys floridana* Complex in the Southeastern United States. Ph.D. diss., Univ. of Fla., Gainesville, 211 pp.

————————. 1955b. The Life History of the Southeastern Spiny Lizard, *Sceloporus undulatus undulatus* Latreille. Amer. Midl. Nat., 54:257-298.

———————— AND F. W. BLAIR. 1959. Relationships in the *Pseudacris nigrita* Complex in Southwestern Georgia. Copeia, 1959:215-222.

DAVIDSON, J. M. 1971. Geographic Variation in the Pond Slider, *Pseudemys scripta*, in Alabama. M.S. thesis, Auburn Univ., Auburn, Ala. 56 pp.

DOBIE, J. L. 1971. Reproduction and Growth in the Alligator Snapping Turtle, *Macroclemys temmincki* (Troost). Copeia, 1971:645-658.

————————. 1972. Correction of Distributional Records for *Graptemys barbouri* and *Graptemys pulchra*. Herpetol. Rev., 4:23.

DONOVAN, LOIS A. AND G. W. FOLKERTS. 1972. Foods of the Seepage Salamander, *Desmognathus aeneus* Brown and Bishop. Herpetologica, 28:35-37.

DOWLING, H. G. 1950a. A New Southeastern Record for the Coal Skink. Copeia, 1950:235.

————————. 1950b. Studies of the Black Swamp Snake, *Seminatrix pygaea* (Cope), with Descriptions of Two New Subspecies. Misc. Pub. Mus. Zool., Univ. Michigan, No. 76:1-38.

————————. 1951. A Proposed Standard System of Counting Ventrals in Snakes. Brit. J. Herpetol. 1:97-99.

DUELLMAN, W. E. AND A. SCHWARTZ. 1958. Amphibians and Reptiles of Southern Florida. Bull. Fla. St. Mus., Biol. Sci. Ser., 3:1-324.

DUNDEE, H. A. 1971. *Cryptobranchus* and *C. alleganiensis*. Cat. Amer. Amphib. Rept.: 101. 1-101.4.

DUNN, E. R. 1920. Some Reptiles and Amphibians from Virginia, North Carolina, Tennessee, and Alabama. Proc. Biol. Soc. Washington, 33:129-137.

————————. 1940. The Races of *Ambystoma tigrinum*. Copeia, 1940:154-162.

EDGREN, R. A. 1955. The Natural History of the Hog-nosed Snakes, Genus *Heterodon*: A Review. Herpetologica, 11:105-117.

ERNST, C. H. 1967. Intergradation between the Painted Turtles *Chrysemys picta picta* and *Chrysemys picta dorsalis*. Copeia, 1967:131-136.

————————. 1970. The Status of the Painted Turtle, *Chrysemys picta*, in Tennessee and Kentucky. J. Herpetol., 4:39-45.

————————. 1971a. Sexual Cycles and Maturity of the Turtle, *Chrysemys picta*. Biol. Bull., 140:191-200.

————————. 1971b. *Chrysemys picta*. Cat. Amer. Amphib. Rept.: 106.1-106.4.

———————— AND R. W. BARBOUR. 1972. Turtles of the United States. Univ. Press of Ky., Lexington. x + 347 pp.

———————— AND B. G. JETT. 1969. An Intergrade Population of *Pseudemys scripta elegans* and *Pseudemys scripta troosti* in Kentucky. J. Herpetol., 3:103.

ESTRIDGE, R. E. 1970. The Taxonomic Status of *Sternothaerus depressus* (Testudinata, Kinosternidae) with Observations on its Ecology. M.S. thesis, Auburn Univ., Auburn, Ala. 49 pp.

FENNEMAN, N. M. 1938. Physiography of Eastern United States. McGraw-Hill Co., Inc., New York. 689 pp.

FITCH, H. S. 1954. Life History and Ecology of the Five-lined Skink, *Eumeces fasciatus*. Univ. Kans. Pub. Mus. Nat. Hist., 8:1-156.

————————. 1958. Natural History of the Six-lined Racerunner. Univ. Kans. Pub. Mus. Nat. Hist., 11:11-62.

————————. 1960. Autecology of the Copperhead. Univ. Kans. Pub. Mus. Nat. Hist., 13:85-288.

————————. 1963. Natural History of the Racer *Coluber constrictor*. Univ. Kans. Pub. Mus. Nat. Hist., 15:351-468.

————————. 1965. An Ecological Study of the Garter Snake, *Thamnophis sirtalis*. Univ. Kans. Pub. Mus. Nat. Hist., 15:493-564.

————————. 1970. Reproductive Cycles in Lizards and Snakes. Univ. Kans. Misc. Pub. Mus. Nat. Hist., No. 52:1-247.

———————— AND R. R. FLEET. 1970. Natural History of the Milk Snake (*Lampropeltis triangulum*) in Northeastern Kansas. Herpetologica, 26:387-396.

FOLKERTS, G. W. 1968a. The Genus *Desmognathus* Baird (Amphibia: Plethodontidae) in Alabama. Ph.D. diss., Auburn Univ., Auburn, Ala. 129 pp.

————————. 1968b. Food Habits of the Stripe-necked Musk Turtle, *Sternotherus minor peltifer* Smith and Glass. J. Herp., 2:171-173.

————————. 1971. Ecotypic Variation in Salamanders of the Southeastern U.S. Herpetol. Rev., 3:106.

———————— AND R. H. MOUNT. 1969. A New Subspecies of the Turtle *Graptemys nigrinoda* Cagle. Copeia, 1969:677-682.

GARTON, S. G., E. W. HARRIS, AND R. A. BRANDON. 1970. Descriptive and Ecological Notes on *Natrix cyclopion* in Illinois. Herpetologica, 26:454-461.

GEHLBACH, F. R. 1967. *Ambystoma tigrinum*. Cat. Amer. Amph. Rept.: 52.1-52.4.

GIBBONS, J. W. 1967. Variation in Growth Rates in Three Populations of the Painted Turtle, *Chrysemys picta*. Herpetologica, 23:296-303.

————————. 1968a. Population Structure and Survivorship in the Painted Turtle, *Chrysemys picta*. Copeia, 1968: 260-268.

————————. 1968b. Reproductive Potential, Activity, and Cycles in the Painted Turtle, *Chrysemys picta*. Ecology, 49:399-409.

————————. 1969. Ecology and Population Dynamics of the Chicken Turtle, *Deirochelys reticularia*. Copeia, 1969:669-676.

GLOYD, H. K., 1935a. The Subspecies of *Sistrurus miliarius*. Occ. Pap. Mus. Zool., Univ. Mich., 322:1-7.

————————. 1935b. The Canebrake Rattlesnake. Copeia, 1935:175-178.

————————. 1940. The Rattlesnakes, Genera *Sistrurus* and *Crotalus*. A Study of Zoogeography and Evolution. Chicago Acad. Sci. Spec. Pub., No. 4:1-300.

————————. 1969. Two Additional Subspecies of North American Crotalid Snakes, Genus *Agkistrodon*. Proc. Biol. Soc. Washington, 82:219-232.

———————— AND R. CONANT. 1938. The Subspecies of the Copperhead, *Agkistrodon mokasen* Beauvois. Bull. Chicago Acad. Sci., 5:163-166.

————————————————————. 1943. A Synopsis of the American Forms of *Agkistrodon* (Copperheads and Moccasins) Bull. Chicago Acad. Sci., 7:147-170.

GOFF, C. C. 1936. Distribution and Variation of a New Subspecies of Water Snake, *Natrix cyclopion floridana*, with a Discussion of its Relationships. Occ. Pap. Mus. Zool. Univ. Mich., 237:1-11.

GOIN, C. J. 1942. Description of a New Race of *Siren intermedia* Le Conte. Ann. Carnegie Mus., 29:211-217.

————————. 1950. A Study of the Salamander *Ambystoma cingulatum* with the Description of a New Subspecies. Ann. Carnegie Mus. 31:299-321.

———————— AND H. G. NETTING. 1940. A New Gopher Frog from the Gulf Coast, with Comments upon the *Rana areolata* Group. Ann. Carnegie Mus., 28:137-140.

GORDON, R. E. 1952. A Contribution to the Life History and Ecology of the Plethodontid Salamander *Aneides aeneus* (Cope and Packard). Amer. Midl. Nat., 47:666-701.

————————. 1967. *Aneides aeneus*. Cat. Amer. Amphib. Rept.: 30.1-30.2.

GROBMAN, A. B. 1950. The Distribution of the Races of *Desmognathus fuscus* in the Southern States. Chicago Acad. Sci. Nat. Hist. Misc., No. 70:1-8.

GROVES, F. 1961. Notes on Two Large Broods of *Haldea v. valeriae* (Baird and Girard). Herpetologica, 17:71.

GUNTER, G. AND W. E. BRODE. 1964. *Necturus* in the State of Mississippi, with Notes on Adjacent Areas. Herpetologica, 20:114-126.

HALTOM, W. L. 1931. Alabama Reptiles. Ala. Geol. Surv. Nat. Hist. Mus. Pap. No. 11. vi + 145 pp.

HANSEN, K. L. 1958. Breeding Pattern of the Eastern Spadefoot Toad. Herpetologica, 14:57-67.

――――――――. 1963. The Burrow of the Gopher Tortoise. Quart. J. Fla. Acad. Sci., 26:353-360.

HARDY, J. D., JR. 1964. A New Frog, *Rana plaustris manseutii*, subsp. nov. from the Atlantic Coastal Plain. Chesapeake Sci., 5:91-100.

HARPER, F. 1939. Distribution, Taxonomy, Nomenclature, and Habits of the Little Treefrog (*Hyla ocularis*). Amer. Midl. Nat., 22:134-149.

HARPER, R. M. 1943. Forests of Alabama. Geol. Surv. Ala., Monogr. 10, 230 pp.

HARRIS, J. P., JR. 1961. The Natural History of *Necturus*, IV. Reproduction. J. Grad. Res. Cent., 29:69-81.

HARRISON, J. R. 1973. Observations on the Life History and Ecology of *Eurycea quadridigitata* (Holbrook). HISS News J., 1:57-58.

HECHT, M. K. 1958. A Synopsis of the Mud Puppies of Eastern North America. Proc. Staten Island Inst. Arts and Sci., 21:1-38.

HELLMAN, R. E., 1953. A Comparative Study of the Eggs and Tadpoles of *Hyla phaeocrypta* and *Hyla versicolor* in Florida. Pub. Res. Div. Ross Allen's Rept. Inst., 1:61-74.

HIGHTON, R. 1961. A New Genus of Lungless Salamander from the Coastal Plain of Alabama. Copeia, 1961:65-68.

――――――――. 1962a. Revision of the North American Salamanders of the Genus *Plethodon*. Bull. Fla. St. Mus., 6:235-367.

――――――――. 1962b. Geographic Variation in the Life History of the Slimy Salamander. Copeia, 1962:597-613.

HOLBROOK, J. E. 1838. North American Herpetology II. Philadelphia, 55 pp.

HOLMAN, J. A. 1961. Amphibians and Reptiles of the Howard College Natural Area. J. Ala. Acad. Sci., 32:77-87.

――――――――. 1971a. *Ophisaurus attenuatus*. Cat. Amer. Amphib. Rept.: 111.1-111.3.

――――――――. 1971b. *Ophisaurus ventralis*. Cat. Amer. Amphib. Rept.: 115.1-115.2.

HOLT, E. G. 1919. Coluber Swallowing a Stone. Copeia, old ser. No. 76:99-100.

――――――――. 1924a. Additional Records for the Alabama Herpetological Catalogue. Copeia, old ser. No. 135:93-95.

――――――――. 1924b. Additional Records for the Alabama Herpetological Catalog. Copeia, old ser. No. 136:100-101.

HORTON, R. T. 1968. *Seminatrix pygaea* in Alabama. J. Herpetol. 1:94.

HOWELL, A. H. 1921. A Biological Survey of Alabama. USDA Div. Biol. Surv., Nor. Amer. Fauna, No. 45:1-88.

HUHEEY, J. E. 1959. Distribution and Variation in the Glossy Water Snake, *Natrix rigida* (Say). Copeia, 1959:303-311.

HUTCHISON, V. H. 1966. *Eurycea lucifuga*. Cat. Amer. Amphib. Rept.: 24.1-24.2.

JACKSON, C. G., JR. AND M. M. JACKSON. 1970. Herpetofauna of Dauphin Island, Alabama. Quart. J. Fla. Acad. Sci., 33:281-287

――――――――――――― AND A. ROSS. 1971. The Occurrence of Barnacles on the Alligator Snapping Turte, *Macroclemys temmincki* (Troost). J. Herpetol., 5:188-189.

------------------------. 1972. (1974). Balanomorph Barnacles on *Chrysemys alabamensis*. Quart. J. Fla. Acad. Sci., 35:173-176.

JACKSON, J. F. 1962. A Second Locality for *Pituophis melanolencus melanolencus* in Alabama. Bull. Phil. Herpetol. Soc., 1962:19.

JORDAN, J. R., JR. 1970. Death-feigning in a Captive Red-bellied Snake, *Storeria occipitomaculata* (Storer). Herpetologica, 26:466-468.

------------------------. 1973. Sexual Dimorphism in the Red Hills Salamander, *Phaeognathus hubrichti* Highton (Amphibia: Caudata: Plethodontidae), with Comments on its Phylogenetic assignment. ASB Bull., 20:62.

------------------------ AND R. H. MOUNT. 1975. The Status of the Red Hills Salamander, *Phaeognathus hubrichti*, J. Herpetol, 9:211-215.

KAUFFELD, C. F. 1941. The Red-tailed Skink, *Eumeces egregius*, in Alabama. Copeia, 1941:51.

------------------------. 1969. Snakes: The Keeper and the Kept. Doubleday and Co., Inc., Garden City, N.Y. xiv + 249 pp.

KEELER, J. E. 1955. An Extension of the Range of the Black Pine Snake in Alabama. J. Ala. Acad. Sci. 27:92-93.

------------------------. 1964. Alligator Snapping Turtle Unique with Hooked Beak, Prominent Shell Ridges. Ala. Conservationist, Oct.-Nov.:22-23.

LAZELL, J. D., JR. AND R. A. BRANDON. 1962. A New Stygian Salamander from the Southern Cumberland Plateau. Copeia, 1962:300-306.

LITTLEJOHN, J. J. AND R. S. OLDHAM. 1968. *Rana pipiens* Complex: Mating Call Structure and Taxonomy. Science, 162:1003-1005.

LÖDING, H. P. 1922. A Preliminary Catalog of Alabama Reptiles and Amphibians. Ala. Geol. Surv. Nat. Hist. Mus., Pap. No. 5:1-59.

McCONKEY, E. H. 1954. A Systematic Study of the North American Lizards of the Genus *Ophisaurus*. Amer. Midl. Nat., 51:133-169.

MARTOF, B. S. AND H. C. GERHARDT. 1965. Observations on the Geographic Variation in *Ambystoma cingulatum*. Copeia, 1965:342-346.

------------------------. 1968. *Ambystoma cingulatum*. Cat. Amer. Amphib. Rept.: 57.1-57.2.

------------------------. 1970. *Rana sylvatica*. Cat. Amer. Amphib. Rept.: 86.1-86.4.

------------------------. 1973a. *Siren intermedia* Cat. Amer. Amphib. Rept.: 127.1-127.3.

------------------------. 1973b. *Siren lacertina*. Cat. Amer. Amphib. Rept.: 128.1-128.2.

------------------------ AND F. L. ROSE. 1963. Geographic Variation in Southern Populations of *Desmognathus ochrophaeus*. Amer. Midl. Nat. 69:376-425.

MEANS, D. B. 1974. The Status of *Desmognathus brimleyorum* Stejneger and an Analysis of the Genus *Desmognathus* (Amphibia: Urodela) in Florida. Bull. Fla. St. Mus., 18:1-100.

MECHAM, J. S. 1954. Geographic Variation in the Green Frog, *Rana clamitans* Latreille. Texas J. Sci., 6:1-24.

------------------------. 1957. Some Hybrid Combinations between Strecker's Chorus Frog, *Pseudacris streckeri*, and Certain Related Forms. Texas J. Sci., 9:337-345.

------------------------. 1960a. Introgressive Hybridization between Two Southeastern Treefrogs. Evolution, 14:445-457.

------------------------. 1960b. Natural Hybridization between the Tree Frogs *Hyla versicolor* and *Hyla avivoca*. J. Elisha Mitchell Sci. Soc., 76:64-67.

------------------------. 1960. Range Extensions for two Southeastern Skinks. Herpetologica, 16:224.

------------------------. 1964. Ecological and Genetic Relationships of the Two Cricket Frogs, genus *Acris*, in Alabama, Herpetologica, 20:84-91.

------------------------. 1965. Genetic Relationships and Reproductive Isolation in Southeastern Frogs of the Genera *Pseudacris* and *Hyla*. Amer. Midl. Nat., 74:269-308.

------------------------. 1967. *Notopthalmus viridescens*. Cat. Amer. Amphib. Rept.: 53.1-53.4.

—————————. 1968. Evidence of Reproductive Isolation between Two Populations of the Frog, *Rana pipiens*, in Arizona. S.W. Nat., 13:35-44.

—————————. 1969. New Information from Experimental Crosses on Genetic Relationships within the *Rana pipiens* Species Group. J. Exp. Zool., 170:169-180.

—————————. 1971. Vocalizations of the Leopard Frog, *Rana pipiens*, and Three Related Mexican Species, Copeia, 1971: 505-516.

—————————, M. J. LITTLEJOHN, R. S. OLDHAM, L. E. BROWN, AND J. R. BROWN. 1973. A New Species of Leopard Frog (*Rana pipiens* complex) from the Plains of the Central United States. Occ. Pap. Mus. Texas Tech. Univ., No. 18:1-11.

MIDDLEKAUFF, W. W. 1943. A Record of the Cave Salamander from Alabama. Copeia, 1943:126.

MILSTEAD, W. W. 1969. Studies on the Evolution of Box Turtles (Genus *Terrapene*) Bull. Fla. St. Mus. 14:1-113.

MITTLEMAN, M. B. 1966. *Eurycea bislineata*. Cat. Amer. Amphib. Rept.: 45.1-45.4.

—————————. 1967. *Manculus* and *M. quadridigitatus*. Cat. Amer. Amphib. Rept.: 44.1-44.2.

MOLL, E. O. AND J. M. LEGLER. 1970. The Life History of a Neotropical Slider Turtle, *Pseudemys scripta* (Schoepff) in Panama. Bull. Los Angeles Co. Mus. Nat. Hist., 11:1-102.

Moss, D. 1955. The Effect of the Slider Turtle *Pseudemys scripta scripta* (Schoepff) on the Production of Fish in Farm Ponds. Proc. 1955 Ann. Meet. S.E. Game and Fish Comm.: 97-100.

MOUNT, R. H. 1963. The Natural History of the Red-tailed Skink, *Eumeces egregius* Baird. Amer. Midl. Nat., 70:356-385.

—————————. 1964. New Locality Records for Alabama Anurans. Herpetologica, 20:127-128.

—————————. 1965. Variation and Systematics of the Scincoid Lizard, *Eumeces egregius* (Baird). Bull. Fla. St. Mus., 9:183-213.

—————————. 1968. *Eumeces egregius*. Cat. Amer. Amphib. Rept.: 73.1-73.2.

—————————. 1969. Distributional Notes on Two Southern Turtles. J. Herpetol., 3:191.

—————————. 1972. Distribution of the Worm Snake *Carphophis amoenus* (Say) in Alabama. Herpetologica, 28:263-266.

————————— AND G. W. FOLKERTS. 1968. Distribution of Some Alabama Reptiles and Amphibians. Herpetologica, 24:259-262.

————————— AND T. D. SCHWANER. 1970. Taxonomic and Distributional Relationships between the Water Snakes *Natrix taxispilota* (Holbrook) and *Natrix rhombifera* (Hallowell). Herpetologica, 26:76-82.

MYERS, C. W. 1967. The Pine Woods Snake, *Rhadinaea flavilata* (Cope), Bull. Fla. St. Mus., 11:47-97.

NEILL, W. T. 1948. A New Subspecies of Tree-Frog from Georgia and South Carolina. Herpetologica, 4:175-179.

—————————. 1949a. The Distribution of Milk Snakes in Georgia. Herpetologica, 5:8.

—————————. 1949b. Juveniles of *Siren lacertina* and *S. i. intermedia*. Herpetologica, 5:19-20.

—————————. 1950. Taxonomy, Nomenclature, and Distribution of Southeastern Cricket Frogs, Genus *Acris*. Amer. Midl. Nat., 43:152-156.

—————————. 1951. Notes on the Natural History of Certain North American Snakes. Pub. Res. Div. Ross Allen's Rept. Inst., 1:47-60.

—————————. 1954. Ranges and Taxonomic Allocations of Amphibians and Reptiles in the Southeastern United States. Pub. Res. Div. Ross Allen's Rept. Inst., 1:75-96.

—————————. 1958. The Occurrence of Amphibians and Reptiles in Salt Water Areas, and a Bibliography. Bull. Marine Sci. Gulf and Carib., 8:1-97.

—————————. 1963a. A New Subspecies of the Queen Snake, *Natrix septemvittata,* from Southern Alabama. Herpetologica, 19:1-9.

—————————. 1963b. Notes on the Alabama Waterdog, *Necturus alabamensis* Viosca. Herpetologica, 19:166-174.

—————————. 1963c. *Hemidactylium scutatum.* Cat. Amer. Amphib. Rept.: 2.1-2.2.

—————————. 1964. Taxonomy, Natural History, and Zoogeography of the Rainbow Snake, *Farancia erytrogramma* (Palisot de Beauvois). Am. Midl. Nat., 71:257-295.

—————————. 1971. The Last of the Ruling Reptiles. Columbia Univ. Press, New York and London. xvii + 486 pp.

NELSON, C. E. 1972. *Gastrophryne carolinensis.* Cat. Amer. Amphib. Rept.: 120.1-120.4.

NELSON, H. N. AND J. W. GIBBONS. 1972. Ecology, Abundance and Seasonal Activity of the Scarlet Snake, *Cemophora coccinea.* Copeia, 1972:582-584.

NELSON, W. F. 1969. Notes on Partruition and Brood Sizes in *Storeria occipitomaculata.* Rept. Reelfoot Lake Biol. Sta., Tenn. Acad. Sci., 44:20-21.

NETTING, M. G. AND C. J. GOIN. 1942. Additional Notes on *Rana sevosa.* Copeia, 1942: 259.

NICKERSON, M. A. AND C. E. MAYS. 1972. The Hellbenders. Milwaukee Public Mus. Pub. in Biol. and Geol. No. 1, viii + 106 pp.

ORGAN, J. A. 1961. The Eggs and Young of the Spring Salamander, *Gyrinophilus porphyriticus.* Herpetologica, 17:53-56.

PALMER, W. M. 1961. Notes on the Eggs and Young of the Scarlet Kingsnake, *Lampropeltis doliata doliata.* Herpetologica, 17:65.

—————————— AND G. TREGEMBO. 1970. Notes on the Natural History of the Scarlet Snake *Cemophora coccinea copei* Jan in North Carolina. Herpetologica, 26:300-302.

—————————— AND G. M. WILLIAMSON. 1971. Observations on the Natural History of the Carolina Pigmy Rattlesnake, *Sistrurus miliarius miliarius* Linnaeus. J. Elisha Mitchell Soc., 87:20-25.

PENN, G. H. 1940. Notes on the Summer Herpetology of DeKalb County, Alabama. J. Tenn. Acad. Sci., 15:352-355.

PISANI, G. R., J. T. COLLINS, AND S. R. EDWARDS. 1972. A Re-evaluation of the Subspecies of *Crotalus horridus.* Trans. Kans. Acad. Sci., 75:255-263.

PLATT, D. R. 1969. Natural History of the Hognose Snakes *Heterodon platyrhinos* and *Heterodon nasicus.* Univ. Kans. Pub. Mus. Nat. Hist., 18:253-420.

PORTER, K. R. 1972. Herpetology. W. B. Saunders Co., Philadelphia. xii + 524 pp.

PRICE, W. H. AND L. G. CARR. 1943. Eggs of *Heterodon simus.* Copeia, 1943:93.

RALIN, D. B. 1968. Ecological and Reproductive Differentiation in the Cryptic Species of the *Hyla versicolor* Complex (Hylidae). Southwest. Nat., 13:283-299.

RANKIN, H. T. 1974. Black Belt Prairie. Montgomery County, Alabama, and Vicinity. Bull. Ala. Agr. Expt. Sta., No. 454:1-24.

ROSE, F. L. 1971. *Eurycea aquatica.* Cat. Amer. Amphib. Rept.: 116.1-116.2.

—————————— AND F. M. BUSH. 1963. A New Species of *Eurycea* (Amphibia: Caudata) from the Southeastern United States. Tulane Stud. Zool., 10:121-128.

—————————— AND J. L. DOBIE. 1963. *Desmognathus monticola* in the Coastal Plain of Alabama. Copeia, 1963:564-565.

ROSSMAN, D. A. 1956. Notes on Food of a Captive Black Swamp Snake, *Seminatrix pygaea pygaea* (Cope). Herpetologica, 12:154-155.

—————————. 1958. A New Race of *Desmognathus fuscus* from the South-central United States. Herpetologica, 14:158-160.

—————————. 1963a. Relationships and Taxonomic Status of the North American Natricine Snake Genera *Liodytes, Regina,* and *Clonophis.* Occ. Pap. La. St. Univ. Mus. Zool., 29:1-29.

—————————. 1963b. The Colubrid Snake Genus *Thamnophis:* a Revision of the *sauritus* group. Bull. Fla. St. Mus., 7:99-178.

————————————. 1965. The Blue Ridge Two-lined Salamander *Eurycea bislineata wilderae*, in Southern Alabama. Herpetologica, 20:287-288.

————————————. 1970. *Thamnophis sauritus*. Cat. Amer. Amphib. Rept.: 99.1-99.2.

————————————. 1973. Evidence for the Conspecificity of *Carphophis amoenus* (Say) and *Carphophis vermis* (Kennicott). J. Herpetol., 7:140-141.

RUBENSTEIN, N. 1969. A Study of the Salamanders of Mt. Cheaha, Cleburne County, Alabama. J. Herpetol., 3:33-47.

SABATH, M. D. AND L. E. SABATH. 1969. Morphological Intergradation in Gulf Coastal Brown Snakes, *Storeria dekayi* and *Storeria tropica*. Amer. Midl. Nat., 81:148-155.

———————————— AND R. WORTHINGTON. 1959. Eggs and Young of Certain Texas Reptiles. Herpetologica, 15:31-32.

SALTHE, S. N. 1973a. *Amphiuma means*. Cat. Amer. Amphib. Rept.: 148.1-148.2.

————————————. 1973b. *Amphiuma tridactylum*. Cat. Amer. Amphib. Rept.: 149.1-149.3.

SCHAFF, R. T., JR. AND P. W. SMITH. 1970. Geographic Variation in the Pickerel Frog. Herpetologica, 26:240-254.

————————————————————————. 1971. *Rana palustris*. Cat. Amer. Amphib. Rept.: 117.1-117.3.

SCHMIDT, K. P. 1953. A Checklist of North American Amphibians and Reptiles, Sixth Ed., Amer. Soc. Ichthyol. and Herpetol., pp. 1-280.

SCHWANER, T. D. 1969. The Systematic and Ecological Relationships between the Water Snakes *Natrix sipedon pleuralis* and *N. fasciata* in Alabama and the Florida Panhandle. M.S. thesis, Auburn Univ., Auburn, Ala., 117 pp.

———————————— AND R. H. MOUNT. 1970. Notes on the Distribution, Habits, and Ecology of the Salamander *Phaeognathus hubrichti* Highton. Copeia, 1970:571-573.

SCHWARTZ, A. 1956. Geographic Variation in the Chicken Turtle, *Deirochelys reticularia* Latreille. Fieldiana, 34:461-503.

————————————. 1957. Chorus Frogs (*Pseudacris nigrita* Le Conte) in South Carolina. Amer. Mus. Novitates, No. 1838:1-12.

SCOTT, A. F. 1973. Geographic Distribution: *Trionyx ferox*. HISS News J., 1:153.

SCOTT, F. AND R. M. JOHNSON. 1972. Geographic Distribution: *Ambystoma texanum*. Herpetol. Rev., 4:95.

SEVER, D. M. 1972. Geographic Variation and Taxonomy of *Eurycea bislineata* (Caudata: Plethodontidae) in the Upper Ohio Valley. Herpetologica, 28:314-324.

SHEALY, R. M. 1973. The Natural History of the Alabama Map Turtle, *Graptemys pulchra* Baur, in Alabama. Ph.D. diss., Auburn Univ., Auburn, Ala. 109 pp.

SHOOP, C. R. 1960. The Breeding Habits of the Mole Salamander, *Ambystoma talpoideum* (Holbrook), in Southeastern Louisiana. Tulane Stud. Zool., 8:65-82.

————————————. 1964. *Ambystoma talpoideum*. Cat. Amer. Amphib. Rept.: 8.1-8.2.

————————————. 1965. Aspects of Reproduction in Louisiana *Necturus* Populations. Amer. Midl. Nat., 74:357-367.

————————————. 1967. *Graptemys nigrinoda* in Mississippi. Herpetologica, 23:56.

———————————— AND G.E. GUNNING. 1967. Seasonal Activity and Movements of *Necturus* in Louisiana. Copeia, 1967:732-737.

SHREVE, B. 1945. *Pituophis melanoleucus mugitis* in Alabama. Copeia, 1945:234.

SMITH, P. W. 1961. The Amphibians and Reptiles of Illinois. Bull. Ill. Nat. Hist. Surv., No. 28. 298 pp.

————————————. 1963. *Plethodon cinereus*. Cat. Amer. Amphib. Rept.: 5.1-5.3.

————————————. 1966. *Hyla avivoca*. Cat. Amer. Amphib. Rept.: 28.1-28.2.

———————————— AND H. M. SMITH. 1952. Geographic Variation in the Lizard *Eumeces anthracinus*. Univ. Kans. Sci. Bull., 34:679-694.

SNEDIGAR, R. 1963. Our Small Native Animals — Their Habits and Care, 2nd Ed., Dover Pub., New York. xvii + 248 pp.

SNYDER, R. C. 1944. Mating of the Gray Rat Snake in Alabama. Copeia, 1944:253.

——————. 1945a. Notes on a Captive Scarlet Snake. Copeia, 1945:54.

——————. 1945b. Notes on the Snakes of Southeastern Alabama. Copeia, 1945:173-174.

SPANGLER, J. A. AND R. H. MOUNT. 1969. The Taxonomic Status of the Natricine Snake *Regina septemvittata mabila* (Neill). Herpetologica, 25:113-119.

SPEAKE, D. W. AND R. H. MOUNT. 1973. Some Possible Ecological Effects of "Rattlesnake Roundups" in the Southeastern Coastal Plain. Proc. 27th Ann. Conf. S.E. Assoc. Game and Fish Comm.: 267-277.

STULL, O. G. 1929. Variations and Relationships of the Snakes of the Genus *Pituophis*. Bull. U.S. Nat. Mus., No. 175. vi + 225 pp.

TAYLOR, E. H. 1935. A Taxonomic Study of the Cosmopolitan Scincoid Lizards of the Genus *Eumeces* with an Account of the Distribution and Relationships of its Species. Univ. Kans. Sci. Bull., 36:1-643.

TELFORD, S. R. 1955. A Description of the Eggs of the Coral Snake, *Micrurus fulvius*. Copeia, 1955:258.

——————. 1966. Variation among the Southeastern Crowned Snakes, Genus *Tantilla*. Bull. Fla. St. Mus., 10:261-304.

THUROW, G. R. 1954. A Range Extension of the Salamander *Gyrinophilus porphyriticus porphyriticus*. Copeia, 1954:221-222.

——————. 1955. A Further Range Extension of *Gyrinophilus p. porphyriticus*. Copeia, 1955:143.

——————. 1966. *Plethodon dorsalis*. Cat. Amer. Amphib. Rept.: 29.1-29.3.

TILLEY, STEPHEN G. 1973. *Desmognathus ochrophaeus*. Cat. Amer. Amphib. Rept.: 129.1-129.4.

TINKLE, D. W. 1958a. The Systematics and Ecology of the *Sternothaerus carinatus* Complex (Testudinata, Chelydridae). Tulane Stud. Zool., 6:1-56.

——————. 1958b. Experiments with Censusing of Southern Turtle Populations Herpetologica, 14:172-175.

——————. 1959. The Relation of the Fall Line to the Distribution and Abundance of Turtles. Copeia, 1959:167-170.

——————. AND R. G. WEBB. 1955. A New Species of *Sternotherus* with a Discussion of the *Sternotherus carinatus* Complex (Chelonia: Kinosternidae). Tulane Stud. Zool., 3:52-67.

TRAPIDO, A. 1944. The Snakes of the Genus *Storeria*. Amer. Midl. Nat., 31:1-84.

ULTSCH, G. R. 1973. Observations on the Life History of *Siren lacertina*. Herpetologica, 29:304-305.

VALENTINE, B. D. 1961. Variation and Distribution of *Desmognathus ocoee* Nicholls (Amphibia: Plethodontidae). Copeia, 1961:315-322.

——————. 1962a. Intergrading Populations and Distribution of the Salamander *Eurycea longicauda* in the Gulf States. J. Ohio Herpetol. Soc., 3:42-55.

——————. 1962b. The Range of the Cave Salamander, *Eurycea lucifuga* Rafinesque, in Alabama. Herpetologica, 18:214.

——————. 1963a. The Salamander Genus *Desmognathus* in Mississippi. Copeia, 1963:130-139.

——————. 1963b. Notes on the Early Life History of the Alabama Salamander, *Desmognathus aeneus chermocki* Bishop and Valentine. Amer. Midl. Nat., 69:182-188.

——————. 1963c. The Plethodontid Salamander *Phaeognathus*: External Morphology and Zoogeography. Proc. Biol. Soc. Washington, 76:153-158.

——————. 1963d. The Plethodontid Salamander *Phaeognathus*: Collecting Techniques and Habits. J. Ohio Herpetol. Soc., 4:49-54.

——————. 1964. *Desmognathus ocoee*. Cat. Amer. Amphib. Rept.: 7.1-7.2.

Viosca, P., Jr. 1937. A Tentative Revision of the Genus *Necturus*, with Descriptions of Three New Species from the Southern Gulf Drainage Area. Copeia, 1937:120-138.

————————. 1938. Notes on Winter Frogs of Alabama. Copeia, 1938:201.

Volpe, E. P. 1957. The Early Development of *Rana capito sevosa*. Tulane Stud. Zool., 5:207-225.

———————— and J. L. Dobie. 1959. The Larva of the Oak Toad, *Bufo quercicus* Holbrook. Tulane Stud. Zool., 7:145-152.

———————— M. A. Wilkens, and J. L. Dobie. 1961. Embryonic and Larval Development of *Hyla avivoca*. Copeia, 1961: 340-349.

Walquist, H. 1970. Sawbacks of the Gulf Coast. Int. Turtle and Tortoise Soc. J., 4:10-13, 28.

———————— and G. W. Folkerts. 1973. Eggs and Hatchlings of Barbour's Map Turtle, *Graptemys barbouri* Carr and Marchand. Herpetologica, 29:236-237.

Wasserman, A. O. 1968. *Scaphiopus holbrookii*. Cat. Amer. Amphib. Rept.: 70.1-70.4.

Waters, J. C. 1974. The Biological Significance of the Basking Habit in the Black-knobbed Sawback, *Graptemys nigrinoda* Cagle. M.S. thesis, Auburn Univ., Auburn, Ala., 81 pp.

Webb, R. G. 1962. North American Recent Soft-shelled Turtles (Family Trionchidae). Univ. Kans. Pub. Mus. Nat. Hist., 13:429-611.

Weber, J. A. 1944. Observations on the Life History of *Amphiuma means*. Copeia, 1944: 61-62.

Wharton, C. H. 1960. Birth and Behavior of a Brood of Cottonmouths, *Agkistrodon piscivorus piscivorus*, with Notes on Tail-luring. Herpetologica, 16:125-129.

Whitaker, J. O., Jr. 1971. A Study of the Western Chorus Frog, *Pseudacris triseriata*, in Vigo County, Indiana. J. Herpetol., 5:127-150.

White, J. B. and George C. Murphy. 1973. The Reproductive Cycle and Sexual Dimorphism of the Common Snapping Turtle, *Chelydra serpentina serpentina*. Herpetologica, 29:240-246.

Williams, K. L. 1970. Systematics of the Colubrid Snake *Lampropeltis triangulum* Lacépède. Ph.D. diss., La. St. Univ., Baton Rouge: 368 pp.

———————— and L. D. Wilson. 1967. A Review of the Colubrid Snake Genus *Cemophora* Cope. Tulane Stud. Zool., 13:103-124.

Wilson, L. D. 1970. The Coachwhip Snake, *Masticophis flagellum* (Shaw): Taxonomy and Distribution. Tulane Stud. Zool. and Bot. 16:31-99.

————————. 1973. *Masticophis flagellum*. Cat. Amer. Amphib. Rept.: 145.1-145.4.

Wimberly, C. A. 1970. Poisonous Snakes of Alabama. Explorer Books, Inc., Birmingham. 46 pp.

Wood, J. T. 1955. The Nesting of the Four-toed Salamander, *Hemidactylium scutatum* (Schlegal), in Virginia. Amer. Midl. Nat., 53:381-389.

Wright, A. H. 1932. Life Histories of the Frogs of the Okefinokee Swamp, Georgia. McMillan Co., New York, 497 pp.

———————— and A. A. Wright. 1949. Handbook of Frogs and Toads of the United States and Canada. Third Ed., Comstock Pub., Ithaca, N.Y. xii + 640 pp.

————————————. 1957. Handbook of Snakes of the United States and Canada. Comstock Pub. Ithaca, N.Y. xviii + 1105 pp.

Yarrow, H. C. 1882. Checklist of North American Reptilia and Batrachia, with Catalogue of Specimens in U.S. National Museum. U.S. Nat. Mus. Bull. 24. 249 pp.

Young, F. N. and C. C. Goff. 1939. An Annotated List of the Arthropods Found in the Burrows of the Florida Gopher Tortoise. Fla. Entomol., 22:53-62.

Zug, G. R. and A. Schwartz. 1971. *Deirochelys* and *D. reticularia*. Cat. Amer. Amphib. Rept.: 107.1-107.3.

APPENDIX

Threatened and Endangered Forms

Following are the Alabama species and subspecies of reptiles and amphibians listed, or approved for listing, as "threatened," "endangered," "special concern," or "status undetermined" by the U.S. Department of the Interior (U.S.D.I.), the panel on reptiles and amphibians at the Symposium on Threatened and Endangered Plants and Animals of Alabama (S.T.E.P.A.A.), or the herpetology panel at the Workshop on Threatened and Endangered Vertebrates of the Southeast (W.T.E.V.S.). The U.S.D.I. national list is contained within *Threatened Wildlife of the United States* (1974 Revised Appendix C) published by the U.S. Fish and Wildlife Service. The results of the state symposium and regional workshop are in press. The abbreviations used are E = endangered; T = threatened; SC = special concern; SU = status undetermined.

Species or Subspecies	USDI	STEPAA	WTEVS
Frogs			
Hyla andersoni (Florida population)[1] (Pine Barrens Treefrog)	----	----	T
Limnaoedus ocularis (Little Grass Frog)	----	SC	—
Rana areolata sevosa (Dusky Gopher Frog)	----	T	T
Rana heckscheri (River Frog)	----	SC	—
Rana sylvatica (Wood Frog)	----	SC	----
Salamanders			
Ambystoma cingulatum (Flatwoods Salamander)	----	E	SU
Cryptobranchus alleganiensis (Hellbender)	----	T	SC
Desmognathus aeneus (Seepage Salamander)	----	SC	----
Desmognathus ochrophaeus (Mountain Dusky Salamander)	----	SC	----
Gyrinophilus palleucus (Tennessee Cave Salamander)	----	SC	SC
Phaeognathus hubrichti (Red Hills Salamander)	----	E	E
Plethodon cinereus polycentratus (Georgia Red-backed Salamander)	----	SC	----
Sirens			
Siren lacertina (Greater Siren)	----	SC	----
Crocodilians			
Alligator mississippiensis (American Alligator)	E	E[2]	SC
Snakes			
Crotalus adamanteus (Eastern Diamondback Rattlesnake)	----	SC	SC
Drymarchon corais couperi (Eastern Indigo Snake)	----	E[3]	T

Species or Subspecies	USDI	STEPAA	WTEVS
Lampropeltis triangulum triangulum (Eastern Milk Snake)	----	SC	----
Lampropeltis triangulum syspila (Red Milk Snake)	----	SC	----
Natrix cyclopion floridana (Florida Green Water Snake)	----	SC	----
Pituophis melanoleucus lodingi (Black Pine Snake)	----	E	T
Pituophis melanoleucus mugitus (Florida Pine Snake)	----	E	SC
Rhadinaea flavilata (Pine Woods Snake)	----	SC	----
Seminatrix pygaea pygaea (Northern Florida Black Swamp Snake)	----	SC	----
Turtles			
Caretta caretta caretta (Atlantic Loggerhead)	----	E	T
Chelonia mydas (Green Turtle)	----	E	E
Dermochelys coriacea coriacea (Atlantic Leatherback)	----	T	T
Eretmochelys imbricata imbricata (Atlantic Hawksbill)	----	E	E
Gopherus polyphemus (Gopher Tortoise)	----	T	T
Graptemys barbouri (Barbour's Map Turtle)	----	SC	----
Lepidochelys kempi (Atlantic Ridley)	----	E	E
Pseudemys alabamensis (Alabama Red-bellied Turtle)	----	T	T
Sternotherus minor depressus (Flattened Musk Turtle)	----	T	T
Trionyx ferox (Florida Softshell)	----	SC	----
Trionyx spiniferus spiniferus (Eastern Spiny Softshell)	----	SC	----

[1] Not known now to occur in Alabama but may ultimately be found in southern portions of Covington or Escambia counties, where the known range closely approaches the Alabama-Florida boundary.

[2] Although proposed for endangered status to comply with Federal guidelines, the alligator is sufficiently abundant in Alabama now to warrant placing it in a lower category of concern.

[3] May be extinct in Alabama.

INDEX

Italicized page numbers refer to principal accounts.

ADDENDA

I. Thomas Yarbrough has recently supplied specimens of *Lampropeltis calligaster* and *L. triangulum* from Madison County in extreme northern Alabama which help solve problems associated with those species. Several specimens of the former were supplied, all from the Redstone Arsenal Reservation. All, including a melanistic individual with an unmarked dorsum, are clearly referable to the subspecies *L. c. calligaster,* confirming the presence of that form in Alabama.

A specimen of *L. triangulum* from the Green Mountain area is clearly *L. t. syspila,* extending the range of that form in Alabama westward for a considerable distance, and raising a question as to the status of milk snake populations in southern central Tennessee, an area which has, for the most part, been included previously within the range of *L. t. triangulum.*

II. The second edition of Roger Conant's field guide (*Field Guide to the Reptiles and Amphibians of Eastern and Central North America,* Houghton Mifflin, Boston) was released in June, 1975. In addition to giving identifying characteristics of each of the various species and subspecies, the guide has color illustrations of most forms, updated range maps, and notes on habitat preference. It should be in the possession of everyone with an interest in herpetology.